The United Nations in the 21st Century

Dilemmas in World Politics

Dilemmas in World Politics offers teachers and students in international relations a series of quality books on critical issues, trends, and regions in international politics. Each text examines a "real world" dilemma and is structured to cover the historical, theoretical, practical, and projected dimensions of its subject.

BOOKS IN THIS SERIES

THIRD EDITION

The United Nations in the 21st Century

KAREN A. MINGST

AND

MARGARET P. KARNS

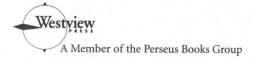

Westview
PRESS

A Member of the Perseus Books Group

Westview Press books are available at special discounts for bulk purchases in the United States by corporations, institutions, and other organizations. For more information, please contact the Special Markets Department at the Perseus Books Group, 11 Cambridge Center, Cambridge MA 02142, or call (617) 252-5298 or (800) 255-1514, or e-mail special.markets@perseusbooks.com.

Library of Congress Cataloging-in-Publication Data

Mingst, Karen A., 1947-
    The United Nations in the 21st century / Karen A. Mingst and Margaret P. Karns.-- 3rd ed.
        p.   cm.—(Dilemmas in world politics)
    Previous eds. published under title: The United Nations in the post-cold war era. Boulder, Colo. : Westview Press, 1995, and 2000.
    Includes bibliographical references and index.
    ISBN-13: 978-0-8133-4346-4 (alk. paper)
    ISBN-10: 0-8133-4346-1 (alk. paper)
    1. United Nations. 2. International cooperation. 3. International relations. 4. Security, International. I. Karns, Margaret P. II. Mingst, Karen A., 1947-. United Nations in the post-Cold War era. 2000.   III. Title. IV. Series.

JZ5005.M56 2006
341.23—dc22
                                                                    2006005877

07 08 09 / 10 9 8 7 6 5 4 3 2 1

Contents

Illustrations

Preface

In revising and updating this book, we have changed far more than we had imagined when Steve Catalano of Westview Press asked us to do a third edition. It is, indeed, a world of rapid change. The title of the first two editions, *The United Nations in the Post–Cold War Era,* no longer seems apt; the world has moved beyond the post–Cold War era into a new millennium marked by the effects of globalization, the September 11, 2001, attacks on the World Trade Center and the Pentagon, divisions provoked by the U.S. war in Iraq and other unilateralist actions by the world's sole superpower, the deepening inequality between North and South, the threats to human security from global climate change and the HIV/AIDS pandemic, and the failure, once again, to respond to genocide in Africa. The United Nations itself has been shaken by the scandal over the Oil-for-Food Programme, sexual misconduct by peacekeepers, and doubts about its capacity for reforms that would enable it to better serve today's rather than yesterday's governance needs.

In updating the book, we reduced material on the earlier history of the UN and sought to deal more with the challenges the UN faces today. We have added a new chapter on human security to encompass this enlarged concept of security that emerged in the late 1990s and bring together treatment of environmental and health issues. The dilemmas of humanitarian intervention are discussed in the chapters on human rights and peace and security; reform-related issues are discussed throughout the book as well as in the concluding chapter. The Millennium Development Goals are addressed in the chapter on economic development as well as in the human rights chapter. In the process, we have benefited from comments from Courtney Smith, who critiqued the second edition, and from feedback and suggestions from other faculty colleagues and students who have used the book. We wish also to thank Jacqueline Chura for her assistance in updating figures and tables; Geenae DeSoto Rivera for help with the index; Dr. Christopher M. Duncan, Chair of the University of Dayton's Department of Political Science, for his encouragement and support; and Lynne Rienner for allowing us to use material on the United Nations from our book *International Organizations: The Politics and Processes of Global Governance* (2004).

We dedicate this third edition to our children and grandchild, Ginger, Brett, Paul, and Anna, whose generations must sustain the United Nations in the twenty-first century. And we wish to thank our husbands, Robert Stauffer and Ralph Johnston, whose continuing patience, support, and encouragement have enabled us to bring this work to fruition.

Karen A. Mingst
Margaret P. Karns

Acronyms

ACT-UP	AIDS Coalition to Unleash Power
AI	Amnesty International
ANC	African National Congress
AU	African Union
BWC	Biological Weapons Convention
CACM	Central American Common Market
CARICOM	Caribbean Community
CBW	chemical and biological weapons
CEDAW	Convention on the Elimination of All Forms of Discrimination Against Women
CERF	Central Emergency Response Fund
CFCs	chlorofluorocarbons
CGIAR	Consultative Group on International Agricultural Research
CSD	Commission on Sustainable Development
CSW	Commission on the Status of Women
CTC	Counter Terrorism Committee
CWC	Chemical Weapons Convention
DPKO	UN Department of Peacekeeping Operations
ECA	Economic Commission for Africa
ECE	Economic Commission for Europe
ECLA	Economic Commission for Latin America
ECOSOC	United Nations Economic and Social Council
ECOWAS	Economic Community of West African States
EPTA	Expanded Programme of Technical Assistance
ESCAP	Economic and Social Commission for Asia and the Pacific
EU	European Union (previously referred to as the European Community [EC] or the European Economic Community [EEC])
FAO	Food and Agriculture Organization
GATT	General Agreement on Tariffs and Trade
GAVI	Global Alliance for Vaccines and Immunization
GEF	Global Environmental Facility
GNP	gross national product
GSP	Generalized System of Preferences
G-7	Group of Seven
G-8	Group of Eight

G-77   Group of 77
HDI   Human Development Index
HIPC   Heavily Indebted Poor Countries Initiative
HIV/AIDS   human immunodeficiency syndrome
HLP   High-Level Panel on Threats, Challenges, and Change
HRC   Human Rights Council
HRW   Human Rights Watch
IAEA   International Atomic Energy Agency
IBRD   International Bank for Reconstruction and Development (also
      known as the World Bank)
ICC   International Criminal Court
ICJ   International Court of Justice
ICPD   International Conference on Population and Development
ICRC   International Committee of the Red Cross
ICSID   International Centre for Settlement of Investment Disputes
ICTR   International Criminal Tribunal for Rwanda
ICTY   International Criminal Tribunal for the Former Yugoslavia
IDA   International Development Association
IDB   Inter-American Development Bank
IFAD   International Fund for Agricultural Development
IFC   International Finance Corporation
IFOR   Implementation Force (NATO force in the former Yugoslavia)
IGO   international intergovernmental organization
ILO   International Labour Organization
IMF   International Monetary Fund
INSTRAW   International Research and Training Institute for the Advancement
      of Women
IR   international relations
ISAF   International Security Assistance Force
KLA   Kosovo Liberation Army
LDCS   less developed countries (also referred to as "the South")
MDG   Millennium Development Goals
MIGA   Multilateral Investment Guarantee Agency
MNC   multinational corporations
NAFTA   North American Free Trade Agreement
NAM   Nonaligned Movement
NATO   North Atlantic Treaty Organization
NEPAD   New Partnership for Africa's Development
NGO   nongovernmental organization
NIC   newly industrializing country
NIEO   New International Economic Order
NPT   Treaty on the Non-Proliferation of Nuclear Weapons
OFFP   Oil-for-Food Programme
OHCHR   Office of the High Commissioner for Human Rights
OIHP   Office International d'Hygiène Publique

ONUC	United Nations Operation in the Congo
ONUCA	United Nations Observer Group in Central America
ONUSAL	United Nations Observer Mission in El Salvador
ONUVEN	United Nations (civilian) Observer Mission in Central America
OPEC	Organization of Petroleum Exporting Countries
OSCE	Organization for Security and Cooperation in Europe
PBC	Peacebuilding Commission
PLO	Palestine Liberation Organization
PRC	People's Republic of China
P-5	permanent members of the UN Security Council
ROC	Republic of China (Taiwan)
RPF	Rwandan Patriotic Front
SARS	severe acute respiratory syndrome
SFOR	NATO Stabilization Force (in the former Yugoslavia)
SUNFED	Special UN Fund for Economic Development
SWAPO	South West Africa People's Organization
UN	United Nations
UNAIDS	United Nations Joint Programme on HIV/AIDS
UNAMA	United Nations Assistance Mission in Afghanistan
UNAMIR	United Nations Assistance Mission in Rwanda
UNCED	United Nations Conference on the Environment and Development
UNCHE	United Nations Conference on the Human Environment
UNCLOS	United Nations Conference on the Law of the Sea
UNCTAD	United Nations Conference on Trade and Development
UNDOF	United Nations Disengagement Observer Force
UNDP	United Nations Development Program
UNDRO	United Nations Disaster Relief Organization
UNEF I, II	United Nations Emergency Force (in Egypt)
UNEP	United Nations Environment Programme
UNESCO	United Nations Educational, Scientific, and Cultural Organization
UNFICYP	United Nations Force in Cyprus
UNFPA	United Nations Fund for Population Activities
UNHCR	United Nations High Commissioner for Refugees
UNICEF	United Nations Children's Fund
UNIDO	United Nations Industrial Development Organization
UNIFEM	United Nations Development Fund for Women
UNIFIL	United Nations Interim Force in Lebanon
UNIIMOG	United Nations Iran-Iraq Military Observer Group
UNIKOM	United Nations Iraq-Kuwait Observer Mission
UNITAF	Unified Task Force on Somalia (also known as Operation Restore Hope)
UNMEE	United Nations Mission in Ethiopia and Eritrea
UNMIH	United Nations Mission in Haiti

UNMIK	United Nations Mission in Kosovo
UNMOVIC	United Nations Monitoring, Verification, and Inspection Commission (in Iraq)
UNOSOM	United Nations Operation in Somalia
UNPROFOR	United Nations Protection Force (in the former Yugoslavia)
UNRWA	United Nations Relief and Works Agency for Palestine Refugees in the Near East
UNSCOM	United Nations Special Commission for the Disarmament of Iraq
UNTAC	United Nations Transitional Authority in Cambodia
UNTAET	United Nations Transitional Administration in East Timor
UNTAG	United Nations Transition Assistance Group (in Namibia)
UNTSO	United Nations Truce Supervision Organization (in Palestine)
WCED	World Commission on Environment and Development
WFP	World Food Programme
WHA	World Health Assembly
WHO	World Health Organization
WID	women-in-development
WIPO	World Intellectual Property Organization
WMD	weapons of mass destruction
WTO	World Trade Organization

1

◄○►

The United Nations in World Politics

In the early twenty-first century, it is hard to imagine a world without the United Nations. Despite many ups and downs over more than sixty years, the UN has not only endured but also played a key role in reshaping the world as we know it. It has embodied humankind's hopes for a better world through the prevention of conflict. It has promoted a culture of legality and rule of law. It has raised an awareness of the plight of the world's poor, and it has boosted development by providing technical assistance. It has promoted concern for human rights, including the status of women, the rights of the child, and the unique needs of indigenous peoples. It has formulated the concept of environmentally sustainable development. It has contributed immensely to making multilateral diplomacy the primary way in which international norms, public policies, and law are established. Along the way, the UN has earned several Nobel Peace Prizes, including the 2005 award to the International Atomic Energy Agency (IAEA) and its chief, Mohamed ElBaradei; the 2001 prize to the UN and Secretary-General Kofi Annan; the 1988 award to UN peacekeepers; and the 1969 honor to the International Labour Organization (ILO).

In each of these and other areas of UN activity, we can point to the UN's accomplishments and also to its shortcomings and failures. Yet, the UN continues to be the only **international intergovernmental organization** (IGO) of global scope and nearly universal membership that has an agenda encompassing the broadest range of governance issues. It is a complex system that serves as the central site for multilateral diplomacy. The UN's General Assembly is center stage: Its three weeks of general debate at the opening of each fall assembly session draw foreign ministers and heads of state from small and large states to take advantage of the opportunity to address the nations of the world and to engage in intensive diplomacy.

As an intergovernmental organization, however, the UN is the creation of its member states; it is they who decide what it is that they will allow this organization to do and what resources—financial and otherwise—they will provide. In this regard, the UN is very much a political organization, subject to the winds of world

1

politics and the whims of member governments. To understand the UN today, it is useful to look back at some of the major changes in world politics and how they affected the UN.

THE UNITED NATIONS IN WORLD POLITICS: VISION AND REALITY

The establishment of the United Nations in the closing days of World War II was an affirmation of the desire of war-weary nations for an organization that could help them avoid future conflicts and promote international economic and social cooperation. As we discuss further in chapter 2, the UN's Charter built on lessons learned from the failed League of Nations created at the end of World War I and earlier experiments with international unions, conference diplomacy, and dispute settlement mechanisms. It represented an expression of hope for the possibilities of a new global security arrangement and for fostering the social and economic conditions necessary for peace to prevail.

The United Nations and Politics in the Cold War World

The World War II coalition of great powers (the United States, the Soviet Union, Great Britain, France, and China), whose unity had been key to the UN's founding, was nevertheless a victim of rising tensions almost before the first General Assembly session in 1946. Developments in Europe and Asia between 1946 and 1950 soon made it clear that the emerging Cold War would have fundamental effects on the UN. How could a **collective security** system operate when there was no unity among the great powers on whose cooperation it depended? Even the admission of new members was affected between 1950 and 1955 because each side vetoed applications from states that were allied with the other.

The Cold War made Security Council actions on threats to peace and security extremely problematic with repeated sharp exchanges and frequent deadlock. Some conflicts, such as the French and American wars in Vietnam and the Soviet interventions in Czechoslovakia and Hungary, were never brought to the UN at all. The UN was able to respond to the North Korean invasion of South Korea in 1950 only because the Soviet Union was boycotting the Security Council at the time.

In order to deal with a number of regional conflicts, the UN developed something never mentioned in its charter, namely, **peacekeeping**; this has involved the prevention, containment, and moderation of hostilities between or within states through the use of multinational forces of soldiers, police, and civilians.

Peacekeeping was a creative response to the breakdown of great-power unity and the spread of East-West tensions to regional conflicts. UN peacekeeping forces were used extensively in the Middle East and in conflicts arising out of the decolonization process during the Cold War period. Thirteen operations were deployed from 1948 to 1988. The innovation of peacekeeping illustrates what the Cold War did to the UN: "It had repealed the proposition that the organization should undertake to promote order by bringing the great powers into troubled situations. . . . Henceforward, the task of the United Nations was to be defined as that of keeping the great powers out of such situations."[1]

The Effects of the Nuclear Revolution.   The UN Charter had just been signed when the use of two atomic bombs on Japan on 6 and 10 August 1945 began a scientific and technological revolution in warfare that would have a far-reaching impact on the post–World War II world. At the United Nations, the earliest and most obvious effect of nuclear weapons was to restore the issue of disarmament (and its relative, arms control) to the agenda. Disarmament as an approach to peace had been discredited during the interwar era. The UN almost from its inception in early 1946 became a forum for discussions and negotiations on **arms control and disarmament**. Hence, the nuclear threat not only transformed world politics but also made the UN the key place where statespersons sought to persuade each other that war had become excessively dangerous, that disarmament and arms control were imperative, and that they were devoted to peace and restraint.

The Role of the United Nations in Decolonization and the Emergence of New States.   At the close of World War II, few would have predicted the end of colonial rule in Africa and Asia. Yet twenty-five years after the UN Charter was signed, most of the former colonies had achieved independence with relatively little threat to international peace and security. Membership in the UN more than doubled from 51 states in 1945 to 118 in 1965, and had tripled by 1980 (see fig. 1.1), the vast majority of these new members being newly independent states. The UN played a significant role in this remarkably peaceful transformation, much of which took place during the height of the Cold War. Twenty-six new states were later seated in the UN after the Cold War's end, mostly as a result of the dissolution of the Soviet Union and Yugoslavia.

The UN Charter endorsed the principle of **self-determination**. Already independent former colonies, such as India, Egypt, Indonesia, and the Latin American states, used the UN as a forum to advocate an end to colonialism and independence for territories ruled by Great Britain, France, the Netherlands, Belgium, Spain, and Portugal. Success added new votes to the growing anticolonial coalition.

By 1960, a majority of the UN's members favored decolonization. General Assembly Resolution 1514 that year condemned the continuation of colonial rule and preconditions for granting independence (such as a lack of preparation for self-rule) and called for annual reports on the progress toward independence for

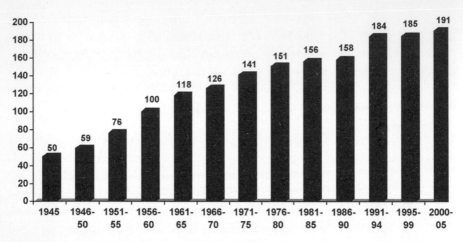

FIGURE 1.1   Growth in UN Membership, 1945–2005

all remaining colonial territories. The UN provided an important forum for the **collective legitimation** of a change in international norms (that is, colonialism and imperialism were no longer acceptable patterns of state behavior, and colonial peoples had a right to self-determination). The international system was fully internationalized to include all sovereign, independent states that sought membership.

The consequences of decolonization and the expanded number of independent states were manifold. The less developed, often newly independent states of Africa, Asia, and Latin America formed a strong coalition within the UN known as the **Group of 77** (G-77); after 1960, this coalition commanded a majority of votes on a broad range of issues. Whereas the Cold War had shaped politics in the UN until 1960, the G-77, and what became known as "North-South issues," shaped much of the politics thereafter. The two sets of issues became entwined in complex ways and political divisions changed. The Soviet Union and many Western European states often sided with the G-77, and the United States frequently found itself in a small minority.

Beginning in the 1960s, new issues proliferated on the UN's agenda, many at the urging of the G-77. For example, in 1967, Arvid Pardo, the representative from Malta, argued on behalf of newly independent states that the resources found on the deep seabed were the "common heritage of mankind," not the property of any specific nation. This would subsequently have an impact on emerging environment issues as well as on law of the sea. Of all the issues pushed by the G-77, none received more attention than the drive for economic and social development.

The North-South Conflict.   By the late 1960s, the agendas of the UN and its subsidiary agencies were dominated by issues of economic and social development and the relations between the developed countries of the industrial North and the less developed countries of the South. The ideological leaning of the G-77 toward a heavy government role in economic development and redistribution of wealth in the 1960s and 1970s shaped many UN programs and activities. In the 1970s, the G-77 pushed for a **New International Economic Order** (NIEO), marshaling support in the UN General Assembly for "A Declaration on the Establishment of a New International Economic Order" and "A Charter of Economic Rights and Duties of States." The NIEO debates dominated and polarized the UN system during the 1970s. The deep divide between North and South at times made agreement on both economic and security issues impossible to achieve.

The North-South conflict continues to be a central feature of world politics, and hence of the UN, although the rhetoric and issues of the NIEO sharply diminished in the late 1980s and 1990s. For example, the UN's treatment of environmental issues, which first emerged at the Stockholm Conference on the Human Environment in 1972, has been permeated by North-South differences. The 1997 Kyoto Conference on Climate Change heard echoes of the North-South conflict when developing countries insisted that industrial countries make the first reductions in carbon dioxide emissions. The G-77, however, is no longer as cohesive a group; its members' interests increasingly diverged in the 1980s when some states, especially in Southeast Asia, achieved rapid economic growth, and as many developing countries shifted from statist-oriented economic policies to neoliberal ones calling for open markets and privatization. Chapter 5 discusses these shifts further as well as the increased emphasis on poverty alleviation that accompanied the **Millennium Development Goals** (MDGs) approved in 2000.

Post–Cold War World Politics

The Cold War's end in 1990 meant not only new cooperation among the five permanent members of the Security Council but also a resurgence of nationalism, civil wars, and ethnic conflicts; the new phenomenon of failed states; and a related series of humanitarian crises. The consequence was greater demands than ever before on the United Nations to deal with threats to peace and security as well as environment and development issues, democratization, population growth, humanitarian crises, and other problems. UN peacekeepers were called on to rebuild Cambodia, create peace in Bosnia, organize and monitor elections in Nicaragua and Namibia, monitor human rights violations in El Salvador, and oversee humanitarian relief in Bosnia, Somalia, Rwanda, Kosovo, Congo, East Timor, and Afghanistan. Beginning with Iraq's invasion of Kuwait, the UN's enforcement powers were used more in the post–Cold War era than at any previous time.

With the spread of **democratization** to all regions of the globe from Latin America, Eastern Europe, and states created from the former Soviet Union to

Africa and Asia, many authoritarian governments in the late 1980s and 1990s were forced to open their political processes to competing political parties, to adopt more stringent human rights standards, and to hold free elections. The UN has been in heavy demand to provide observers for elections in countries around the world. UN–sanctioned intervention in Haiti in 1993 marked the first time the UN took action to restore a democratically elected government. In Namibia, Kosovo, Bosnia, and East Timor, the UN was called upon to assist with organizing the elements of newly independent states, including the provision of transitional administrations, the writing of constitutions, and the organization of elections.

By 1995, however, the early post–Cold War optimism about the United Nations had diminished substantially. The peacekeepers in Somalia, Bosnia, and Rwanda found little peace to be kept, although their presence did alleviate much human suffering. Despite almost continuous meetings of the UN Security Council and numerous resolutions, the UN's own members lacked the political will to provide the military, logistical, and financial resources needed to deal with these complex situations. In addition, the UN faced a deep financial crisis caused by the increased cost of peacekeeping and other activities and the failure of many members, including the United States, to pay their assessed contributions. The UN celebrated its fiftieth anniversary in 1995, but failed to use the occasion to enact necessary reforms in its administration, financing, and structure.

The UN, Globalization, and World Politics in a New Millennium

Because the **Bretton Woods institutions** have always operated largely independently, the UN has never played a central role in international economic relations; indeed, rising globalization in the 1990s made this fact even clearer. **Globalization** is the process of increasing worldwide integration of politics, economics, social relations, and culture, often appearing to undermine traditional state sovereignty. Although topics related to globalization appeared on the agendas of the General Assembly and the United Nations Economic and Social Council (ECOSOC), the major decisionmaking was clearly taking place elsewhere: in the World Bank, the International Monetary Fund (IMF), the World Trade Organization (WTO), and the **Group of Seven** (G-7), as well as in Washington, Tokyo, Berlin, London, and the headquarters of major corporations. A clear indicator of the UN's marginal importance to globalization issues was protesters' focus on the other institutions. To be sure, some of the UN specialized agencies, such as the International Labour Organization (ILO), the World Health Organization (WHO), and World Intellectual Property Organization (WIPO), became very much involved in globalization-related issues of labor, health, and intellectual property rights. Still, globalization's role in fueling the growth of **nongovernmental orga-**

nizations (NGOs) was felt within the UN system in the pressures for a greater voice for **global civil society**.

Globalization's effects on a nexus of **interdependence** issues have also increased pressures within the UN for the series of global conferences and summits on the environment, human rights, population and development, women, and social development (issues discussed in chapter 2 and elsewhere). Each of these conferences has been important for articulating new international norms; expanding international law; setting agendas for governments, as well as for the UN itself, through programs of action; and promoting linkages among NGOs, the UN, and governments.

The emergence of the United States as the world's sole superpower is a related aspect of post–Cold War world politics, the era of globalization, and the new millennium. The economic and military capabilities of the United States far exceed those of any other state, and, at present, the superpower has no serious rival. Many have worried that this development would result in the UN's marginalization, particularly if, or when, the United States chose to act unilaterally. An alternative view is that the UN could become a puppet of the sole superpower, dependent upon its goodwill for funding, subservient in authorizing U.S. actions. Yet, the United States has always been important to the United Nations (discussed further in chapter 3). The interesting phenomenon today is the willingness of groups of states and of NGOs to push ahead with policy initiatives even when the United States has opposed them, examples being the International Criminal Court, the Convention on Landmines, and the Kyoto Protocol on Climate Change. And the United States, too, has carried out initiatives without the support of others, as it did with the invasion of Iraq in 2003, with neither the approval of many major allies nor the authorization of the UN Security Council.

The UN used the occasion of the new millennium to convene a Millennium Summit in 2000 with a special report from Secretary-General Kofi Annan, *We the Peoples,* providing his views of the state of the world, the major global challenges, and the need for structural reform. In suggesting the special gathering, the secretary-general hoped "to harness the symbolic power of the millennium to the real and urgent needs of people everywhere."[2] The three days of meetings drew the largest gathering of world leaders ever: There were 147 heads of state or government, and representatives from forty-four other countries.

The Millennium Declaration adopted at the close of the extraordinary summit reflected the high degree of consensus on two priorities: peace and development. Different leaders had stressed different aspects of the issues ranging from globalization to nuclear weapons, fairer economic systems, ethnic tolerance, and HIV/AIDS; they had disagreed about how to restructure the UN, but not about the importance of the world organization; they concurred with lofty language about values and principles, but they also committed themselves to a series of specific

objectives known as the **Millennium Development Goals** (MDG) that include
halving the number of people living on less than one dollar a day by the year 2015
and reversing the spread of HIV/AIDS, malaria, and other major diseases. The declaration outlined special measures to meet the needs of Africa, and it intensified
efforts to reform the Security Council, to strengthen ECOSOC and the International Court of Justice (ICJ), to make the General Assembly a more effective delib-
erative and policymaking body, and to ensure that the UN is provided the
resources needed to carry out its mandates.

The answer to whether the Millennium Summit and Declaration succeeded in
mobilizing new energy will lie in efforts to meet the ambitious goals set and to
overcome the persistent problems within the UN system that have made other ambitious declarations empty promises. The MDG and their implementation are discussed further in chapters 5 and 7.

Because the terrorist attacks of September 11, 2001 took place in New York City
just as the General Assembly was about to convene there for its annual session, the
UN was powerfully affected. The attacks made clear the nature of the global
threat posed by Al Qaeda and other terrorist organizations. This was a new type
of threat to international peace and security, not just an attack on the United
States, and one that took advantage of globalization's impact on the ease of moving people, money, communications, and arms across borders. In light of these
changes, the very possibility that weapons of mass destruction could find their
way into the hands of terrorist organizations makes the threat real and the need to
coordinate action all the more urgent. Responses to these threats require major
new approaches: Some could be taken through the United Nations system (such
as gathering regular reports from states on counterterrorism steps); others would
involve many other actors. All approaches would require much more extensive
coordination in sharing information, monitoring financial transactions, and
other steps.

To understand the links between world politics and the United Nations, it is also
important to examine the major international relations (IR) theories to see how
they explain global changes and the roles of IGOs such as the UN.

CONTENDING INTERNATIONAL
RELATIONS THEORIES

During much of the post–World War II era, **realist theory,** or realism, provided
the dominant explanation for international politics. Realists see states as the most
important actors in the international system. They view states as unitary actors
that define their national interests in terms of maximizing power and security.
States' **sovereignty** means that they coexist in an anarchic international system
and, therefore, must rely primarily on themselves to manage their own insecurity

through balance of power, alliances, and deterrence. International rules (law) and norms, as well as international organizations, do not carry much weight with realists because they lack enforcement power. In realists' view, IGOs and NGOs are marginal actors. IGOs, in particular, do not enjoy autonomy or capability for independent action on the world stage. Rather, they reflect the interests of their members, especially the most powerful ones. In this view, the UN is constrained by its members' willingness to work through it in dealing with specific problems; to comply with and support its actions; to provide peacekeeping contingents (military or civilian); and to pay for its regular operations and special programs. In realist theory, cooperation among states is not impossible, but states have little incentive to enter into international arrangements, and they are always free to exit from them.[3]

For many international relations scholars, however, realist theory is an inadequate theoretical framework for analyzing world politics, and especially the rapid changes since the Cold War's end as well as the expanded practice of **multilateralism** and the activities of the UN and other IGOs. One major alternative is **liberalism**.[4]

Liberals regard states as important actors, but they place importance on a variety of other actors in the international system, including IGOs, NGOs, multinational corporations (MNCs), and even individuals. States, in their view, are pluralistic, not unitary, actors. Moral and ethical principles, power relations and bargaining among different domestic and transnational groups, and changing international conditions shape states' interests and actions. There is no single definition of national interest; rather, states vary in their goals, and their interests change. Liberal theorists characterize the international system as an interdependent one in which there is both cooperation and conflict and where actors' mutual interests tend to increase over time. States' power matters, but it is exercised within a framework of international rules and institutions that help to make cooperation possible.

Liberalism posits that IGOs such as the United Nations make a difference in world politics by altering state preferences and establishing rules that constrain states. They are not merely pawns of the dominant powers but actually modify state behavior by creating habits of cooperation and serving as arenas for negotiation and policy coordination. For some liberal theorists, the growth of multilateralism, IGOs, and international law is indicative of a nascent international society in which actors consent to common rules and institutions and recognize common interests as well as a common identity or sense of "we-ness." Within this emerging society, international institutions are changing the way states and other actors interact with each other. Many scholars argue that the growing role of nongovernmental actors represents an emerging global civil society.[5]

A third, relatively recent approach to international relations is **constructivism,** which has become important for studying various aspects of **global governance,** particularly the role of norms. Constructivism has several variants, and questions have arisen about whether it is a theory of politics. Yet it offers a valuable way of studying how shared beliefs, rules, organizations, and cultural practices shape the behavior of states and other actors. Among the key norms affecting state behavior in constructivists' view is multilateralism. Several studies have examined the impact of norms and principled beliefs on international outcomes such as the evolution of the international human rights regime, bans on certain types of weapons, and humanitarian intervention in which the UN and other IGOs have played a role. They have found that international organizations can be not only "teachers" but also "creators" of norms; as such, they can socialize states into accepting certain political goals and values.[6]

Constructivists tend to see IGOs as actors that can have independent effects on international relations and as arenas in which discussions, persuasion, education, and argument take place that influence government leaders', businessmen's, and NGO activists' understandings of their interests and of the world in which they live. The consequences are not always positive, however, because IGOs can also stimulate conflicts; their actions may not necessarily be interests of their member states; and independent bureaucracies may develop agendas of their own.[7]

Realism, liberalism, and constructivism, then, are different "lenses" through which scholars view world politics and the United Nations.

DILEMMAS IN THE NEW MILLENNIUM

No matter which theory one finds most valuable, understanding the role of the UN in the twenty-first century requires the exploration of three dilemmas.

Dilemma One: Needs for
Governance Versus the UN's Weaknesses

The United Nations and other IGOs have faced increasing demands that they provide peacekeeping and peacebuilding operations, initiate international regulation to halt environmental degradation, alleviate poverty and inequality in the world, promote greater human economic and social wellbeing, provide humanitarian relief to victims of natural disasters and violence, and protect human rights for various groups. These are demands for global governance—not world government, but rules, norms, and organizational structures intended to address transboundary or interdependence problems that states acting alone cannot solve, such as crime, drugs, environmental degradation, and human rights violations.[8]

These demands test the capacity and the willingness of states to commit themselves to international cooperation and the capacity of the UN and other international organizations to function effectively. Can they meet these new demands without simply adding more programs? How can the initiatives be funded? Can the UN be more effective in coordinating the related activities of various institutions, states, and NGOs? Can it improve its own management and personnel practices? Can the UN adapt to deal with the changing nature of conflicts and persistent poverty and inequality in the era of globalization? The most important issues concerning the global economy are discussed and decided outside the UN system. The UN Charter's provisions are designed for interstate conflicts, yet most post–Cold War conflicts have been intrastate civil wars. The UN's membership has grown from 50 to 191 states.

Clearly the UN needs to reform to increase its capacity to meet new demands and to reflect the changing distribution of power and authority in the twenty-first century. One of the UN's strengths to date has been its flexibility in response to new issues and an expanded membership more than three times the size of the original membership. Its weakness is the rigidity of its central structures, its slowness to accommodate nonstate actors and the changing realities of geopolitics, and the continuing inability of member states to agree about major reforms. It has also been weakened by states' failure to meet their commitments to fund the UN. The demands for global governance require the commitment of states and enhanced institutional capacity in the UN; they therefore also require that states give up more of their sovereignty. This leads to the second dilemma.

Dilemma 2: Sovereignty Versus Challenges to Sovereignty

The long-standing principles of state sovereignty and nonintervention in states' domestic affairs are affirmed in the UN Charter, yet sovereignty has eroded on many fronts and is continually challenged in this era of globalization by issues and problems that cross states' borders and that states cannot solve alone. Historically, sovereignty empowered each state to govern all matters within its territorial jurisdiction. **Nonintervention** is the related principle that obliges other states and international organizations not to intervene in matters within the internal or domestic jurisdiction of a sovereign state. Global telecommunications, including the Internet and economic interdependencies such as global financial markets, international human rights norms, international election monitoring, and environmental regulation, are among the many developments that infringe on states' sovereignty and traditional areas of domestic jurisdiction. The growing activities of IGOs and NGOs erode the centrality of states as the primary actors in world politics. For example, Amnesty International (AI) and the International Commission of Jurists have been key actors in promoting human rights, sometimes exerting more influence than states themselves. **Multinational corporations** with operations in several countries and industry groups such as paper, oil, automobiles, and shipping are important players in trade negotiations, some having more resources than some states.

How is sovereignty challenged by these developments? Global telecommunications and economic interdependence diminish the control that governments can exercise over the information their citizens receive, the value of their money, financial transactions, and the health of their country's economy. NGOs can influence legislators and government officials both from within countries and from outside through transnational networks and access to the media.

International norms and rules, such as those on trade, the seas, intellectual property rights, ozone-depleting chlorofluorocarbons (CFCs), and women's rights, have been established through UN-sponsored negotiations. They set standards for states and relevant industries as well as for consumers and citizens. When states themselves accept commitments to uphold these standards (by signing and ratifying international treaties and conventions), they are simultaneously exercising their sovereignty (the commitment they make) and accepting a diminution of that sovereignty (the agreement to international standards that will then be open to international monitoring).

Although multilateral institutions in theory take actions that constitute intervention in states' domestic affairs only with their consent, there is now a growing body of precedent for **humanitarian intervention,** which has emerged as a new norm to justify international actions to alleviate human suffering during violent conflicts without the consent of the "host" country. It was invoked to provide food relief and to reestablish civil order in Somalia in 1993–1994, to justify the North Atlantic Treaty Organization's (NATO) bombing of Yugoslavia and Kosovo in 1999, and to call for international action against genocide in the Darfur region of Sudan in 2005–2006.

Increasing multilateralism, humanitarian intervention, and the challenges to sovereignty are linked to the third dilemma: needs for leadership.

Dilemma 3: The Need for Leadership
Versus the Dominance of a Sole Superpower

World politics in the early twenty-first century is marked both by the dominance of the United States as the sole superpower and a diffusion of power among many other states, the European Union as a key actor, and a wide variety of nonstate actors that exercise influence in different ways. Yet traditional measures of power in international politics do not necessarily dictate who will provide leadership or be influential within the UN and other IGOs.

Multilateral institutions such as the UN create opportunities for small and middle powers as well as for NGOs, groups of states, and IGOs' executive heads to exercise initiative and leadership. The UN secretary-general has become an increasingly important figure in the international arena; he is in demand for mediating conflicts and articulating international responses to a wide range of problems. Other key individuals even from small states—such as Tommy Koh, the former Singaporean ambassador to the UN who brought the nine-year-long negotiations in the UN Conference on the Law of the Sea (UNCLOS) to closure in 1982—can exercise leadership through technical expertise or diplomatic skill. Middle powers such as Australia, Canada, Brazil, and India have been influential in international trade negotiations on agricultural issues, as they have long been in peacekeeping and development. Brazil and India took the lead with a handful of other states in 2005 to promote Security Council reform. Within certain issue areas such as human rights, development, and environment, NGOs have not only gained voice but also provided key input for institutional and policy development.

With the demise of the Soviet Union in 1991, the United States became the sole remaining superpower—that is, the only state with intervention capabilities and interests in many parts of the globe. Democracy and market capitalism have spread to many more countries, and only three diehard Communist regimes, Vietnam, Cuba, and North Korea, remain. The United States is enjoying a new period of dominance in the world, but that dominance has been tempered by domestic debate over American interests and by other countries' fears of U.S. dominance, **unilateralism,** and irresponsibility in an era of expanded multilateralism. In the late 1990s, U.S. opposition to the creation of the International Criminal Court, the convention banning antipersonnel landmines, the Comprehensive Test Ban Treaty, and the Kyoto Protocol on Climate Change signaled a "go-it-alone" pattern that has continued in the early years of the twenty-first century with the Bush administration's opposition to international treaties that might limit U.S. actions.[9] This has worried proponents of multilateralism and international law; it has led many countries and NGOs to push ahead with these initiatives without U.S. participation; it has made many less willing to accept U.S. dominance.[10] The pattern was evident during the divisive debate in 2002–2003 about U.S. desire for military action against Iraq when Germany and France, as well as the smaller countries on the Security Council, refused to support a resolution authorizing U.S. and British use of force. In the eyes of many, the U.S. invasion of Iraq had huge consequences for the UN. Secretary-General Kofi Annan, for one, noted, "If . . . nations discount the legitimacy provided by the UN, and feel they can and must use force unilaterally and pre-emptively, the world will become even more dangerous."[11] Some would call the United States a "rogue superpower" today—one that like Gulliver, the hero of Jonathan Swift's *Gulliver's Travels,* needs to be "tied down" by the Lilliputians of the world through webs of rules and norms. Yet the dilemma for other countries and for the UN is that a superpower determined to pursue what it perceives to be its vital interests cannot readily be "tied down."

U.S. economic, military, technological, and other resources vastly exceed those of all other countries: The U.S. gross domestic product is more than 2.5 times the nearest rival, Japan; and the American military budget is more than twice as large as the budget of all NATO's European members. Power disparity such as this may make the United States "bound to lead," but the style of leadership required in a world marked by multilateralism is not one of unilateral action but one geared to building coalitions and consensus and achieving active consultation and cooperation.[12] Some would argue that the United States itself could become the enforcer of global rules. One former government official put it this way: "The sheer preeminence of American power could, in itself, be the ordering and taming principle of a disorderly and dangerous world."[13] Dominance alone, however, tends to inspire resistance. A dominant power can rely on its sheer weight to play hardball and gets its way—up to a point—and the prolonged insurgency and failures in Iraq following U.S. military intervention in 2003 demonstrate the limits of hard power. Leadership (and inspiring follower-ship) depend on soft power's inspiration and cultivation. But in a United Nations of 191 member states, many of which are small, weak, and not democratic, the multiplicity of voices makes the task of coalition building cumbersome and slow. Some neoconservatives in the United States have, for example, suggested that a coalition of liberal democracies might be a better source of legitimacy for dealing with global security threats than the UN.

The third dilemma, then, is that a sole superpower doesn't necessarily provide the leadership needed for initiatives and action within the UN and other multilateral institutions. And, to the degree to which that superpower pursues its own interests in defiance of the concerns of others, or of established international norms and rules, it may inspire resistance and opposition.[14]

CONCLUSION

Subsequent chapters explore these dilemmas in the context of different areas of UN activity. Chapter 2 outlines the historical foundations of the United Nations and describes the various structures, politics, and processes within it. Chapter 3 considers the major actors in the UN system, including NGOs, coalitions and blocs, small states and middle powers, and the United States and other major powers, as well as the UN secretary-general and the Secretariat. Chapter 4 deals with the UN's role in peace and security issues, including peacekeeping, enforcement, the challenges of peace building, humanitarian intervention, and nuclear proliferation. In chapter 5, which covers the role of the UN system in promoting development, we explore case studies of the women-in-development (WID) agenda, North-South conflict over the NIEO, and the debates over MNCs and poverty alleviation. Chapter 6 analyzes the role of the UN in the evolution of international human rights norms with case studies of the anti-apartheid movement, the women's rights agenda, the movement against slavery and slave-like practices, and the issues of genocide, crimes against humanity, and war crimes. Chapter 7 deals with two types of so-called human security issues: environmental degradation and health. Chapter 8 explores the need to reform the UN so that it can function more effectively and so retain legitimacy in the twenty-first century; the final chapter also discusses the leadership and role of the United States.

NOTES

1. Inis L. Claude Jr., *The Changing United Nations* (New York: Random House, 1965), 32.

2. Christopher S. Wren, "Annan Says All Nations Must Cooperate," *New York Times*, September 6, 2000.

3. See for example, Hans Morgenthau, *Politics Among Nations*, 4th ed. (New York: Knopf, 1967), and John J. Mearsheimer, "The False Promise of International Institutions," *International Security* 13, no. 3 (Winter, 1994–1995): 5–49.

4. See, for example, Michael W. Doyle, "Liberalism and World Politics," *American Political Science Review* 80, no. 4 (December 1986): 1151–1169; Hedley Bull, *The Anarchical Society: A Study of Order in World Politics* (New York: Columbia University Press, 1977); and Robert O. Keohane and Joseph Nye, *Power and Interdependence*, 3rd ed. (New York: Longman, 2001).

5. See, for example, Ronnie Lipschutz, "Reconstructing World Politics: The Emergence of Global Civil Society," *Millennium: Journal of International Studies* 21, no. 3 (1992): 398–399, and Craig Warkentin, *Reshaping World Politics: NGOs, the Internet, and Global Civil Society* (Lanham, Md.: Rowman and Littlefield, 2001).

6. See, for example, John Gerard Ruggie, "Multilateralism: The Anatomy of an Institution," in *Multilateralism Matters: The Theory and Praxis of an Institutional Form*, ed. John Gerard Ruggie (New York: Columbia University Press, 1993), 3–47; Martha Finnemore, *National Interests in International Society* (Ithaca: Cornell University Press, 1996); and Martha Finnemore and Kathryn Sikkink, "Taking Stock: The Constructivist Research Program in International Relations and Comparative Politics," *Annual Review of Political Science* 4 (2001): 391–416.

7. Michael Barnett and Martha Finnemore, *Rules for the World: International Organizations in Global Politics* (Ithaca: Cornell University Press, 2004).

8. Margaret P. Karns and Karen A. Mingst, *International Organizations: The Politics and Processes of Global Governance* (Boulder: Lynne Rienner, 2004).

9. Stewart Patrick and Shepard Forman, eds., *Multilateralism and U.S. Foreign Policy: Ambivalent Engagement* (Boulder: Lynne Rienner, 2002).

10. David M. Malone and Yuen Foong Khong, eds. *Unilateralism and U.S. Foreign Policy: International Perspectives* (Boulder: Lynne Rienner, 2003).

11. Quoted in "Binding the Colossus," *Economist* 369, no. 8351 (November 22, 2003): 25.

12. Joseph S. Nye, Jr., *Bound to Lead: The Changing Nature of American Power* (New York: Basic Books, 1990), and Joseph S. Nye, Jr., *The Paradox of American Power: Why the World's Only Superpower Can't Go It Alone* (Oxford: Oxford University Press, 2002).

13. Quoted in "Binding the Colossus," *Economist* 369, no. 8351 (November 22, 2003): 26.

14. Stephen Walt, *Taming American Power: The Global Response to U.S. Primacy* (New York: W. W. Norton, 2005).

2

◄○►

The Evolution of the
United Nations System

Political communities historically have tried to establish norms and rules for interacting with their neighbors. Many early schemes sought methods specifically designed to manage or eliminate conflict between differing parties. For example, the Chinese sage Confucius (551–479 BC) preached moderation in interstate relations and condemned the use of violence. The Greek city-states sought to establish more permanent protective alliances and mechanisms to deal with conflict before war broke out. Yet none of these arrangements was in reality either an "international" entity or an "organization." Groups were limited to a specific geographical area, and organizations were generally ad hoc arrangements lacking permanent institutionalized relationships.

More than a millennium later, European philosophers began to elaborate schemes for world unity. The Roman Catholic Church and its head, the pope, provided the focal point for many of these. For example, the medieval French writer Pierre Dubois (1250–1322) proposed that Christian (at that time, Catholic) leaders should form political alliances against those who violated prevailing norms. He even proposed that disputes be arbitrated by the pope. When the European states began to challenge religious authority, Hugo Grotius (1583–1645), an early Dutch legal scholar, proposed a new legitimacy based on international law.

The **Grotian tradition** elucidated a number of fundamental principles that serve as the foundation not for only modern international law but also for international organization.[1] For Grotius, all international relations were subject to the rule of law; that is, a law of nations and the law of nature, the latter serving as the ethical basis for the former. He rejected the idea that states can do whatever they wish and that war is the supreme right of states, the hallmark of their sovereignty. Grotius believed that states, like people, are basically rational and law-abiding entities capable of achieving cooperative goals.

17

Although the Grotian tradition posits an order in international relations based on the rule of law, Grotius himself was not concerned with an organization for administering this rule of law. Many subsequent theorists, however, have seen an organizational structure as a vital component in realizing the legal principles on which international relations are based. For example, the French writer Émeric Crucé (1590–1648) proposed a universal organization within which groups of ambassadors would hear disputes among complainants and decide how to approach the problem. Enforcement would occur through mutual military sanctions.

The Grotian tradition provided a foundation for the development of international law that is a crucial element in developing international organizations, rooted as they are in agreements between states and in commitments to cooperation. Yet state sovereignty—the idea that states have exclusive governing authority within their borders—became the cornerstone of European politics, as symbolized by the Treaty of Westphalia in 1648. A tension thus arose between the **Westphalian tradition,** with its emphasis on sovereignty, and the Grotian tradition, with its focus on law and order. Did the affirmation of state sovereignty mean that international law was irrelevant? Could international law threaten state sovereignty? Would states join an international body that might challenge or even undermine their sovereignty? Until the nineteenth century, the tensions were largely intellectual, and the impact on practice minimal. Then the Westphalian and Grotian traditions were joined.

NINETEENTH-CENTURY ROOTS OF CONTEMPORARY INTERNATIONAL ORGANIZATIONS

In the nineteenth century, ideas for international organizations and the practice of governments began to bear fruit. In a pioneering textbook on international organization, *Swords into Plowshares,* Inis Claude described how three major strands of thinking and practice emerged.[2] The first strand involved recognizing the utility of multilateral diplomacy in contrast to the standard practice of bilateral diplomacy. Beginning in 1815, the European states participated in the **Concert of Europe.** Under the Concert system, the leaders of the major European powers came together in multilateral meetings to settle problems and coordinate actions. Meeting more than thirty times between 1815 and 1878, the major powers legitimized the independence of new European states such as Belgium and Greece. At the last meeting in Berlin in 1878, they extended the reach of European imperialism by dividing up the previously uncolonized parts of Africa. These Concert meetings solidified some important practices followed by later international organizations, including multilateral consultation, collective diplomacy, and special status for great "powers." As Claude summarized: "The Concert system was the manifestation of a rudimentary but growing sense of interdependence and community of interest among the states of Europe."[3] A community of interest such as this was a vital prerequisite for modern international organizations.

The second strand involved the formation of public international unions. These agencies were initially established among European states to deal with problems stemming from the expanding commerce, communications, and technological innovation of the industrial revolution; for example, health standards for travelers, shipping rules on the Rhine River, increased mail volume, and the cross-boundary usage of the newly invented telegraph. The practical problems of expanding international relations proved amenable to intergovernmental cooperation through organizations such as the International Telegraphic Union, formed in 1865, and the Universal Postal Union, established in 1874. As they became increasingly interdependent, the European states found it necessary to cooperate on a voluntary basis to accomplish nonpolitical tasks. Thus, the public international unions gave rise to **functionalism**—the theory that IGOs can help states deal with practical problems in their international relations.

The public international unions spawned several procedural innovations; among them were international secretariats, that is, permanent bureaucrats hired from a variety of countries to perform specific tasks. They also developed the practice of involving specialists from outside ministries of foreign affairs as well as private interest groups in their work. Multilateral diplomacy was no longer the exclusive domain of traditional diplomats. In addition, the public unions began to develop techniques for multilateral conventions—law- or rule-making treaties. Many additional such organizations have been established in the twentieth century, including the International Maritime Organization and the International Civil Aviation Organization.

The third strand revolved around the **Hague system.** Czar Nicholas II of Russia convened two conferences in The Hague (Netherlands) of European *and* non-European states to consider techniques that would prevent war and the conditions under which arbitration, negotiation, and legal recourse would be appropriate. Exploring such issues in the absence of a crisis was a novelty. The Hague conferences of 1899 and 1907 led to the Convention for the Pacific Settlement of International Disputes, ad hoc international commissions of inquiry, and the Permanent Court of Arbitration, which still exists and has been used in recent years for handling claims arising from the 1979–1980 Iran hostage crisis.

The Hague conferences also produced several major procedural innovations. This was the first time that participants included both small and non-European states. The Latin American states, China, and Japan were given an equal voice, an advance that not only established the principle of universality but also bolstered legal equality. Thus, what had been largely a European state system until the end of the nineteenth century became a truly international system at the beginning of the twentieth. For the first time, multilateral diplomacy employed such techniques as the election of chairs, the organization of committees, and roll call votes, all of which became permanent features of twentieth-century organizations. The Hague conferences also advanced the codification of international law and promoted the novel idea that humankind has common interests.

Thus, the nineteenth-century innovations served as vital precursors to the development of international organizations in the twentieth century. Ideas and state action gelled. Governments established new approaches to dealing with problems of joint concern, including the multilateral diplomacy of the Concert system, the Hague system's legalistic mechanisms, and the functional public international unions. Innovative procedures were developed, participation was broadened, and international secretariats were institutionalized. Each has been extensively utilized during the twentieth century. These developments owed much to the changes associated with the industrial revolution: growing economic interdependence, technological innovations, and the increasing human and material destructiveness of war.

The institutional arrangements of the nineteenth century, however, did not prevent war among the major European powers. The Concert system broke into two competing military alliances at the turn of the twentieth century. Cooperation in other areas of interest proved insufficient to prevent war when national security was at stake. Hence, the outbreak of World War I pointed vividly to the weaknesses and shortcomings of the nineteenth-century arrangements. The twentieth century has been marked by the progressive expansion of international law and organizations and by the wide acceptance of multilateralism as a general practice in international relations. It was also the most violent and destructive century in history.

THE LEAGUE OF NATIONS

World War I had hardly begun when private groups and prominent individuals in Europe and the United States began to plan for the postwar era. Nongovernmental groups such as the League to Enforce Peace in the United States and the League of Nations in Great Britain were eager to develop more permanent frameworks for preventing future wars. President Woodrow Wilson's proposal to create a permanent international organization in the Versailles Peace Treaty was based on these plans.

The League of Nations reflected the environment in which it was conceived.[4] Almost half of the League Covenant's twenty-six provisions focused on preventing war. Two basic principles were paramount: Member states agreed to respect and preserve the territorial integrity and political independence of states and to try different methods of dispute settlement. If they failed, the League had the power under Article 16 to enforce settlements through sanctions. The second principle was firmly embedded in the proposition of collective security, namely, that aggression by one state should be countered by all members acting together as a "league of nations" with economic sanctions and force if necessary.

The League Covenant established an assembly and a council, the latter recognizing the special prerogative of great powers, a lasting remnant of the European Concert system, and the former giving pride of place to universality of membership (about sixty states at that time). Authority rested with the council, composed of four permanent and four elected members. The council was to be the settler of disputes, the enforcer of sanctions, and the implementer of peaceful settlements. The requirement of unanimity, however, made action difficult.

Although often considered a failure, the League did enjoy a number of successes, many of them on territorial issues. It conducted plebiscites in Silesia and the Saar, and then demarcated the German-Polish border. It settled territorial disputes between Lithuania and Poland, Finland and Russia, and Bulgaria and Greece, and it guaranteed Albanian territorial integrity against encroachments by Italy, Greece, and Yugoslavia.

The failure of the League's Council to act when Japan invaded Manchuria in 1931 pointed to the organization's fundamental weaknesses. The League Assembly, at the urging of small states, seized the initiative, though it lacked the power needed to respond to acts of aggression.

The League's response to the Italian invasion of Ethiopia in 1935 further undermined its legitimacy. The Ethiopians appealed to the League Council, to be met only by stalling actions for nine months. France and Great Britain had assured the Italian dictator Benito Mussolini that they would not interfere in his operations. The smaller states (and Russia) were horrified by the lack of support for Ethiopia. Eventually, the Council approved voluntary sanctions. But without unanimity, they carried little effect and were lifted in 1936. The sanctions were an example of the League's acting too little and too late. When the great powers proved unwilling to uphold the League's principles, the institution's power and legitimacy deteriorated. Nowhere was the absence of great-power support for the League felt more than in the failure of the United States, as a result of congressional opposition and a resurgence of isolationism, to join the organization.

The League of Nations was unable to act decisively against the aggression of Italy and Japan in the 1930s. Collective security failed as Britain and France pursued their own national interests. The League could not prevent the outbreak of World War II, yet it represented an important step forward in the process of international organization. Planning for the post–World War II peace began shortly before the United States entered the war and involved several high-level meetings of the Allied leaders—Roosevelt, Churchill, and Stalin—as well as other officials in Allied governments. Most important, this planning built on the lessons of the League in laying the groundwork for its successor, the United Nations. Despite the League's shortcomings, there was consensus on the importance of such an international organization, albeit one whose scope would be far greater than the League's. President Roosevelt, a firm believer in the importance of such an organization, early on sought to ensure domestic support for U.S. participation.

THE ORIGINS OF THE UNITED NATIONS

The Atlantic Charter of 14 August 1941—a joint declaration by President Franklin Roosevelt and Prime Minister Winston Churchill calling for collaboration on economic issues and a permanent system of security—served as the foundation for the Declaration by the United Nations in January 1942. Twenty-six nations affirmed the principles of the Atlantic Charter and agreed to create a new universal organization to replace the League of Nations. The UN Charter was then drafted in two sets of meetings, between August and October 1944, at Dumbarton Oaks in Washington, D.C. The participants agreed that the organization would be based on the principle of the sovereign equality of members and that all "peace-loving" states would be eligible for membership, thereby excluding the Axis powers—Germany, Italy, Japan, and Spain. It was also agreed that decisions on security issues would require unanimity of the permanent members of the Security Council, the great powers.

When the United Nations Conference on International Organization convened in San Francisco on 25 April 1945, delegates from the fifty participating states modified and finalized what had already been negotiated among the great powers. On 28 July 1945, with Senate approval, the United States became the first country to ratify the Charter, and it would take only three more months to obtain a sufficient number of ratifications (legal consents) from other countries. (An abridged and amended version of the UN Charter can be found in the appendix.)

One conference participant made the following comments after the Charter was signed:

> One of the most significant features was the demonstration of the large area of agreement which existed from the start among the 50 nations. . . . Everyone exhibited a serious minded determination to reach agreement on an organization which would be more effective than the League of Nations. . . . Not a single reservation was made to the Charter when it was adopted. . . . The conference will long stand as one of the landmarks in international diplomacy. . . . [Nonetheless] one wonders—will the conversations of men prove powerful enough to curb the might of military power or to harness it to more orderly uses?[5]

THE ORGANIZATION OF THE UNITED NATIONS

Basic Principles

Several principles undergird the structure and operation of the UN and represent fundamental legal obligations of all members. These are contained in Article 2 of the Charter as well as in other Charter provisions.

The most fundamental principle is the sovereign equality of member states. Since the Peace of Westphalia of 1648, states as political units do not recognize any higher governing authority. "Equality" refers to the legal status of states, not to their size, military power, or wealth; Russia, Lithuania, China, and Singapore, for instance, are thus equals. Sovereign equality is the basis for each state having one vote in the General Assembly. Yet inequality is also part of the UN framework, embodied in the permanent membership and veto power of five states in the Security Council: the United States, Russia, China, Great Britain, and France.

Closely related to the UN's primary goal of maintaining peace and security are the twin principles that all member states shall refrain from threatening or using force against the territorial integrity or political independence of any state, and from acting in any manner inconsistent with UN purposes; and that they shall settle their international disputes by peaceful means. During the last fifty years, states have often failed to honor these principles, and they have often failed even to submit their disputes to the UN for settlement. Yet the UN continues to demonstrate strong support for these core principles, as evidenced by its response to Iraq's occupation of Kuwait in 1990.

Members also accept the obligation to support **enforcement actions,** such as economic sanctions, and to refrain from giving assistance to states that are the objects of UN preventive or enforcement action. They have the collective responsibility to ensure that nonmember states act in accordance with these principles as necessary for the maintenance of international peace and security.

A further key principle is the requirement that member states fulfill in good faith all the obligations assumed by them under the Charter; this affirms a fundamental norm of all international law and treaties, *pacta sunt servanda*—treaties must be carried out. One of the UN Charter obligations is payment of assessed annual contributions (dues) to the organization.

The final principle in Article 2 asserts that "nothing in the present Charter shall authorize the United Nations to intervene in matters which are essentially within the domestic jurisdiction of any state or shall require the Members to submit such matters to settlement under the present Charter . . . [although] this principle shall not prejudice the application of enforcement measures under Chapter VII." This provision underscores the long-standing norm of nonintervention in the domestic affairs of states. But who decides what is an international problem and what is a domestic one? Since the UN's founding in 1945, the scope of what is considered international has broadened with UN involvement in human rights, development, and environmental degradation. In the post–Cold War era, many UN peacekeeping operations have involved intrastate rather than interstate conflicts, that is, conflicts within rather than between states. The UN's founders recognized the tension between the commitment to act collectively against a member state and the affirmation of state sovereignty represented in the nonintervention principle. They could not foresee the dilemmas that changing definitions of security, new issues, and ethnic conflicts would pose.

The Preamble and Article 1 of the UN Charter both contain references to human rights and obligate states to show "respect for the principle of equal rights and self-determination of peoples." Hence, discussions about human rights have always been regarded as a legitimate international activity rather than solely a domestic concern. Actions to promote or enforce human rights have been more controversial.

In Article 51 the Charter affirms states' "right of individual or collective self-defence" against armed attack. Thus, states are not required to wait for the UN to act before undertaking measures in their own (and others') defense. They are obligated to report their responses, and they may create regional defense and other arrangements. This "self-defence" principle, not surprisingly, has led to many debates over who initiated hostilities and who was the victim of aggression. For example, in the Middle East conflicts, was it Israel or the Arab states that first used force? Indeed, a special committee labored for many years over the problem of defining aggression itself before concluding that the UN Security Council has the ultimate responsibility of determining acts of aggression.

Structure

The structure of the United Nations as outlined in the Charter includes six major bodies: the Security Council, the General Assembly, the Economic and Social Council (ECOSOC), the Trusteeship Council, the International Court of Justice, and the Secretariat. Each has changed during the life of the organization in response to external realities, internal pressures, and interactions with other organs.[6] In reality, however, we speak of the **United Nations system,** because the UN has evolved into far more than these six organs.[7] Articles 57 and 63 of the Charter called for the affiliation with the UN of various agencies established by separate international agreements to deal with particular issues, as discussed later in this chapter.

The General Assembly, the Security Council, and the Economic and Social Council have also used their powers to create separate and subsidiary bodies, particularly since 1960; in doing so, they have illustrated the phenomenon of "IGOs creating other IGOs."[8] For example, in 1964, developing countries, with their large majority in the General Assembly, created the United Nations Conference on Trade and Development (UNCTAD) in order to focus more attention on the specific trade and development problems of newly independent and developing states. Figure 2.1 captures the complexity of the UN system; yet even this chart does not show, for example, the large number of UN-sponsored global conferences held since the 1970s that have been an important part of the UN's activities.

In the sections that follow, we discuss how the six major UN organs have evolved in practice and some of their political dynamics. We also provide brief discussions of one specialized agency and of UN global conferences.

The Security Council.   Under Article 24 of the Charter, the Security Council has primary responsibility for maintaining international peace and security and the authority to act on behalf of all members of the UN. The provisions for carrying out this role are spelled out in Chapters VI and VII of the Charter. Chapter VI deals with the peaceful settlement of disputes and provides a wide range of techniques for investigating disputes and helping parties achieve resolution without using force. Chapter VII specifies the Security Council's authority to identify aggressors and to commit all UN members to take enforcement measures, such as economic sanctions, or to provide military forces for joint action. Prior to 1990, the Security Council used its enforcement powers under Chapter VII on only two occasions. During the Cold War years, it relied on the peaceful settlement mechanisms under Chapter VI to respond to the many conflicts on its agenda; for example, prior to 1992, all UN peacekeeping forces were authorized under Chapter VI. One dramatic change of the post–Cold War era, therefore, is the Security Council's increased use of Chapter VII, including its provisions for economic sanctions and military enforcement action. (We discuss the Security Council's activities further in chapter 4.)

The Security Council was deliberately designed to be small so that it could facilitate swifter and more efficient decisionmaking in dealing with threats to international peace and security. It is also the only UN body that incorporates permanent and nonpermanent members. The five permanent members (P-5)—the United States, Great Britain, France, Russia (successor state to the seat of the Soviet Union in 1992), and the People's Republic of China (PRC, replacing the Republic of China [ROC] in 1971)—are key to Security Council decisionmaking because each has **veto** power. The nonpermanent members, originally six in number and expanded to ten in 1965, are elected for two-year terms and participate fully in the council's work. At least four nonpermanent members must vote in favor of a resolution for it to pass. Under current rules, no country may serve successive terms as a nonpermanent member. Following an "informal agreement" in the 1940s to allocate specific seats by geographic region, the General Assembly in 1965 adopted a resolution allocating five of the nonpermanent seats to Africa and Asia, two each to Latin America and Western Europe, and one to Eastern Europe.

The designation of permanent members reflected the distribution of military power in 1945. The logic of their designation was to ensure the UN's ability to respond quickly and decisively to aggression. Their veto power reflected the unwillingness of either the United States or the Soviet Union to accept UN membership without such a provision. It also reflected a realistic acceptance by others that the

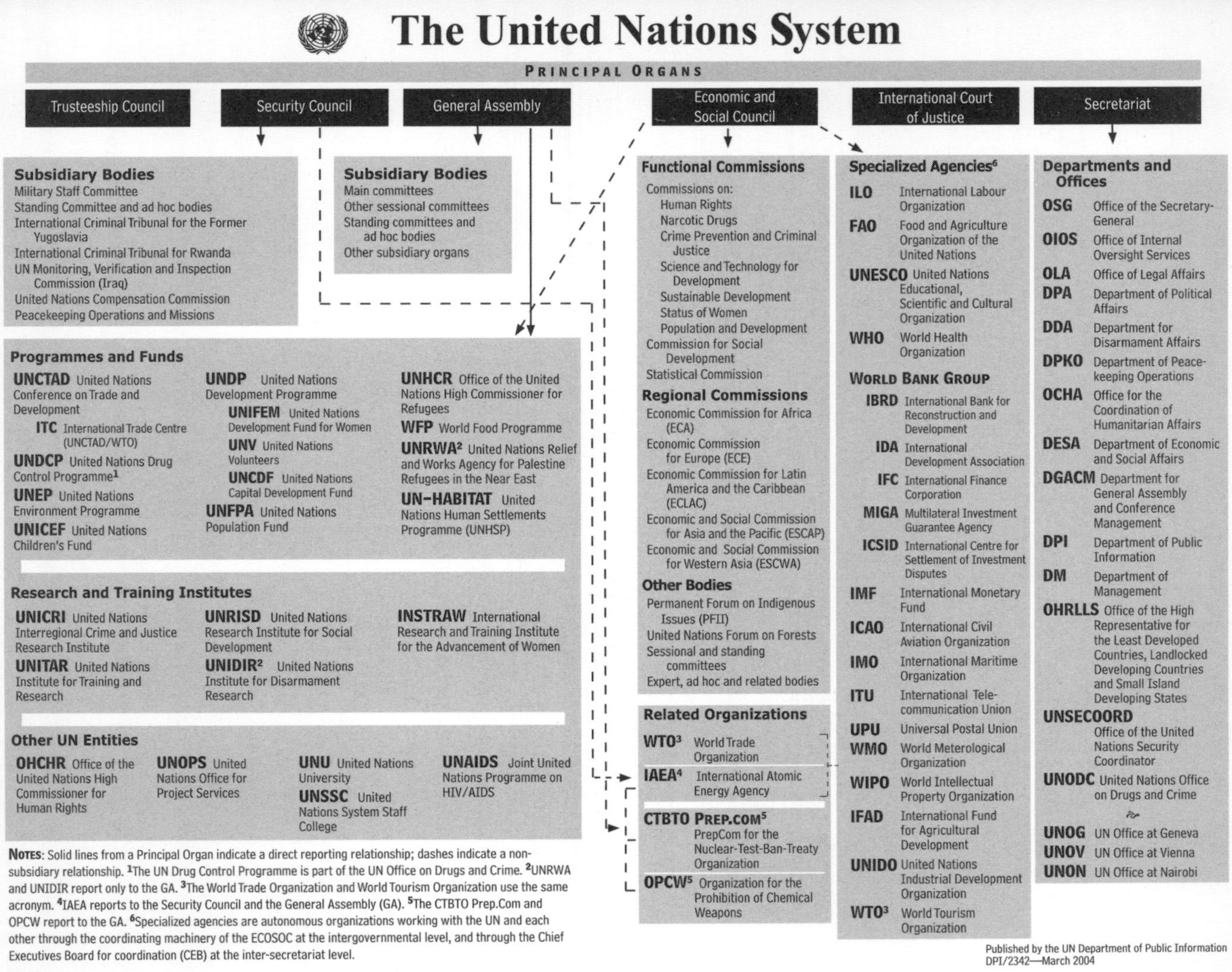

The United Nations System

PRINCIPAL ORGANS

| Trusteeship Council | Security Council | General Assembly | Economic and Social Council | International Court of Justice | Secretariat |

Trusteeship Council

Security Council

Subsidiary Bodies
Military Staff Committee
Standing Committee and ad hoc bodies
International Criminal Tribunal for the Former Yugoslavia
International Criminal Tribunal for Rwanda
UN Monitoring, Verification and Inspection Commission (Iraq)
United Nations Compensation Commission
Peacekeeping Operations and Missions

General Assembly

Subsidiary Bodies
Main committees
Other sessional committees
Standing committees and ad hoc bodies
Other subsidiary organs

Programmes and Funds
UNCTAD United Nations Conference on Trade and Development
ITC International Trade Centre (UNCTAD/WTO)
UNDCP United Nations Drug Control Programme[1]
UNEP United Nations Environment Programme
UNICEF United Nations Children's Fund

UNDP United Nations Development Programme
UNIFEM United Nations Development Fund for Women
UNV United Nations Volunteers
UNCDF United Nations Capital Development Fund
UNFPA United Nations Population Fund

UNHCR Office of the United Nations High Commissioner for Refugees
WFP World Food Programme
UNRWA[2] United Nations Relief and Works Agency for Palestine Refugees in the Near East
UN–HABITAT United Nations Human Settlements Programme (UNHSP)

Research and Training Institutes
UNICRI United Nations Interregional Crime and Justice Research Institute
UNITAR United Nations Institute for Training and Research

UNRISD United Nations Research Institute for Social Development
UNIDIR[2] United Nations Institute for Disarmament Research

UNU United Nations University
UNSSC United Nations System Staff College

INSTRAW International Research and Training Institute for the Advancement of Women

Other UN Entities
OHCHR Office of the United Nations High Commissioner for Human Rights

UNOPS United Nations Office for Project Services

UNAIDS Joint United Nations Programme on HIV/AIDS

Economic and Social Council

Functional Commissions
Commissions on:
Human Rights
Narcotic Drugs
Crime Prevention and Criminal Justice
Science and Technology for Development
Sustainable Development
Status of Women
Population and Development
Commission for Social Development
Statistical Commission

Regional Commissions
Economic Commission for Africa (ECA)
Economic Commission for Europe (ECE)
Economic Commission for Latin America and the Caribbean (ECLAC)
Economic and Social Commission for Asia and the Pacific (ESCAP)
Economic and Social Commission for Western Asia (ESCWA)

Other Bodies
Permanent Forum on Indigenous Issues (PFII)
United Nations Forum on Forests
Sessional and standing committees
Expert, ad hoc and related bodies

Related Organizations
WTO[3] World Trade Organization
IAEA[4] International Atomic Energy Agency
CTBTO PREP.COM[5] PrepCom for the Nuclear-Test-Ban-Treaty Organization
OPCW[5] Organization for the Prohibition of Chemical Weapons

International Court of Justice

Specialized Agencies[6]
ILO International Labour Organization
FAO Food and Agriculture Organization of the United Nations
UNESCO United Nations Educational, Scientific and Cultural Organization
WHO World Health Organization
World Bank Group
IBRD International Bank for Reconstruction and Development
IDA International Development Association
IFC International Finance Corporation
MIGA Multilateral Investment Guarantee Agency
ICSID International Centre for Settlement of Investment Disputes
IMF International Monetary Fund
ICAO International Civil Aviation Organization
IMO International Maritime Organization
ITU International Telecommunication Union
UPU Universal Postal Union
WMO World Meteorological Organization
WIPO World Intellectual Property Organization
IFAD International Fund for Agricultural Development
UNIDO United Nations Industrial Development Organization
WTO[3] World Tourism Organization

Secretariat

Departments and Offices
OSG Office of the Secretary-General
OIOS Office of Internal Oversight Services
OLA Office of Legal Affairs
DPA Department of Political Affairs
DDA Department for Disarmament Affairs
DPKO Department of Peacekeeping Operations
OCHA Office for the Coordination of Humanitarian Affairs
DESA Department of Economic and Social Affairs
DGACM Department for General Assembly and Conference Management
DPI Department of Public Information
DM Department of Management
OHRLLS Office of the High Representative for the Least Developed Countries, Landlocked Developing Countries and Small Island Developing States
UNSECOORD Office of the United Nations Security Coordinator
UNODC United Nations Office on Drugs and Crime

UNOG UN Office at Geneva
UNOV UN Office at Vienna
UNON UN Office at Nairobi

NOTES: Solid lines from a Principal Organ indicate a direct reporting relationship; dashes indicate a non-subsidiary relationship. [1]The UN Drug Control Programme is part of the UN Office on Drugs and Crime. [2]UNRWA and UNIDIR report only to the GA. [3]The World Trade Organization and World Tourism Organization use the same acronym. [4]IAEA reports to the Security Council and the General Assembly (GA). [5]The CTBTO Prep.Com and OPCW report to the GA. [6]Specialized agencies are autonomous organizations working with the UN and each other through the coordinating machinery of the ECOSOC at the intergovernmental level, and through the Chief Executives Board for coordination (CEB) at the inter-secretariat level.

Published by the UN Department of Public Information
DPI/2342—March 2004

FIGURE 2.1   UN System Chart

UN could not undertake enforcement action against its strongest members. The veto, however, has always been controversial among small states and middle powers. Today, with the many changes in world politics and the reality that other states contribute more financially than three of the permanent members, there are serious questions about the legitimacy and effectiveness of the geographical composition of permanent membership and its economic representation. (We explore these issues further in chapter 8.)

The functioning and prestige of the Security Council have waxed and waned. The founders envisioned the Security Council as the UN's premier body, charged with the most essential security tasks and participating in other key tasks such as the election of the secretary-general, justices to the International Court of Justice, and new members in collaboration with the General Assembly. During the 1940s, the council held approximately 130 meetings a year. The Cold War diminished its use, and 1959 saw only five meetings. The Soviet Union used its veto power frequently during the Cold War to block action on many peace and security issues. The United States did not exercise its veto until the 1970s, a reflection of its early dominance and many friends. (See table 2.1 for a summary of vetoes cast and note how infrequently the veto has been used since 1995.) One practice that keeps the number of vetoes low is that abstentions are not counted as negative votes (that is, as vetoes). China, for example, used this strategy on many occasions in the 1990s to register its unhappiness but avoid blocking council action.

Since the late 1980s, the Security Council's activity, power, and prestige have once again grown. Between 1987 and 1993, the number of meetings each year rose from 49 to 171; after dropping somewhat in the mid-1990s, the number rose to more than 225 in 2004. The Security Council conducts more of its business, however, in informal consultations rather than in formal meetings, and it reaches many decisions by consensus rather than by formal voting. Past criticisms of the private, informal meetings that were common in the early 1990s led the council to open these sessions to nonmembers and to circulate draft agendas. In addition, in the late 1990s, the council began the practice of consulting with countries that contributed troops for peacekeeping operations, and with NGOs involved in humanitarian and peacebuilding missions. Council presidents are active in facilitating discussions and building consensus, and they determine when the members are ready to reach a decision and vote formally. The president also confers regularly with the secretary-general and with relevant states and other actors that are not represented on the council. The council presidency rotates monthly among the fifteen members. Since 1987, the permanent members have engaged in their own informal consultations as a group, a practice that enhanced their close cooperation in the Gulf conflict and other crises. Their cooperation was a key factor in the Security Council's post–Cold War activism, but it also fueled perceptions of great-power collusion.

TABLE 2.1   Vetoes in the Security Council, 1946–2005

Period	China	France	Britain	U.S.	USSR/Russia	Total
1946–1955	1	2	—	—	80	83
1956–1965	0	2	3	—	26	31
1966–1975	2	2	10	12	7	33
1976–1985	0	9	11	34	6	60
1986–1995	0	3	8	24	2	37
1996–1999	2	0	0	2	0	4
2000–2005	0	0	0	8	1	9
Total	4.5	18	32	80	122	257

*Between 1946 and 1971 the Chinese seat on the Security Council was occupied by the Republic of China (Taiwan), which used the veto only once (to block Mongolia's application for membership in 1955). The first veto by the present occupant, the People's Republic of China, was therefore not exercised until 25 August 1972.

SOURCE: http://www.globalpolicy.org/security/data/vetotab.htm.

Since 1987, the Security Council has taken action on more armed conflicts, made more decisions under Chapter VII of the Charter, and authorized more peacekeeping operations and enforcement actions, such as sanctions, than at any previous time. It has taken the unprecedented step of creating ad hoc war-crimes tribunals to prosecute individuals responsible for ethnic cleansing in Rwanda, the former Yugoslavia, and Sierra Leone. These trends reflect the absence of Cold War hostility and the permanent members' greater solidarity. Yet this very increase in the Security Council's activity has led other members to push for reform in the council's membership so that it reflects the world of the twenty-first century, not the world of 1945. Because many of the council's Chapter VII decisions in the 1990s proved more ambitious than either the member states were willing to support with resources and troops or the secretariat could effectively manage (e.g., the Iraqi Oil-for-Food Programme, or OFFP), the Security Council damaged its own and the UN's credibility. There were some hard-learned lessons also about the limits of the UN's capacity to launch and manage large-scale enforcement operations (discussed further in chapter 4). Since the late 1990s, the council has addressed a number of broader issues, rather than just specific conflicts; these include children and armed conflict, HIV/AIDS as a security threat in Africa, humanitarian intervention, women and conflict resolution, and terrorism. The expansion of the agenda underscores the new, transnational human security issues the council confronted and the need to design effective responses.

The Security Council's agenda has always been selective—influenced by geopolitical and regional realities. Colombia's long civil war has never been on the

PHOTO 2.1   UN Security Council authorizes deployment of European Union force during Democratic Republic of Congo elections, 25 April 2006. *UN Photo 117124/Evan Schneider.*

agenda because it and other Latin American states prefer not to see this internationalized. The United States preferred not to bring the conflict in Vietnam to the Security Council in the 1960s. India resists allowing the issue of Kashmir to be discussed by the council even though one of the oldest peacekeeping observer groups is stationed along the line of control between Indian and Pakistani forces in Kashmir. This selectivity has been particularly problematic with respect to humanitarian crises (as we discuss in chapter 4), because the council has responded to some crises, such as Somalia, but largely ignored others, such as the long civil wars in the Sudan and Congo.

The determination of the United States and NATO to undertake bombing of Yugoslavia (Serbia) in 1999 to halt the humanitarian crisis in Kosovo, as well as military action against Iraq in 2003, both without Security Council authorization, raised serious questions about the Security Council's continuing legitimacy and authority. Had the council degenerated into a failed body that no longer was capable of carrying out its responsibilities or could it continue to perform vital tasks?[9]

Under the Charter, the Security Council is given enormous formal power, but not direct control over the means to use that power. The council depends upon the voluntary cooperation of states willing to contribute to peacekeeping missions, to enforce sanctions, to pay their dues, and to support enforcement actions either under UN command or by a coalition of the willing. Most important, states' voluntary compliance depends on their perceptions of the legitimacy of the Security

Council and its actions. The increase in council activity since 1990 has made the issues of reform in membership far more urgent because they relate closely to ensuring the continuing legitimacy of the council's authority and its ability to function effectively. (These issues are discussed in chapter 8.) The Security Council, however, also shares a number of responsibilities with the General Assembly, and it is to that central organ of the UN that we now turn.

The General Assembly.   The General Assembly, like its predecessor in the League of Nations, was designed as the general debate arena where all members would be equally represented according to a one-state/one-vote formula. It is the organization's hub, with a diverse agenda and the responsibility for coordinating and supervising subsidiary bodies but with power only to make recommendations to members, unlike the Security Council, which can make decisions on behalf of all members. The assembly has important elective functions: electing the nonpermanent members of the Security Council, ECOSOC, and the Trusteeship Council; appointing judges to the International Court of Justice; and, upon the recommendation of the Security Council, admitting states to UN membership and appointing the secretary-general. The words of one observer, however, capture the essence of the General Assembly's role as "the favorite principal organ of weak states, which have always constituted a majority of the UN's membership, because it gives them an influence over decisions that they lack anywhere else in the international system."[10] To paraphrase Shakespeare, if "all the world's a stage," the UN General Assembly is center stage—one particularly important for states such as Malta, Singapore, Zambia, Costa Rica, and Fiji.

The General Assembly, based on its right to consider any matter within the purview of the Charter (Article 10), also may undertake initiatives in peace and security matters if the Security Council cannot. The **Uniting for Peace Resolution** passed during the Korean War in 1950, however, ignited controversy over the respective roles of these two organs. Under the resolution, the General Assembly claimed authority to recommend collective measures when the Security Council was deadlocked by a veto. It was subsequently used to deal with crises in Suez and Hungary (1956), the Middle East (1958), and the Congo (1960). In all, nine emergency special sessions of the General Assembly dealt with threats to international peace when the Security Council was deadlocked. The P-5 have now tacitly agreed that only the Security Council should authorize the use of armed force, and this is widely accepted. Neither in 1999 nor in 2003, when the United States could not gain council approval for interventions in Kosovo and Iraq respectively, did it invoke the Uniting for Peace precedent and seek General Assembly affirmation. Nonetheless, the General Assembly does have the right to make inquiries and studies with respect to conflicts (Articles 13, 14), and the right to be kept informed by the Security Council and the secretary-general (Articles 10, 11, 12).

The General Assembly is a cumbersome body, however, for dealing with delicate situations concerning peace and security. It is a far better organ for the symbolic politics of agenda setting and for mustering large majorities in support of resolutions.

The Security Council and General Assembly share responsibilities for Charter revision. The assembly can propose amendments with a two-thirds majority; two-thirds of the member states, including all the permanent members of the Security Council, must then ratify the changes. The General Assembly and Security Council together may also call a general conference for the purpose of Charter review. There have been only two instances to date, however, of Charter amendment, both taken to enlarge the membership of the Security Council (1965) and the Economic and Social Council (1965 and 1973).

Regular meetings of the General Assembly are held for three months (or longer) each fall; they begin with a "general debate" period when heads of state, prime ministers, and foreign ministers by the score come to New York to speak before the assembly. In addition, there have been more than twenty special sessions called to deal with specific problems (for example, with financial and budgetary problems in 1963; with development and international economic cooperation in 1975; with small island developing states in 1999; and with children in 2002). These special sessions should not be confused with the emergency special sessions convened under a Uniting for Peace Resolution.

The bulk of the General Assembly's work is done in six functional committees on which all members sit: the First, or Disarmament and International Security Committee; the Second, or Economic and Financial Committee; the Third, or Social, Humanitarian, and Cultural Committee; the Fourth, or Special Political and Decolonization Committee; the Fifth, or Administrative and Budgetary Committee; and the Sixth, or Legal Committee. The assembly also has created other, smaller committees to carry out specific tasks, such as studying a question (the ad hoc Committee on International Terrorism) or framing proposals and monitoring (the Committee on Peaceful Uses of Outer Space, the Disarmament Commission, and the Human Rights Committee).

Each year, the General Assembly elects a president and seventeen vice presidents who serve for that year's session. By tradition, presidents come from small and middle power states. Only once (in 1969) has a woman been elected. The president's powers come largely from personal influence and political skills in guiding the assembly's work, averting crises, bringing parties to agreement, ensuring that procedures are respected, and accelerating the large agenda.

Almost from the UN's inception, politics within the General Assembly has mirrored world politics and the effects of the egalitarian voting principle of one-state/one-vote. The General Assembly became the place to set the agendas of world politics, to get ideas endorsed or condemned, to have actions taken or rejected. Any state can propose an agenda item, and the assembly has been an especially valued tool of small and developing states. As membership in the UN changed with de-colonization, the assembly's agendas and voting patterns changed as well, so that by 1960 developing countries commanded a majority of votes; by 1963, they could muster a two-thirds majority. The assembly's agenda was dominated by Cold War and decolonization issues in the 1950s, but from the 1960s to the 1980s, developing countries used their voting power to push a number of Third World goals, especially the proposed New International Economic Order (discussed in chapter 5). The lopsided voting and frequent condemnations of U.S. policies led the United States, in particular, to regard the General Assembly as a "hostile place" by the mid-1970s. Assembly agendas still largely reflect developing coun-tries' interests in self-determination, economic development, global inequalities, and neocolonialism.

Early in the UN's history, states from the same geographic region as well as those having shared economic or political interests formed **voting blocs** to coordinate positions on particular issues and build support for them. The Soviet Union and Eastern Europe formed the most cohesive bloc and voted together almost 100 per-cent of the time. Since the end of the Cold War, Russia and other East European states have tended to vote with the West Europeans or with a larger "Northern" group that emerged during the 1980s. The countries of the North, however, have never been as cohesive as those of the South because many European states have been more supportive of developing countries' concerns than the United States. A small subgroup, led by the United States, that included a few West European coun-tries and Israel (but not Japan), for example, has constituted a minority on many issues. Since the 1960s, when Latin American, African, and Asian states formed the Group of 77 (G-77), it, together with the **Nonaligned Movement** (NAM)—whose membership is very similar—has dominated General Assembly agendas and vot-ing. In the late 1980s, the G-77's cohesion began to break down somewhat with the rapid economic growth of various **newly industrializing countries** (NIC), includ-ing the so-called Asian tigers such as Singapore, Malaysia, and South Korea, and the resulting divergence in interests among developing countries. Voting in the General Assembly still shows the North-South divide, but differences in social and economic conditions among Asian, African, and Latin American countries make common policy positions difficult to forge. Chapter 3 explores further the phe-nomenon of blocs and coalitions.

Beginning in the 1990s, a key division has formed over a global agenda dealing with **human security** that incorporates human rights, development, international security, and the environment. Self-determination, formerly associated with colo-nialism, has taken on a broader interpretation associated with concerns about neo-colonialism, Northern dominance, the right to development, nuclear testing, and disarmament by the nuclear powers. Political rights and UN intervention have also emerged as major issues; resolutions addressing human rights problems in particular countries and UN aid to countries holding free and democratic elections have divided members. Resolutions related to the Middle East that target Israel or deal with "Palestine" draw lopsided majorities, the United States and Israel frequently being left in a tiny, isolated minority. "The North-South division now overwhelmingly defines the terms of political debate in the Assembly," concluded one study of voting alignments. "And views of self-determination and economic development . . . reflect the continuing great differences between rich and poor nations."[11]

Many criticisms directed at the UN are really criticisms of the General Assembly. The number of resolutions passed in the General Assembly steadily increased over time, from about 117 annually during the first five years to 133 in 1961–1965, 188 in 1971–1975, and 343 in 1981–1985, when efforts to reduce the number began. That effort was short-lived, however. In 2001–2002, the assembly reached a new high of 360 resolutions, leveling off to around 300 in recent sessions. It is estimated that over time, between 75 and 80 percent of these resolutions were adopted by consensus, often "ritual resolutions"—their texts repeated almost verbatim year after year. At the height of the North-South conflict in the 1970s, resolutions dealing with the proposed New International Economic Order were repeatedly passed over the strong objections of most developed countries, whose support and action were essential to accomplishing any of the changes being called for by the General Assembly's majority.

A similar pattern has been repeated in the post–Cold War era: Large Southern majorities approve resolutions on self-determination and disarmament with little concern for enforcement. This situation has led many to argue that there are too many resolutions with redundant or watered down content; in addition, the resolutions call for too many reports, and the delegates show too little concern about following up on commitments made.[12]

Despite the criticism, the General Assembly has nevertheless played an important role in the development of international law through the work of the Sixth (Legal) Committee and the International Law Commission, an elected group of thirty-four individuals that drafts international conventions (law-creating treaties). General Assembly resolutions may lay the groundwork for new international law by articulating new principles, such as one that called the seas the "common heritage of mankind." These principles then may (or may not) be embodied in conventions. The "common heritage" principle ultimately shaped the 1982 Convention on the Law of the Sea and the 1967 Treaty on Outer Space. In 2005, the General Assembly called on the international community to conclude the comprehensive convention on international terrorism.

With the end of the Cold War, the General Assembly's importance within the UN system declined. The epicenter of UN activity shifted back to the Security Council and the Secretariat, a development that dismayed the South because it would like to have more consultation between the General Assembly and the Security Council on peace and security issues if it cannot secure changes in the membership of the council itself. Likewise, with the UN Secretariat forced by its most powerful members (and largest contributors) to downsize and streamline in the name of efficiency and improved management, the South has worried that its interests are being given shorter shrift. Unquestionably, the General Assembly needs reform and revitalization—more than just a shorter agenda and fewer resolutions. The difficulty lies in gaining the approval of a majority of member states.

The Economic and Social Council.   ECOSOC, with its fifty-four members, is supposed to coordinate the UN's economic and social programs, various subsidiary bodies, functional commissions, regional commissions, and the specialized agencies. The sections of the UN Charter (Chapters IX and X) dealing with ECOSOC are short and very general, but it is the most complex part of the UN system because it covers the broadest areas of activity, the majority of expenditures, and the greatest number of programs. The founders of the UN envisaged that the various specialized agencies, ranging from the ILO and WHO to the World Bank and the IMF, would play primary roles in operational activities devoted to economic and social advancement and that ECOSOC would be responsible for coordinating those activities. Hence, the Charter speaks of ECOSOC's functions in terms of that coordination and also charges it with undertaking research and preparing reports on economic and social issues, making recommendations, preparing conventions, and convening conferences. Of those tasks, coordination has been the most problematic because so many activities lie outside the effective jurisdiction of ECOSOC.

With respect to the specialized agencies, for example, Articles 61–66 of the Charter empower ECOSOC only to issue recommendations and to receive reports from them. It has no control over their budgets or secretariats. Recommendations and conventions drafted by ECOSOC require General Assembly approval. ECOSOC is supposed to coordinate various bodies, including the UN Development Programme (UNDP), the UN Fund for Population Activities (UNFPA), the UN Children's Fund (UNICEF), and the World Food Programme (WFP). Compounding the confusion, those programs report to ECOSOC as well as the General Assembly. ECOSOC's agenda includes such diverse topics as housing, narcotic drug control, water resources, population, trade, rights of children, industrial development, literacy, the status of women, the environment, and the rights of indigenous peoples. Of these, human rights and development form the two largest subject areas.

Part of ECOSOC's work is done in ten functional commissions dealing with social development, human rights, narcotic drugs, the status of women, science and technology for development, sustainable development, population, forests, crime prevention, and statistics. The latter reflects the importance of statistical studies and analysis to economic and social programs, and the major contribution the UN system makes annually to governments, researchers, and students worldwide through its statistical studies. A series of regional commissions and standing committees are also part of the ECOSOC sphere. It is a complex system (see fig. 2.1), one whose work is not easy to follow. It is also not hard to see why ECOSOC's mandate for coordination has been almost impossible to fulfill.

ECOSOC's membership has been expanded twice through Charter amendments. The original eighteen members were increased to twenty-seven in 1965 and to fifty-four in 1973. Members are elected to three-year terms, and the regional blocs ensure geographic representation. It is also through consultative status with ECOSOC that some NGOs have official relationships with the UN and its activities. ECOSOC meets once a year and alternates between UN headquarters in Geneva and New York. Motivated by recognition that states with the ability to pay should be continuously represented, four of the five permanent members of the Security Council (all but China) have been regularly reelected. Decisions are subject to simple majority votes.

Because the huge expansion of UN economic and social activities has left ECOSOC with an unmanageable task, there have been persistent but largely unsuccessful calls for reform since the mid-1960s. (We discuss this further below.)

The Secretariat.   The 7,500 professional and clerical staff based in New York, Geneva, Vienna, Nairobi, and elsewhere around the world who are employed by the UN Secretariat are international civil servants—individuals who, though nationals of member countries, represent the international community. The first IGO secretariats were established by the Universal Postal Union and the International Telegraphic Union in the 1860s and 1870s, but their members were not independent of national governments. The League of Nations established the first truly international secretariat; though responsible for carrying out the will of the League's members, it was impartial or neutral in serving the organization as a whole and dedicated to its principles. This same practice carried over to the United Nations and the specialized agencies; Secretariat members were recruited from an ever-broader geographic base as the membership expanded. Secretariat members are expected to refrain from promoting national interests, but not to give up their national loyalty—a difficult task at times in a world of strong nationalisms. Articles 100 and 101 deal with the issues of the Secretariat's internationalism and independence.

Functions of the Secretariat.   The UN Secretariat is subject to many problems common to other complex organizations, such as growth in number of personnel and budgets, inefficiency, and weak management. The Secretariat has frequently been criticized for lapses in its neutrality, duplication of tasks, and poor administrative practices. (We discuss these later in this chapter.) Only about one-third of Secretariat personnel are based at headquarters in New York or Geneva; others are posted in more than 140 countries. Their work often has little to do with the symbolic politics of the General Assembly, or even with the highly political debates of the Security Council. Rather, Secretariat members implement the many economic and social programs that represent much of the UN's tangible contribution to fulfilling the Charter promises to "save succeeding generations from the scourge of war . . . promoting social progress and better standards of life in larger freedom." The Secretariat is also responsible for gathering statistical data, issuing studies and reports, servicing meetings, preparing documentation, and providing translations of speeches, debates, and documents in the UN's six official languages.

The Secretary-General.   The UN secretary-general's position has been termed "one of the most ill-defined: a combination of chief administrative officer of the United Nations and global diplomat with a fat portfolio whose pages are blank."[13] The secretary-general is the chief administrator or manager of the organization, responsible for providing leadership to the Secretariat, preparing the UN's budget, submitting an annual report to the General Assembly, and overseeing studies conducted at the request of the other major organs. Article 99 of the Charter authorizes the secretary-general "to bring to the attention of the Security Council any matter which in his opinion may threaten the maintenance of international peace and security."

Over time, secretaries-general also have come to play significant political roles as spokespersons for the organization and as mediators drawing on the Charter's spirit as the basis for taking initiatives. Yet the secretary-general is simultaneously subject to the demands of two constituencies—member states and the Secretariat itself. States elect the UN's chief administrator and do not want to be either upstaged or publicly opposed by the person in that position. As chief executive officer, the secretary-general also has to have good personnel management and budgetary skills.

The secretary-general holds office for a five-year renewable term on the recommendation of the Security Council and election by two-thirds of the General Assembly. The process of nomination is intensely political, with the P-5 having key input. For example, when the United States opposed the reelection of Boutros Boutros-Ghali in 1996, it forced members to agree on an alternate candidate, Kofi Annan. Efforts to establish a better means of selecting this global leader have not succeeded. Not surprisingly, the persons elected have tended to come from relatively small and neutral states (see box 2.1). Because of differences in personality and skills as well as in the challenges faced, each secretary-general has undertaken his tasks in a different way, with varying consequences for the organization. Collectively, however, the secretaries-general have been a key factor in the emergence of the UN as a key actor in world politics. (We explore the secretary-general's role more fully in chapter 3.)

BOX 2.1   UN Secretaries-General, 1946–Present

Secretary-General	Nationality	Dates of Service
Trygve Lie	Norway	1946–53
Dag Hammarskjöld	Sweden	1953–61
U Thant	Burma	1961–71
Kurt Waldheim	Austria	1972–81
Javier Pérez de Cuéllar	Peru	1982–91
Boutros Boutros-Ghali	Egypt	1992–96
Kofi Annan	Ghana	1997–2006

The International Court of Justice.   Although its predecessor, the Permanent Court of International Justice, enjoyed only a loose association with the League of Nations, the International Court of Justice as the judicial arm of the UN, headquartered in The Hague, shares responsibility with the other major organs for ensuring that the principles of the Charter are followed. Its special role is providing states with an impartial body for settling legal disputes in accordance with international law and giving advisory opinions on legal questions referred to it by international agencies. All members of the UN are *ipso facto* parties to the ICJ Statute.

The ICJ has **noncompulsory jurisdiction,** meaning that parties to a dispute (only states) must all agree to submit a case to the court; it has no executive to enforce its decisions and no police to bring a party to justice. Enforcement therefore depends on the perceived legitimacy of the court's decisions, the voluntary compliance of states, and the "power of shame" if states fail to comply. The fifteen ICJ justices are expected to act independently of their national affiliations. They are elected by the General Assembly and the Security Council for nine-year terms (five are elected every three years) on the basis of qualifications befitting appointment to the highest judicial body in their home countries and recognized competence in international law. Together, the judges represent the "main forms of civilization and principal legal systems of the world."[14]

Empowered to interpret treaties and to determine the legal status of states' customary practices (two primary sources of international law), the ICJ had 109 contentious cases brought before it between 1946 and 2005. The court has never been heavily burdened, although its case load has increased significantly in recent years. During the Cold War, major powers preferred other means to settle their disputes. Usage declined markedly in the 1970s when many developing states rejected its jurisdiction. The increased caseload since 1990 is a result of greater trust in the court by developing countries and in part because many newer international conventions require the use of the ICJ to resolve disputes. Also, the court has instituted the option of using a chamber of five justices to hear and determine cases by summary procedure, thus speeding up what is often a lengthy process.

ICJ cases have seldom reflected the major political issues of the day because few states want to trust a legal judgment for the settlement of a largely political issue. Several cases addressed decolonization questions (for example, South West Africa or Namibia and Western Sahara). The ICJ has helped states resolve numerous territorial disputes (for example, the Case Concerning the Land and Maritime Boundary between Cameroon and Nigeria), disputes over delimitation of the continental shelf (in the North Sea, for example), and fisheries jurisdiction (such as in the Gulf of Maine and fisheries jurisdiction cases). The ICJ has also ruled on the legality of nuclear tests, hostage taking, the right of asylum, use of force, environmental protection, and expropriation of foreign property.

In addition to dealing with contentious cases between states, the ICJ has issued twenty-five **advisory opinions** to international agencies. Such opinions have involved the various UN organs asking for legal advice. Among the more prominent have been the *Reparation for Injuries Suffered in the Service of the United Nations* opinion (1949), in which the UN's international legal personality was clarified, and the *Certain Expenses* opinion (1962). In the former, the UN was accorded the right to seek payment from a state held responsible for the injury or death of a UN employee; in the latter, peacekeeping expenses were ruled to be part of the fiscal obligation of member states. Most recently, the court provided an advisory opinion on the legality of the barrier wall being erected by Israel in the Occupied Territories of the West Bank.

The ICJ is complemented by other international tribunals within the UN system. Some are tied to specialized agencies, such as the International Labour Organization's Administrative Tribunal and the Centre for the Settlement of Investment Disputes within the World Bank. Others have been established to adjudicate specific issues such as the Law of the Sea Tribunal and the International Criminal Court. Still others are temporary bodies designed to deal with a particular problem, for example, the UN Compensation Commission dealt with claims against Iraq following its invasion of Kuwait; and ad hoc war crimes tribunals adjudicate crimes in the former Yugoslavia, Rwanda, and Sierra Leone.

The establishment of the International Criminal Court (ICC) in 1998 was a response to a long-standing movement to create a permanent international criminal court and the difficulties posed by the ad hoc nature of the Yugoslavia and Rwanda tribunals. With this step, UN members moved international adjudication and international law in the direction of accepting individuals as subjects of international law. Historically, only states have had such status. In contrast to the ICJ, the new court has both compulsory jurisdiction and jurisdiction over individuals who are charged with "serious" war crimes that represent a "policy or plan" rather than just random acts committed by personnel in wartime. Crimes must also have been "systematic or widespread," not single abuses. Among the types of crimes covered are genocide, crimes against humanity, war crimes, and crimes of aggression. The ICC is discussed in detail in chapter 6.

The Trusteeship Council.   This council was originally established to oversee the administration of the non-self-governing trust territories that carried over from the mandate system of the League of Nations. These territories were former German colonies, mostly in Africa, that were placed under the League-supervised control of other powers (Great Britain, France, Belgium, and Japan) because they were deemed unprepared for self-determination or independence. The eleven UN trust territories also included Pacific islands that the United States had liberated from Japan during World War II. The council's supervisory activities include reporting on the status of the people in the territories, making annual reports, and conducting periodic visits to the territories. The council terminated the last trusteeship agreement when the people of the Trust Territory of the Pacific Islands voted in November 1993 for free association with the United States. Thus, the very success of the Trusteeship Council spelled its demise. To avoid amending the UN Charter, the council continues to exist, but it no longer meets in annual sessions.

In recent years, there has been discussion about new functions for the Trusteeship Council, though no action has yet been taken. One proposal calls for giving the council responsibility for monitoring conditions that affect the global commons (seas, seabed, and outer space). Another calls for using it to assist "failed states." A third proposal would transform the council into a forum for minority and indigenous peoples.

The Specialized Agencies.   Although the origins of functionally specialized international organizations can be found in the nineteenth-century public international unions, their full development and maturation occurred in the twentieth century in response to growing needs to deal with increasingly specialized problems. The founders of the UN envisaged that functional agencies would play key roles, particularly in activities aimed at economic and social advancement. Indeed, Articles 57 and 63 of the Charter called for the affiliation with the UN of various organizations established by separate international agreements to deal with issues such as health (the World Health Organization, or WHO), food (Food and Agriculture Organization, or FAO), science, education, and culture (UN Educational, Scientific and Cultural Organization, or UNESCO), and economics (the International Monetary Fund, or IMF, and the World Bank). Today, nineteen specialized agencies are formally affiliated with the UN through agreements with ECOSOC and the General Assembly (see fig. 2.1). Like the UN itself, they have global responsibilities, but separate charters, memberships, budgets, and secretariats, as well as their own interests and constituencies. They operate largely independent of UN control, despite ECOSOC's efforts to coordinate their vast areas of activity.

The economic institutions are discussed further in chapter 5. We provide a brief overview here of one specialized agency: the International Labour Organization (ILO); other specialized agencies, such as the WHO and FAO, are discussed in subsequent chapters.

The origins of the ILO can be traced to the nineteenth century, when two industrialists, the Welshman Robert Owen and the Frenchman Daniel Legrand, advocated an organization to protect labor from abuses of industrialization and the development of the labor movement in Europe and the United States. Labor's growing political importance and Owen and Legrand's ideas led to the adoption of the Constitution of the International Labour Organization in 1919 by the Paris Peace Conference. The constitution was based on the belief that world peace could be accomplished only by attention to social justice. Thus, the ILO became an autonomous organization within the structure of the League of Nations, an institutional model utilized for other functional organizations related to the United Nations.

Setting standards for treatment of workers is the ILO's major activity. Since 1919, more than two hundred labor conventions have been signed and 180 recommendations made. In many countries, the international labor codes on such issues as the right to organize and bargain, the ban on slavery and forced labor, the regulation of hours of work, agreements about wages, and workers' compensation and safety are translated directly into domestic law. Among the conventions designated "fundamental" by the ILO are the conventions against forced labor, freedom of association, discrimination, and child labor. Sixty-eight states have ratified all these conventions; the United States has ratified but two, the forced labor and child labor conventions.

Under Article 33, the ILO can take action against states to secure compliance, but in practice, the ILO generally promotes compliance through the less coercive means of gathering member state reports and hearing complaints of noncompliance. Using peer pressure and persuasion rather than hard sanctions, it makes recommendations to states on how their records can be improved and offers technical assistance programs to facilitate state compliance.

The ILO, headquartered in Geneva, Switzerland, accomplishes its work through three major bodies, each of which includes a tripartite representation structure involving government officials, employers, and workers. This integration of governmental and nongovernmental representatives is a unique approach not duplicated in any other IGO. Nonetheless, the arrangement has been uniquely suited to represent both governmental and societal interests. Much like the General Assembly, the International Labour Conference meets annually; the Governing Body—the executive arm of the ILO—establishes programs, and a Committee of Experts examines governments' reports on compliance with ILO conventions.

BOX 2.2   Global Conferences

Aging, 1982, 2002
Agrarian Reform and Rural Development, 1984
Children, 1990
Climate, 1979, 1990
Desertification, 1977
Environment, 1972
Environment and development, 1992
Food, 1974, 1996, 2002
Habitat, Human Settlements, 1976, 1996
Human Rights, 1968, 1993
Law of the Sea, 1958, 1973–1982
New and Renewable Sources of Energy, 1981
Population, 1974, 1984
Population and Development, 1994
Racism, 1987, 2001
Science and Technology for Development, 1979
Social Development, 1995
Sustainable Development, 2002
Sustainable Development of Small Island Countries, 1995
Water, 1972
Women, 1975, 1980, 1985, 1995

Global Conferences.   Multilateral global conferences date back to the period after World War I when the League of Nations convened conferences on economic affairs and disarmament. They increased in the 1970s with a series of UN-sponsored conferences relating to the environment, food supply, population, women's rights, water supplies, and desertification, as listed in box 2.2. The conferences focus international attention on salient issues of the day and bring together diverse constituencies.

There are basically two types of global conferences, each having different processes and outcomes. The first is a traditional intergovernmental conference the purpose of which is to negotiate a law-creating treaty for states subsequently to ratify. The UN Conference on Law of the Sea (UNCLOS) between 1973 and 1982 is illustrative. It was a protracted political process involving more than 160 governments in complex negotiations triggered by the need to update the law of the sea following the independence of many new states in the 1960s and the endorsement by the UN General Assembly in 1967 of the principle that the high seas and deep seabed are part of the "common heritage of mankind." The Law of the Sea Convention, concluded in 1982, came into effect in 1994, and has been ratified now by more than 120 states. Participants in the law of the sea negotiations were official representatives of states; there was no formal participation by NGOs. Items were negotiated in committees of the whole and the outcome was a legal document, not statements of goals and aspirations.

In contrast, for other UN global conferences, preparatory meetings involving NGOs and states are a critical part of the political process where decisions are made on many key agenda items, experts are brought in, and NGO roles at the conference itself are determined. By one estimate, at least 60 percent of the final global conference outcomes are decided during the preparatory process.[15] The preparatory processes frequently also include in-depth studies that provide background data for the conference and may serve as wake-up calls to the international community. For example, studies prior to the 1982 World Assembly on Aging showed that developing countries would be confronted by challenges of aging populations comparable to those in industrial countries in less than fifty years. Often, two conferences are held in the same location—an intergovernmental conference and a parallel NGO conference. This arrangement permits extensive interaction between the two with NGOs proposing measures, governments reacting, and negotiations shaping specific outcomes that had not been previously agreed during the preparatory process. Yet how much NGOs are allowed to participate in the official global conference has varied widely (we discuss this topic further in chapter 3).

The outcomes of global conferences usually include a number of goals, sometimes new institutions and programs to meet those goals, calls on states to take action, and, in several cases, a charge to NGOs with key roles in implementation. For example, the First World Conference for Women in 1975 led to the creation of the UN Development Fund for Women (UNIFEM) to support projects run by women in developing countries. The Platform of Action approved by the 1995 Fourth World Conference on Women in Beijing called for "empowering women" through access to all kinds of economic resources.

Subsequent chapters analyze the outcomes of specific global conferences, such as the Rio Earth Summit in 1992, the Vienna human rights conference in 1994, and the Beijing women's conference in 1995, as well as follow-up conferences. These and other conferences have been important for articulating new international norms, expanding international law, creating new structures, setting agendas for the UN itself and for governments through programs of action, and promoting linkages among the UN, the specialized agencies, NGOs, and governments. They have contributed to the growth of NGOs and civil society in many parts of the world, and, in doing so, have raised important questions about who participates in global governance. They have also increased understanding of the links among issues as seemingly disparate as environmental protection, human rights (especially for women), poverty alleviation, development, trade, and technology dissemination. The conferences have served as a counter hierarchy to established international organizations.

Critics have argued that these large and expensive media events are too unwieldy, often duplicate the work of other bodies, and are an inefficient way to identify problems and solutions. Undoubtedly, the global conferences are political events, and their outcomes are products of political compromises that merely exhort governments to accept general principles and frameworks to guide their policies. With the combined outputs of all the conferences in the 1990s, the issue was how to monitor what was actually being done and how to integrate the implementation of those outcomes with the work of the main UN organs, especially ECOSOC.

PERSISTENT ORGANIZATIONAL PROBLEMS AND THE NEED FOR REFORM

Like any organization, the UN has had institutional problems. The most persistent of these involve financing, coordination, management, and structural weaknesses. Each can be linked to the proliferation of issues addressed by the organization and the corresponding challenges to the system's capacity for effective response. There are also deep political disagreements among the UN's members, and strong and weak states either attempt to steer the organization in directions congruent with their objectives or try to prevent it from infringing on their interests. Everyone agrees that the UN needs reforming, but there are sharp disagreements about what kind of reform is needed and for what purpose. Chapter 8 is devoted to reform issues, but we focus here on three specific sets of issues: financing, management, and coordination.

Financing

Like the UN system itself, the UN's budget is complex; in fact, it comprises several budgets. And as is true of other organizations, the size of that budget and, more important, members' contributions have proven controversial.

The UN's regular budget covers its administrative machinery, major organs, and their auxiliary agencies and programs. It grew from less than $20 million in 1946 to more than $1.4 billion in 2004. Peacekeeping expenses constitute a separate budget, and each of the specialized agencies also has a separate budget. These three types of budget expenditures are funded by contributions assessed among member states according to a formula based on ability to pay. In addition, however, many economic and social programs (such as UNICEF, UNDP, WFP, and UN High Commissioner for Refugees [UNHCR]) are funded by states' voluntary contributions, which frequently exceed the amounts of their assessments. Table 2.2 illustrates the relative size of each of these categories of budget expenditure based on assessed and voluntary contributions and changes between 1986 and 2004. The escalation of peacekeeping costs in the early post–Cold War years (1992–1995) is particularly notable. Also evident are the effects of the major powers' insistence on "no growth" in the UN's regular budget since the early 1990s, despite developing countries' interests in increased UN social and economic activities. Prior to that time, UN budgets had grown with the membership increases, new programs and agencies, inflation, and currency rate fluctuations.

The formulas for member states' assessed contributions for the regular budget and for peacekeeping operations are reevaluated every three years. The General Assembly's Committee on Contributions considers national income, per capita income, economic dislocations (such as from war), and members' ability to obtain foreign currencies. Initially, the highest rate (for the United States) was set at 40 percent of the assessed budget. The minimum rate was 0.04 percent for states with the most limited means. Over time, these rates have been adjusted: The U.S. share was reduced to 22 percent, and the minimum dropped to 0.01 in 1978 and 0.0001 in 1997. Between 1985 and 2002, for example, Japan's share increased significantly from 11.82 percent to 18.9 percent; but the Soviet/Russian figure declined from 11.98 percent to 1.15 percent, a reflection of Russia's reduced size and increased economic difficulties. Russia now contributes less than Brazil, South Korea, and Canada. Figure 2.2 shows the scale of assessments for major contributors and the majority of UN members for the three-year period 2001–2004. Two things are particularly striking: First, Russia and China's assessments are too small to appear on the chart; and second, 182 UN members contribute less than 25 percent of the budget. The nine remaining states contribute more than 75 percent of the UN's regular budget.[16]

Not surprisingly, the UN has frequently experienced difficulties in getting states to pay their assessments. States fail to fulfill their legal obligations to pay for reasons ranging from budget technicalities to poverty to politics or unhappiness with the UN in general or with specific programs and activities. The result has been periodic financial crises. The only sanction provided by the Charter in Article 19 is the denial of voting privileges in the General Assembly if a member falls more than two years in arrears.

In the early 1960s, the first financing crisis arose over UN peacekeeping operations in the Congo and Middle East: The Soviet Union, other Communist countries, and France refused to pay their assessments because, in their view, peacekeeping authorized by the General Assembly under Uniting for Peace resolutions was illegal. The second crisis arose in the 1980s when the United States began withholding part of its dues. Congress and the Reagan administration were unhappy with specific UN policies and with the **politicization** of many agencies; the

TABLE 2.2   UN System Expenditures, 1986–2004 (in $U.S. millions)

Year	Assessed Contributions				Voluntary Contributions			Total
	Regular	Peacekeeping	Agencies	Total Assessed	Organs	Agencies	Total Voluntary	
1986	725	242	1,142	2,109	3,075	951	4,026	6,135
1990	838	379	1,495	2,712	4,436	1,346	5,782	8,494
1995	1,181	3,281	1,847	6,309	5,778	1,159	6,937	13,246
2000	1,113	2,139	1,766	5,018	4,023	1,406	5,429	10,447
2004	1,389	3,345	2,000	6,734	—	—	—	6,734

SOURCE: http://www.globalpolicy.org/finance/tables/tabsyst.htm, ttp://www.globalpolicy.org/finance/tables/finvol.htm.

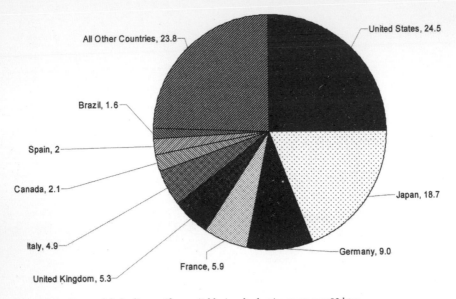

Source: http://www.globalpolicy.org/finance/tables/reg-budget/percentassess03.htm.

FIGURE 2.2   Assessments for Major Contributors to the UN Budget

General Assembly's procedures, which gave the United States, though the largest contributor, little weight in budget decisions; UN administration and management; and the size of the U.S. assessment relative to that of other wealthy states, specifically Japan and Germany.

In the late 1990s, the UN faced its most serious financial crisis. Member states owed the UN more than $2.5 billion for current and past assessments to cover regular expenses and peacekeeping expenses. Only 100 of 185 members had paid in full. The United States, by far the biggest debtor, owed $1.6 billion, or two-thirds of the total due. Many members faced major economic problems that made payments difficult. The financial crisis prompted by these **arrearages** (unpaid assessments or debts) threatened the organization's ability to fulfill the various mandates given it by member states and illustrated the second dilemma: the tension between demands for governance and institutional weakness arising from states' unwillingness (the United States being one example) or inability (the situation of many states in economic difficulties) to pay their assessed contributions. The crisis was partially resolved by an agreement struck in the U.S. Congress and with the UN General Assembly to reduce the U.S. assessments for the regular budget and peacekeeping and for payment of all arrears by 2003, subject to certain conditions.[17] Nonetheless, the financing problem persists. In 2005, arrearages to the UN's regular budget totaled $777 million, the United States alone owing 78 percent, or $607 million. And after the General Assembly session in September that year, the Bush administration proposed approving only interim budgets until UN reforms are passed, a controversial way of trying to manage reform through budgetary manipulation.

Beyond states' assessed and voluntary contributions, the UN is limited in finding ways to finance its activities and programs. It has neither the authority to borrow money nor a history of private fund-raising. Although the current financial crisis would be significantly reduced if the United States paid its debts, the long-term problem would persist, namely, how to fund adequately the many economic, social, and security activities that member states have approved. Secretary-General Kofi Annan's millennial report, *We the Peoples,* noted,

> When the scope of our responsibilities and the hopes invested in us are measured against our resources, we confront a sobering truth. The budget for our core functions . . . is about 4 percent of New York City's annual budget and nearly a billion dollars less than the annual cost of running Tokyo's fire department. Our resources are simply not commensurate with our global tasks.[18]

Administration and Management

UN effectiveness has also been plagued by administrative problems. The UN Secretariat grew almost continuously until the 1990s: from 300 persons in 1946 to 3,237 in 1964; rising to 11,303 in 1974 and reaching a peak of 14,691 in 1994; declining to less than 8,000 in the early years of the new millennium. This spurt of growth stemmed from the proliferation of programs and activities, which ranged from peacekeeping missions to technical assistance, and the expansion of the UN's membership. As the UN bureaucracy expanded, charges of political bias and administrative inefficiency surfaced. The United States has been particularly vocal in this regard.

During the 1950s and early 1960s, Soviet Secretariat personnel were charged with maintaining too close a relationship with their government. During the 1970s, the charge was that heads of some specialized agencies, particularly UNESCO's Amadou-Mahtar M'Bow, FAO's Edouard Saouma, and WHO's Halfdan Mahler, were serving as spokespersons for the Third World.

The UN has also been charged with mismanagement and inefficiency. In the 1970s, the UN's own studies concluded that lack of coordination within UN economic development programs made them costly and ineffective. Such criticisms grew in the 1980s when many programs were approved with little consideration of financing and program evaluation was weak to nonexistent.

The first five secretaries-general paid little attention to internal management of the Secretariat and also had little incentive for change. Thus, it took the UN more than fifty years to adopt management systems such as program reviews, internal audits, performance evaluations for staff members, and effective recruitment and promotion practices. Even then, developed countries were more concerned about effective management, financial control, and clear objectives than were many developing countries.

When Kofi Annan became secretary-general in January 1997, he was pressured by the United States in particular to reduce the size of the Secretariat by 25 percent and implementing other reforms. These included merging departments, cutting administrative costs, strengthening the UN resident coordinators' roles as leaders of UN country teams, preparing a code of conduct for the staff, and reducing documentation by 25 percent. In addition, Annan's "quiet revolution" involved a number of important structural changes, such as grouping thirty departments into four sectoral areas (peace and security, humanitarian affairs, development, and economic and social affairs); creating an executive committee to coordinate the work of each; establishing a senior management group to bring coherence to the UN's work and serve as a cabinet; inaugurating the post of deputy secretary-general; setting up a kind of think tank for the Secretariat to provide analytical and research capacity independent of member governments; centralizing development administration in the UN Development Group; reorganizing the Department of Humanitarian Affairs into a new Office for the Coordination of Humanitarian Affairs; and consolidating human rights bodies under the Office of the High Commissioner for Human Rights (OHCHR). He could make these changes because they did not require charter amendments.

Much more serious than the questions of the size and effectiveness of the UN Secretariat has been a series of scandals that surfaced early in the new millennium. These raised issues of mismanagement and accountability. The most highly publicized was the scandal about the UN's management of the Oil-for-Food Programme.

Initiated in 1996, the Oil-for-Food Programme (OFFP) program was an exception to the comprehensive sanctions imposed on Iraq in 1990 that permitted limited sales of Iraqi oil to finance food supplies and medicine as humanitarian relief. About $67 billion were transferred through the program. In 2004, sources revealed that Saddam Hussein's government had pocketed more than $10 billion from smuggling and kickbacks. The control of smuggling and the approval of contracts were responsibilities of the P-5, but administration of the contracts was a Secretariat task. Among those accused of receiving kickbacks were companies, European politicians, the Palestine Liberation Organization (PLO), and UN administrators, including the UN director of the OFFP.

Six investigations of the UN and the OFFP have been conducted by the U.S. government. Paul Volcker, the former U.S. Federal Reserve chairman, oversaw a UN investigation that examined contractor overcharges, violations of bidding rules, and insufficiently monitored contractors. Although Secretary-General Kofi Annan was not found guilty, his son was implicated, and others at the UN resigned or were fired. The scandal provided plenty of fuel for UN critics in the United States and elsewhere. It raised major questions about the UN's ability to manage large, long-term projects and, hence, the wisdom of ambitious Security Council actions. Yet, who was more responsible for the failures: the P-5 or the Secretariat? Regardless of the answer, the UN's reputation was tarnished.

In response to the OFFP scandal, the Secretariat introduced measures to improve the performance of senior management, including a better selection system for senior officials, the monitoring of individual performance, and a new, independent Office of Internal Oversight Services. With the adoption of policies covering anti-fraud and corruption, whistleblower protection, financial disclosure, conflict of interest, and procurement contracts, the Secretariat is being reorganized to prevent the type of personnel abuses found in the oil for food scandal. In short, the Secretariat needs to grow in capacity, adapt its management and working procedures, and introduce efficiency measures to maintain its effectiveness and legitimacy.

Coordination

The problem of multiple uncoordinated agencies engaged in similar tasks has plagued the UN system from the beginning. Yet, ironically, the founders designed the organization to be decentralized because this would increase the capacity of different groups to participate while minimizing the potential for politicization. Although increasingly issues do not fit into clear sectoral or regional boundaries, a call persists for the better coordination of programs, agencies, and activities within the UN system.

There are a plethora of reports and recommendations for improving ECOSOC's effectiveness as the main coordinating agency for economic and social programs and for reform of the UN's development activities. Three prominent ones are UNDP's 1969 Jackson Report, the 1991 Nordic UN Project, and the 1995 Commission on Global Governance. Incremental changes are easier to effect, however, than revolutionary ones. Furthermore, the coordination problems have been compounded by the global conferences of the 1990s. Each conference spawned a special commission to follow up on the program of action, yet because of zero-growth budgets, there have been fewer resources to meet greater demands. Recent changes have involved refocusing ECOSOC's activities around cross-cutting issues and strengthening its authority to ensure the implementation of resolutions, decisions, and agreed conclusions.[19]

Coordination for economic and social development, however, also involves dialogues with the World Bank and IMF; more effective relationships with the specialized agencies, funds, and programs; and the greater involvement of NGOs in policymaking processes. The various reforms of the late 1990s have had the effect of making it politically in the interest of specialized agencies to become more oriented to the UN system as a whole. The Millennium Development Goals approved in 2000 represent a major shift towards greater coordination (we explore this subject further in chapter 5).

Coordination and management issues have also plagued UN efforts to deal with humanitarian crises produced by war and natural disasters—whether they be those that emerge over time, such as drought, or sudden incidents, such as the Indian Ocean tsunami, earthquakes, and storms. Typically, there is a functional division of responsibilities: UNHCR manages refugee camps; UNICEF handles water and sanitation; WFP is responsible for food supplies; and WHO handles the health sector. In a number of situations, peacekeeping forces were mandated to safeguard relief workers and supplies. Yet, as one observer described, "the United Nations did not respond as a system but rather as a series of separate and largely autonomous agencies. Each had its own institutional dynamics, formulated its own priorities, and moved according to a timetable of its own devising."[20] Complaints about uncoordinated emergency responses have become increasingly frequent. In 1998, the Office for the Coordination of Humanitarian Affairs was created, headed by an undersecretary-general who is responsible for coordinating all emergency relief within and outside the UN system. Still, UN specialized agencies and private relief NGOs frequently resist giving up their independence and compete for a share of the action. The 2004 tsunami in the Indian Ocean and the devastating 2005 earthquake in Kashmir drew attention once more to the need for more coordinated action. Finally, transnational human security issues such as the HIV/AIDS epidemic particularly demand better coordination and management. The UN system's adaptations since the mid-1980s to deal with the epidemic illustrate a model of better coordination (we explore this subject further in chapter 7).

Efforts to address coordination issues in the UN system often lead to greater centralization of activities. These steps are controversial because any proposal to bring agencies under more effective centralized control conflicts with the deliberately decentralized nature of the system. In addition, each proposal for change advantages some agencies, states, and NGOs while disadvantaging others. That is why the process of reform is so challenging.

CONCLUSION

Differing interests and value systems contribute to the controversies over these organizational issues. The major industrialized countries tend to be interested in promoting order in the international system as well as managerial and financial efficiency. The developing countries tend to be more concerned with promoting justice, that is, with achieving greater economic and political equity through the redistribution of resources and enhanced participation in key decisionmaking.

IGOs like the UN have been created largely to promote and protect the interests of states. They enhance the opportunities for participation and influence by small states, coalitions of states, and NGOs. They have also facilitated their own emergence as actors in the international system. We explore the opportunities for these various actors in the UN system in chapter 3.

NOTES

1. Hersch Lauterpacht, "The Grotian Tradition in International Law," in *The British Year Book of International Law* (London: Oxford University Press, 1946), 1–56.

2. Inis L. Claude Jr., *Swords into Plowshares: The Problems and Progress of International Organization,* 3rd rev. ed. (New York: Random House, 1964), esp. ch. 2.

3. Ibid., 22.

4. On the League, see F. S. Northledge, *The League of Nations: Its Life and Times, 1920–1946* (New York: Holmes and Meier, 1986); and F. P. Walters, *A History of the League of Nations* (New York: Oxford University Press, 1952).

5. Norman J. Padelford (executive officer for Commission IV of the UN Conference Secretariat), letter to family and friends, June 26, 1945.

6. Paul Taylor and A. J. R. Groom, eds., *The United Nations at the Millenium: The Principal Organ* (New York: Continuum, 2000). Works on the specific organs include Sydney D. Bailey, *The Procedure of the UN Security Council,* 3rd ed. (New York: Oxford University Press, 1999); David M. Malone, ed., *The UN Security Council: From the Cold War to the 21st Century* (Boulder: Lynne Rienner, 2004); Edward Newman, *The UN Secretary-General: From the Cold War to the New Era: A Global Peace and Security Mandate* (New York: Palgrave, 1998); Miguel Marin-Bosch, *Votes in the UN General Assembly* (The Hague: Kluwer Law International, 1998).

7. The difference is exemplified in the two UN Web sites: one for the central organs, http://www.UN.org; and one for the system as a whole, http://www.unsystem.org.

8. Harold K. Jacobson, *Networks of Interdependence: International Organizations and the Global Political System,* 2nd ed. (New York: Random House, 1984), 39.

9. See the debate between Michael J. Glennon, "Why the Security Council Failed," *Foreign Affairs* 82, no. 3 (May-June 2003): 16–35, and Edward C. Luck, "Stayin' Alive/The End of an Illusion: A Response to Michael J. Glennon," *Foreign Affairs* 82, no. 4 (July-August 2003): 201–202.

10. M. J. Peterson, *The General Assembly in World Politics* (Boston: Unwin Hyman, 1986), 2.

11. Soo Yeon Kim and Bruce Russett, "The New Politics of Voting Alignments in the General Assembly," in *The Once and Future Security Council,* ed. Bruce Russett (New York: St. Martin's Press, 1997), 37, 55.

12. Dutch Permanent Mission to the UN, "General Assembly Reform: The Role and Impact of Resolutions," www.pvnewyorki.org/statements/general_assembly (November 16, 2005).

13. Brian Hall, "Blue Helmets," *New York Times Magazine,* January 2, 1994, 22.

14. Statute of the International Court of Justice, article 9. This statute is a separate document from the UN Charter but was also approved at the founding conference in San Francisco in 1945.

15. Michael Schechter, "Making Meaningful UN-Sponsored World Conferences of the 1990s: NGOs to the Rescue?" in *United Nations-Sponsored World Conferences: Focus on Impact and Follow-up*, ed. Michael G. Schechter (Tokyo: UNU Press, 2001), 189. For a thorough study of global conferences, see Michael G. Schechter, *United Nations Global Conferences* (New York: Routledge, 2005).

16. Excellent data can be found on the Global Policy Web site, www.globalpolicy.org.

17. See Margaret P. Karns and Karen A. Mingst, "The United States as 'Deadbeat'? U.S. Policy and the UN Financial Crisis," in *Multilateralism and U.S. Foreign Policy. Ambivalent Engagement*, ed. Stewart Patrick and Shepard Forman (Boulder: Lynne Rienner, 2002), 267–294.

18. Kofi Annan, *We the Peoples: The Role of the United Nations in the 21st Century* (2000), http://www.un.org/millennium/sg/report/full.htm.

19. Paul Taylor, "Managing the Economic and Social Activities of the United Nations System: Developing the Role of ESOSOC," in *The United Nations at the Millenium*, ed. Paul Taylor and A.J.R Groom (New York: Continuum, 2007), 128.

20. Larry Minear, "Humanitarian Action in the Former Yugoslavia: The UN's Role, 1991–1993," occasional paper no. 18, Thomas J. Watson Institute for International Studies, Providence, R.I., 1994, 28.

3

—◇—

Actors in the United Nations System

When the well meaning 'man from Mars' arrived at the headquarters of the United Nations in New York City and asked to be taken to that organization's leader, personnel at the security desk assumed that the Secretary-General was being sought. They, thus, proceeded to direct the visitor to the 38th floor. But diplomats encountered in the corridors promptly suggested to the misdirected Martian that he was in the wrong building. 'Cross First Avenue,' they instructed. 'The leader of the United Nations is in the US mission.' The United States, however, denied this statement and assured the by now very confused Martian that, far from leading the United Nations, they were not even very interested in the organization. 'Go and talk to the Cubans, the Algerians, the Indians, or others from the Group of 77. They are leading the United Nations, and that is precisely why we Americans are not very interested.' But the leaders of the Group of 77 explained to the alien visitor that their hold even on their own Third World group was at best tenuous. 'The United Nations,' they rather ruefully acknowledged, 'is economically dominated by the North and politically controlled by the West,' who, the bewildered Martian discovered, are essentially the same people, although they have no address.[1]

This fanciful story speaks to the core question in this chapter: Who are the key actors in the United Nations today—the most powerful member states, the dominant bloc or coalition, the secretary-general, the Secretariat, or the NGOs? The United Nations was formed by states, it depends on states for its sustenance, and it is directed by states on the supposition that its existence and operation may be useful to them. The Charter accords special status to five states, giving them permanent membership on the Security Council and veto power. One reason the Martian may have sought out the United States is its privileged position on that body and its acknowledged superpower status as the "Permanent One."[2] But middle powers and small states have historically played important roles, particularly when organized in blocs and coalitions—hence the Martian's quest for the Group of 77, or the West.

If the UN is but a venue for states, or just another diplomatic instrument for states to utilize, that is compatible with a realist view. But if it has become an actor in its own right, and if NGOs play influential roles within the UN system, the liberal perspective is more appropriate. In fact, the members of the Secretariat, particularly the secretary-general and other major officials, have acquired authority, influence, and legitimacy that enable them to act at times without the explicit direction of the governing bodies and a majority of member states. And the UN's bureaucracy may influence the actions of member states and others because of their expertise and position. Our discussion of actors in the UN system, then, must consider not only various member states but also coalitions and blocs, the secretary-general and the Secretariat, and the NGOs. Increasingly, "the peoples" in whose name the UN Charter was drafted are exerting their voices through NGOs and other civil society groups.

THE UN AS AN INSTRUMENT OF STATES OR AN INDEPENDENT ACTOR?

If the realist position is correct, the UN is only an instrument of its member states, particularly the most powerful ones, one among many diplomatic tools used by states to serve their national interests. States may use the UN to gain a collective stamp of approval on specific actions, points of view, principles, and norms; they may seek to create new rules, enforce existing ones, and settle disputes. The UN and many of its agencies serve useful functions: They gather and analyze information, improving the quality of information available to governments. They bring representatives of states together regularly, thereby affording them opportunities to gather information about other governments' attitudes and policies to the benefit of their own decisionmaking. This continuing interaction also enhances the value of maintaining a good reputation. The UN's decisionmaking processes encourage states to form coalitions and to link specific issues so as to enhance their bargaining power on those issues. States have used the UN system to create a variety of valuable programs and activities for addressing global problems; these range from development assistance, disease eradication, and aid to refugees to peace-keeping, election monitoring, and human rights promotion. To realists, the UN is not more than this and, as such, it is controlled by dominant states and hegemonic coalitions.

The UN, however, may be more than just an instrument of its member states. The organization also exercises influence and imposes constraints on its members' policies and the processes by which those policies are formed. Year in and year out, the meetings of the UN General Assembly, and all other bodies, set international, and hence national, agendas, and force governments to take positions on issues such as the Middle East, environmental degradation, Cuba's human rights record, and the status of women. These meetings and ongoing data gathering on each state's economy, trade, balance of payments, population, and compliance with treaties also subject states' behavior to international surveillance. UN-approved rules, norms, and principles, whether on human rights, the law of the sea, ozone depletion, or the financing of terrorism, force states to realign their policies if they wish to maintain a reputation for law-abiding behavior and to enjoy the benefits of reciprocity from other states. Particularly in democratic, pluralist societies, norms and rules created by the UN may be used by domestic interest groups to press for changes in national policies.[3] This is the liberal institutionalist position: that the UN operates through the interaction between state members, coalitions, and groups, the mutual flow of influence being between the organization and its member states.

Another possibility is that the UN not only influences states but is a strong independent actor in itself. Some constructivists have made the argument that international organizations such as the UN have autonomy because they are bureaucracies and their authority is based on impersonal rules. As two scholars described the process, "IOs, through their rules, create new categories of actors, form new interests for actors, define new shared international tasks, and disseminate new models of social organization around the globe."[4] Acting autonomously may mean that the bureaucracy develops its own views and manipulates material and information resources. These characteristics may eventually lead to undesirable outcomes such as tunnel vision, bias, and a reluctance to embrace reform. In this chapter we explore the actors in the UN and the nature of their interactions.

THE ROLE OF STATES

Intergovernmental organizations such as the UN whose members are states depend on their member states. And no state is more critical than the United States. To be effective, the UN must be able in some ways and to some extent influence the largest, most powerful states in the system. It must be valued by them as a means of inducing other states to change their behavior, to redefine their interests, and to accept certain constraints. In this regard, the United States has a long history of conveying "mixed messages" concerning its support for international organizations.[5]

The Key Role of the United States

As the dominant power after World War II, the United States played an important role in shaping the international system structure, including the establishment of many IGOs, from the UN to the Bretton Woods institutions, the International Atomic Energy Agency (IAEA), and the United Nations Environment Programme (UNEP). The provisions of the UN Charter, for example, were consistent with U.S. interests, and until the 1960s the United States could often count on the support of a majority on most major issues. This enabled the United States to use the UN and its specialized agencies as instruments of its national policies and to create institutions and rules compatible with U.S. interests.

Over time, the United States has used the UN, the specialized agencies, and UN-authorized regional organizations for collective legitimation of its own actions, examples being Korea in 1950, the Cuban revolution in 1960, the Dominican Republic in 1965, the Iran hostage crisis in 1979, the first Gulf War in 1990–1991, and the terrorist attacks on the World Trade Center and the Pentagon on September 11, 2001.

From the late 1960s to mid-1980s, however, the United States was much more ambivalent about international institutions in general, and about parts of the UN system in particular. It withdrew from the ILO in 1978 (rejoining it more than two years later) and from UNESCO in 1984 (rejoining it in 2003), because of politicization and bureaucratic inefficiency. Developing countries' demands in the 1970s for a New International Economic Order, their repeated resolutions linking Zionism with racism, and their criticisms of American policies led Washington to oppose many UN-sponsored development programs and to view the UN as a hostile place. U.S. alienation from the UN was borne out in the steep drop in U.S. voting with majorities in the General Assembly in 1981. In the Security Council, the United States used its veto thirty-four times between 1976 and 1985 (see table 2.1). In 1985, when Congress imposed conditions on contributions and withheld full payment as a strategy to force change, congressional support for paying UN dues started to decline.[6]

U.S. antipathy to the UN moderated somewhat in the late 1980s. Changes in Soviet policy under Mikhail Gorbachev created opportunities for UN efforts to settle regional conflicts (discussed below). The UN's success in handling new peacekeeping challenges, and the war against Iraq in 1991, generated widespread optimism about an expanding UN role in the post–Cold War era. Yet U.S. voting with the majority on roll call votes in the UN General Assembly reached its lowest point ever in 1990 (10 percent), and it improved only slightly in subsequent years. In

1993, the Clinton administration articulated assertive multilateralism, a foreign policy designed to share responsibilities for global peace with other countries by working through an invigorated UN. The stance was short-lived.

The U.S. post–Cold War record on multilateralism has, in fact, been more mixed and fragile than the public rhetoric suggests. By the mid-1990s, problems with UN missions in Somalia, Rwanda, and Bosnia overshadowed successes elsewhere. The U.S. experience in Somalia, in particular, had a devastating effect on its willingness to engage its own military personnel in UN peacekeeping operations, and on its support for new types of peacekeeping in general. The United States lost confidence in then Secretary-General Boutros Boutros-Ghali and undertook a unilateral campaign to deny him a second term in 1996. Other unilateralist actions followed, including the rejection of the Comprehensive Test Ban Treaty in 1999, the International Criminal Court (1998), the convention banning antipersonnel landmines (1997), and the Kyoto Protocol (1997). In addition, the Congress contributed to the UN's financial crisis by continuing to withhold U.S. dues for the regular budget and for peacekeeping, as discussed in chapter 2.

Given George W. Bush's past statements and the records of many of his close associates, no one expected this president to be a strong supporter of the UN. His unprecedented decision in 2001 to renounce U.S. signature of the Kyoto Protocol provoked widespread condemnation, as has the U.S. active campaign against the International Criminal Court. That the Bush administration used the UN as one of many tools in responding to the terror attacks of September 11, 2001, reinforced realists' views. A year later, the U.S. undertook protracted negotiations in the UN in an effort to address the problem of Iraq and its weapons of mass destruction. The blatant willingness of the United States to go to war against Iraq in 2003 without authorization from the Security Council, however, was widely seen as evidence that it did not consider itself bound by the obligations of the UN Charter. Yet, the United States subsequently returned to the Security Council to secure help with the challenges of dealing with postwar Iraq. The United States has long supported organizational reform, a position given greater urgency by the 2004–2005 oil-for-food scandal, although when the particularities of reform are introduced, the United States often finds its position substantially at variance with other member states. In short, the record on multilateralism generally, and the UN specifically, is mixed.

Several factors have shaped the U.S. view of the UN and the various specialized agencies over time. The often critical view the United States takes of the global environmental agenda "is not the result of a fundamental policy shift under the current Bush administration," one scholar noted. "It reflects a long-standing skepticism among Congressmen, and especially Republicans, about the merits of an undifferentiated commitment to multilateralism."[7] More than that of other states, U.S. policy is shaped by domestic politics, including presidential leadership (or lack thereof), executive-legislative relations, lobbying by domestic groups, and public opinion. It is also shaped by more general attitudes of American political culture, notably a belief in U.S. **exceptionalism.** America's unique history, its record of democracy, and its support for human rights all give it a special role in international relations. This belief, reinforced in the twenty-first-century by its lone superpower status, leads to greater tendencies toward unilateralism. The dilemma is that the UN needs the support of the world's superpower if it is to remain a vital institution.

Nonetheless, historically, "American preferences on many issues, embodied in US policies and backed by US power, have explained a great many . . . public policies emanating from the United Nations, its associated specialized agencies, and the managing institutions of the global economy."[8] Yet the UN has "always been and continues to be a Western organization," Puchala argued, because "the 'West' . . . never was, nor is it now, solely the United States."[9] He and others recognize that the United States, along with the countries of Western Europe and Japan, collectively make up the club of the powerful that controls much of the wealth, trade, and military capability of the world. In short, the main actors include other major powers.

Other Major Powers

Among the major powers are the other permanent members of the Security Council. The Soviet Union (now Russia), France, Great Britain, and China have each had significant roles in shaping the organization's development, and, like the United States, they have not always been ready to commit themselves to using the UN as the major arena for their foreign policy.

The Soviet Union/Russia.   The Soviet Union played a key (though largely negative) role in the UN during the Cold War period, clashing frequently with the United States and its allies. Between 1945 and 1975, the Soviet Union used its veto 114 times; more than half of the vetoes were on membership applications in the early 1950s, and the impasse over the membership of the divided states of Korea, Vietnam, and Germany continued until the 1970s. The Soviet Union also clashed with the United States about China's representation.

In the 1960s and 1970s, the Soviet Union, siding often with the newly independent states in the General Assembly, supported self-determination for colonial peoples, the Palestine Liberation Organization, and the New International Economic Order agenda. This strategy permitted it to vote with the majority in the General Assembly a high percentage of the time. For ideological reasons, the Soviet Union and other bloc members were not part of the Bretton Woods institutions, but they did participate in many other specialized agencies.

The actions and attitudes of the Soviet Union changed dramatically in 1987. After years of opposition, the Soviet Union adopted a facilitative attitude toward using the UN to monitor and legitimize its troop withdrawal from Afghanistan and to end the Iran-Iraq War. The new attitude was particularly evident in the Gulf War of 1990–1991. The Soviet Union abandoned its former ally, Iraq, and supported U.S.-UN actions in the Gulf, although not without expressing reservations, especially about the use of force. The Soviets wished not only to prevent bloodshed but also to assert what little influence they had left; they were also trying to limit damage to their future interests in the region.[10] Eventually they went along with the UN-authorized operation. The Soviet Union's need for U.S. economic and emergency aid to deal with its own internal problems and its desire for support in dealing with the crumbling empire overrode other considerations.

These changes were hastened by the speed and thoroughness of the Soviet Union's dismemberment in 1991. That led to a period during the early 1990s when U.S.-Russian cooperation reached a peak, voting together 89 percent of the time in the General Assembly. That consensus dropped dramatically by the end of the decade, when agreement between the two fell to 40 percent and Russia opposed U.S. and NATO intervention in Kosovo, for example, and endeavored to put together enough votes in the Security Council to condemn the action. Russia was then moving in a different direction than either the United States or its allies.[11]

Today, although Russia is a diminished power, and its economic means are meager, it still exercises influence as a major power. As one indicator of its diminished capability, Russia's UN assessment dropped from 8.7 percent in 1991 to 1.15 percent in 2000. Yet its veto power makes its support essential to Security Council actions. In parts of the former Yugoslavia, as well as in former Soviet republics, the Middle East, and elsewhere, Russia still exerts significant influence. This was evident during the 2003 debate over Iraq. Initially, Russia joined France and Germany in opposing the U.S. invasion of Iraq. Like its European counterparts, Russia preferred to extend UN-mandated inspections of Iraqi sites and a peaceful settlement. Although less vocal than the Europeans, Russia opposed UN authorization of U.S. action in Iraq. Subsequently, however, as violence in Chechnya grew, along with evidence that Islamic militants were entering Russian territory, Russia's President Putin assumed a more pragmatic position and gave the United States more latitude.[12]

In 2005, Russia emerged as a major player in international efforts to deal with Iran's nuclear program: Its veto power gave it influence when the matter was referred to the Security Council for sanctions, and its status as a major nuclear power allowed it to offer an alternative diplomatic solution involving an agreement to enrich Iranian uranium in Russian facilities.

France and Great Britain.   France and Great Britain continue to be major actors in the UN and world politics despite their diminished status. As members of the P-5, they hold veto power; both continue to be significant donors, their assessments being roughly equal at 6 percent ($107 and $109 million respectively); and both have played active roles in post–Cold War UN peacekeeping and enforcement operations by providing troops in the Gulf War, Bosnia, and Afghanistan. During the Cold War, they played secondary yet important supporting roles on East-West issues in the UN Security Council. Both were placed in a defensive position by pressures in the 1950s to move their colonies to independence. Since 1990, each has also assumed responsibility for a subcontracted enforcement operation—Great Britain in Sierra Leone, and France in Rwanda, Côte d'Ivoire, and Congo. As prominent players in the World Bank and International Monetary Fund, both contribute senior personnel and financial resources and vote consistently with other large developed countries. Both have supported such initiatives as the International Criminal Court, the Kyoto Protocol on climate change, the landmines treaty, and the Comprehensive Test Ban Treaty, all of which were rejected by the United States.

In UN politics, however, Great Britain and France have also carved different niches. During the 1970s and 1980s, France's role can best be described as mediator between the South's NIEO agenda and the North's opposition to change. More than other developed countries, France was ready to accept state intervention in regulating commodity markets and financial compensation to developing countries for market failure. It has always been a stronger supporter of UNESCO, which is based in Paris and has traditionally been headed by a Frenchman. On other issues, France's positions have paralleled those of other developed countries—for example, France voted with the United States and Great Britain in opposition to mandatory economic sanctions against South Africa. Yet France has also shown greater interest than Great Britain in developing and enforcing a common European position—that is, a common position on major issues among members of the European Union (EU).

The desire to assert a common EU position in opposition to military action in Iraq in 2003 pitted France against the United States and Great Britain in the UN Security Council. Supporting the IAEA request for more time to conduct UN-led weapons inspections, France opposed any military action against Iraq not approved by the council. During a tense five-month period, President Chirac and President Bush engaged in active lobbying to convince nonpermanent members of the Security Council to support their respective positions. In the end, facing clear opposition, the United States dropped its attempt to get UN authorization; it blamed the failure on French obstructionism and the general incapacity of the UN to enforce its resolutions.[13] The French view is that a Security Council mandate is indispensable for intervention in another country.

Britain, France's partner in the European Union, took a different position on that and other issues. Britain's Prime Minister Tony Blair attempted to sell the U.S. position on Iraq to the EU and was a strong member of the U.S.-led coalition. Great Britain has always had a prominent position in the UN, not only as a permanent member of the Security Council but also as a member of other restricted-member committees, notably the Geneva Group for review of budgets and programs. It is always voted to membership in ECOSOC, and a British jurist has always held a seat on the ICJ. This privileged position also carries over to the specialized agencies: Britain has occupied leadership positions in the International Labour Organization and the World Health Organization.[14]

Even though its financial contribution is only 5.3 percent of the assessed budget, Britain holds these positions for several reasons. First, British delegates and Secretariat members are frequently called on to exercise their skill in drafting. Second, continued ties to Africa and Asia through the Commonwealth give the British established contacts with many of the UN's members. Third, Britain has been a leader, along with the United States, in promoting UN financial reform and accountability. Fourth, through special voluntary contributions, Britain does pay a larger share of expenses than its assessment. Britain wants to keep its privileged position and has opposed efforts to restructure the Security Council.

Despite its strong involvement in UN peacekeeping operations and its participation in the 1991 Gulf War and 2003 Iraq War, Great Britain has generally been reluctant to send troops outside of Europe. It has preferred a noncombat role, favored humanitarian emergencies, and shied away from placing its troops within the UN command structure.[15]

Continuing ties with their former colonies help Great Britain and France retain substantial influence and interests in Africa, and in the Third World more generally. Yet both are part of the North, and that limits the extent of their influence. The same cannot be said for China, the only developing and non-Western country among the P-5; indeed, China's influence in the Third World and in the UN generally has been growing steadily.

China.   The fifth permanent member of the Security Council, China, historically was far less active or interested in international institutions generally and the UN in particular, but that pattern changed in the late 1990s. The Republic of China (ROC) originally held China's Security Council seat, which it continued to occupy long after the Chinese revolution brought the People's Republic of China (PRC) to power in Beijing and sent the ROC government to Taiwan. In 1971, Third World votes granted the PRC the Chinese seat and Taiwan walked out of the body. Up to that time, the PRC had been a member of only one IGO. One scholar noted, "The PRC's newcomer status in the world of international organizations has meant that the last thirty years have involved a steep learning curve, mediated by its own ambitions, changing perceptions, and unique perspectives."[16]

During its first decade of UN membership, the PRC kept a low profile. Although it supported the G-77 and the nonaligned group positions on decolonization and economic development issues, it remained uninvolved in security issues. Only in 1981, when threatened with the loss of voting rights under UN's Article 19, did China begin to pay its share of peacekeeping assessments. In the late 1980s, China's move to a market economy, its subsequent rapid economic growth, and its increasing share of world trade made admission to the IMF, World Bank, and World Trade Organization (WTO) essential. The PRC assumed China's seats in the IMF and World Bank in 1980, and gained its own seat on the Executive Board. In 2001, after fifteen years of negotiations over the terms of entry, China was accepted into the World Trade Organization.

Over time, China's participation in various UN bodies has led it to redefine its interests and policies. For example, despite its resistance to international human rights norms, it fought hard to host the 1995 Fourth World Conference on Women because it believed that a successful conference would bring prestige to China. Also in the same year, China agreed to accept selected ILO labor standards, and, in doing so, it initiated a process to modify domestic law to accommodate the changes. In 1992, it reversed its previous support for nuclear proliferation and signed the Nuclear Nonproliferation Treaty. In the mid- and late 1990s, China also introduced domestic legislation that reflected its awareness of human rights norms and its obligations as a party to various environmental conventions, including the Convention on Biological Diversity and the Montreal Protocol on Ozone Depletion. Still, adjusting domestic practices to international norms in human rights and the environment has been a slow and incomplete process.

China's foreign policy has historically been marked by strong adherence to the principles of sovereignty and noninterference in the domestic affairs of states. Increasingly, these have created conflicts with its growing desire to be accepted as part of the international community. The June 1989 Tiananmen Square massacre highlighted the divergence between the conception of popular sovereignty held by most of the world and China's belief in state sovereignty. Its actions were widely condemned in the UN and in human rights circles. In 1990, China was confronted with a test of its commitment to the principle of collective security. Although it opposed using force to remove Iraq from Kuwait, it did not want to be the "odd country out." This led it to abstain on key votes in the Security Council, a strategy that allowed it to register its objections but not bear responsibility for blocking international action. These same dilemmas came up repeatedly during the 1990s with the advent of more assertive peacekeeping operations under Chapter VII; China abstained on forty-one votes. By threatening to use the veto, then agreeing not to block action, China could exercise influence consistent with its great-power status. "It is likely that China normally abstains rather than uses its veto because of its concern to keep the UN international machinery intact and in use," concluded one scholar.[17] Another noted, "As an aspiring great power, it is learning from others to use its power in more subtle ways than before."[18]

China's dramatic economic growth in the 1990s has bolstered its status as a major power. In 2000, its assessment was still only 0.9 percent of the UN budget. In 2005, that had risen to 2 percent ($37 million). With a rising sense of national pride, increasing assertiveness, a burgeoning economy, and P-5 membership, China's views have to be taken into account.

This has become increasingly evident on security issues. Threat of a Chinese veto (as well as Russian) led the United States and NATO to intervene in Kosovo in 1999 without Security Council approval. The U.S. bombing of China's embassy in Belgrade, Yugoslavia, severely damaged relations between the two countries. China, in fact, exercised its veto to end the UN's preventive deployment of peacekeepers in Macedonia, albeit on the grounds of that country's ties with Taiwan! In the lead up to the 2003 Iraq War, China preferred that the dispute be settled peacefully through the UN and quietly joined the coalition against the United States. China did not want to jeopardize its oil supply from the Middle East. By offering humanitarian aid and actively vying for reconstruction contracts once the war started, China worked for a quick resolution. Unable to exert much influence on the United States, China acted in its own economic interests, underlining its traditional support for state sovereignty.[19] In 2004, China contributed for the first time to a UN peacekeeping operation by sending police to Haiti. Its veto power has given it leverage with respect to efforts to deal with the crises in Darfur (Sudan) and Iran. In both, China's rapidly rising need for oil along with its antipathy to sanctions and humanitarian interventions lead it to oppose Security Council actions under Chapter VII.

China was a strong supporter of the proposed NIEO, but it has not sought to pose as a leader of the Third World. Rather, China is a "Club of One," balancing its own interests and representing those of other developing nations.[20] It has supported Third World candidates for important UN posts and greater representation in the Security Council. It has pled for special treatment as a developing nation. Yet, its long history as one of the world's great civilizations and its rising economic status lead China to see itself as a major power; indeed, its interests are often more similar to those of other powerful states than to those of the developing countries.

Germany and Japan. The ranks of the world's major powers include Germany and Japan, yet neither is a permanent member of the Security Council; indeed, their historical experiences as the defeated World War II powers have had a major impact on their individual willingness and capacity to make certain types of international commitments. Because of Germany's pivotal geographic position in Cold War Europe, there was a concerted effort to bring it into organizations such as NATO and the European Economic Community (precursor of the EU). Yet it was not until 1973 that the two German states—the Federal Republic, or West Germany, and the German Democratic Republic, or East Germany—were admitted into the UN.

Japan joined the UN almost twenty years earlier in 1956. During those early years, Japan kept a lowprofile; it concentrated on a few selective issues, such as keeping the People's Republic of China out of the UN and supporting the UN as a guarantor of the peace. In the 1970s, Japan's role in UN politics shifted markedly. Japan joined with the less developed countries to uphold the right of self-determination for the Palestinian people, accept the role of the Palestine Liberation Organization in the UN, and support other Arab causes. These positions reflected Japan's national interest given its resource (particularly oil) vulnerability. The UN was just one of the forums where Japan supported the Middle East oil producers.[21]

The decade of the 1990s was pivotal for Germany and Japan in the UN. In both countries, the 1991 Gulf War stimulated debates over their international roles. Both had been asked to make significant monetary contributions to the war, yet neither was a member of the Security Council, nor had they been consulted. Klaus Kinkel, the German foreign minister, remarked, "As a reunited and sovereign country we must assume all the rights and obligations of a member of the United Nations to avoid any discrepancy between our verbal commitment to peace and human rights and our active involvement in their defense."[22] In response, a German field hospital was deployed to Cambodia in 1992, and German military personnel flew and maintained helicopters supporting UN arms inspection teams in Iraq, beginning in late 1991.

Germany and Japan both had constitutional impediments to participation in any collective enforcement or peacekeeping operation, however. The result was that in 1992, the Japanese Diet (Parliament) approved legislation permitting up to 2,000 Japanese troops to be deployed in UN peacekeeping missions under limited conditions. Thus, the Japanese joined the UN operation in Cambodia, known as the United Nations Transitional Authority in Cambodia (UNTAC). This development set a precedent for subsequent Japanese participation in other UN operations; and, although it was largely limited to humanitarian tasks, it was an important step toward Japan's full contribution to the UN.

The German Constitutional Court ruled in 1994 that German military forces could participate in UN peacekeeping operations and those of other international organizations. Germany sent 4,000 soldiers and 150 police officers to the former Yugoslavia, and it provided military and civilian personnel for UN operations in Angola, Kuwait, Liberia, Macedonia, and Kosovo. Germany has played a particularly vital role in the UN-authorized NATO operation in Afghanistan, supporting the reconstruction program, providing security assistance forces, funding humanitarian programs in education and culture, and training police forces.[23]

Why did Germany and Japan change their constitutions to participate in UN peacekeeping? Both are, after all, major UN financial supporters. Japan is the second largest contributor to the UN, its assessed contribution being set at 19 percent, more than the combined share of France, Great Britain, China, and Russia. Germany is third, its assessment being 9 percent. Both are major contributors to the IMF, World Bank, and WTO. German and Japanese participation in peacekeeping can best be explained by self-interest. Both seek permanent seats on the UN Security Council and both realize that participation in peace and security activities is an essential criterion.

Major powers are not the only states that matter in the UN. In fact, multilateral diplomacy in the UN system opens many opportunities for a group of states known as middle powers, as well as small states, to exercise influence. Categorizations such as these are always subject to dispute, but they provide a way of identifying and analyzing the roles of different states.

Middle Powers

The so-called middle powers have played and continue to play an important role in UN politics. This group of states was uniquely able to facilitate valuable UN activity during the Cold War era, when disputing parties were wary of great-power involvement, but less so of middle-power mediation. These states act less out of their own interests than out of a belief in international responsibility.

Western and non-Western, developed and developing countries that fit the category of middle powers can be characterized according to their relative power or size in the international community. More important, they can be characterized according to the kinds of policies they pursue, including multilateralism, compromise positions in disputes, and coalition building to secure reform in the international system. Canada, Australia, Norway, Sweden, Argentina, Brazil, India, South Africa, and Nigeria are all considered middle powers. During the 1944 Dumbarton Oaks conference, Prime Minister Mackenzie King of Canada called for a special position in the UN for Canada and others. His argument was that states ought to have a role commensurate with their contribution and that a division between the great powers and the rest was unworkable. Although a provision for special status for middle powers failed to become part of the UN Charter, the notion persisted.

When UN peacekeeping was developed in the 1950s, several middle powers became frequent contributors of peacekeeping troops. Among them were Canada, Australia, Finland, Sweden, India, Brazil, Chile, Argentina, Iran, Nigeria, and the former Yugoslavia. The Canadian niche, for example, has been in the early phases of peacekeeping, helping to train peacekeepers, setting up command structures, and providing communication facilities, linguistic facility, and medical expertise. Canadian, Australian, and Indian generals have been prominent among the commanders of UN peacekeeping forces.

Of the middle powers, Canada has played a particularly vital role. Its political culture has influenced Canada's preferences in the UN "for pragmatic non-ideological compromise, a belief in pluralism and tolerance, and a commitment to the orderly mediation and resolution of conflicts."[24] During the Cold War, Canada tried to maintain a line between taking independent action through the UN and supporting its neighbor to the south. During the Gulf War, Canada was reluctant to support military action, preferring to give sanctions more time. That was true in

2003 as well, when Canada offered no support to the U.S. position on Iraq, but preferred to continue inspections.

During the 1990s, Canada's role in the UN came under greater domestic scrutiny. Could it support more than one-quarter of its troops in UN peacekeeping when other domestic policy commitments were pressing? The widely publicized misconduct of Canadian troops in Somalia and Yugoslavia, and the subsequent government cover-up, stimulated a public debate over training and racism in the Canadian military and its continued ability and willingness to serve in more expensive and dangerous operations. Canada removed troops from the UN peacekeeping operation in Cyprus in 1992 after twenty-nine years of participation, even though the conflict had not been resolved. Canadian troops in Afghanistan were called home after six months because of insufficient replacements.[25]

Since the late 1990s, Canada has played important roles on human security issues. Lloyd Axworthy, the former minister of foreign affairs, for example, was instrumental in managing the negotiations for the convention banning anti-personnel landmines. Canada has helped to draft guidelines for humanitarian intervention, and it hosted the first conference of parties to the Kyoto Protocol on climate change in late 2005.

Australia is also a strong supporter of the UN, although the extent of its participation has varied according to the exigencies of domestic politics. Its major commitment to peacekeeping has tended to be concentrated on conflicts in Southeast Asia. It played a key diplomatic role in Cambodia and provided the force commander for UNTAC. Even closer to home, Australia was involved in Papua New Guinea and East Timor. With respect to the latter, Australia provided military forces, police, and civilian personnel, totaling about one-half of the 11,000 person force.[26]

Beyond peacekeeping, Australia has been a crucial player in leading and supporting coalitions. It helped establish the Cairns Group of Fair Trading Nations to push reform in international agricultural trade during the GATT trade negotiations in the early 1990s, for example. This coalition crossed both divides: East/West and North/South. Australia provided the intellectual leadership and managed the difficult negotiations in support of a freer, open, and nondiscriminatory international trade regime in agriculture.[27]

India's long-standing participation in peacekeeping operations in the Middle East and Africa has served its aspiration for international recognition and for a permanent seat on the Security Council. Indian generals commanded operations in Korea, Africa (Congo and Sierra Leone), Bosnia, and the Middle East. Participation in peacekeeping also helped India project its image as a nonaligned state and claim to leadership in the Nonaligned Movement (NAM). India helped create the movement in the 1950s and then used it to reinforce its activist multilateral agenda. In the first UN General Assembly session in 1946 and later in the nonaligned summits, India spoke out about racism in South Africa and led the push to end apartheid and colonialism. Yet, through its refusal to sign the Treaty on the Non-Proliferation of Nuclear Weapons (1970) and the Comprehensive Nuclear Test Ban Treaty (1996), and by testing a nuclear device in 1998, India has also been a spoiler in the UN's efforts to curb nuclear nonproliferation.

Much like India, Nigeria also has seen contributions to peacekeeping operations as an important strategy. Thus, Nigeria volunteered troops for service in the Congo (1960) even before its own independence was official. It participated in UN peacekeeping in Lebanon in the late 1970s as well as in Namibia in 1989–1990. In the 1990s, Nigeria orchestrated the Economic Community of West African States' (ECOWAS) intervention in Liberia; later, in Sierra Leone, it provided financing and three-quarters of the manpower for the operations. In 2005, it provided much of the manpower for the UN-authorized African Union peacekeeping force in Darfur (Sudan) and hosted negotiations between the Sudanese government and the rebels.

Brazil, along with Argentina, became a significant contributor to peacekeeping operations in the 1990s, but concentrated on those within other former Portuguese colonies (Angola and Mozambique) where common language provided a link. By hosting the 1992 UN Conference on the Environment and Development (UNCED), it sought to enhance its reputation as an emerging power. It also used its jurisdiction over the world's largest expanse of tropical forest to resist efforts to negotiate a binding regime for tropical forests. Since 2003, Brazil has played a leading role in the so-called Group of 21 advanced developing countries that have pushed hard for greater concessions on agricultural and other trade in WTO negotiations.

The essence of the middle powers' role lies in the importance of secondary players in international politics; there must be followers as well as leaders. They can be both. Fostering cooperation in the future is likely to require leadership based not only on military capability and economic strength but also on diplomatic skill and policy initiatives—precisely the strengths that middle powers can contribute.

Small and Developing States

For small states everywhere, and for the majority of less developed countries, the UN has facilitated a number of foreign policy objectives. First, membership in the UN is a symbol of statehood and sovereignty. Second, small states in particular use the UN and the specialized agencies as the arena in which they can carry on bilateral and multilateral discussions, even if they concern non-UN matters. With limited diplomatic and economic resources, less-developed countries find in the UN a cost-efficient forum where they can forge multilateral ties and conduct bilateral talks on a range of issues. The fall General Assembly sessions are vehicles for conducting other business among representatives and visiting ministers. Third, small states, especially the small European and Latin American states, have used the UN to promote the expansion of international law in an effort to constrain the major powers and protect small-power interests. Fourth, the UN enlarges the "voice" of small states and offers opportunities to set the global agenda. For example, because Kuwait was a UN member, Iraq's invasion and occupation in 1990 immediately gained attention and there was strong support for sanctions and even the use of force. Costa Rica was influential in the formation of the Commission on Human Rights in the 1940s and the new post of UN High Commissioner for Human Rights in the 1990s, viewing each as essential to the pursuance of its human rights agenda.[28] Since it assumed leadership of the Nonaligned Movement and the Organization of the Islamic Conference in 2003, Malaysia has assumed a proactive role on a number of issues within the UN. Noted one scholar, "Malaysia's influence in world politics has been far greater than its national power potential, almost approximating to that of a middle power, and in the main this was due to its imaginative foreign policy and high profile diplomacy."[29]

Because small and less powerful states do not have the diplomatic resources to deal with all issues in depth, participation in the UN has tended to force them either to specialize in particular issues or in some cases to follow the lead of larger states within the Group of 77 or other coalitions. Participation in the UN not only aids in achieving foreign policy objectives directly but also provides small states with more avenues. The UN presents opportunities for interest aggregation by facilitating the formation of coalitions to enhance weak states' influence. With the proliferation of UN-related bodies, small states may also seek the body most favorable to their interests—a phenomenon known as "forum shopping."

Small and weak states have been able to bargain with major powers in the UN for their support on certain important issues in return for economic concessions. In the Gulf War, for example, some small states that were nonpermanent members of the Security Council at the time agreed to support U.S.-UN action in return for favors. Ethiopia extracted a promise from the United States to broker a peace between the government and Eritrean rebels. Egypt and Malaysia received financial "rewards." For Yemen, however, the consequence of opposition to the Gulf War was the withdrawal of U.S. aid and commitments.

Developing countries are the direct major beneficiaries of most UN economic and development programs. They may apply to the World Bank and UN development agencies for project, technical assistance, and structural adjustment funds to augment their economic development plans. They are also the beneficiaries of funds from the UN specialized agencies, including the World Health Organization, the World Food Programme, the International Fund for Agricultural Development, UNHCR's refugee programs, and the UN Disaster Relief Organization's emergency disaster funds.

Although small and developing countries have frequently enhanced their "voice" and influence through coalitions and blocs, all member states participate in one or more such groupings. As in any parliamentary or legislative body, coalition building is a primary strategy for garnering a majority of votes in favor of or opposition to proposals for action.

COALITIONS, BLOCS, AND THE IMPORTANCE OF CONSENSUS

Early in the UN's history, states in the same geographic region, or those sharing economic or political interests, formed coalitions to shape common positions on particular issues and to control a bloc of votes.[30] The UN Charter itself specified that the General Assembly should give consideration to "equitable geographic distribution" in electing the nonpermanent members of the Security Council and members of ECOSOC, though it offered no guidance about how to do so or on what the appropriate geographic groups should be. By informal agreement, these groups came to correspond roughly to the major regions of the world: Western Europe, Eastern Europe, Africa, Latin America, Asia, and the Middle East. Each region has adopted different rules and procedures for selecting candidates. For the Security Council, the Latin America group tends to give preference to the larger states (Argentina, Brazil, and Colombia), but the African group rotates candidates among the respective member states.

The European Union has developed the most formalized process for continual consultation among its member states and for delegating responsibility to articulate common policies. The union increasingly acts as a single unit in the UN, voting as a bloc on social and economic issues. On issues of security, however, the EU members have found it difficult to take common positions, as illustrated in the divisions over apartheid in South Africa, decolonization, the Middle East, and the 2003 Iraq War.

Subregional groups often show remarkable unity in the General Assembly as well as in other bodies where they might participate. High cohesion can be found among the five Nordic states and the Caribbean members of the Caribbean Community (CARICOM).

Coalitions are important because the General Assembly body functions like a national parliament, each state having one vote and decisions being made by a majority (either simple or two-thirds under specified circumstances). Just as a majority political party (or a coalition) can control most decisions, so can a stable coalition of states comprising a majority of UN member states. These coalitions within the UN have tended to persist for long periods; the presence of such groups led to the practice of consensus voting in the General Assembly, as described in chapter 2.

During the Cold War, two competing coalitions were composed of states aligned with either the United States or the Soviet Union. The Eastern European states could be counted on to vote consistently with the Soviet Union, thus forming a true bloc.

Throughout the mid-1950s, the Western European, Latin American, and British Commonwealth states also voted closely with the United States on issues that involved Cold War competition, and also often on human rights, social concerns, and UN administration. Despite some internal tensions, that U.S.-dominated coalition held a controlling position in UN General Assembly voting until 1955.

Beginning in 1960 with the influx of new African and Asian states, a new coalition emerged, the Group of 77 (G-77), whose members constituted more than two-thirds of the UN's membership. By 1971, the G-77 had become the dominant coalition, based upon its high level of cohesion on development-related issues in particular. As such, it was able to set agendas in the General Assembly, ECOSOC, and many specialized agencies. The G-77 was often supported by the Eastern European bloc when the Soviet Union took advantage of opportunities to escape its minority position and accuse the West of being responsible for the problems of less developed countries. Once the People's Republic of China held the Chinese seat, it also supported G-77 demands for economic change. The cohesion among the G-77 reached its peak in the mid-1970s. Thereafter, differences in social and economic conditions among Asian, African, and Latin American countries made common policy positions more difficult to forge and the G-77's influence declined. Still, in the 2005 WTO negotiations on a new trade agreement, the G-77 once again became a "booming voice," an alliance of 110 developing members seeking to shape an outcome favorable to their interests.[31] Thus, in many UN bodies, including the General Assembly, the North-South divide still shapes coalitions on issues of economic inequality and development.

Other interests also serve as the basis for coalitions, however. For example, the thirty landlocked countries have tended to vote together on specific issues of trade and transportation; they have also convened UN-sponsored meetings to address their particular needs. So, too, have the forty-five small-island states. The member states of the Organization of Petroleum Exporting Countries (OPEC) who once provided leadership for the G-77 and calls for a New International Economic Order in the 1970s now play a key role as a group in the international financial institutions.

States sharing particular political interests have used their contacts with each other to influence politics within the UN. For example, the Commonwealth—fifty-four states formerly part of the British Empire—operates as a coalition at the UN as well as at the intergovernmental and societal levels. The Nonaligned Movement (NAM), previously a strong bloc of like-minded states opposing colonialism, racism, and Cold War alignments, has refocused its energies since the Cold War's end on representing small non-Western states. The NAM tries to promote common positions within the Security Council and elsewhere, and it works closely with the G-77. Since China joined the NAM in 1992, it has used its membership to call on NAM votes, for example in the Commission on Human Rights.[32]

A relatively recent coalition has emerged among the democratic states, the UN Democracy Caucus. That informal group has pushed for inclusion of good gover-

---

BOX 3.1   Regional and Caucusing Groups in the United Nations

Number of Member States

Regional Groups

African states (53)
Asian states (52)
Latin American and Caribbean states (33)
Western European states and others (27)
Eastern European states (21)

Other Multilateral Organizations

African Union (53)
Arab League (22)
Association of South East Asian Nations (10)
CARICOM (15)
Commonwealth (53)
Economic Community of West African States (16)
European Union (25)
Nordic Group (4)
Organization of the Islamic Conference (56)
Organization of Petroleum Exporting Council (11)

Other Special Interest Groups

Group of 77 (132)
Nonaligned Movement (ca. 130)
UN Democracy Caucus (100)
Land-Locked Developing States (30)
Small-Island Developing States (45)

---

nance norms not only in UN development programs but also in the international financial institutions' aid conditions. That group has also urged the adoption of a concerted human rights agenda. The United States, in particular, has favored collaboration with this group of like-minded (and governed) states.

In addition to coalitions and blocs, the UN members also increasingly rely on ad hoc informal groups of states particularly to support UN peace-related actions. In the late 1970s, the so-called Contact Group on Namibia worked alongside the Security Council in the search for a peaceful solution to the problem of South West Africa, or Namibia, which had been under South African control as a League of Nations mandate since the end of World War I. That group involved high-ranking members of five UN missions (Canada, France, Germany, Great Britain, and the United States) in a decade-long series of negotiations that eventually led to independence for a democratic Namibia. Subsequently, contact groups were formed as part of efforts to settle conflicts in Central America and the former Yugoslavia.

In the 1990s, such groups proliferated. Some of the member states, usually between three and six, organized as "Friends of the Secretary-General" and included at least one interested member of the P-5. The "friends" keep in close contact with the secretary-general and support his efforts to find a peaceful solution to a crisis. The group is kept small so that meetings can be quickly convened. More than one country is used to exert pressure on parties and present a common view that speaks for the international community at large. The purpose is to keep a peace process on track and coordinate the work of mediators, either before reaching a formal agreement or in implementing an agreement. "Friends" groups have been formed, for example, for Haiti (Canada, France, the United States, Venezuela); Georgia (France, Germany, Russia, Great Britain); and Tajikistan (Afghanistan, Iran, Turkey, the United States, Uzbekistan). One study identifies fourteen "Friends of the Secretary-General."[33] In an effort to advance peaceful settlement of the Israeli-Palestinian conflict, the UN, the United States, Russia, and the EU form the so-called Quartet—a further illustration of the value attached to collaborative approaches.

Groups and coalitions, then, provide order and some coherence in a UN of 191 member states and an already crowded agenda. Some serve primarily parliamentary-style functions of putting issues on the table, establishing negotiating positions, garnering votes, and engaging in bargaining. Still others have complemented the UN secretary-general's role as a mediator by bringing the assets of several countries to bear on efforts to find a peaceful settlement to a difficult conflict.

THE SECRETARY-GENERAL AND THE UN BUREAUCRACY AS KEY ACTORS

The growing international prominence of the UN's secretary-general has contributed to the emergence of the UN itself as an autonomous actor in world politics. Both the secretary-general and the UN's bureaucracy, however, wield significant influence within the UN itself and, in some circumstances, over member states. Both command authority to shape agendas and the ways issues are framed. Both are often asked to recommend "what is the right thing to do." Both tend to emphasize their "neutrality, impartiality, and objectivity in ways that make essentially moral claims against particularistic self-serving states."[34]

The Secretary-General

For more than fifty years a pattern of leadership has evolved: Secretaries-general have taken advantage of opportunities for initiatives, applied flexible interpretations of Charter provisions, and sought mandates from UN policy organs as necessary. Seven successive secretaries-general have contributed to developing their own political roles and that of the institution (see box 2.1). Their personalities and interpretations of the UN Charter, as well as of world events, have combined to increase the power, resources, and importance of the position. More than just a senior civil servant, the UN secretary-general has become an international political figure "subject to the problems and possibilities of political leadership."[35]

The UN secretary-general is well placed to serve as a neutral communications channel and intermediary for the global community. Although he represents the institution, he can act independently of the policy organs even when resolutions have condemned a party to a dispute, maintaining lines of communication and representing the institution's commitment to peaceful settlement and alleviation of human suffering. Although these tasks call for diplomatic skills, it has become essential for the secretary-general also to have strong managerial and budgetary skills.

The most important resource for UN secretaries-general is the power of persuasion. The "force" of majorities behind resolutions may lend greater legitimacy to initiatives, though it may not ensure any greater degree of success. Autonomy is also a source of the secretary-general's influence. For example, during the Security Council's 2002–2003 debate over Iraq's failure to disarm and cooperate with UN inspections and whether to authorize a U.S.-led war, Kofi Annan steered an independent course by pushing for Iraqi compliance, council unity, and peace. This type of approach facilitates a secretary-general's ability to serve as a neutral intermediary. U Thant stated, "The Secretary-General must always be prepared to take an initiative, no matter what the consequences to him or his office may be, if he sincerely believes that it might make the difference between peace and war."[36] Annan put it more bluntly: "I know some people have accused me of using diplomacy. That's my job."[37]

Dag Hammarskjöld, the second secretary-general, played a key part in shaping the role and the UN during the critical period 1953–1961. Hammarskjöld articulated principles for UN involvement in peacekeeping. He demonstrated the secretary-general's efficacy as an agent for peaceful settlement of disputes, beginning with his successful 1954–1955 mediation of the release of eleven U.S. airmen under the UN command in Korea who had been imprisoned by the Communist Chinese. This accomplishment was particularly notable because the People's Republic of China was then excluded from the UN. Hammarskjöld also oversaw the initiation of UN peacekeeping operations with the creation of the United Nations Emergency Force (UNEF) at the time of the 1956 Suez crisis.

Javier Pérez de Cuéllar, the fifth secretary-general, presided over the UN's transformation from the brink of irrelevance in the 1980s to an active instrument for resolving conflicts and promoting international peace at the end of the Cold War.

In his persistent, patient, low-key approach to Israel's 1982 invasion of Lebanon, the Falklands/Malvinas War, the Iran-Iraq War, and the ongoing problems in Cyprus, Namibia, and Afghanistan, he epitomized the ideal intermediary.

Secretary-General Boutros Boutros-Ghali pushed the boundaries of the office further with the benefit of independent UN information-gathering and analytical capability. He prodded states, including the U.S., to take action in Somalia. He engaged the UN in civil conflicts in Cambodia, Bosnia, and Haiti. This activism and his antagonistic relationship with the United States that led to his defeat for a second term in 1996. Instead, Kofi Annan, a Ghanaian national, became the seventh secretary-general and the first from within the UN bureaucracy. Among his previous posts were under-secretary general for peacekeeping operations, special representative to the secretary-general to the former Yugoslavia, and special envoy to NATO. A much quieter individual, Annan pledged change, yet has been even more of an activist than his predecessor. In 2001, he won the Nobel Peace Prize for himself and the organization. He has carried out extensive administrative and budgetary reforms within the UN, including structural changes within the Secretariat, to use the UN's limited resources more efficiently. He strengthened liaison between various departments and NGOs, and initiated dialogue with business leaders. Annan is the first secretary-general to make a special effort to build a better relationship with the U.S. Congress, an important step given American predominance and Congress's failure to appropriate full funding for U.S. dues to the UN for much of the 1990s.

A widely respected Annan won reelection in 2001. He has used his "bully pulpit" as UN head, including his annual reports to the General Assembly, to speak out on controversial issues such as HIV/AIDS and support for the norm of humanitarian intervention, and to initiate programs such as the Global Compact with private corporations. He has taken the unprecedented step of publishing reports on the UN's failures in the disastrous massacre in the UN-declared safe area of Srebrenica, in the Rwandan genocide, and in security for UN personnel in Iraq. His prestige and authority were damaged, however, by the oil-for-food scandal discussed in chapter 2.

Annan's second five-year term ends in December 2006. Politicking for the office of the secretary-general is intense. The successful candidate must be acceptable to all of the P-5. Groups wanting geographic diversity in the office support one among many Asian candidates. Others suggest the need for particular qualifications. Still others have argued that it is time to have the first female secretary-general. Referring obliquely to the oil-for-food scandal, the U.S. representative to ECOSOC made this observation: "Obviously we're looking at a candidate that has strong management experience, that can bring a commitment to accountability, transparency and, in a sense, clean up the organization a little bit, making it more lean and efficient."[38]

PHOTO 3.1 UN Secretary-General
Kofi Annan addresses the media after the
Security Council meeting on Sudan, 13
December 2005. *UN photo 106645/Mark
Garten.*

The United States and other dominant states seek an efficient manager for the post of secretary-general. That is compatible with the view that the UN and its secretary-general should be but an instrument of states, to be used by states to promote their own interests. For those, the words of one former UN official are telling: "They will never again choose anyone as independent as this man [Kofi Annan] has turned out to be."[39] Those seeking a more independent figure, a secretary-general who is willing to take initiatives and direct a powerful bureaucracy, have a very different view of the organization. To them, the UN and its secretary-general can and must be an independent actor. The tension between these two very different positions persists.

In addition to the secretary-general, other individuals within the UN system can exercise significant influence. They include the various special representatives of the secretary-general who are now appointed in conjunction with all UN peacekeeping missions and often serve as mediators in negotiations to end conflicts. They also include the high commissioners for refugees and for human rights as well as special rapporteurs on human rights. All these officials can be highly influential in building awareness of issues and calling attention to specific problems such as child soldiers or violence against women. They may criticize countries openly, as a special rapporteur has done on torture in China, or work more quietly to foster constructive dialogue. One rapporteur has made this comment: "We must always bear in mind, though, that the nature of our mandates involves fact-finding and not political advocacy."[40] Chapter 6 examines the leadership that high commissioners for human rights have played since the post was created in 1993.

The directors-general of the specialized agencies also wield considerable power. Diplomatically, they carry the same rank as the secretary-general, historically a factor complicating efforts of the latter to coordinate initiatives across different parts of the UN system. But the role of the UN as bureaucracy extends beyond these high-level officials, and it is to that we turn briefly.

The UN as Bureaucracy

The UN's Secretariat and the secretariats of the specialized agencies share some of the characteristics of bureaucracies more generally. They derive authority in performing "duties of office" from their rational-legal character and from their expertise; they derive legitimacy from the moral purposes of the organization and from their claims to neutrality, impartiality, and objectivity; they derive power from their missions of serving others. The different agencies within the UN system tend to be staffed by technocrats—individuals with specialized training and knowledge who shape policy options consistent with that expertise. "In fact," Barnett and Finnemore note, "the organization will not readily entertain policy options not supported by its expertise. Professional training, norms, and occupational cultures strongly shape the way experts view the world. They influence what problems are visible to staff and what range of solutions are entertained."[41]

The UN's bureaucrats play a significant role in shaping the agendas of various meetings. The ways in which they understand particular conflict situations can also influence how member states view them. For example, Barnett and Finnemore show how the UN staff defined the situation in Rwanda in 1994 as a civil war and failed to see that the unfolding genocide was quite different from violence against civilians in other ethnic conflicts. "Because Rwanda was a civil war there was no basis for intervention," they noted. "The rules of peacekeeping . . . [at that time] prohibited peacekeeping in a civil war and in the absence of a stable cease-fire . . . but also shaped its [the Secretariat's] position on how peacekeepers might be used in this volatile situation"[42] Furthermore, Secretary-General Boutros-Ghali did not make the argument for intervention. Thus, the UN's failure to stop the genocide in Rwanda was "the predictable result of an organizational culture that shaped how the UN evaluated and responded to violent crises."[43]

Examples can be drawn from many other UN agencies. In the mid-1980s, HIV/AIDS (as we discuss in chapter 7) was viewed as solely a health problem and, hence, the province of the medical professionals in WHO. Only gradually did other UN agencies demonstrate the scope of the epidemic's effects and the necessity for interagency collaboration in dealing with the problem. The influence of liberal economists in the IMF and World Bank has long been noted as a major factor shaping the way those institutions' bureaucracies think about and address development issues and financial crises.

Yet, influence in international institutions is not limited to states, secretaries-general, directors-general, or bureaucrats. Increasingly, nonstate actors and nongovernmental organizations in particular have come to play leading roles.

NONGOVERNMENTAL ORGANIZATIONS IN THE UN SYSTEM

Although the UN's members are states, the organization has long recognized the importance of NGOs. The members of these organizations are not states but include private individuals and groups that form the basis of a global civil society. NGOs are interest or pressure groups that operate across national borders in not-for-profit activities.

Article 71 of the UN Charter authorized ECOSOC (but not the General Assembly) to grant consultative status to NGOs. By 1948, 40 NGOs had been formally accredited to ECOSOC; by 1968, 180 NGOs had been recognized; twenty years later, in 2005, there are 2,719 recognized NGOs.[44] Resolution 1296 (1968) formalized that arrangement into three categories. Category I NGOs include those whose multifaceted goals and activities reach virtually all areas of ECOSOC's responsibilities; Category II NGOs are those that specialize in a particular area of economic and social activity, such as health or human rights; Category III NGOs are organizations that may have an occasional interest in UN activities. Consultative status permits NGOs to attend ECOSOC meetings, submit written statements, testify before ECOSOC meetings, and, in certain cases, propose items for the agenda.

Although originally NGOs were limited to consultation with ECOSOC, the distinction between those NGOs with ECOSOC consultative status and those without it has become largely academic because NGOs have found various means for influencing global policymaking and implementation.[45] In the General Assembly, four NGOs—the International Federation of the Red Cross and Red Crescent Societies, the International Committee of the Red Cross (ICRC), the Inter-parliamentary Union, and the Sovereign Military Order of Malta—have special privileges to participate as observers in all assembly sessions. Since the late 1980s, NGOs have access as petitioners to some assembly committees, notably the Third Committee (Humanitarian and Cultural) and the Second Committee (Economic and Financial). In 1997, NGOs first gained limited access to Security Council meetings. Through the NGO Working Group on the Security Council, NGOs that provide relief aid in humanitarian emergencies have gained a voice in council activities. Informal consultations between NGOs, the council president, and council members are now a common practice.

NGOs are also active in the specialized agencies. Only in the International Labour Organization are such contacts formalized in the unique tripartite system of representation; in other agencies, the practice of consultation is widespread, as illustrated by the work of more than six hundred NGOs with UNESCO. In IGOs performing services in the field, such as UNHCR, World Food Programme, UNICEF, and other development organizations, NGOs are vital partners because they distribute goods and provide services.

NGO participation in the international financial organizations has been longer in coming. In the late 1970s and throughout the 1980s, women's and environmental NGOs pressured the World Bank, for example, to adopt a women-in-development agenda and advisor post and an Environment Department, environmental impact statements, and lending for environmental projects. The environmentalists also targeted specific bank projects such as big dams. Since 1994, when the bank turned to a more participatory development approach, it increasingly used NGOs to collaborate on and administer projects. This shift in the World Bank's approach was part of a broader shift toward civil society empowerment among development agencies that NGOs helped bring about. In contrast, the IMF has been slow to develop formal contacts with NGOs because its specialized focus on monetary policy has not lent itself easily to NGO input. Yet, even the IMF felt NGO influence during the Jubilee 2000 campaign for debt reduction orchestrated by a wide range of NGOs, religious groups, trade unions, and business associations.

When in the 1970s the UN began to sponsor global conferences on issues such as women, the environment, human rights, population, and sustainable development, NGOs found valuable new outlets for their activity. In many cases, groups participated in preconference meetings with delegates, organized their own parallel meetings on topics of interest, published materials to increase public awareness of the issues, and developed networks with other NGO to enhance their influence. At the conferences themselves, the rules for NGO participation have varied. Some conferences have permitted NGO lobbying and NGO roles in implementation; others have limited participation to informal activities. (See chapters 5, 6, and 7 for discussion of specific conferences.)

For several decades, proposals have been floated to give civil society actors a forum of their own. The People's Millennium Assembly held in 2000 was an ad hoc version of such a forum that brought together representatives of more than one hundred NGOs. Although the names have varied—including a UN Parliamentary Assembly, a Forum of Civil Society, a Second Assembly—the ideas are basically the same. To proponents, nonstate actors—including NGOs—should have a venue for consultations among themselves and should be given standing within the UN system. Such an assembly would give voice to heretofore unrepresented groups, add

PHOTO 3.2   The proliferation of NGO posters outside the local offices of NGOs in Burkina Faso. *Photo by Jeremy Hartley/Panos Pictures, London.*

transparency to the international political process, and potentially add accountability. Some of these proposals would necessitate change in the UN Charter, however, an issue we examine in chapter 8.

CONCLUSION

States remain major actors in the UN system, although their sovereignty may be eroding, and their centrality may be diminished by the activism of the UN bureaucracy and NGOs. Across the years, they have used the United Nations for foreign policy purposes and have been affected in turn by the organization's actions. Since the Cold War's end, there have been proliferating demands for UN action on security, economic, and other issues. The political will, or commitment, of member states has become an increasingly critical factor in determining whether or not sufficient action is taken and sufficient resources are made available. One key is the willingness of the United States to provide leadership and funding as well as to build coalitions involving other states in UN decisionmaking and implementation.

As we have discussed, domestic politics in the United States, including presidential leadership, congressional support, and public acquiescence, are factors determining whether the world's sole superpower chooses to provide that leadership. The willingness of other economically powerful states to contribute to the financial burden, and of middle powers to be leaders or followers, is also essential. Likewise, the ability and willingness of small states to support global initiatives and to fulfill their own commitments are part of the picture. The proliferation of NGOs, the emergence of global civil society, and the roles of the secretary-general and UN bureaucracy as actors are developments that complicate and enrich the cast of characters on the UN's stage.

NOTES

1. Donald J. Puchala, "World Hegemony and the United Nations," *International Studies Review* 7, no. 4 (December 2005): 571.

2. Ibid., 574.

3. Margaret P. Karns and Karen A. Mingst, eds., *The United States and Multilateral Institutions: Patterns of Changing Instrumentality and Influence* (Boston: Unwin Hyman, 1990).

4. Michael Barnett and Martha Finnemore, *Rules for the World: International Organizations in Global Politics* (Ithaca: Cornell University Press, 2004), 3.

5. Edward C. Luck, *Mixed Messages: American Politics and International Organization 1919–1999* (Washington, D.C.: Brookings Institution Press, 1999).

6. Margaret P. Karns and Karen A. Mingst, "The United States as 'Deadbeat'? U.S. Policy and the UN Financial Crisis," in *Multilateralism and U.S. Foreign Policy: Ambivalent Engagement,* ed. Stewart Patrick and Shepard Forman (Boulder: Lynne Rienner, 2002), 267–294.

7. Robert Falkner, "American Hegemony and the Global Environment," *International Studies Review* 7, no. 4 (December 2005): 592. See pages 592–595 for further discussion of domestic factors in U.S. environmental policy.

8. Puchala, "World Hegemony and the United Nations," 575.

9. Ibid., 576.

10. See Ken Matthews, *The Gulf Conflict and International Relations* (London: Routledge, 1993), 81.

11. Michael Grossman, "Role Theory and Foreign Policy Change: The Transformation of Russian Foreign Policy in the 1990s," *International Politics* 42, no. 3 (September 2005): 334–351.

12. Dmitry Shlapentokh, "Outside View: Russian Troops in Iraq," *The Washington Times* (2004), www.washingtontimes.com/upi-breaking/2004.

13. B. Gregory Marfleet and Colleen Miller, "Failure after 1441: Bush and Chirac in the UN Security Council," *Foreign Policy Analysis* 1, no. 3 (November 2005): 333–360.

14. For extensive treatment of the British position, see A. J. R. Groom and Paul Taylor, "The United Kingdom and the United Nations," in *The United Nations System and the Politics of Member States,* ed. Chadwick F. Alger, Gene M. Lyons, and John E. Trent (Tokyo: United Nations University Press, 1995), 376–409.

15. Tom Woodhouse and Alexander Ramsbotham, "The United Kingdom," in *The Politics of Peacekeeping in the Post-Cold War Era,* ed. David S. Sorenson and Pia Christina Wood (London: Frank Cass, 2005), 100–103.

16. Ann Kent, "China's International Socialization: The Role of International Organizations," *Global Governance* 8, no. 3 (July-September 2002): 345.

17. Sally Morphet, "China as a Permanent Member of the Security Council," *Security Dialogue* 31, no. 2 (June 2000): 165.

18. Kent, "China's International Socialization," 358.

19. Yitzhak Shichor, "Decisionmaking in Triplicate: China and the Three Iraqi Wars," in *Chinese National Security Decisionmaking Under Stress,* ed. Andrew Scobell and Larry M. Wortzel (Carlisle, Penn.: Strategic Studies Institute, U.S. Army War College, 2005), 191–228.

20. Kent, "China's International Socialization," 349.

21. See Sadako Ogata, "Japan's Policy Towards the United Nations," in *The United Nations System and the Politics of Member States,* ed. Chadwick F. Alger, Gene M. Lyons, and John E. Trent (Tokyo: United Nations University Press, 1995), 231–270. See also Reinhard Drifte, *Japan's Quest for a Permanent Security Council Seat: A Matter of Pride or Justice?* (New York: St. Martin's Press, 2000).

22. Quoted in Paul Lewis, "Germany Asks Permanent UN Council Seat," *New York Times,* September 24, 1992.

23. Mary N., Hampton, "Germany," in *The Politics of Peacekeeping in the Post-Cold War Era,* ed. David S. Sorenson and Pia Christina Wood (London: Frank Cass, 2005), 43–44.

24. Keith Krause, David Dewitt, and W. Andy Knight, "Canada, the United Nations, and the Reform of International Institutions," in *The United Nations System and the Politics of Member States,* ed. Chadwick F. Alger, Gene M. Lyons, and John E. Trent (Tokyo: United Nations University Press, 1995), 171.

25. David Rudd, "Canada," in *The Politics of Peacekeeping in the Post-Cold War Era,* ed. David S. Sorenson and Pia Christina Wood (London: Frank Cass, 2005), 173.

26. Hugh Smith, "Australia," in *The Politics of Peacekeeping in the Post-Cold War Era,* ed. David S. Sorenson and Pia Christina Wood (London: Frank Cass, 2005), 9–13.

27. Andrew F. Cooper, Richard A. Higgott, and Kim Richard Nossal, *Relocating Middle Powers: Australia and Canada in a Changing World Order* (Vancouver: University of British Columbia Press, 1993).

28. Alison Brysk, "Global Good Samaritans? Human Rights Foreign Policy in Costa Rica," *Global Governance* 11, no. 4 (2005): 445–466.

29. Quoted in Sally Morphet, "Multilateralism and the Non-Aligned Movement: What Is the Global South Doing and Where Is It Going?" *Global Governance* 10, no. 4 (October-December 2004): 533.

30. Courtney B. Smith, *Politics and Process at the United Nations: The Global Dance* (Boulder: Lynne Rienner, 2006). See especially chap. 3.

31. Greg Hitt and Scott Miller, "Booming Voice for New Bloc," *Wall Street Journal,* December 17–18, 2005.

32. Morphet, "Multilateralism and the Non-Aligned Movement," 528–530.

33. Jochen Prandt and Jean Krasno, "Informal Ad Hoc Groupings of States and the Workings of the United Nations" (New Haven: International Relations and the United Nations Occasional Papers, no. 3, ACUNS, 2002).

34. Michael Barnett and Martha Finnemore, "The Power of Liberal Organizations," in *Power in Global Governance,* ed. Michael Barnett and Raymond Duvall (New York: Cambridge University Press, 2005), 170, 173.

35. Oran R. Young, *The Intermediaries: Third Parties in International Crises* (Princeton: Princeton University Press, 1967), 283.

36. Ibid, 284.

37. Barbara Crossette, "Kofi Annan Unsettles People, As He Believes U.N. Should Do," *New York Times,* December 31, 1999.

38. Sichan Siv, quoted in Colum Lynch, "An Early Lineup," *Washington Post National Weekly Edition,* December 5–11, 2005.

39. Quoted in Warren Hoge, "U.N. Is Transforming Itself, But Into What Is Unclear," *New York Times,* February 28, 2005.

40. Paulo Sergio Pinheiro, "Musings of a UN Special Rapporteur on Human Rights," *Global Governance* 9, no. 1 (January-March 2003): 11.

41. Barnett and Finnemore, "The Power of Liberal International Organizations," 174. The ideas in this section draw heavily from pages 171–178.

42. Barnett and Finnemore, *Rules for the World,* 151–152.

43. Ibid., 155.

44. These figures were compiled and reported by Ann Marie Clark, "Human Rights NGOs at the United Nations," paper prepared for Multi-Level Governance and Civil Society Workshop, Berlin, October 14–15, 2005.

45. This section relies heavily on Smith, *Politics and Process at the United Nations,* chap. 5.

4

———◄○►———

Peace and Security:
International Organizations
as Venues for Security

We acknowledge that we are living in an interdependent
and global world and that many of today's threats
recognize no national boundaries, are interlinked and
must be tackled at the global, regional, and national levels
in accordance with the Charter and international law.

—2005 World Summit Outcome

War, *the* fundamental problem in international politics, has been the primary factor motivating the creation of IGOs from the Concert of Europe in the nineteenth
century to the League of Nations and the United Nations in the twentieth century.
Despite being the most destructive century in human history, the twentieth century was also the century of creating ways to address security issues. These new approaches are being tested and revised in the twenty-first century.

The nature of wars and conflicts has changed in significant ways in the last fifty
years. Studies have shown a sharp decrease in the incidence of interstate war, or
wars between two or more states. Since 1992, the number has declined by more
than 40 percent, the deadliest (those with 1,000 or more battle deaths) having
dropped by 80 percent. The number of intrastate conflicts, or conflicts within
states, resulting from the collapse of an already weak state, ethnic conflict, or civil
war has increased dramatically to more than 95 percent of all armed conflicts, but

has leveled off in recent years.[1] Civil wars that become internationalized through the intervention of other states or groups represent a further problem. These developments are the result of three major political changes: the end of colonialism, the Cold War's end, and increased international activities, especially by the United Nations in the 1990s, to stop ongoing wars and prevent new ones.

Yet, the UN's Charter was designed to deal with interstate conflicts, and most states remain jealous of their sovereignty. Thus, they are wary of commitments that compromise the principle of nonintervention in states' domestic affairs. Since the Cold War's end, however, the UN's member states have empowered it to play a much more active role in dealing with conflicts within states, many of which have also involved humanitarian disasters resulting from the fighting, from ethnic cleansing or genocide, from the collapse of governmental authority (failed state), or from famine and disease. These have provoked debates about the legitimacy of international armed intervention under UN auspices to protect human beings, yet the growth of international human rights norms in the second half of the twentieth century has shifted the balance between the rights of states and the rights of people to provide legitimacy for armed intervention to protect human beings from violence.

The changing nature of conflicts and complex humanitarian crises are two challenges to peace in the twenty-first century. Other threats include the spread of weapons of mass destruction (chemical, biological, and nuclear) and terrorism. These threats are not new, but the linkages between them are, and these present major challenges to the UN and international efforts to maintain peace and security.

MAINTAINING PEACE AND SECURITY: THE UN CHARTER AND ITS EVOLUTION

Maintaining peace and security has always been the primary purpose of the UN. But how the UN undertakes this task has changed over time in ways never envisaged by the founders. Many provisions of the Charter that lay largely unused during the forty years of the Cold War have seen far more use since 1989.

The United Nations Charter in Article 2 (sections 3, 4, and 5) obligates all members to settle disputes by peaceful means, to refrain from the threat or use of force, and to cooperate with UN-sponsored actions. The Security Council has primary responsibility for maintenance of international peace and security (Article 24).

Chapter VI specifies the ways in which the Security Council can promote **peaceful settlement** of disputes. For example, under Article 34, "the Security Council may investigate any dispute, or any situation which might lead to international friction or give rise to a dispute, in order to determine whether the continuance of the dispute or situation is likely to endanger the maintenance of international peace and security." For the most part, the Security Council has relied on the Charter's peaceful settlement mechanisms in responding to the many situations placed on its agenda over the years.

Chapter VII specifies actions the UN can take with respect to threats to the peace, breaches of the peace, and acts of aggression. The Security Council can identify aggressors (Articles 39 and 40), decide what enforcement measures should be taken (Articles 41, 42, 48, and 49), and call on members to make military forces available, subject to special agreements (Articles 43–45).

Chapter VIII recognizes the rights and responsibilities of regional organizations to "make every effort to achieve peaceful settlement of local disputes" before referring them to the Security Council. When a regional organization seeks to use force, however, Security Council authorization is required to maintain the UN's primacy with respect to enforcement.

For more than sixty years, the UN has addressed security threats in ways that reinforced Chapters VI and VII of the Charter such as through **preventive diplomacy** and deployment, patient mediation by the secretary-general, targeted sanctions, and enhanced monitoring procedures. It has also invented new approaches such as peacekeeping, humanitarian intervention, peacebuilding or nation-building, ad hoc criminal tribunals to prosecute war crimes and crimes against humanity, and counterterrorism measures. These newer approaches illustrate how the UN has evolved as an institution.

MECHANISMS FOR PEACEFUL SETTLEMENT AND PREVENTIVE DIPLOMACY

As early as the Greek city-states, there was agreement about the desirability of settling disputes peacefully. The 1899 and 1908 Hague Conferences laid the foundations for mechanisms still in use today when they produced the Convention for the Pacific Settlement of International Disputes. These conventions assume that war is a deliberate choice for settling a dispute and that it is possible to create mechanisms that will influence actors' choices. Mechanisms were created for third-party roles variously labeled good offices, inquiry, mediation, conciliation, adjudication, and arbitration. These were incorporated into the League of Nations Covenant and Chapter VI of the UN Charter.

Among the peaceful settlement approaches, the UN has been most involved through good offices and mediation led by the secretary-general, a special envoy appointed by the secretary-general, or an ad hoc group of states (usually including at least one permanent member of the Security Council) called a "contact group" or "Friends of the Secretary-General," as discussed in chapter 3.[2] Secretary-General Javier Pérez de Cuéllar and Alvaro de Soto, his special assistant, for example, mediated an end to the conflicts in El Salvador in the 1980s, and secured agreement on the Soviet Union's withdrawal from Afghanistan.

Adjudication and arbitration take place in the International Court of Justice, ad hoc war crimes tribunals, the International Criminal Court, the World Bank's Centre for Settlement of Investment Disputes, and arbitration panels.

Preventive diplomacy, an approach to peaceful settlement introduced by UN Secretary-General Dag Hammarskjöld in the late 1950s, is "action to prevent disputes from arising between parties, to prevent existing disputes from escalating into conflicts and to limit the spread of the latter when they occur."[3] Most often, preventive diplomacy takes the form of diplomatic efforts, sometimes coupled with economic sanctions or arms embargoes. Preventive deployment, an important innovation, is intended to change the calculus of parties regarding the purposes to be served by political violence and to deter them from choosing to escalate the level of conflict. It is estimated that the UN's deployment of 1,000 peacekeeping troops to Macedonia from late 1992 to 2001 cost $0.3 billion as opposed to an estimated $15 billion had the violence in other regions of the former Yugoslavia spread to Macedonia.[4] Successful preventive diplomacy depends on timeliness; indeed, the costs of waiting tend to be much higher than those for preventive action. But preventing conflicts is rarely easy, and opportunities are frequently missed. Still, there are numerous success stories. Likewise, other approaches to peaceful settlement have not always met with success. Hence, the founders of the League of Nations and the UN recognized the importance of provisions for collective security and enforcement actions.

COLLECTIVE SECURITY, ENFORCEMENT, AND SANCTIONS

The concept of collective security was at the heart of President Woodrow Wilson's proposal for the League of Nations as an alternative to the traditional balance-of-power politics that had frequently led to wars. That concept carried over to the UN.

Under collective security, states attempt to prevent aggression by agreeing to unite in collective action against an aggressor with the overwhelming united threat of counterforce, mobilized through an international organization such as the League or the UN. States do not act on the basis of their own individual national interests, but on the perceived collective interest of the international community to counter aggression. Collective security requires mutual trust, the belief of each state that other states will come to its rescue should it be a target of aggression. The goal of collective security is to prevent the use of force, the proposition being that potential aggressors will refrain from attack when they know their actions will be met by the actions of the international community.

Writers of the UN Charter had assumed great power unity; indeed, effective functioning of the Security Council requires the concurrence of the P-5. Their veto power ensured that from the outset the UN was a limited collective security organization during the Cold War. Indeed, only two situations—Korea in 1950 and Iraq's 1990 invasion of Kuwait—resemble collective security actions.

Korea and the Gulf War: Collective Security in Action?

The sanctioning of UN forces to counter the North Korean invasion of South Korea in 1950 was made possible by the temporary absence of the Soviet Union from the Security Council in protest against the UN's refusal to seat the newly established Communist government of the People's Republic of China. Thus, the UN provided the framework for legitimizing U.S. efforts to defend the Republic of Korea and mobilizing other states' assistance. An American general was designated the UN commander, but he took orders directly from Washington. Some fifteen states contributed troops during the three-year war.

Iraq's invasion of Kuwait in the summer of 1990 triggered a period of unprecedented activity by the UN Security Council as members sought ways to respond effectively to this act of aggression against a UN member state. Unity among the P-5, including the Soviet Union (despite its long-standing relationship with Iraq), facilitated the passage of twelve successive resolutions during a four-month period activating Chapter VII of the Charter. These included, most importantly, Resolution 678 of 29 November 1990, which authorized member states "to use all necessary means" to reverse the occupation of Kuwait.

The military operation launched under the umbrella of Resolution 678 and Article 42 of the Charter was a U.S.-led multinational effort resembling a subcontract on behalf of the organization. U.S. commanders did not regularly report to the secretary-general, nor did senior UN personnel participate in military decision-making. Coalition forces did not use the UN flag or insignia. After the fighting ceased in late February 1991, a traditional, lightly armed peacekeeping force known as the United Nations Iraq-Kuwait Observer Mission (UNIKOM) was organized to monitor the demilitarized zone between Iraq and Kuwait.

The U.S.-led military action in the Gulf was widely regarded as exemplifying a stronger post–Cold War UN, but also came under critical scrutiny.[5] Germany and Japan, which contributed substantial monetary resources, were excluded from decisions on the Security Council because they were not members; consequently, they became interested in securing permanent membership on the Council, as discussed in chapter 3. Many developing countries supported the action, but they were also troubled by the autonomy of the U.S.-led operation. The Gulf War marked only the beginning, however, of efforts to deal with Iraq's threats to regional peace.

Enforcement Actions and Sanctions

Iraq's invasion of Kuwait in August 1990 and the Cold War's end initiated unprecedented cooperation among the P-5 and extensive use of Charter provisions. Chapter

VII has since been invoked on many occasions to authorize the use of force or various types of sanctions. In Bosnia, Haiti, East Timor, Afghanistan, and Sierra Leone, the Security Council authorized the use of force either by a regional organization such as NATO (Bosnia and Afghanistan) or by a **"coalition of the willing"** led by a country willing to commit military forces to the effort, such as the United States (Somalia and Haiti), Australia (East Timor), France (Rwanda), and Great Britain (Sierra Leone).

Chapter VII of the UN Charter outlines a variety of enforcement mechanisms— including economic, diplomatic, and financial sanctions—to prevent or deter threats to international peace or to counter acts of aggression. During the Cold War, these Chapter VII provisions were used only twice: to impose economic sanctions on the white minority regime in Southern Rhodesia after it unilaterally declared its independence from Great Britain in 1965, and to impose an arms embargo on South Africa in 1977. Beginning with the Iraq crisis in 1990, the Security Council extensively utilized the Chapter VII sanctions provisions—leading two experts to dub the 1990s "the sanctions decade."[6] These enforcement actions have included arms embargoes against Yugoslavia, Angola, Rwanda, and Afghanistan, as well as comprehensive sanctions against Iraq and Haiti. In an effort to hurt those most responsible for conflicts rather than ordinary people, the Security Council imposed targeted sanctions such as freezing the assets of governments or individuals (Libya and Afghanistan), travel bans for government and rebel leaders and their families (Sudan, Sierra Leone, Liberia, Afghanistan), and import/export bans for specific commodities such as oil, tropical timber, and diamonds (Liberia, Sierra Leone, Angola, and Haiti) (see table 4.1). The purposes for which these sanctions were employed also broadened. Sanctions have been employed to counter aggression (Iraq), to restore a democratically elected government (Haiti), to respond to human rights violations (Yugoslavia, Rwanda, and Somalia), to end wars (Angola, Sierra Leone, Ethiopia, and Eritrea), and to bring suspected terrorists to justice (Libya).

The most extensive enforcement undertaking was the effort to persuade Iraq to comply with the complex terms of the April 1991 cease-fire agreement. Security Council Resolution 687 enumerated terms of the cease-fire agreement and a far-reaching plan for dismantling Iraq's weapons of mass destruction (WMD). It called for Iraq to accept the destruction, under international supervision, of all its chemical and biological weapons and ballistic missiles; it had to agree not to acquire or develop nuclear weapons and to place all nuclear-usable material (such as for power plants) under international control. The resolution also required Iraq to compensate victims for losses and damages using money from the sale of oil, and it created a Compensation Commission to administer the fund and resolve claims against Iraq. The earlier sanctions were to continue until all the provisions were carried out to the Security Council's satisfaction. The only exception was oil sales authorized under the 1995 Oil-for-Food Programme to pay for food and medical supplies.

TABLE 4.1   Selected UN Sanctions

Type of Sanction	Target Country	Years
Arms Embargo	South Africa	1978–93
	Iraq	1990–2003
	Yugoslavia	1991–96, 1998–2001
	Angola and UNITA	1993–2002
	Libya	1992–99
	Liberia	1992–2001
	Rwanda	1992–95
	Afghanistan	1990–2001
	Sierra Leone	1997
	Sierra Leone (rebels only)	1998
	Eritrea	2000
	Ethiopia	2000
Export or Import Limits (ban exports of diamonds, timber, etc, or embargo on imports of oil, etc.)	Cambodia (logs, oil)	1992–94
	Haiti (oil)	1993–94
	Angola (diamonds)	1993, 1998–2002
	Sierra Leone (oil, diamonds)	1997–98, 2000
	Liberia (diamonds)	2001
Asset Freeze	Iraq	1990–2003
	Libya	1993–99
	Yugoslavia	1992–95, 1998–2000
	Haiti	1994 (junta only), 1993–94
	Angola	1998 (UNITA only)
	Afghanistan	1999–2001
	Liberia	2001–
Withdrawal of Diplomatic Relations	Sudan	1996–2001
	Angola	1997 (UNITA only)
Denial of Visas (travel bans)	Libya	1992–99
	Haiti	1994
	Angola	1997 (UNITA only)
	Sudan	1996–2001
	Sierra Leone (rebels only)	1998
	Iraq	1999–2003
	Afghanistan	1999–2001
	Liberia	2001
Cancellation of Air Links	Iraq	1990–2003
	Yugoslavia	1992–95
	Libya	1992–99
	Angola (UNITA)	1997–2002
	Afghanistan	1999–2001
Comprehensive Sanctions	Southern Rhodesia	1965–80
	Iraq	1990–2003
	Yugoslavia	1992–95
	Haiti	1993–94

The disarmament sanctions regime involved the most intrusive international inspections ever established. The UN Special Commission (UNSCOM) was created to oversee the destruction of Iraq's chemical and biological weapons and their production and storage facilities, and to monitor compliance. The International Atomic Energy Agency (IAEA), a UN specialized agency established in the 1950s, was responsible for eliminating Iraq's nuclear weapons program. Between 1991 and 1998, inspectors moved all over Iraq, carrying out surprise inspections of suspected storage and production facilities, destroying stocks of materials, and checking documents. Iraq continually thwarted UNSCOM and IAEA inspectors: It removed equipment, claimed to have destroyed material without adequate verification, argued that some sites were off limits, and complained about the makeup of the commission. When Iraq severed all cooperation in November 1998, inspectors were withdrawn.[7] Although the successor to UNSCOM, the UN Monitoring, Verification, and Inspection Commission (UNMOVIC), was allowed to begin inspections anew in November 2002, its work was cut short by U.S. military action against Iraq in March 2003.

The Iraq sanctions became highly controversial as they produced a mounting humanitarian crisis among ordinary Iraqis (aggravated by the government's diversion of funds from the Oil-for-Food Programme). Evidence of malnutrition, contaminated water supplies, increased infectious disease, and high infant and child mortality rates generated widespread sympathy and calls for ending sanctions. The Iraqi government also exacerbated the crisis for political purposes and rejected international proposals to alleviate it. In addition, over time, sanctions fatigue grew among neighboring and other nations that had traditionally relied on trade with Iraq, and compliance eroded as unauthorized trade and transport links multiplied.

Although the IAEA succeeded in destroying Iraq's existing nuclear weapons materials and production facilities, UNSCOM was unable to certify that it knew the full extent of Iraq's chemical and biological weapons production facilities because materials are easily concealed. Destroying weapons stocks and production facilities did not destroy the knowledge base that Iraq had developed, nor did it curtail its access to alternative technologies, especially for biological and chemical weapons. This would require a long-term program of monitoring and the political will to maintain it. Yet at another level, the sanctions were successful—no weapons of mass destruction or active programs have been found in Iraq, despite search efforts following the U.S. invasion in 2003.

The experience with sanctions against Iraq and other countries in the 1990s not only produced a set of lessons about the importance of targeted as opposed to general sanctions but also led to recognition by the Security Council that monitoring was crucial to getting states and other actors to comply with sanctions. For example, sanctions were among several approaches used by the UN in efforts to end the fighting in Angola during the 1990s; they had little impact until 1999, however, when an independent panel of experts was created to investigate sanctions violations and recommend ways to enhance compliance. By mid-2001, the monitoring group reported that arms deliveries were greatly reduced; countries were no longer providing safe havens to officials of the rebel National Union for the Total Independence of Angola known as UNITA; and diamond export revenues (targeted by the sanctions) had dropped. Long considered a failure, Angola became "one of the most important developments in sanctions policy in recent years."[8] Furthermore, the lessons learned in Angola were applied to the conflict in Sierra Leone and to target states supporting terrorism before and after the September 11, 2001, attacks on the World Trade Center.

The Security Council drew two important lessons from the experience with comprehensive sanctions on Iraq: the importance of tailoring what and who is sanctioned to the specific situation to reduce ambiguity, close loopholes, and avoid unacceptable humanitarian costs, and the importance of monitoring compliance. Independent expert panels have gathered data on violators, supply routes, networks, and transactions; the council has named and shamed violators by publicly identifying them; regional and nongovernmental organizations as well as private corporations have been recruited as partners in implementing and monitoring sanctions. Thus, sanctions continue to be a major tool in enforcement efforts.

Legitimizing Enforcement Actions: Afghanistan and Iraq II

A major issue relating to the UN's collective security and enforcement role concerns the debate over whether and when states, including the world's only superpower—the United States—must obtain authorization from the Security Council to use force. In the post–Cold War era, the issue was first joined in the debate over the legitimacy of NATO-led action in Kosovo in 1999 (discussed later in this chapter). It arose again after September 11, 2001, when the United States intervened in Afghanistan on the grounds of self-defense to bring down the Taliban government that had harbored Al Qaeda training camps for terrorists. The issue was most sharply debated in 2002–2003; this was when the United States pushed for Security Council endorsement of military action to bring down the government of Saddam Hussein in Iraq on the grounds that Iraq had repeatedly failed to implement Security Council resolutions, had ousted UN weapons inspectors, and was developing weapons of mass destruction. In short, the United States announced that it would act with or without Security Council approval because Iraq constituted a threat to regional and global peace and security. It is useful to compare the cases of Afghanistan in fall 2001 and Iraq in 2002–2003.

Within twenty-four hours of the September 11, 2001, attacks, the UN Security Council approved Resolution 1368, which, among other things, recognized the U.S. right to self-defense under Article 51. Although states inherently have the right to self-defense, the United States interpreted the Security Council resolution as providing an international legal basis for its military action against the Taliban regime and Al Qaeda camps in Afghanistan one month later. Following the Bonn Conference establishing the Afghan Interim Authority in December 2001, UNSC Resolution 1386 authorized a British-led International Security Assistance Force (ISAF) with enforcement power under Chapter VII to help the Afghan transitional authority maintain security. It also established a UN peacebuilding mission, the UN Assistance Mission in Afghanistan (UNAMA), to coordinate the work of sixteen UN agencies. In 2003, NATO took control of ISAF and, with Security Council authorization, has expanded its jurisdiction.

The greatest problems regarding the legitimacy of the use of force arise when it is neither a clear case of self-defense (individual or collective) in response to an armed attack nor authorized by the Security Council. Hence, the story of U.S. efforts to secure Security Council authorization for enforcement actions against Iraq in late 2002 and 2003—Iraq II—is a very different and controversial one.

The United States expended a great deal of diplomatic effort during the fall and winter of 2002–2003 in trying to muster Security Council support for action against Iraq. Following President George W. Bush's address to the General Assembly on September 12, 2002, in which he warned Iraq that force would be used to uphold the objectives set by the Security Council unless it agreed to be peacefully disarmed of all weapons of mass destruction, the Iraqi government accepted the immediate and unconditional return of weapons inspectors. In October 2002, the U.S. Congress authorized the president to use armed forces if necessary. In November, the Security Council unanimously passed a new resolution (1441) reinforcing the inspections regime and giving Iraq a last opportunity to provide "a currently accurate, full and complete declaration of all aspects of its programs to develop" WMD and missiles. Although council members were unwilling to authorize states in advance to use force against Iraq in the event of noncompliance, they did state that lack of cooperation, lies, and omissions would constitute a material breach that could lead to action. Despite IAEA and UNMOVIC reports showing that Iraq was cooperating with the strengthened inspections regime, the United States and Great Britain sought Security Council authorization in February and March 2003 for military action to disarm Iraq. They were forced to withdraw their draft resolution in the face of opposition from three other P-5 members (France, Russia, and China), as well as most nonpermanent members, including Germany. As one analyst has noted, this was "a resolution too far" and their skepticism or opposition was "not surprising, given their different interests, their different views of war, their different assessments of any threat posed by Iraq, and their stated concerns about U.S. dominance."[9]

By deciding to go to war in Iraq in March 2003 in defiance of the majority of the Security Council, however, the United States, Great Britain, and their coalition allies posed a serious challenge to the authority of the council to authorize the use of force in situations other than self-defense. And, because a major argument for military action involved what has been called "anticipatory self-defense" —or preventive action—the question was one of whether military action can be taken unilaterally in response to nonimminent threats. In short, the war in Iraq raised a host of questions of principle and practice concerning the UN's role in enforcement, including the fundamental question of the UN's relevance. Did the Security Council's failure to support the U.S. action in Iraq illustrate the UN's ineffectiveness and confirm its waning legitimacy, especially in the face of a superpower with overwhelming military power and a willingness to pursue its own agenda without Security Council authority, as some have argued? Or did the Security Council work as its founders envisioned, not supporting UN involvement unless all the P-5 members and a majority of nonpermanent council members concurred? The debate has taken on a new intensity, the supporters of the U.S. position deriding the UN for its lack of follow-up to the sanctions, and opponents of the U.S.-led war applauding the UN's stance and appreciative of the UN role in postconflict **peacebuilding.**[10]

One observer, however, noted, "The suggestion . . . that the UN was on the verge of irrelevance and political bankruptcy, has turned out to be profoundly misplaced . . . [as] the occupying powers soon realized . . . that *some* form of UN involvement was essential to help overcome the difficulties created by the occupation's lack of legitimacy and public support."[11] In Iraq and Afghanistan, the UN's assistance is best seen in the context of peacebuilding activities and has been more extensive in Afghanistan.

Although the UN has used the enforcement powers embodied in Chapter VII far more extensively since 1990 than in the forty-five previous years, its conflict management role before and after 1990 has been most notable in the evolution of peacekeeping and the complex activities related to peacebuilding. Despite the debate over the UN's continuing relevance and effectiveness following the U.S. intervention in Iraq and the deep divisions within the Security Council that engendered, there has been a dramatic increase in UN peacekeeping and peacebuilding operations since 2003. This illustrates the continuing vitality of these innovative approaches to conflict management that evolved during and after the Cold War.

PEACEKEEPING

Peacekeeping, first developed to provide observer groups for cease-fires in Kashmir and Palestine in the late 1940s, was formally proposed by Lester B. Pearson, the Canadian secretary of state for external affairs, at the height of the Suez crisis in 1956 as a means for securing the withdrawal of British, French, and Israeli forces from Egypt pending a political settlement. Its development demonstrates that the members did not allow the Cold War to block efforts to use the UN to promote and maintain international security. Peacekeeping enabled the UN to play a positive role in dealing with regional conflicts at a time when hostility between East and West prevented the use of the Charter provisions for collective security and enforcement.

It has taken different forms and evolved dramatically since the Cold War's end removed superpower involvement in many regional and civil conflicts and opened a political space for expanding peacekeeping operations. The UN defines peace-keeping as "an operation involving military personnel, but without enforcement powers, undertaken by the United Nations to help maintain or restore interna-tional peace and security in areas of conflict."[12] Since there is no Charter provision for peacekeeping, it lies in a "grey zone" between the peaceful settlement provisions of Chapter VI and the military enforcement provisions of Chapter VII and is sometimes referred to as Chapter VI and a half. Some operations in the 1990s crossed that "grey zone" and more closely resembled enforcement, creating contro-versy and operational problems that we address below. It has become common, therefore, to distinguish between **traditional peacekeeping** (often referred to as first generation peacekeeping) and the often more muscular **complex peacekeep-ing** and peacebuilding operations (second and third generations). The latter may involve greater use of force and an absence of parties' consent, combined with ef-forts to enforce an end to violence and rebuild a viable state.

Inasmuch as the permanent UN military forces envisioned by the Charter were never created, peacekeeping operations have relied on ad hoc military (civilian or police) units, or subcontracting to a coalition of states. During the Cold War these were drawn almost exclusively from the armed forces of nonpermanent members of the Security Council (often small, neutral, and nonaligned members, such as Canada, India, Sweden, Ghana, and Nepal) to keep the superpowers out of re-gional conflicts or, for postcolonial problems, to keep former colonial powers from returning. The size of peacekeeping forces has varied widely from small monitor-ing missions numbering less than one hundred to major operations in the Congo in the 1960s, and Cambodia, Somalia, and Bosnia in the early 1990s, requiring more than 20,000 troops. Since the end of the Cold War, and especially with the undertaking of much larger operations, major powers, including the United States, Great Britain, France, and Russia, have also contributed forces. China first made personnel (civilian police) available for the stabilization mission deployed in Haiti in 2004. Still, the majority of peacekeeping contingents continue to come from countries other than the P-5.

Traditional Peacekeeping

During the Cold War, peacekeeping forces were used most extensively in the Mid-dle East and in conflicts arising out of decolonization in Africa and Asia when the

PHOTO 4.1   UN peacekeeper in Burundi, November 2004.
UN photo 55855/Martine Perret.

interests of the United States and the Soviet Union were not directly at stake. Participants were either unarmed or lightly armed, often stationed between hostile forces to monitor truces and troop withdrawals or to provide a buffer zone. Meanwhile, negotiations for a political settlement would be proceeding. So-called first-generation peacekeeping provided impartial and neutral assurance to the parties desiring a settlement (or at least a cease-fire) and a guarantee that the United States and the Soviet Union would not directly intervene.

The Suez crisis of 1956 (provoked by the British, French, and Israeli attack on Egypt after its nationalization of the Suez Canal and threat to ban Israeli shipping) marked the first major instance of traditional peacekeeping. The General Assembly, acting under a Uniting for Peace Resolution, created the United Nations Emergency Force (UNEF I) to help defuse the crisis. UN peacekeepers separated the combatants, supervised the withdrawal of British, French, and Israeli forces, and thereafter patrolled portions of the Sinai Peninsula, notably the Straits of Tiran and the Gaza Strip. This force was withdrawn, at Egypt's request, just before the 1967 Six-Day War.

In 1973, following the Yom Kippur War, UNEF II was established to monitor that cease-fire and to facilitate the disengagement of Egyptian and Israeli forces by supervising a buffer zone between the combatants. Two other Middle East operations begun in the 1970s—the United Nations Disengagement Observer Force (UNDOF) on the Golan Heights and the United Nations Interim Force in Lebanon (UNIFIL)—continue today. UNEF II was terminated in 1979 following the Camp David peace agreement between Egypt and Israel.

Kashmir and Cyprus provide two other examples of longstanding traditional peacekeeping missions that continue. In Kashmir, UN observers have monitored a cease-fire line between Indian and Pakistani forces in the disputed area of Kashmir since 1948 with little movement toward a settlement. The United Nations Force in Cyprus (UNFICYP) was established in 1964 to monitor a cease-fire between local Greek and Turkish Cypriot forces. UNFICYP remained in place even during the Turkish invasion in 1974, and it continues to patrol a buffer zone between the two communities today. The presence of UN peacekeepers and a variety of diplomatic initiatives have failed, however, to produce a settlement of the Cyprus conflict.

In the late 1980s, traditional peacekeepers facilitated the withdrawal of Soviet troops from Afghanistan and supervision of the cease-fire in the eight-year war between Iran and Iraq. These actions were possible because of the increasing consensus among the P-5 following dramatic changes in Soviet foreign policy initiated by General Secretary Mikhail Gorbachev. They also built on years of quiet diplomacy by Secretary-General Pérez de Cuéllar. The Nobel Peace Prize for 1988 was awarded to UN peacekeeping forces in recognition of their "decisive contribution toward the initiation of actual peace negotiations."

Traditional peacekeeping continues to be useful in interstate conflicts where there is a cease-fire agreement and a limited mandate. In 2000, for example, after two years of fighting, Eritrea and Ethiopia signed a peace agreement, although Ethiopia subsequently refused to accept the decision of the independent arbitration commission created to demarcate the boundary between the two countries. The UN Mission in Ethiopia and Eritrea (UNMEE), with up to 4,000 personnel, was created to monitor a buffer zone between the two countries and the deployment of their troops.

Sir Brian Urquhart, a former undersecretary-general for political affairs and widely regarded as one of the founders of peacekeeping, summarizes the political requirements for successful traditional peacekeeping as follows:

- The consent of the parties involved in the conflict
- The continuing and strong support of the operation by the Security Council
- A clear and practicable mandate
- The nonuse of force except as a last resort in self-defense
- The willingness of troop-contributing countries to provide adequate numbers of capable military personnel
- Less often noted: the willingness of the member states, and especially the permanent members of the Security Council, to make available the necessary financial and logistical support[13]

These conditions have not always been fully satisfied. Nevertheless, peacekeeping provided a valuable means during the Cold War for limiting superpower involvement in regional conflicts (with their consent) and for coping with the threats to peace and security posed by the emergence of new states, border conflicts between those states, and the intractable conflicts in the Middle East. Most peacekeeping operations since the Cold War's end, however, have been complex ones with broader mandates, often involving Chapter VII authorization to use force, and a variety of tasks intended to lay the foundations for long-term stability in internal or civil conflicts (see table 4.2 and box 4.1).

Post–Cold War Complex Peacekeeping

The successful experience with UN peacekeeping during the 1980s and the UN's active role in responding to Iraq's invasion of Kuwait increased world leaders' enthusiasm for employing UN peacekeepers in still more missions in the emerging post–Cold War era. Indeed, many observers believed that the new international climate provided the UN with opportunities for ending persistent civil conflicts in Central America, southern Africa, and Southeast Asia. In addition, collapsing state institutions, violent civil conflicts, and complex humanitarian emergencies in the former Yugoslavia, Angola, Mozambique, Somalia, Rwanda, Congo, and Sierra Leone demanded new approaches. This often meant committing peacekeepers in intrastate conflicts before the warring parties had reached agreement, with authorization to use greater force, and involvement in complex peacebuilding efforts such as organizing elections, training police and judicial officials, administering government agencies, and monitoring human rights violations after fighting had ceased.

In post–Cold War conflicts where UN peacekeepers have been deployed without a cease-fire in place, there has been no consent from all parties, and operations have been expected to protect refugees and civilians from attack or genocide and perhaps to compel parties to end fighting. Thus, these operations have cost more and had a greater probability of casualties for peacekeepers. They have often required the "muscle" of major military powers (e.g., the United States, Britain, and France) with their logistical capability, large numbers of trained personnel, heavy equipment, and even air power. They have been controversial because they blur the line between peacekeeping and enforcement actions under Chapter VII, the result being that the requisite "muscle" was not always readily forthcoming because states were reluctant to provide sufficient military forces to backup a Security Council mandate; they were also unwilling to risk casualties in a situation where they did not have major interests at stake. The UN operations in Somalia and Yugoslavia exemplified the difficulties of these more complex operations.

Somalia.   In 1991 and 1992, the UN confronted a situation in Somalia in which civil order had totally collapsed and warring clans had seized control of the country. Widespread famine and chaos accompanied the fighting. The control of food

TABLE 4.2 Selected Complex UN Peacekeeping and Peacebuilding Missions

Country		Namibia	Somalia		Mozambique	Rwanda	El Salvador	Cambodia		E. Timor	Bosnia/-Croatia	Croatia/Slavonia	Kosovo	Afghanistan
Mission		UNTAG	UNOSOM I	UNOSOM II	UNOMOZ	UNAMIR	ONUCA	UNAMIC	UNTAC	UNTAET	UNPROFOR	UNTAES	UNMIK	UNAMA
Dates		4/89–5/90	4/92–5/93	5/93–5/95	12/92–12/94	10/93–5/96	11/88–1/92	10/92–5/92	7/91–4/95	10/99–5/02	2/92–12/95	1/96–1/97	9/99–	1/02–
Military Tasks	Monitor cease-fire	X	X	X	X	X	X	X	X	X	X	X		
	Peace enforcement			X							X	X		
	Disarmament	X		X	X	X			X			X		
	Demine	X		X	X	X		X	X			X		
Refugees and Humanitarian Assistance	Refugee Return	X		X	X	X	X	X	X	X	X	X	X	
	Assist civilians	X	X	X	X	X			X	X	X	X	X	
	Protect intl. workers			X	X	X							X	X
Civil Policing	Police retraining	X			X	X	X			X	X	X	X	X
Electoral Assistance	Monitor elections	X			X	X	X		X	X		X		X
Legal Affairs	Constitution/Judicial reform	X		X	X		X		X	X		X	X	X
	Human rights oversight					X	X		X	X		X	X	X
Administrative Authority		X							X	X		X	X	

BOX 4.1   Types of Peacekeeping Tasks

	Traditional	Complex	Peacebuilding/ Nation-Building
Observation and Monitoring			
Cease fires and withdrawal of forces	✓		
Democratic elections		✓	
Human rights		✓	
Arms control		✓	
Separation of combatant forces			
Establish buffer zones	✓		
Deter onset of spread of war	✓		
Limited Use of Force			
Maintain or restore civil law and order	✓	✓	
Restore peace		✓	
Deliver aid		✓	
Humanitarian Assistance/Intervention			
Open food & medical supply lines; guard supplies		✓	
Protect aid workers		✓	
Protect refugees		✓	
Create safe havens		✓	
Peacebuilding/Nation-Building			
Rebuild and train police			✓
Repatriate refugees			✓
Provide interim civil administration			✓
Oversee transition to local authority			✓

was a vital political resource for the Somali warlords and supplies of food a currency with which to pay the mercenary militias. The Security Council was initially slow to react, assuming it needed the consent of the Somali warlords to provide humanitarian assistance, consistent with the norms of traditional peacekeeping. A small contingent of five hundred lightly armed Pakistani troops (the UN Operation in Somalia, or UNOSOM I) was finally deployed in August 1992 with a mandate to protect relief workers, but was inadequate for the task at hand.

Finally, in December 1992, with the mounting humanitarian crisis, the Security Council authorized a large U.S.-led military-humanitarian intervention (Unified Task Force or UNITAF, known to the American public as Operation Restore Hope) to secure ports and airfields, protect relief shipments and workers, and assist humanitarian relief efforts. The secretary-general also wanted UNITAF to impose a cease-fire and disarm the factions, but U.S. leaders (in the outgoing Bush and the incoming Clinton administrations) were reluctant to enlarge the mission's objectives in this fashion. This disagreement complicated relations among the participants.

Despite these problems, UNITAF was largely successful in achieving its humanitarian objectives, supplying food to those in need, and imposing a de facto cease-fire in specific areas. In 1993, the United States scaled back its presence in Somalia and the Security Council created UNOSOM II—a larger and more heavily armed force than a traditional peacekeeping contingent but smaller than UNITAF and lacking much of the heavy equipment and airpower the United States had brought to Somalia. UNOSOM II, with 20,000 troops and 8,000 logistical personnel from thirty-three countries, included 5,000 U.S. soldiers (as compared to 26,000 in UNITAF). Because it was authorized to use force when disarming the factions, the peacekeepers were exposed to increased risk when some of the militias resisted such efforts. When twenty-three Pakistani soldiers were killed in June 1993, UNOSOM II gave up all pretense of impartiality and targeted General Mohamed Farah Aidid for elimination. Thus, the UN became one of the players in the conflict. Four months later, eighteen American soldiers were killed by Aidid's soldiers—an episode captured in the film *Blackhawk Down*—leading President Bill Clinton to announce that the U.S. contingent would be withdrawn by March 1994 and that future American participation in UN peacekeeping operations would be re-evaluated. It became only a matter of time before all UN forces were withdrawn. UN operations in Somalia ceased in March 1995, having successfully ended the humanitarian emergency (famine), but not having helped the Somalis to establish an effective government, nor end their internal strife.

UNOSOM remains a controversial and uncertain undertaking.[14] Although begun at the height of the post–Cold War enthusiasm for UN peacekeeping, UNOSOM's difficulties led to reluctance, especially on the part of the United States, to undertake such activities in the future. It had major implications for the UN's handling of the conflicts that broke out almost simultaneously in the former

Yugoslavia, and particularly for its handling of the 1994 genocide in Rwanda, as we shall explore below.

Former Yugoslavia and Bosnia-Herzegovina.   Yugoslavia had played a unique role in the Cold War competition between East and West, and was a country where the fault lines of ethnic, religious, and political differences were buried for half a century. The efforts of Serbian leader Slobodan Milosevic in the late 1980s to push Serbian nationalism yet maintain Yugoslavia's unity provoked strong separatist movements in Slovenia, Croatia, and Bosnia-Herzegovina and, ultimately, war. Nationalist leaders of each group fueled ancient suspicions and hostilities; each group's military and paramilitary forces attempted to enlarge and ethnically cleanse its territorial holdings. The resulting war killed more than 200,000 people, produced millions of refugees, and subjected thousands to concentration camps, rape, torture, and genocide. Yugoslavia's disintegration into five separate states in the early 1990s unleashed the fiercest fighting in Bosnia-Herzegovina, where Muslim Bosniaks, Croats, and Serbs were heavily intermingled, and raised political and legal issues such as self-determination, individual versus group rights, and the use of force to serve humanitarian ends.

Between 1991 and 1996, the Security Council devoted a record number of meetings to debates over whether to intervene, to what end, and with what means in the former Yugoslavia. Initially in 1991, the UN deferred to European Union diplomatic efforts first to find a peaceful settlement and then to negotiate repeated cease-fire agreements, consistent with Chapter VIII of the Charter. The mandate of the peacekeeping mission (UN Protection Force, or UNPROFOR) organized in 1992 was gradually broadened from maintaining a cease-fire in Croatia, disbanding and demilitarizing regular and paramilitary forces, and delivering humanitarian assistance to creating safe areas for refugees in Bosnia, relieving the besieged city of Sarajevo, protecting basic human rights, and using NATO to enforce sanctions, a "no-fly zone," and safe areas, as well as conduct air strikes. In short, what began as a traditional peacekeeping mission was transformed into a much more complex one involving much more use of force. The lightly armed UN peacekeepers encountered massive and systematic violations of human rights, a situation demanding more vigorous military action, and very little interest by the parties in making peace. By late 1992, the Security Council had invoked Chapter VII calling on member states to "take all necessary measures," and would repeatedly invoke it to expand UNPROFOR's mandate. The request for NATO assistance in monitoring compliance with sanctions and implementing a "no-fly zone" over Bosnia was the first experiment in cooperation between UN peacekeepers and a regional military alliance.

Security Council resolutions alone did not produce the manpower, logistical, financial, or military resources needed to fulfill the mandates, however. All sides interfered with relief efforts and targeted UN peacekeepers and international aid personnel. UN personnel were reluctant to use the authority given them to employ NATO airstrikes. The UN "safe areas" were anything but safe for the civilians who had taken refuge in them. Srebrenica, in particular, became a humiliating defeat when UN peacekeepers failed to prevent the massacre of more than 7,000 Bosnian Muslim men and boys by Bosnian Serbs in July 1995.[15] The International Criminal Tribunal for the Former Yugoslavia was established in 1993, but UN members lacked the political will for a full-scale enforcement action against the Bosnian Serbs and their Serbian backers.

The UN's peacekeeping role in Bosnia and Croatia ended with the U.S.-brokered Dayton Peace Accords of November 1995, and UN blue helmets were replaced by the NATO Implementation Force (IFOR) of 60,000 combat-ready troops; these included 20,000 Americans and units from almost twenty non-NATO countries, including Russia (subsequently replaced by a smaller NATO Stabilization Force, or SFOR, and, in 2005, by an EU peacekeeping force). Alongside NATO, many other IGOs and NGOs have been involved in implementing different parts of the Dayton Accord and dealing with Bosnia's extensive needs. The UN itself was charged with monitoring and reforming Bosnia's police forces—a difficult task because of the shortage of international police personnel and high levels of distrust among the three Bosnian groups, each of which had its own police. UN specialized agencies were active, for example, in aiding children (UNICEF) or promoting development projects (UNDP and the World Bank). UNHCR was responsible for refugee resettlement and return.[16]

The Bosnian experience demonstrates the dangers of complex peacekeeping operations that require greater use of force without parties' consent. Since the late 1990s, the UN has confronted similar challenges where the line between the need for enforcement and traditional peacekeeping was blurred in a number of subsequent conflict situations. These include Liberia, Sierra Leone, Côte d'Ivoire, the Democratic Republic of Congo, Burundi, and Haiti. For example, the UN Mission in Sierra Leone, initiated in 1999, has been responsible for enforcing a cease-fire agreement between the government and rebel forces. It also had tasks associated with complex peacebuilding missions, including running elections, training police, and demobilizing and reintegrating combatants into society. The same is true in Sudan, where a UN peacekeeping force authorized in 2005 is charged with monitoring the cease-fire agreement between the government and the Sudan People's Liberation Movement and has both authority under Chapter VII to take necessary actions involving use of force and a range of peacebuilding responsibilities. Hence, the complexity of many peacekeeping missions since the early 1990s has related not only to issues of "muscularity" but also to mandates to carry out what are variously referred to as peacebuilding or nation-building tasks.

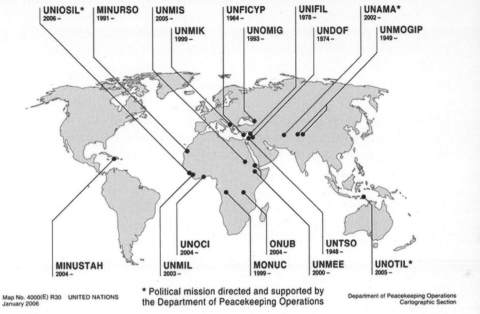

FIGURE 4.1   Ongoing UN Peacekeeping Missions

Peacebuilding/Nation-Building

More complex peacekeeping operations involve both civilian and military activities. While troop contingents may be engaged in observer activities characteristic of traditional missions, other military personnel and civilians, along with humanitarian NGOs and personnel from different UN agencies, may be involved in organizing elections, reorganizing police forces, delivering relief, and carrying out other activities aimed at creating viable states. This is the essence of peacebuilding.

Nambia: The First Experiment.   A former German colony (South West Africa) that was administered by South Africa from the end of World War I until 1989, and the object of intense international efforts to secure its independence, Namibia represented the first experiment with peacebuilding. The UN Transition Assistance Group in Namibia (UNTAG), deployed in April 1989, had the most ambitious and diverse mandate of any UN mission to that time. It included the supervision of the cease-fire between South African and rebel forces (known as the South West African Peoples Organization, or SWAPO); monitoring the withdrawal of South African forces from Namibia and the confinement of SWAPO forces to a series of bases; supervising the civil police force; securing the repeal of discriminatory and restrictive legislation; arranging for the release of political prisoners and the return of exiles; and creating conditions for free and fair elections, which were subsequently conducted by South Africa under UN supervision. With military and civilian personnel provided by 109 countries, UNTAG played a vital role in managing the process by which Namibia moved step by step from war to a cease-fire and then to full independence. This success led the UN to undertake other complex missions, not all of which enjoyed the same success.

Cambodia: Experimenting with Interim Administration.   In October 1991, the Agreements on a Comprehensive Political Settlement of the Cambodia Conflict were signed in Paris with strong U.S., Soviet, Chinese, and Vietnamese support. They included a cease-fire among the rival forces, along with the mandate to demobilize the armies, repatriate refugees, and organize elections. The agreements ending the twenty-year civil war in Cambodia "charged the UN—for the first time in its history—with the political and economic restructuring of a member state as part of the building of peace under which the parties were to institutionalize their reconciliation."[17]

A small advance mission helped the four Cambodian parties implement the cease-fire. In March 1992, the UN Transition Authority in Cambodia (UNTAC) was deployed. The Security Council mandate called for up to 22,000 military and civilian personnel. UNTAC's military component was charged with supervising the cease-fire and disarming and demobilizing forces. Civilian personnel assumed full responsibility for administering the country for an eighteen-month transition period, during which they controlled Cambodia's foreign affairs, defense, finance, and public security. UN personnel also monitored the police, promoted respect for human rights, assisted in the return of 370,000 Cambodian refugees from camps in Thailand, organized the 1993 elections that returned civil authority to Cambodians, and rehabilitated basic infrastructure and public utilities. According to Boutros Boutros-Ghali, then secretary-general, "Nothing the UN has ever done can match this operation."[18]

UNTAC's presence helped end the civil war and bring peace of sorts to most of the country. UNTAC was unable, however, to achieve a complete cease-fire, demobilize all forces, or complete its civil mission. Cambodia, therefore, illustrates the difficulty of carrying out all aspects of a complex peacekeeping and peacebuilding mission. Although the peacekeeping mission itself largely accomplished its goals and the UN conducted a successful election in 1993, Cambodia was not a stable state as UNTAC's mandate had not included building an effective legal system and constitutional process or promoting economic development.

Kosovo and East Timor: Failure and Success?   The UN built on its experience in Namibia and Cambodia when, in the late 1990s, it undertook even more extensive nation-building responsibilities in Kosovo and East Timor. In neither case, however, was there a prior peace agreement or an existing state; both were provinces of other countries (Yugoslavia and Indonesia); both involved the use of force by a coalition of the willing—the United States and NATO for Kosovo, and a UN-authorized Australian-led force for East Timor. And, in the case of Kosovo, its international legal status was among the questions to be determined.

Following NATO bombing of Serbia and intervention to protect Kosovar Albanians in 1999 from ethnic cleansing by Serbian/Yugoslav military forces, Security Council Resolution 1244 (1999) called for the UN Mission in Kosovo (UNMIK) to undertake wide-ranging civilian administrative functions in conjunction with a NATO peacekeeping force (known as KFOR) ; these included maintaining civil law and order, aiding in the return of refugees, coordinating humanitarian relief, and supporting the reconstruction of key infrastructure. Additionally, UNMIK was given the important political tasks of promoting Kosovo's autonomy and self-government and helping determine Kosovo's future legal status. The head of UNMIK, a special representative of the secretary-general, coordinates the work of several non-UN organizations, among which various functions are divided. The UN has chief responsibility for police and justice and civil administration; the Organization for Security and Cooperation in Europe (OSCE) handles democratization and institution building; the EU is responsible for reconstruction and development; and the UNHCR is responsible for all humanitarian matters. The Kosovo mission is pathbreaking in its nature and scope.

There have, however, been critical problems with the Kosovo mission in general and Resolution 1244 in particular. First, the mandate is not only vague but also potentially contradictory. Second, the Albanian Kosovars want independence, but the mandate calls for the respect of Yugoslavia's sovereignty and the protection of Serbs living in Kosovo who want to be part of Yugoslavia (now Serbia and Montenegro); thus, it is unclear when and how the UN's interim administration could end. Third, security is provided by NATO under KFOR, yet there is no clear division of responsibility between NATO and the UN, EU, and OSCE. Fourth, although the international community supports local governance, there has been inadequate consultation, and little actual power has been transferred to locals. Fifth, policies such as privatization, a key strategy for promoting economic development, have been poorly organized and implemented. All these difficulties lead to skepticism about the long-term outcome of this international effort at peacebuilding.[19]

Skepticism has been reinforced by the experience in East Timor (now Timor-Leste), where the transition to independence under UN auspices was successful; the new government has little capacity beyond its capital, however, and critical issues remain unresolved. This mission was undertaken in 1999 after almost fifteen years of UN-mediated efforts to resolve the status of East Timor—a former Portuguese colony seized by Indonesia in the mid-1970s—after violence broke out,

Indonesian troops failed to restore order, and almost a half million East Timorese were displaced. The Security Council initially authorized Australia to lead a multilateral force to restore order; later it created the UN Transitional Administration in East Timor (UNTAET), its ambitious and wide-ranging mission ranging from exercising all judicial, legislative, and executive powers to assisting in the development of civil and social services, providing security, ensuring the delivery of humanitarian aid, promoting sustainable development, and building the foundation for stable liberal democracy. As in Kosovo, the UN's role involved collaboration with other IGOs as well as with NGOs.

But unlike Kosovo, where its future status was unspecified, UNTAET's charge was unequivocal: to lead the territory to statehood. Three years later, in 2002, elections were held and an independent Timor-Leste was recognized. The task was not easy because there was no roadmap to follow. Sergio Vieira de Mello, the Special Representative of the Secretary-General in charge, noted, "We had to feel our way, somewhat blindly, towards [the two-phased strategy of devolving executive power] wasting several months in doing."[20] Following independence, the UN stayed on in a small operation; in 2005, it officially ended its responsibilities.

Timor-Leste is viewed as a relative international success at peacebuilding, but one scholar concluded that the operation was a "midwife to an incomplete state."[21] Ambitious, large-scale peacebuilding missions such as Cambodia, Kosovo, and East Timor are only beginning to be subjected to careful analysis. Although the length of interim administration was circumscribed in Cambodia and East Timor, that is not true in Kosovo (nor in Bosnia, where an EU-appointed High Representative remains in overall control). They have been variously described as forms of international trusteeship, protectorates, and even neoimperialism.[22] To address some of the evident shortcomings, a Peacebuilding Commission (PBC) was established by the 2005 World Summit as an intergovernmental advisory body to bring together all relevant actors within and outside the UN, marshal resources, and advise on strategies for reconstruction, institution building, and sustainable development. The summit also approved a multiyear standing peacebuilding fund for postconflict reconstruction, to be financed by voluntary contributions, and a small support office within the Secretariat. Peacebuilding is a long process where success may not be seen for years, perhaps decades. The hope is that the new PBC will ensure longer-term attention by the UN to the tasks of postconflict recovery (discussed further in chapter 8).

Evaluating Success and Failure in Peacekeeping and Peacebuilding

What defines success in peacekeeping and peacebuilding? An end to fighting? A political solution in the form of a peace agreement? A period of years (two, five, ten?) without renewed violence? The establishment of a viable state? A democratic state? In reality, different types of missions should be evaluated with different criteria. Traditional peacekeeping missions, therefore, might be assessed according to their ability to prevent the resumption of interstate war and, here, the evidence is strong that the presence of peacekeepers reduces the risk of another war.[23] The first UN Emergency Force (UNEF I) averted war between the Arab states and Israel for eleven years, and the UN Disengagement Observer Force (UNDOF) has kept peace between Israel and Syria on the Golan Heights since 1974. The UN Force in Cyprus (UNFICYP) has averted overt hostilities between the Greek and Turkish communities on Cyprus, although it could not prevent the 1974 invasion by Turkish forces. There has been no renewal of hostilities either between Iraq and Iran or between Iraq and Kuwait; and for years UN monitors' presence helped India and Pakistan to avoid war and contain intermittent hostilities along the line of control in disputed Kashmir.

Yet fifty years of experience demonstrates that having international monitors for a truce does not resolve the underlying conflict. Fighting may resume, even with UN monitors in place, especially as the UN has historically been reluctant to condemn states for violations for fear of jeopardizing its impartiality. "This unfortunately undermined the organization's ability to use the spotlight of international attention to help maintain peace," noted one scholar.[24] Closer examination also shows that peacekeepers are most likely to be deployed in the most difficult cases where the military outcome has been indecisive, where belligerents have a long history of conflict, and, hence, where peace is most fragile. The tension, however, between credibility and impartiality is a dilemma for the UN, one that has changed somewhat since the Cold War's end with greater willingness to condemn belligerents and even to take military action against those who threaten peace.

UN missions involving arms control verification, human rights monitoring, and election supervision tend to be successful because they are most similar to traditional peacekeeping; that is, they involve unarmed observers. They are generally linked to a peace agreement and therefore involve the consent of the parties to a peacekeeping operation. Thus, UN peacekeepers have compiled an excellent record in facilitating elections in Namibia, Cambodia, Mozambique, Eastern Slavonia, East Timor, and elsewhere.

Missions that differ most from traditional peacekeeping operations tend to have the greatest difficulties, often because the forces are not designed to carry out multiple functions. "Peacekeepers are not necessarily suitable for developing government infrastructure," wrote Paul Diehl. "Highly coercive missions may also be incompatible with peacekeeping philosophy, functions, and design."[25] Precisely because complex peacekeeping missions combine different types of tasks as well as civilian and military components, the assessment of these operations may be mixed. In Somalia, as noted above, UN and U.S. forces were successful in achieving the humanitarian tasks, but they failed in the pacification and nation-building tasks. Cambodia is now regarded as a short-run success with longer-term mixed reviews. Likewise, Timor-Leste has achieved independence, but the long-term prognosis is uncertain. In Kosovo, the outcome remains in doubt, as it does in the several African conflicts in which the UN has most recently been involved—Sierra Leone, Liberia, Côte d'Ivoire, the Democratic Republic of Congo, and Sudan. One study notes:

> The UN success rate among the missions studied—seven out of eight societies left peaceful, six out of eight left democratic—substantiates the view that nation-building can be an effective means of terminating conflicts, ensuring against their recurrence, and promoting democracy. The sharp overall decline in deaths from armed conflict around the world over the past decade also points to the efficacy of nation-building.

The author also notes that such UN operations are comparatively low cost, especially compared to peacebuilding missions led by the United States or NATO, and they offer the greatest degree of international legitimacy.[26]

Factors that can facilitate success in these complex operations include the parties' desire for peace; the political will of member states to make necessary resources available (including sufficient forces and authority to use them); the wide deployment of police monitors along with police and judicial reform; the extensive training of election monitors; the energy, skill, and improvisation of the secretary-general's special representative in the country; the even-handed treatment of the parties; and, most critically, continuous political support. The UN itself cannot ensure all these factors; it depends on the commitments of states and, most especially, the major powers. Wars characterized by an ethnic or religious component and large number of factions are less likely to be resolved and less susceptible to peacebuilding efforts. Where parties, such as in Angola and Sierra Leone, depend on the export of primary products, such as diamonds or oil, for buying arms and for personal enrichment, peacebuilding is also less likely to be successful because the temptation to renew war and to loot resources is too great to be resisted.[27] Two studies conclude that learning and adaptation by UN personnel make a critical difference.[28] Another found that turning warring parties into political parties through the demobilization and demilitarization of soldiers is critical.[29]

Almost half of all UN peacekeeping operations, before and since the Cold War's end, have been in Africa. As one observer noted, this shows that "conflicts and problems of governance continue to haunt Africa more than ever."[30] Yet, ever since the debacle in Somalia in 1993, the UN has had difficulty in mustering adequate resources—especially military forces—for African operations, leaving them woefully shorthanded and susceptible to charges of racism. As a result, through the

Economic Community of West Africa States and the recently invigorated African Union (AU), there have been significant efforts to mount African peacekeeping efforts in conjunction with (and often authorized by) the Security Council.

The UN undertook a number of steps in response to increased demand for peacekeeping in the 1990s and the difficulties and failures encountered. There were major reforms of the Department of Peacekeeping Operations (DPKO) and a 50 percent increase in staff, including the addition of military staff from member states and experts in de-mining, training, and civilian police. The 2000 Brahimi Report, commissioned by Secretary-General Kofi Annan, called for strengthening the planning and management of complex peace operations, the Secretariat's information gathering and analysis capacity in order to improve conflict prevention, and the staffing of DPKO to increase its size and competence. The report also signaled doctrinal changes, namely, the need to prepare for more robust peacekeeping.[31] Some of its recommendations have been implemented, including the creation of strategic deployment stocks and the use of rapid deployment teams.

Many post–Cold War complex peacekeeping operations have also involved major humanitarian emergencies. These crises have called for international responses to human suffering, despite the longstanding norm of noninterference in states' domestic affairs. This has triggered debate about an emerging norm of humanitarian intervention; it is based on the evolution of both humanitarian and human rights norms and a "responsibility to protect" as well as on the emerging concept of "human security."

Humanitarian Intervention

Horrific as some earlier twentieth-century conflicts had been, many post–Cold War conflicts were marked by the humanitarian disasters they produced: displaced populations, refugees, mass starvation, deliberate targeting of civilians, rape as a tool of ethnic cleansing, widespread abuses of human rights, and genocide. In the last decade of the twentieth century, it is estimated that 35 million people faced humanitarian crises. In this "revolutionary decade for humanitarian action . . . the Security Council authorized more than a dozen Chapter VII operations in response to conscience-shocking human catastrophes; regional organizations were seized with these issues and responded; militaries and humanitarian agencies adopted new policies and practices . . . [and] the lives of literally hundreds of thousands were saved."[32] This marked a sea change as during the Cold War, not one Security Council resolution mentioned humanitarian intervention.

The UN Charter specifically precludes the United Nations from intervening "in matters which are essentially within the domestic jurisdiction of any state" (Article 2, section 7). Yet over the life of the UN, the once-rigid distinction between domestic and international issues has weakened. Because human rights are often abrogated, citizens are made refugees, and weapons are moved across borders, civil wars and other internal conflicts have increasingly been viewed as international, thereby justifying UN action. In April 1991, after the Gulf War's end, Western allies created safe havens and no-fly zones to protect Iraqi Kurds in northern Iraq and Shiites in the south. The UN's intervention in Somalia was initiated for humanitarian reasons, as was NATO's in Kosovo. Other interventions motivated in part by humanitarian crises included Haiti, Bosnia, Rwanda, Sierra Leone, East Timor, and Kosovo. Yet the UN is more known for its failures than its successes in humanitarian intervention. Rwanda offers the most striking example.

Rwanda—A Failure of Political Will.   The UN was still engaged in Somalia when humanitarian disaster on a massive scale erupted in yet another small African country, Rwanda. In April 1994, following the death of President Juvenal Habyarimana (a Hutu) in a mysterious plane crash, Hutu extremists in the Rwandan military and police began slaughtering the minority Tutsi as well as moderate Hutus. In a ten-week period, more than 750,000 Tutsis were killed out of a total Rwandan population of 7 million. When Tutsi rebels of the Rwandan Patriotic Front (RPF) seized the capital of Kigali, approximately 2 million Rwandans fled their homes in the largest and most rapid migration of the twentieth century. With media reports of this "third genocide," public outcry mounted to "do something." Yet the UN's experience in Somalia produced a pattern of paralysis, halfhearted action, and then intervention, spearheaded this time by France.[33]

The roots of the Rwandan conflict between the Hutu and the Tutsi go back to colonial times when first German and then Belgian rulers favored the minority Tutsi over the majority Hutu. Periodic outbreaks of devastating ethnic violence gave way to open fighting in 1990 between the Hutu-dominated government and the RPF, based in neighboring Uganda. A 1993 peace agreement led to establishment of the UN Assistance Mission in Rwanda (UNAMIR) to monitor the ceasefire and investigate allegations of noncompliance. The Rwandans (both Hutu and Tutsi) never had much confidence in UNAMIR's impartiality, however, and growing violence in the country made the continuation of its mandated tasks impossible. In April 1994, despite early reports of massacres in Rwanda, the Security Council voted to reduce UNAMIR's strength from 2,539 to 270. Four weeks later, responding to public pressure for action, the council voted to deploy 5,500 troops to protect civilians and the delivery of humanitarian aid. Few countries were willing to volunteer troops, however, and the human tragedy mounted, as is graphically shown in the film *Hotel Rwanda*.

Ten weeks after the massacres began, the Security Council finally invoked Chapter VII to authorize member states (lead by France) to set up a temporary multinational operation in Rwanda and pave the way for a reconstituted UNAMIR. Only then, under an onslaught of media coverage, did the United States itself finally send in charter flights bearing personnel, supplies, and equipment to aid the refugees (but not the victims of genocide within Rwanda). UNAMIR belatedly established a humanitarian protection zone in southeast Rwanda in an attempt to ensure the safety of threatened civilians. It provided security for relief supply depots and escorts for aid convoys. Its personnel restored roads, bridges, power supplies, and other infrastructure destroyed by the civil war. The Rwandan mission ended in April 1996, not because peace had been restored or humanitarian needs fulfilled but because the new (Tutsi-led) government requested the departure of UN troops.

Rwanda is linked in many people's minds with Somalia, both symbolizing ethnic or factional conflict within states and of humanitarian disaster. Yet their origins were fundamentally different. Somalia was and is a "failed state" in which no one faction is strong enough to prevail. Rwanda's massacres, on the other hand, were the product of a planned campaign of genocide by Hutu extremists, the evidence of which led the Security Council to establish the International Criminal Tribunal for Rwanda (ICTR) in 1995. In both situations, however, earlier action by the Security Council could almost certainly have reduced the scale of humanitarian disaster. The Independent Inquiry on Rwanda reported that "the responsibility for the failings of the United Nations to prevent and stop the genocide in Rwanda lies with a number of different actors, in particular the Secretary-General [then Boutros Boutros-Ghali], the Secretariat [in which Annan was Head of the Department of Peacekeeping Operations at the time], the Security Council, UNAMIR and the broader membership of the United Nations."[34] All agreed that "never again" would they fail to respond to genocide.

Kosovo Intervention—the Solution or the Problem?   Although it was not the only armed intervention without prior authorization from the UN Security Council, the 1999 NATO action in Kosovo was by far the most controversial; indeed, it was a watershed in the debate about humanitarian intervention. It was triggered by Yugoslav (Serbian) rejection of a political settlement for Kosovo, the development of a paramilitary force known as the Kosovo Liberation Army (KLA), Serbia's war against the KLA, and growing evidence of ethnic cleansing against the Kosovar Albanian population—terror, atrocities, and displacement from homes and villages. The humanitarian crisis itself involved both the danger to civilian Kosovar Albanians remaining within Kosovo and a massive, rapid outflow of almost 1 million refugees into Albania, Macedonia, Montenegro, Bosnia, and other countries, all within the space of a few weeks.

Two key questions emerged from the Kosovo case. First, could the use of force by NATO for humanitarian purposes be justified if it lacked an authorizing UN Security Council resolution? Although Russia, China, and other countries protested the illegality, a Russian-sponsored draft resolution condemning the NATO action failed, suggesting that many felt there was a legitimate case to be made for humanitarian intervention. The months of diplomacy preceding NATO's intervention had failed to change Serbian policy. Even Secretary-General Kofi Annan had concluded, "The bloody wars of the last decade have left us with no illusions about the difficulty of halting internal conflicts by reason or by force particularly against the wishes of the government of a sovereign state. But nor have they left us with any illusions about the need to use force, when all other means have failed."[35] The second question that arose, however, was whether NATO bombing alleviated or worsened the humanitarian crisis by accelerating the flight of refugees and humanitarian suffering, civilian casualties, and destruction of major infrastructure. Legal scholars and policy analysts debated the issue for months. There was no consensus, but the Independent International Commission on Kosovo concluded that the intervention was "illegal but legitimate."[36]

Two senior UN officials summarized the controversy over humanitarian intervention: "To its proponents, it marks the coming of age of the imperative of action in the face of human rights abuses, over the citadels of state sovereignty. To its detractors, it is an oxymoron, a pretext for military intervention often devoid of legal sanction, selectively deployed and achieving only ambiguous ends."[37] The large-scale crises of the 1990s showed that force may be the only way to halt genocide, ethnic cleansing, and other crimes against humanity. Given their colonial experiences, however, many Asian and African countries are skeptical about altruistic claims by Western countries. Along with Russia and China, they have insisted on Security Council authorization as a prerequisite for intervention. The controversy over NATO's intervention in Kosovo led Secretary-General Kofi Annan to create the International Commission on Intervention and State Sovereignty to examine the legal, moral, operational, and political questions relating to humanitarian intervention. Its report endorsed the **"responsibility to protect"** and set forth criteria for military intervention dealing with right authority, just cause, right intention, last resort, proportional means, and reasonable prospects.[38] Annan himself had vowed in accepting the report, "Of all my aims as Secretary-General, there is none to which I feel more deeply committed than that of enabling the United Nations never again to fail in protecting a civilian population from genocide or mass slaughter."[39] Yet the collective political will of UN members to intervene for humanitarian purposes is being tested yet again, this time in the Darfur region of the Sudan, raising questions about the strength of the emerging norm of humanitarian intervention.

Darfur—Never Again?   Beginning in 2003, the western region of Darfur in the Sudan presented yet another horrific humanitarian disaster. Fighting between government forces and rebels from the Sudanese Liberation Army and the Justice and Equality Movement forced thousands to flee their homes after attacks from gov-

CARTOON 4.1   Genocide in Darfur. By Tom Toles/*Washington Post. Reprinted with permission of Universal Press Syndicate. All rights reserved.*

ernment-backed Arab militias (known as *Janjaweed*), many seeking shelter in neighboring Chad. During the next year, the humanitarian disaster grew to 100,000 refugees and more than 1 million internally displaced persons; estimates of those killed started at 10,000. Although various UN specialized agencies were active in providing food, establishing refugee camps, initiating a massive vaccination program, and warning of human rights abuses, their efforts were frequently blocked by the Sudanese government. It was May 2004, however, before the Security Council addressed the issue, and then it merely called for the Sudan to disarm the *Janjaweed* and cease fighting. That toothless action was followed by promises to aid the African Union's deployment of cease-fire monitors. A subsequent Security Council resolution suggested the possibility of action if Sudan failed to curb the violence, but four members, including two of the P-5 (China and Russia), abstained. Through it all, Secretary-General Annan pushed for more concerted action, supported by U.S. Secretary of State Colin Powell, who labeled Darfur a clear case of genocide in mid-2004.[40] In March 2005, the Security Council, acting under Chapter VII, referred the Darfur crisis to the new International Criminal Court for action against those responsible for the genocide. By that time, between 180,000 and 300,000 people had died and 2.4 million individuals had been displaced and the Sudanese government announced it would not cooperate with the ICC. The "never again" promise following Rwanda's genocide again looked hollow.

Darfur highlights three essential problems that the UN and international community face with humanitarian intervention. The first is selectivity. Why did the UN intervene in Somalia but ignore Sudan and Liberia, both of which in the early 1990s were suffering large-scale loss of life as a result of deliberate starvation, forced migrations, and massive human rights abuses? Why did the UN and NATO focus on the former Yugoslavia but ignore the war in Chechnya? More recently, why did the international community mobilize so rapidly to aid the victims of the 2004 Indian Ocean tsunami, yet fail to respond to the humanitarian crises in the Congo and Darfur? The experience with Darfur has led many to conclude that the UN no longer is prepared to act in Africa because of racism and/or donor fatigue. Second is the problem of timely action. International action was too little and too late to save thousands of human lives in Somalia, Srebrenica, Rwanda, Sierra Leone, and now Darfur. Mobilizing a force takes time—unless one or more major powers deem it in their national interest to act. That is one of the reasons there have been repeated recommendations for some type of small rapid-reaction force available to the secretary-general to protect civilians caught in humanitarian disasters. Still, learning from peacekeepers' experience, the best such a force might do is to draw international attention to a crisis and hope that a larger response will be forthcoming, including sanctions against the responsible party(s).

Perhaps most importantly, Darfur highlights the problem of political will for humanitarian intervention. The P-5 states have conflicting interests in many situations; Russia and China have economic interests in the Sudan, and both states have traditionally opposed using enforcement measures for internal disputes. The Europeans and the United States put priority on the 2004 peace accord ending the long civil war in southern Sudan. Also, the United States does not want to jeopardize cooperation with the Sudanese government in the war against terrorism, nor does it want to commit its own troops to intervene, although it initiated discussions of a UN force for Darfur in 2006. Islamic countries do not support sanctions against an Islamic state; in their view, the Islamic world is already under siege in Iraq and Afghanistan. "Major and minor powers alike are committed only to stopping killing that harms their national interests," a *Washington Post* article concluded. "Why take political, financial and potential military risks when there is no strategic or domestic cost to remaining on the sidelines?"[41]

Regardless of selectivity, egregious errors, and continuing controversy, the very fact that debate is taking place over the legitimacy of humanitarian intervention and that the Security Council repeatedly in the 1990s referred to humanitarian crises as threats to international peace and security under Chapter VII marks a change. In the minds of many, there is an emerging norm of international responsibility to protect civilians from large-scale violence when states cannot protect their own and there is recognition that the principle of nonintervention in internal affairs cannot be used to protect large-scale humanitarian violations. Yet Darfur illustrates that the political will to stop humanitarian disasters, let alone prevent them, is still lacking.

Humanitarian concerns have long motivated advocates of arms control and disarmament who have seen particular weapons as inhumane or who want to eliminate wars entirely by eliminating the weapons of war. The history of disarmament and arms control efforts is a mixed one, however. Advocates have been highly successful in getting the subject established permanently on the UN's agenda. But Claude noted that "it is important to avoid confusing long hours of international debate, vast piles of printed documents, and elaborate charts of institutional structure with meaningful accomplishment."[42] Still, there have been some notable achievements, particularly with regard to controlling chemical, biological, and nuclear weapons of mass destruction.

ARMS CONTROL AND DISARMAMENT

The UN Charter did not envision a major role for the UN with respect to arms control and disarmament, although Article 26 does give the Security Council responsibility for formulating plans for the regulation of armaments. At the initiative of middle powers, the General Assembly nonetheless created a variety of locales for the discussion of arms control and disarmament issues over the years, including the Conference on Disarmament, the General Assembly's own First Committee, and the Disarmament Commission. Here, we compare efforts to address the proliferation of nuclear weapons on the one hand with efforts to prevent the spread of chemical and biological weapons on the other.

The Challenges of Limiting Proliferation of Nuclear Weapon Capability

The development of nuclear weapons at the end of World War II spawned numerous responses within the UN system. Even at the height of the Cold War, following President Dwight D. Eisenhower's Atoms for Peace proposal in 1954, the United States and the Soviet Union collaborated in creating an international agency to help spread information about the peaceful uses of atomic energy and to provide a system of safeguards designed to prevent the diversion of fissionable material. The International Atomic Energy Agency was established in 1957 as a specialized agency of the UN. The Cuban Missile Crisis in 1963 provided impetus for the two superpowers to sign the Partial Test Ban Treaty. They then participated in UN-organized negotiations for a treaty banning the spread of nuclear weapons. The Treaty on the Non-Proliferation of Nuclear Weapons (NPT) was signed by the two superpowers in 1967 and then opened to other nations to sign. It entered into force in 1970. Currently, 187 UN member states are parties to the NPT.

The essence of the NPT is a bargain that in return for the pledge of nonnuclear-weapon states not to develop weapons, they will be aided in gaining access to peaceful nuclear technologies. In addition, the declared nuclear weapons states promised to give up their weapons at some future time. In essence, the NPT created a two-class system: The five declared nuclear weapons states (the United States, the Soviet Union/Russia, Britain, France, and China) were in one class, and everyone else was in the other. Although accepted by most states, this two-class system has always been offensive to some, most notably India, which conducted a peaceful nuclear test in 1974 and five weapons tests in 1998. All but five states (North Korea, which withdrew in 2004, India, Pakistan, Cuba, and Israel) are now parties to the NPT. Three states that previously had nuclear weapons programs—South Africa, Brazil, and Argentina—became parties in the 1990s along with three states—Belarus, Kazakhstan, and Ukraine—that gave up nuclear weapons left on their territory after the dissolution of the Soviet Union. In 1995, the UN NPT Review Conference approved an indefinite extension of the treaty, conditioned on renewed efforts toward disarmament and a pledge by the nuclear weapons states to conclude a Comprehensive Test Ban Treaty. The latter was drafted under UN auspices in 1996, but ratification stalled in 1998 when the U.S. Senate rejected the treaty and India and Pakistan conducted weapons tests.

Critical to the nuclear nonproliferation regime is the IAEA-managed safeguard system of inspections. Although the system appeared operational and reliable for many years, the discovery of a secret Iraqi nuclear weapons program in 1991—in direct violation of Iraq's safeguard agreements with the IAEA and its obligations under the NPT—brought the entire system under scrutiny. The IAEA Board of Governors agreed to strengthen nuclear safeguards through increased access to information and to facilities and sites.

Further doubts about the system, however, were fueled by four developments. First was the problem of North Korea's nuclear ambitions, which surfaced with the expulsion of IAEA inspectors in 1993, then the abrogation in 2002 of a 1994 agreement that renewed inspections, its withdrawal from the NPT, and admission that it was enriching uranium. In 2003 came an announcement that it already had nuclear weapons. Second, lax security controls on nuclear materials and scientists in the former Soviet Union fueled concerns from 1991 on about the possible proliferation to so-called "rogue states" and terrorist groups. Third is the problem with Iran, the extent of whose nuclear program eluded IAEA inspectors until 2003 and which has announced its intention to develop nuclear capacity for peaceful purposes with Russian aid. Many of Iran's activities are permissible under the NPT, but because they have been carried out surreptitiously, the United States and Europeans in particular worry that it actually seeks to develop the capacity to build and deliver nuclear weapons. Finally, following the discovery in early 2004 that Pakistan's chief nuclear scientist Abdul Qadeer Khan was part of a secret sales network of nuclear materials, technology, and knowledge, it was clear that new strategies would be needed to stop proliferation to states or terrorist groups determined to acquire nuclear weapons capability. Mohamed ElBaradei, the director-general of IAEA, said that the revelations regarding Khan's network were "the most dangerous thing we have seen in proliferation in many years," and required a major reform of the export control system.[43] Each of these developments constitutes a major threat to the NPT-based **regime**.

With respect to Iran (or any other country that is party to the NPT), when the IAEA determines that it is not in compliance with its treaty obligations with respect to full inspections, uranium enrichment, or potential weapons development, the issue may be referred to the Security Council for enforcement action. The EU led negotiations with Iran to try to secure an agreement that would bring it into compliance. China and Russia, as well as some nonpermanent council members, have opposed the use of sanctions, which underscores the difficulty of dealing with states (let alone other actors) determined to acquire nuclear weapons capability. Nonetheless, in September 2005, the IAEA's board voted 22 to 1, with 12 abstentions, to report Iran's "many failures and breaches of its [NPT] obligations" to the Security Council.[44] When the council took up the issue in 2006, Iran threatened to withdraw from the NPT and to retaliate if sanctions were imposed. In contrast, Libya, a party to the NPT, but one of several "rogue" states known to be bent on acquiring nuclear weapons, gave up its program and all related materials in 2004, in large part to regain standing in the international community and end U.S. sanctions imposed on it in the 1990s for its sponsorship of terrorism.

Chemical and Biological Weapons

Since 1969, the issue of chemical and biological weapons (CBW) has appeared regularly on the agenda of the UN General Assembly. Pressures for controls on these weapons stemmed from the known existence of large stockpiles of various CBW in a number of countries and the use of CBW in several conflicts, for example, by the United States in Vietnam and by Iraq in the Iran-Iraq War. Chemical weapons, if effectively used, have the potential to kill tens of thousands of people; the potential toll from biological weapons could number in the hundreds of thousands. Both could also be used against livestock, water supplies, and crops, thereby magnifying the potential economic, health, or environmental damage. Because one of the major principles behind arms control efforts is to reduce the destructiveness of armed conflicts, major efforts for more than a century have been directed at suppressing chemical and biological weapons as instruments of warfare. These gained added impetus with the threat that terrorist groups could acquire and use CBW.

The Biological Weapons Convention (BWC) negotiated in the UN Committee on Disarmament came into force in 1975. Although 146 parties to the treaty have agreed to destroy existing stocks and to restrict materials for research purposes, there is no provision in the treaty for inspections. Several states, most notably Iran, Libya, Egypt, Syria, and Russia, are suspected of possessing such weapons. Efforts to draft a protocol to strengthen the effectiveness of the BWC have stalled on U.S. opposition.

On the issue of chemical weapons, no discussions were conducted until the Cold War's end in 1990; then, the United States and Russia agreed to reduce their chemical weapon stocks and so opened the way for the Conference on Disarmament to draft the long-awaited Chemical Weapons Convention (CWC). In 1993, the convention was signed banning the production, acquisition, stockpiling, retention, and usage of such weapons. Signed by 167 states and now ratified by 147 states (excluding Iraq, Libya, Syria, Egypt, North Korea, and Israel), the CWC, unlike the Biological Weapons Convention, includes verification provisions and the threat of sanctions against violators, including those who have not signed the treaty. Since 1997, the UN-related Organization for the Prohibition of Chemical Weapons has conducted hundreds of inspections at military and industrial facilities and aided in the destruction of chemical weapon stockpiles in three of four countries known to possess chemical weapons.

The key difference between the chemical and biological weapons conventions and the NPT is the acceptance by all parties of a total ban on the possession, development, and use of these weapons of mass destruction. In other words, there is no two-class system. All three treaties have in common an agreement between the two superpowers. In the case of the Biological Weapons Convention, Britain's support was also important. For the Comprehensive Test Ban Treaty, the commitments of France and China were key; the failure of the United States to ratify was deadly. Only by having these major powers "on board" could the treaties take effect. Yet the failure of the declared nuclear weapon states under the NPT's two-class system to move in the direction of disarmament continues to rankle. The U.S. invasion of Iraq in 2003 on the grounds that its supposed WMD programs threatened regional and global security appears to have led some states, such as North Korea and Iran, to conclude that their only defense or leverage against the world's sole superpower will come through the acquisition of nuclear weapons. Thus, the challenge of preventing nuclear proliferation has become more, not less, serious since the Cold War's end. The fear that nuclear, chemical, or biological weapons could be acquired and used by terrorist groups is likewise very real.

COPING WITH TERRORISM

Terrorism is an old threat to individual, state, and regional security that has taken on a number of new guises, making it a much greater threat to international peace and security. The Middle East conflict spawned a cycle of terror following the 1967 Arab-Israeli War and Israeli occupation of the West Bank, Gaza, and the Golan Heights when Palestinian groups began using terrorism to draw attention to their cause of establishing a homeland (or destroying Israel). Contemporary terrorism frequently targets innocent civilians. The goals are not limited to overthrowing a government or leader, or to gaining an independent Tamil, Palestinian, or Basque homeland, but include eliminating Western, and especially American, presence in Islamic holy lands. The increased ease of international travel and telecommunications have made transnational terrorism less confined to a particular geographic place and enabled terrorist groups not only to form global networks but also to move money, weapons, and people easily from one area to another—thus creating a global problem.

International efforts to address terrorism have long been hobbled by inability to agree on a definition. The problem is "how to formulate the term without criminalizing all armed resistance to oppressive regimes[,] . . . how to distinguish legitimate armed struggle from terrorism and how much emphasis to place on identifying root causes of grievances that lead individuals and groups to adopt terrorist methods."[45] This is often cast as the problem of distinguishing "freedom fighters" from terrorists.

The UN General Assembly first began to address the general issue of terrorism in 1972 in the wake of several incidents and worked to develop a normative framework defining terrorism as a common problem (without agreeing on a definition of terrorism itself) and to conclude a series of international treaties. Hijackings, so prevalent in the 1970s, led to three treaties on airline and airport safety that declared terrorist acts against civil aviation illegal and sought to ensure the safety of the flying public. Concern about similar problems at sea led to the conclusion in the late 1980s of several conventions that guarantee the safety of maritime navigation and fixed platforms on the continental shelf (i.e., drilling rigs). A 1979 convention addressed the problem of hostage taking. One approved in 1980 established a legal framework to protect nuclear material during transport. In 1996, the UN General Assembly drafted the Comprehensive International Convention on Terrorism, but differences about how to define terrorism held up adoption. The struggle over definition was sidestepped in treaties on specific issues by avoiding language on terrorism's causes.

The Security Council began to address the question of terrorism only in the 1990s in response to specific events, particularly the downing of Pan Am and UTA flights, the assassination attempt against President Hosni Mubarek of Egypt, and the 1998 bombings of American embassies in Africa. These led the United States to push the council into an activist stance on terrorism and to sanctions against three countries—Libya, the Sudan, and Afghanistan—for their roles in supporting terrorism.

To pressure Libya into giving up the two men indicted for the bombings of Pan American Flight 103 and France's UTA 772 (1989), the Security Council in 1992 and 1993 imposed travel sanctions, flight bans, diplomatic sanctions, an embargo on aircraft parts, and a ban on payments for flight insurance. In 1999, after Libya delivered the two suspects in the Pan Am case for trial in the Netherlands, the UN suspended sanctions.

Sanctions against the Taliban regime in Afghanistan imposed in 1999 included an arms embargo, aviation and financial sanctions, a ban on sale of acetic anhydrine (which is used in processing opium into heroin), diplomatic restrictions, and a travel ban. UN members concluded in 1999 that a neutral UN role was impossible and only the Taliban's removal would end its support for terrorism (including harboring Osama bin Laden after he fled Sudan), its continuing civil war, its role in the heroin trade, and its harsh treatment of women. The Security Council set up an office for sanctions-monitoring along with a panel of experts because the six neighboring countries had such weak border control capabilities that there was no hope of making sanctions effective without assistance. Although diplomatic isolation was effective, other sanctions did not persuade the Taliban to end their support for terrorism until after the U.S. intervention in October 2001 gave them an incentive for regime change.

In the case of the Sudan, diplomatic sanctions quickly led the government to expel Osama bin Laden and other groups, but a ban on international flights was never implemented because of the already severe humanitarian situation in the country as well as Egypt's refusal to support a ban. Even before September 11, 2001, the Sudan had taken other measures to counter terrorism and had signed several of the UN conventions; thereafter, thanks to its help with intelligence on Al Qaeda, the Security Council lifted diplomatic sanctions.

Broader concerns were also at work in the council's increased attention to terrorism. They included the rising number of casualties per incident; the growing evidence that some groups were operating as part of a global network; fears that terrorists might acquire chemical, biological, or nuclear weapons and use them; and the role of certain states in supporting and sponsoring terrorism, enhancing the power and reach of terrorist groups.[46] It took the attacks on September 11, 2001, however, to make terrorism a priority for the UN, and especially for the Security Council.

UN Post–9/11 Responses to Terrorism

The September 11, 2001, attacks on the World Trade Center and the Pentagon elicited immediate and general condemnation by the international community. A day after the attacks, the UN Security Council passed Resolution 1368 condemning the heinous acts of terrorism and calling for international cooperation to punish those responsible. Most importantly, the resolution affirmed that the attacks were a breach of international peace under Chapter VII, thus giving the council authority to take action and recognizing "the inherent right of individual or collective self-defense" as a legitimate response. Chapter VII had never been invoked in connection with terrorist attacks. This was also the first time the use of force in self-defense was authorized in response to terrorism; and because it was completely open-ended, it allowed wide latitude for interpretation by the United States and others. It was Resolution 1368 that the United States used as the basis for its attack on Afghanistan to root out terrorist training camps, the Taliban government that had sanctioned Al Qaeda and other terrorist groups, and the Al Qaeda leadership.

On September 28, 2001, the Security Council adopted Resolution 1373 and thereby obliged all states to clamp down on the financing, training, and movement of terrorists, and to cooperate in a campaign against them, even with force if necessary. The resolution called on states to take measures that included suppressing the financing of terrorist groups, freezing their assets, blocking the recruitment of terrorists, and denying them safe haven. Under Chapter VII, the measures outlined in Resolution 1373 are binding on all 191 UN member states, in contrast to the twelve treaties that bind only those states that accede to them. The resolution also established the Counter Terrorism Committee (CTC), comprised of all fifteen council members, to review regular reports from all states on their counterterrorism actions, and to monitor states' capability to deny funding and/or haven to terrorists.

The CTC has been hobbled by the lack of resources to undertake comprehensive monitoring and follow up on state reports, and many states lack the capabilities to carry out the requirements; some states are reluctant to do so for other reasons. In 2004, the Security Council took steps to revitalize the CTC by creating a Counter Terrorism Executive Directorate responsible for carrying out technical assistance programs to bolster states' capacity for compliance as well as engaging in proactive dialogue with states and cooperation with international, regional, and subregional organizations. Concerning the steps taken by the Security Council in response to September 11, 2001, two scholars noted the dichotomy between the intrusive measures of Resolution 1373 and the council's choice to exercise no control or oversight on the use of military force in response to terrorism.[47] The danger is that the council's authority will be eroded and the UN weakened if states fail to implement the former.[48]

In 2004, the secretary-general's High-level Panel on Threats, Challenges and Change recommended a broad-ranging strategy to address root causes of terrorism and more immediate measures to counter terrorism such as intelligence sharing and controlling dangerous materials. The panel report also proposed a definition of terrorism and called on the General Assembly to conclude a comprehensive convention on terrorism.[49] The 2005 World Summit Outcome endorsed these recommendations, including language that condemned terrorism "in all its forms and manifestations, committed by whomever, wherever and for whatever purposes, as it constitutes one of the most serious threats to international peace and security."[50] Defining terrorism may be insufficient and conflict-prevention efforts alone ineffective, however, in preventing terrorism whose causes lie in the structure of the global system itself. The international community has not yet addressed those issues, although the 2005 summit reaffirmed the importance of initiatives on "dialogue among cultures and civilizations, including the dialogue on interfaith cooperation . . . to promote a culture of peace."[51] Yet they are linked to fundamental questions of the UN's relevance and legitimacy in today's world and of the need for major UN reform on the one hand and broad global changes on the other.

FUTURE CHALLENGES FOR THE
UN'S ROLE IN PEACE AND SECURITY

The UN's experience over more than sixty years in dealing with changing threats to international peace and security has highlighted a number of lessons that represent important issues for the future. These tie directly to the three dilemmas around which this book is organized: the needs for governance versus the struggle over the UN's role and its legitimacy; the persistence of sovereignty versus challenges to sovereignty; and the need for leadership versus the dominance of a sole superpower and the unwillingness of many countries and other actors to accept U.S. domination.

Dilemma One: Changing Threats
Versus the Limits on the UN's Role

A major lesson of sixty years of UN efforts to provide collective security and enforcement, and especially of the operations in Somalia, Bosnia, Haiti, East Timor, and Sierra Leone in the 1990s, is that although international military action (in contrast to sanctions) should be authorized by the UN, the actual work of applying force has to be subcontracted to what has become known as a "coalition of the willing" led by one or more major powers with sufficient military capabilities. States never have and never will empower the UN with the means to exercise coercion. "The U.N. itself can no more conduct military operations on a large scale on its own than a trade association of hospitals can conduct heart surgery," Michael Mandelbaum has noted.[52]

In peacekeeping operations where the line between peacekeeping and enforcement is blurred and the situation requires some use of military force, UN-appointed commanders need operational mandates from the Security Council and

DPKO spelling out how they can use force other than in self-defense to disarm local militias, deliver humanitarian relief, and protect civilians. All too often in the 1990s, such mandates were not forthcoming. Consideration must be given to the "precise rules of engagement" covering when, and under what circumstances, they can employ deadly force in the pursuit of their objectives. More than this, they will require sufficient military strength and the political support of member states to carry out their tasks under circumstances of adversity. When UN peacekeepers use force, they give up the UN's impartial position to confront one or more belligerent groups, as was clear in Somalia and Bosnia. They also run greater risk that peacekeepers will lose their lives. Even so, ambitious objectives and substantial support cannot guarantee desired outcomes.

What is often referred to as the problem of political will of member states has several dimensions. First, it is important to note that as an intergovernmental organization, the UN depends on its members' support to act. Thus, when the necessary political will is lacking that may mean (a) failure of the Security Council to address or act on a given issue, for example, ignoring the long civil war in the Sudan in the 1980s and 1990s, and/or (b) failure of member states to provide the personnel, financial, or logistical support necessary to implement resolutions passed by the council. Funding for peacekeeping operations has long been a problem, but it was aggravated in the 1990s. Observer missions are generally funded from the UN's regular budget, whereas full-scale peacekeeping operations are funded through special peacekeeping assessments. Yet member states, large and small, are frequently in arrears, and as more peacekeeping operations were mounted in the 1990s, the financial strains increased. In 1987, the cost of peacekeeping was $240 million; in 1995 it peaked at $3.36 billion, and stood at $2.26 billion in 2003. Total arrearages in 2004 were $2.5 billion—the highest ever—with the United States alone owing more than one-third of that total.[53]

The recruitment of forces for peacekeeping operations has also become a significant problem for the UN. Historically, peacekeeping contingents have been drawn from middle and smaller powers, especially nonaligned and neutral countries; as peacekeeping demands have increased, military units have been drawn from many more countries, including major powers. For many poor developing countries, there are financial benefits because UN pay scales are far higher than their own (but arrearages of richer countries can make payments slow in coming). The greater risks of casualties, however, in post–Cold War operations made many European countries, as well as Canada and the United States, more reluctant to participate. The participation by major powers also entails political risks either because they have a history of past involvement (for example, the United States in Haiti, or France in Rwanda) or because the national interests of the major powers and international interests may not coincide.[54] Many states, however, have become much more reluctant to provide troops for UN operations because of the increased risk of casualties where fighting has not yet ceased. In addition, the reluctance of most developed countries now to commit their own armed forces to UN peacekeeping operations in Africa raises "major ethical and operational questions," in the words of David Malone, a former Canadian ambassador to the UN. "The industrialized countries," he said, "need to think hard about their attitudes toward Africa."[55] The practice of "subcontracting" the task of organizing an intervention force, as occurred in Somalia, Rwanda, Haiti, and East Timor, raises difficult issues. In particular, the leading power is unlikely to place its troops under UN command, a situation that compromises the UN's control over the force's actions. The trend of "subcontracting" various peacekeeping tasks to a regional organization, especially to the African Union, may seem logical, but there are significant limits on the capacity of regional organizations other than NATO.

With respect to peacebuilding, implementation is generally a lengthy process, complex, and expensive. The long-term success of such efforts is still being tested, just as the very concepts and approaches themselves are being applied still in Kosovo, Bosnia, Afghanistan, and Iraq. The UN's ability, acting on behalf of the international community, to build conditions for stable peace and viable states remains to be seen.

Finally, the UN's managerial capacity, especially with respect to peacekeeping operations, has been an increasingly contentious issue as operations have become larger, more complex, and more expensive, and have involved coordination among military and civilian components, various UN agencies, and NGOs. Although the UN Secretariat has taken a number of initiatives since the mid-1990s to provide better coordination and improve responses to international threats, much more remains to be done in this regard. In 2005, accusations of rape, pedophilia, and prostitution involving UN peacekeepers from Morocco, Nepal, Pakistan, and Uruguay, among others, in the Democratic Republic of Congo highlighted the UN's inability to exert adequate control over field operations. With respect to such problems of the personal conduct of peacekeepers themselves, although the UN conducted an investigation of the abuses, it has been hindered at all turns by the contributing states that refused to prosecute offenders or to impose discipline on their troops.

In 2004–2005, as noted in chapter 2, the UN was also rocked by revelations of mismanagement of the Oil-for-Food Programme that raised major questions about the UN's ability to manage large, long-term projects. At issue, however, was not only the reliability and capability of UN Secretariat officials but also the commitment of member states including the P-5 to carry out decisions they had taken in the Security Council. Although the UN could have prevented contract abuses in OFFP, states were responsible for enforcing the sanctions by monitoring Iraq's borders and they failed to do so. Still, it was the UN's reputation that was tarnished.

For many, however, the most serious issue relating to the UN's ability to address changing threats to international peace is the very composition and operation of the Security Council. Although enlarged in the 1960s to enhance representation of developing countries, the council's membership, and especially the five permanent members, does not adequately reflect the political realities of the twenty-first century. This undermines the legitimacy of the council as the primary world body charged with making decisions on maintaining peace in the world and on the use of military force for purposes other than self-defense. (We examine these issues as well as the politics of and proposals for Security Council reform in chapter 8.)

Dilemma Two: Changing Norms and Challenges to Sovereignty

Although consent of parties is key to traditional peacekeeping, attitudes on both the political and legal necessity of consent of the parties for complex peacekeeping and humanitarian intervention have been changing, as our earlier discussion outlined. This reflects the consequences of evolving human rights norms and perceptions of the meaning of state sovereignty. As Secretary-General Kofi Annan said in his 1999 address to the General Assembly:

> State sovereignty . . . is being redefined by the forces of globalization and international cooperation. The State is now widely understood to be the servant of its people, and not vice versa . . . [with] renewed consciousness of the right of every individual to control his or her own destiny. These parallel developments . . . demand of us a willingness to think anew—about how the United Nations responds to the political, human rights, and humanitarian crises affecting so much of the world.[56]

The UN Charter itself makes clear that sovereignty cannot stand in the way of responses to aggression and threats to peace or states' obligations to meet their commitments under the charter. International customary and treaty law also limit sovereignty. Thus, Iraq could not use sovereignty as a defense against the intrusive arms control inspections and sanctions after the Gulf War. Nor did states raise objections on the grounds of sovereignty to the extensive reporting requirements of Resolution 1373 and the CTC following the terrorist attacks of September 11, 2001. And, increasingly, sovereignty is interpreted as carrying responsibilities, including the responsibility to protect persons. "Surely," Annan concluded, "no legal principle—not even sovereignty—can ever shield crimes against humanity."[57]

The issue of sovereignty and states' consent also arises with respect to the conflicts that are referred to the Security Council for action. Some conflicts, such as the U.S. war in Vietnam, India and Pakistan's conflict over Kashmir, and the civil war in Colombia, remain off the council's agenda because one or more of the protagonists opposes council involvement. Likewise, sovereignty is a variable in the problem of states' political will to carry out Security Council decisions discussed in dilemma one.

Dilemma Three: The Need for Leadership Versus U.S. Dominance

As Kosovo and the U.S. invasion of Iraq in 2003 made clear, although international legitimacy matters, a sole superpower determined to take action will not be deterred by the absence of Security Council authorization. The acrimonious, divisive debate in the UN about the war in Iraq was widely regarded as raising serious issues about the future effectiveness of the UN, and especially of the Security Council. It was "at least as much about American power and its role in the world as about the risks posed by Iraq's weapons."[58]

A major dilemma for the UN is that as security threats have required more complex and more coercive responses, the only state with the capability to carry out Security Council mandates involving the use of force is the United States, perhaps in cooperation with a few other developed states. Thus, if the council is to enforce its decisions, the United States must participate. Or, if the United States identifies a security threat and others do not, the UN is threatened with irrelevance if the United States acts without council authorization, as it did in Iraq.

The status of the United States today is augmented by the absence of meaningful opposition to its power. It has no serious rival at present, although China is widely perceived as a potential future rival. China and the other P-5 members share to varying degrees a desire to regulate U.S. power; they and smaller countries alike fear U.S. unilateralism.

As discussed in chapter 3, the United States' record on multilateralism in general and the UN in particular has been one of "mixed messages" throughout the twentieth century. The United States has not infrequently clashed with others at the UN, but, given the margin of U.S. dominance as sole superpower and the lack of U.S. leadership on many issues, the current situation is clearly different. Historically, the United States was supportive of traditional UN peacekeeping and provided logistical support and equipment to most operations. In the early post–Cold War era, Washington was strongly supportive of (and willing to participate in) an expanded UN role in international peacekeeping. Somalia was a watershed, however. By setting restrictive conditions for participation thereafter, demanding reimbursement for logistical support, and continuing to be in financial arrears, the United States sowed doubt about the political and financial support that the world's only superpower would contribute to UN efforts to deal with future conflicts. And, from the standpoint of U.S. leadership, the Gulf War highlighted an important problem of the post–Cold War era: "The ambivalence of many states toward a stronger UN . . . coupled with apprehension about a pax Americana, even a UN-centered one, without a Soviet counterweight."[59] Yet, the second Bush administration, despite its unilateral bent, turned to the UN immediately after the attacks of September 11, 2001, to seek authorization for self-defense, and it expended great diplomatic effort in difficult negotiations on a resolution about how to deal with Iraq. These actions suggest that even for the world's sole superpower, the UN has a unique capacity to confer legitimacy, and that "international legitimacy counts."[60]

Still, the United States' military predominance and current preference for minimizing international legal and political constraints on decisions concerning its national security make other states wary of U.S. power and intentions. This has consequences both for the solidity of the UN's role and for U.S. ability and willingness to provide the necessary leadership for such issues as humanitarian intervention in Darfur, curbing Iran's nuclear program, and sustaining peacebuilding operations in Afghanistan, Kosovo, and Iraq.

CONCLUSION

Traditionally, international peace and security have meant states' security and the defense of states' territorial integrity from external threats or attack. As suggested by our discussion of the emerging norm of humanitarian intervention and a responsibility to protect, the concept of human security—the security of human beings in the face of many different kinds of threats—is beginning to take hold. These concerns are reflected in the discussions in chapters 5, 6, and 7 about the need to eradicate poverty and reduce the inequalities exacerbated by globalization, to promote sustainable development and greater respect for human rights norms, and to address the growing security threats posed by pandemics, population pressures on scarce resources, and environmental degradation.

NOTES

1. For these and other data, see *The Human Security Report 2005* (New York: Oxford University Press, 2005), www.humansecurityreport.info.

2. On the subject of "Friends of the Secretary-General," see Jochen Prandt and Jean Krasno, "Informal Ad Hoc Groupings of States and the Workings of the United Nations" (New Haven: International Relations Studies and the United Nations Occasional Papers, no. 3, ACUNS, 2002).

3. Boutros Boutros-Ghali, *An Agenda for Peace: Preventive Diplomacy, Peacemaking, and Peacekeeping* (New York: United Nations, 1992), 45.

4. Michael E. Brown and Richard N. Rosecrance, *The Costs of Conflict: Prevention and Cure in the Global Arena* (Lanham, Md.: Rowman and Littlefield, 1999), 225.

5. Two helpful sources are Abram Chayes, "The Use of Force in the Persian Gulf," in *Law and Force in the New International Order,* ed. Lori Fisler Damrosch and David J. Scheffer (Boulder: Westview Press, 1991), 3–11, and Ken Matthews, *The Gulf Conflict in International Relations* (London: Routledge, 1993).

6. For a set of excellent studies of the "sanctions decade," see David Cortright and George A. Lopez, *The Sanctions Decade: Assessing UN Strategies in the 1990s* (Boulder: Lynne Rienner, 2000).

7. For an analysis of UNSCOM's efforts, see "Iraq: The UNSCOM Experience," SIPRI factsheet (October 1998), http://editors.sipri.se/pubs/Factsheet/unscom.html.

8. David Cortright and George A. Lopez, *Sanctions and the Search for Security* (Boulder: Lynne Rienner, 2002), 71.

9. Adam Roberts, "The Use of Force," in *The UN Security Council: From the Cold War to the 21st Century,* ed. David M. Malone (Boulder: Lynne Rienner, 2004), 141.

10. See Michael J. Glennon, "Why the Security Council Failed," *Foreign Affairs* 82, no. 3 (May-June 2003): 16–35, and responses, Edward C. Luck, "The End of an Illusion," Anne-Marie Slaughter, "Misreading the Record," and Ian Hurd, "Too Legit to Quit," all published in *Foreign Affairs* 82, no. 4 (July-August 2003): 201–205. See also the debate, "The United Nations Has Become Irrelevant," *Foreign Policy,* no. 138 (September-October 2003): 16–24.

11. Mats Berdal, "The UN after Iraq," *Survival* 46, no.3 (Autumn 2004): 82.

12. United Nations, *The Blue Helmets: A Review of United Nations Peace-Keeping,* 3rd ed. (New York: UN Department of Public Information, 1996), 4. The *Blue Helmets* volume is an excellent resource on peacekeeping operations up to the mid-1990s. The UN Web site is a resource for more recent information (http://www.un.org/Depts/dpko/home.htm) as well as articles and data published in the journal *International Peacekeeping.*

13. Sir Brian Urquhart, *A Life in Peace and War* (New York: Harper and Row, 1987), 198.

14. For further discussion, see Walter Clarke and Jeffrey Herbst, "Somalia and the Future of Humanitarian Intervention," *Foreign Affairs* 75, no. 2 (March-April 1996): 70–85; Enrico Augelli and Craig N. Murphy, "Lessons of Somalia for Future Multilateral Humanitarian Assistance Operations," *Global Governance* 1, no. 3 (September-December 1995): 339–366.

15. United Nations, *Report of the Secretary-General Pursuant to General Assembly Resolution 53/35: The Fall of Srebrenica,* UN Doc.No.A/54/549, 15 November 1999, http://www.un.org/peace/srebrenica.pdf.

16. See Georgios Kostakos, "Division of Labor among International Organizations: The Bosnian Experience," *Global Governance* 4, no. 4 (October-December 1998): 461–484.

17. Michael W. Doyle, *UN Peacekeeping in Cambodia: UNTAC's Civil Mandate* (Boulder: Lynne Rienner, 1995), 26.

18. United Nations, *Chronicle,* "The 'Second Generation': Cambodia Elections 'Free and Fair,' but Challenges Remain," (November-December 1993), 26.

19. Alexandras Yannis, "The UN as Government in Kosovo," *Global Governance* 10, no. 1 (January-March 2004): 67–81.

20. Sergio Vieira de Mello, "Message to the UNITAR-IPS-JIIA Conference." See also Sergio Vieira de Mello, "How Not to Run a Country: Lessons from Kosovo and East Timor," UNITAR-IPS-JIIA Conference to assess the Report on UN Peace Operations, Singapore, February 2001.

21. Anthony Goldstone, "UNTAET with Hindsight: The Peculiarities of Politics in an Incomplete State," *Global Governance* 10, no. 1 (January-March 2004), 95.

22. For extended discussion of the issues of international administration, see Richard Caplan, *International Governance of War-Torn Territories: Rule and Reconstruction* (New York: Oxford University Press, 2005), and the special issue of *Global Governance* 10, no. 1 (January-March 2004).

23. Paul F. Diehl, "Forks in the Road: Theoretical and Policy Concerns for 21st Century Peacekeeping," *Global Society* 14, no. 3 (2001): 337–360.

24. Virginia Page Fortna, "Interstate Peacekeeping: Causal Mechanisms and Empirical Effects," *World Politics* 56 (July 2004), 510.

25. Diehl, "Forks in the Road," 352.

26. James Dobbins, "Nation-Building: UN Surpasses U.S. on Learning Curve," *Rand Review* (Spring 2005), http://www.rand.org/publications/randreview/issues/spring2005/nation.html. For the full study, see James Dobbins et al., *The UN's Role in Nation-Building: From the Congo to Iraq* (Santa Monica, Calif.: RAND Corp., 2005).

27. Among recent assessments, see for example, Michael J. Doyle and Nicholas Sambanis, "International Peacebuilding: A Theoretical and Quantitative Analysis," *American Political Science Review* 94, no. 4 (December 2000): 779–801.

28. See Lise Morjë Howard, "Learning to Keep the Peace? United Nations Multidimensional Peacekeeping in Civil Wars" (Ph.D. diss., University of California, Berkeley, 2001), and Dobbins, "Nation-Building: UN Surpasses U.S. on Learning Curve."

29. Stephen John Stedman, "International Implementation of Peace Agreements in Civil Wars: Findings from a Study of Sixteen Cases," in *Turbulent Peace: The Challenges of Managing International Conflict,* ed. Chester A. Crocker, Fen Osler Hampson, and Pamela Aall (Washington, D.C.: United States Institute for Peace, 2001), 737–752.

30. Assefaw Bariagaber, "Africa," in *Global Agenda: Issues Before the 59th General Assembly of the United Nations,* ed. Angela Drakulich (New York: UNA/USA, 2004), 109.

31. United Nations General Assembly and Security Council, *Report of the Panel on United Nations Peace Operations,* A/55/305-S/2000/809, 21 August 2000, http://www.un.org/peace/reports/peace_operations/.

32. International Commission on Intervention and State Sovereignty (ICISS), *The Responsibility to Protect: Research, Bibliography, Background: Supplementary Volume to the Report* (Ottawa: International Development Research Centre for ICISS), 220. The report and supplementary volume are available online at http://www.iciss-cisse.gc.ca.

33. For one perspective, see Alain Destexhe, "The Third Genocide," *Foreign Policy* no. 97 (Winter 1994-1995): 3–17.

34. United Nations, *Report of the Independent Inquiry into the Actions of the United Nations During the 1994 Genocide in Rwanda,* S/1999/1257, 15 December 1999, http://www.un.org./news/ossg/rwanda_report.htm.

35. United Nations press release SG/SM/6878, 28 January 1999.

36. Independent International Commission on Kosovo, *The Kosovo Report: Conflict, International Response, Lessons Learned* (Oxford: Oxford University Press, 2000).

37. Shashi Tharoor and Sam Daws, "Humanitarian Intervention: Getting Past the Reefs," *World Policy Journal* 18, no. 2 (Summer 2001): 23. The debate over humanitarian intervention has spawned a growing literature. In addition to the ICISS supplementary volume cited in

note 28, see, for example, *Hard Choices: Moral Dilemmas in Humanitarian Intervention,* ed. Jonathan Moore (Lanham, Md.: Rowman and Littlefield, 1998); Nicholas J. Wheeler, *Saving Strangers: Humanitarian Intervention in International Society* (Oxford: Oxford University Press, 2000); Thomas G. Weiss and Cindy Collins, *Humanitarian Challenges and Intervention,* 2nd ed. (Boulder: Westview Press, 2000); Martha Finnemore, *The Purpose of Intervention: Changing Beliefs About the Use of Force* (Ithaca: Cornell University Press, 2003); and *Humanitarian Intervention: Ethical, Legal, and Political Dilemmas,* ed. J. L. Holzgrefe and Robert O. Keohane (New York: Cambridge University Press, 2003).

38. ICISS, *The Responsibility to Protect: Report of the International Commission on Intervention and State Sovereignty* (Ottawa: International Development Research Centre for ICISS), 32.

39. United Nations press release, SG/SM/7263, AFR/196, 16 December 1999, http://www.un.org/Docs/SG/sgsm.htm.

40. Secretary Powell's remarks were contained in testimony before the U.S. Senate Foreign Relations Committee and reported in the news; see http://www.washingtonpost.com/wp-dyn/articles/A8364–2004Sep9.html.

41. Morton Abramowitz and Samantha Power, "A Broken System," *Washington Post,* September 13, 2004.

42. Inis L. Claude, Jr., *Swords into Plowshares: The Problems and Progress of International Organization,* 3rd ed. (New York: Random House, 1964), 267.

43. Jonathan Dean, "Beyond Iraq: Controlling Weapons of Mass Destruction Worldwide," *Global Agenda: Issues Before the 59th General Assembly of the United Nations,* ed. Angela Drakulich (New York: UNA/USA, 2004), 175.

44. Mark Landler, "Nuclear Agency Votes to Report Iran to U.N. Security Council for Treaty Violations," *New York Times,* September 25, 2005.

45. M. J. Peterson, "Using the General Assembly," in *Terrorism and the UN: Before and After September 11,* ed. Jane Boulden and Thomas G. Weiss (Bloomington, Ind.: Indiana University Press, 2004), 178.

46. Chantal de Jonge Oudraat, "The Role of the Security Council," in *Terrorism and the UN: Before and After September 11,* ed. Jane Boulden and Thomas G. Weiss (Bloomington, Ind.: Indiana University Press, 2004), 152.

47. Jane Boulden and Thomas G. Weiss, "Whither Terrorism and the United Nations?" in *Terrorism and the UN: Before and After September 11,* ed. Jane Boulden and Thomas G. Weiss (Bloomington, Ind.: Indiana University Press, 2004), 11.

48. Chantal de Jonge Oudraat, "The Role of the Security Council," in *Terrorism and the UN: Before and After September 11,* ed. Jane Boulden and Thomas G. Weiss (Bloomington, Ind.: Indiana University Press, 2004), 153.

49. See the High-level Panel's report, *A More Secure World,* http://www.un.org/secureworld/.

50. 2005 World Summit Outcome, General Assembly A/60/L.1, section 81, http://www.un-ngls.org/un-summit-FINAL-DOC.pdf.

51. Ibid., sections 144–145.

52. Michael Mandelbaum, "The Reluctance to Intervene," *Foreign Policy,* no. 93 (Summer 1994): 11.

53. See http://www.globalpolicy.org/finance/tables/inxpckp.htm.

54. For a discussion, see Robert C. Johansen, "Reconciling National and International Interests in UN Peacekeeping," in *A Crisis of Expectations: UN Peacekeeping in the 1990s,* ed. Ramesh Thakur and Caryle A. Thayer (Boulder: Westview Press, 1995), 281–302.

55. David M. Malone, "Conclusion," in *The UN Security Council: From the Cold War to the 21st Century,* ed. David M. Malone (Boulder: Lynne Rienner, 2004), 640.

56. Kofi Annan, *Annual Report of the Secretary-General to the General Assembly*, SG/SM7136 GA/9596, 20 September 1999.

57. Ibid.

58. Boulden and Weiss, "Whither Terrorism and the United Nations?," 17.

59. Edward L. Luck and Tobi Trister Gati, "Whose Collective Security?" *Washington Quarterly* (Spring 1992): 43.

60. Ibid., 17.

5

⊸◦⊷

Economic Development and Sustainability

A world not advancing towards the Millennium
Development Goals will not be a world at peace. And a
world awash in violence and conflict will have little chance
of achieving the goals. . . . We need to consider whether the
United Nations itself is well-suited to the challenges ahead.

—Kofi Annan, Message to the Conference on
Global Economic Governance and Challenges of
Multilateralism, Dhaka, 17 January 2004.

Since the UN's founding, fundamental changes have taken place in international
economic relations and in understandings of development. The global economy
has been reshaped by many dichotomies, including globalization tempered by state
fragmentation, unprecedented wealth in some locations coupled with the deepening of poverty in others, and major advances in technology complicated by the
unanticipated, sometimes unwanted, consequences of technological advancement.

The paradigms used to explain these global economic trends are also changing.
Where once development was conceived largely in terms of national economic
growth and measured by changes in aggregate and per capita income, a more
holistic view has emerged in the broad concept of **human development**: the notion that the general improvement in human wellbeing and poverty alleviation are
primary development objectives. Much of the activity related to managing international economic relations more generally has taken place historically in what are
called the Bretton Woods institutions (the World Bank, International Monetary

Fund, and General Agreement on Tariffs and Trade, now the World Trade Organization) and, since the mid-1970s, in the Group of Seven (G-7), which is composed of the major industrialized countries, not in the UN. And, although the World Bank and IMF are UN specialized agencies, they have traditionally operated largely outside the UN system. Nonetheless, the UN and UN-sponsored global conferences have provided much of the intellectual leadership in developing key ideas and frameworks for thinking about development, and UN programs and the specialized agencies have undertaken major development tasks. The UN system has also been *the* principal source of data for development planning, including global economic projections that enable states to measure their own performance against that of others.

THE UN AND THE EVOLUTION OF DEVELOPMENT THINKING

Views about development historically have been linked to competing schools of thought in political economy: economic liberalism, mercantilism or statism, and Marxism. These schools differ in their concepts of human nature; the relationship between individuals, the state, and markets; and the appropriate relationship between domestic and international economies. They have shaped debates within the UN system as well as within individual countries. To understand the UN's role in the evolution of development thinking, we need first to look at these three schools of thought.

Liberal View of Economic Development

Liberal economic views heavily shaped development thinking in the immediate post–World War II period, particularly in Western Europe and North America. The major international economic institutions established following the 1944 Bretton Woods Conference were all firmly rooted in this school of thought.

Economic liberalism, based on ideas from Adam Smith to contemporary thinkers, asserts that human beings are rational and acquisitive and will seek to improve their condition in the most expeditious manner possible. Markets develop to ensure that individuals are able to carry out the necessary transactions to improve their wellbeing. To maximize economic welfare and efficiency and to stimulate individual (and therefore collective) economic growth, markets must operate freely, economics and politics must be separated as much as possible, and governments must permit the free flow of trade and economic intercourse. If they do not interfere in the efficient allocation of resources provided by markets, the increasing interdependence between domestic economies will lead to greater cooperation and aggregate economic development. Since multinational corporations were first created in the 1960s, liberals have viewed them as key engines of growth.

Consistent with the thinking of liberal economists in Great Britain and the United States, the World Bank, International Monetary Fund, and the General Agreement on Tariffs and Trade (GATT) were established to facilitate international cooperation in aiding reconstruction after the war (World Bank), ensuring a stable international monetary system to undergird the flow of capital and goods (IMF), and in opening markets through negotiated reductions in barriers to trade and the principle of nondiscrimination (GATT). Economic development, it was thought, could best be achieved through open markets for goods and capital with an international infrastructure to provide limited amounts of assistance.

Alternatives to Economic Liberalism

Two other schools of economic thought have long challenged the liberal paradigm. The oldest is **mercantilism,** or **statism,** developed between the fifteenth and eighteenth centuries when powerful European states sought to regulate all international economic transactions. The modern version of mercantilism emphasizes the role of the state and the subordination of all economic activities to state interests, including its security and military power. Where liberals see the mutual benefits of international trade, mercantilists see states competing with each other to maximize their economic potential. Statist policies stress national self-sufficiency rather than interdependence, limited imports of foreign goods through the substitution of domestic products and high tariffs, and restricted foreign direct investment. The school of thought has been widespread in parts of Latin America and Asia. The "tigers" of East Asia, including South Korea, Singapore, and Taiwan, successfully used this approach to economic development during the 1980s and early 1990s. Much of the controversy about approaches to economic development pits those of a liberal persuasion against states and individuals that espouse statist approaches.

The other contending view, **Marxism,** had strong appeal among developing countries in the 1950s and 1960s, as did the Soviet model of central planning and its success in achieving rapid industrialization. Marxism and its various permutations are united by four beliefs:

1. Society is broadly conflictual as well as dynamic.
2. Conflict is caused largely by the contradictions and struggles between social classes over the distribution of resources.
3. Capitalist economic systems are inherently deterministic and expansionary; they require new resources and the colonization of less developed regions in order to generate continual profits. Thus, the international system is basically conflictual.
4. There must be a more equitable distribution of resources within societies and between societies in the international system.[1]

In the late 1950s, a variation on Marxist thinking emerged in the writings of some Latin American economists, many of whom worked in the UN. They focused on the need for radical change in the distribution of international political and economic power if the disadvantaged position of developing countries was to be altered.[2] This view, known as **dependency theory,** argued that the capitalist international system divided states into two groups: those on the periphery and those at the core. Those on the periphery were locked into a permanent state of dependency, irrespective of the domestic policies they pursued or the external assistance they received. Multinational corporations that had extensive operations within such peripheral states were criticized for exacerbating the dependency, making these companies targets for nationalization.

In essence, dependency theory argued that development could not take place without fundamental changes in international economic relations to redress the inequalities of power and wealth. These views had strong appeal and came to undergird much of the agenda of developing countries in the UN in the 1960s and 1970s.

These three schools of thought infused debates within the UN about approaches to economic development. With the strong presence of Latin American economists in the UN Secretariat in the 1950s and 1960s, and the growing membership of developing countries, the UN was often seen as a critic of liberalism, while the IMF, World Bank, and GATT were considered bastions of liberalism. In reality, at the same time it has provided a forum for the demands of the less developed world, as well as an alternative perspective to that of the Bretton Woods institutions, the UN has played a vital role in the evolution of a more complex view of development.

Only recently has there been increasing convergence of development thinking. Marxism was discredited with the end of the Cold War, the dissolution of the Soviet Union, and the revelations of economic and environmental failures in all the former Communist countries. Statism and dependency theory waned in the 1980s and 1990s as well after developing countries failed to achieve the sustained growth they sought, or the reforms in the international economic relations they advocated. Instead, they were pushed and pulled into adopting liberal economic policies by conditions for World Bank and IMF loans and U.S. influence. Thus, in the 1990s, economic liberalism (or neoliberalism) emerged as the dominant school of economic thought. Almost all national economies are now open to some degree and linked in patterns of complex interdependence that include vastly expanded world trade, global financial markets, and globalized production in some industries. Multinational corporations are important actors alongside states and NGOs that are making their voices heard. Markets function as key mechanisms in the international economy.

The UN and Evolving Ideas About Development

Over the years, thinking about what development entailed underwent considerable change, thanks in large part to work done under UN auspices, since before the late 1940s there had been very few studies of economic and social development. Much attention was initially directed to the ways to get development and industrialization, in particular, moving. What role should governments play? What role did outside factors, including aid and capital investment, play? One of the UN's earliest intellectual contributions was the notion that economic development did not just happen; planning was important, as was the development of needed skills, education, health, hygiene, and national administrative services. A second contribution stemmed from the conviction that foreign assistance in remedying capital shortages should only supplement domestic efforts, but was nonetheless critical, especially if provided on concessionary terms. A third contribution concerned the value of agreements and international buffer stocks to prevent short-term fluctuations in the prices of primary products and commodities such as wheat, sugar, copper, and tin. The fourth area in which the UN had a major influence was the idea of **technical assistance**—"providing developing countries with the human skills and human resources to make capital inputs effective."[3] These contributions all came in the late 1940s and 1950s.

By the end of the 1960s, the UN again led the way in a further evolution of development thinking away from an emphasis on economic growth rates. The persistence of hunger, illiteracy, and poverty, growing income inequality, and employment problems prompted a new emphasis on the importance of addressing these issues. The UN played a major role in the increased focus on equity among different socioeconomic groups, between North and South, between men and women, and between present and future generations that marked the 1970s. Collaboration between development scholars and various UN agencies, including the World Bank, produced new approaches oriented to basic human needs focusing on the redistribution of income from growth to the needs of the poorest. Where these ideas focused largely on strategies for national action, another set of initiatives through the UN proposed to establish a new international economic order. Later, those ideas were incorporated into the proposed New International Economic Order (NIEO), becoming enormously influential throughout the 1970s and much of the 1980s, and echoes can still be heard today. In these same years, the UN advanced thinking and practice with respect to the roles of women in development and the links between environmental sustainability and development. We discuss all three of these later in this chapter.

As a result of this evolutionary process, by the 1990s thinking about development centered on a synthetic approach captured in the concept of human development.

The UN-sponsored global conferences contributed greatly to blueprints of actions required at national and global levels to realize the political, social, and economic objectives set forth in the conference declarations and platforms for action. The annual *Human Development Reports* show how much human development and economic growth rates can vary. Many of these ideas have been adopted by the Bretton Woods institutions, although they have not always altered World Bank and IMF policies.[4]

The UN's seminal role in the evolution of development thinking owed much to its strong research capacity and ability to tap the small community of development scholars. That capacity declined over time, and the scholarly community grew larger and more dispersed. From its earliest days, however, the UN system also evolved a variety of operational approaches to promote economic and social development.

THE ORGANIZATION OF THE UN SYSTEM FOR PROMOTING ECONOMIC DEVELOPMENT

The UN Charter

The UN Charter's provisions on economic and social development reflected a liberal vision of building institutions and programs to promote prosperity and peace through international cooperation and industrial change. These were strongly influenced also by European social democracy and the American New Deal of the 1930s that envisioned expanding the role of government to deal with social and economic problems. Thus, achieving "international co-operation in solving international problems of an economic, social, cultural, or humanitarian character" is among the provisions of Chapter I and is described in Article 55 as "necessary for peaceful and friendly relations among nations." Yet the specific provisions for carrying out this broad mandate are limited, particularly when contrasted with the extensive sections on managing threats to international peace and security.

In Article 13, the General Assembly is given responsibility for providing general direction, coordination, and supervision for economic and social activities through its Second Committee. Chapter X empowers ECOSOC specifically to undertake studies and prepare reports, make recommendations, prepare conventions, convene conferences, create specialized agencies, and make recommendations for their coordination. And, as discussed in chapter 2, the founders of the UN envisaged that the specialized agencies affiliated with the UN would play key roles in carrying out operational activities aimed at economic and social advancement, coordinated through ECOSOC.

For more than sixty years now, the attention to economic and social issues and the number of entities within the UN system engaged in development activities have steadily grown. As a result, the UN has faced the ongoing challenge of ratio-nalizing and coordinating a complex network of agencies and activities. With the Third World commanding a majority of votes in the General Assembly, it has also proved difficult to terminate programs that may have outlived their usefulness (at least in the eyes of developed countries). About 80 percent of the UN's budget goes to its economic functions and activities, but these resources represent only a small fraction of the current world funding for development-related activities. The World Bank's resources, for example, are seldom included in calculations of UN development aid, and they far exceed those of the UN itself. More important, pri-vate capital flows have vastly outstripped official multilateral and bilateral develop-ment aid since the early 1990s.

Even though economic liberalism shaped the Charter and Bretton Woods insti-tutions, there was no consensus among the three schools of thought in the General Assembly, ECOSOC, and the UN Secretariat. All affected debates concerning norms and operational activities, as well as the evolution of key ideas about devel-opment discussed earlier. The studies and reports in which those ideas emerged were conducted by the Secretariat (and by scholars enlisted in UN-sponsored pro-jects) under mandates from the assembly and ECOSOC.

UN Development Activities

The UN has developed several approaches to fulfill the operational side of its man-date to promote economic and social advancement. These include the creation of a series of regional commissions to decentralize planning and programs; the commit-ment to technical assistance—providing educational and training programs as well as expert advice; setting international goals for development; and seeking to redress the imbalance in less developed countries' international trade relationships.

Regional Commissions.   In 1947, two of what became a network of five regional commissions were established: the Economic Commission for Europe (ECE) and the Economic Commission for Asia and the Far East (renamed in the 1970s the Economic and Social Commission for Asia and the Pacific, or ESCAP, after the Commission for Western Asia was formed). Shortly thereafter, in 1948, the Eco-nomic Commission for Latin America (ECLA) came into being; and ten years later, the Economic Commission for Africa (ECA) was formed. These commis-sions were designed to stimulate regional approaches to development with studies and initiatives to promote regional projects. Many, however, feared a duplication of efforts, added expense, and needless fragmentation.

The UN's regional approach has met with considerable success, nonetheless. The European commission under the leadership of the Swedish development economist Gunnar Myrdal provided early impetus to European integration. The

Latin American group played an important role during the 1950s in critiquing the liberal economic model's applicability to dependent states. Under the leadership of Raul Prebisch, ECLA encouraged states to adopt import substitution policies to escape economic dependency. Many of its ideas formed the theoretical basis for the New International Economic Order proposals of the 1970s, especially in the area of commodity policy. ECLA also contributed to the establishment of the Central American Common Market (CACM) and the Inter-American Development Bank (IDB). In 1966, thanks to India's early awareness of the problem of population growth, ESCAP organized one of the first meetings to discuss the sensitive issue of family planning at a time when population growth was just emerging as a major development-related topic.[5] The Economic Commission for Africa in the late 1960s helped draw attention to women's roles in development when it organized the first regional workshop on the topic. With the World Bank and IMF's subordination of basic needs approaches to neoliberal stabilization and structural adjustment policies in the 1980s, ECA, along with the ILO and UNICEF, formulated critiques of their adverse impact on the poorest countries.[6]

All the commissions have produced high-quality economic surveys of their respective regions, as well as country plans used by national governments and other multilateral institutions. All have addressed the diverse issues of trade, industry, energy, and transportation. Yet disputes among members, such as Arab versus non-Arab states in the Commission for Western Asia, and lack of resources and expertise in Africa have hampered the work of some commissions.

Funding for Development.   In the late 1940s, experts realized that less developed countries lack the necessary capital for infrastructure development. Early debate in the UN therefore centered on that institution's role in providing funding for investment needs. The World Bank was limited in its ability to fund private enterprises and NGOs, and its lending terms were too strict for many developing countries. One answer was to create an affiliate of the bank, the International Finance Corporation (IFC), to make loans to private enterprises without a governmental guarantee. The other proposal was to create a UN fund for economic development to overcome the shortcomings of the bank.

Debate over a UN fund lasted for nine years in the 1950s and was marked by conflicts between developed and developing countries. The latter were keenly interested in the proposed special fund because it would "provide a systematic and sustained assistance in fields essential to the integrated technical, economic and social development of the less developed countries . . . [and] it would facilitate new capital investments of all types—private and public, national and international— by creating conditions which would make such investments either feasible or more effective."[7] But what started out as a proposal for a large fund that would have depended heavily on U.S. financial support emerged as a much smaller fund to establish research institutes, finance regional training centers, conduct natural resources surveys, and support other pre-investment projects. The Special UN Fund for Economic Development (SUNFED) would not give loans or provide investment capital, but it would be managed under the UN Expanded Programme for Technical Assistance, which, by the late 1950s, had emerged as the primary UN development agency.[8]

Technical Assistance.   The provision of technical assistance to developing countries has been a major contribution of the UN system. Although it was unable to provide substantial amounts of capital, the UN could supply people skills and new technologies. This approach grew out of a December 1948 General Assembly mandate and U.S. President Harry Truman's 1949 inaugural address, which presented his ideas for aiding peoples in economically underdeveloped areas. It was institutionalized in the 1950 Expanded Programme of Technical Assistance (EPTA). The UN has awarded fellowships for advanced training, supplied equipment for training purposes, and provided project experts recruited from around the world. Many projects are jointly funded by the UN and the specialized agencies, such as the WHO, the FAO, UNESCO, or one of the regional economic commissions. EPTA pioneered the approach of asking governments to review their needs and develop plans and administrative machinery for country programs to establish the principle of country ownership and control. Regular UN budget funds for technical assistance are frequently augmented by voluntary contributions from member states. This development assistance consists of grant aid, not loans; hence, it does not create future burdens for recipient countries.

In 1965, the General Assembly approved the merger of SUNFED and EPTA into the new United Nations Development Program (UNDP) to enhance coordination of the various types of technical assistance programs within the UN system. As a result of changes instituted thereafter, UNDP resident representatives in recipient countries are expected to assess local needs and priorities, be the focal point of UN development activities, coordinate technical assistance programs, function as "country representatives" for some of the specialized agencies, and link the United Nations with the recipient government. Although the resident representative positions have grown in significance, the resources at their disposal are still dwarfed by those of the World Bank and major bilateral aid donors, let alone private investors. This limits their power to coordinate country-based activities, as does the autonomy of the specialized agencies.

Information Gathering.   The UN also has played a key role in gathering and disseminating information—data and statistics—to aid development planning and the translation of ideas into initiatives. Beginning in 1945, the UN Statistical Commission worked to set international standards for gathering and reporting

statistics. In the early years, this meant establishing standards for national ac-
counts, for example. Then, as new ideas permeated the system, various UN
agencies recognized the need to collect data that had not previously been col-
lected by member states, let alone analyzed and disseminated worldwide. This
included trends in world trade, population growth, food, and industrial
production.

In the 1970s and 1980s, the UN emphasis turned to standardizing social statistics on such issues as fertility, hunger, and nutrition. As more attention was being
paid to the roles of women in development and the status of women generally,
there was a recognized need to collect data by gender. As a result, the UN Commission on the Status of Women compiled and published *The World's Women: Trends
and Statistics 1970–1990,* the first such compilation.[9] As poverty reduction ideas
permeated the system, UNDP introduced the human development index (HDI) in
the early 1990s to emphasize that development is about improving the quality of
life for human beings, not just promoting economic growth. The index is based on
a composite of indicators, including infant mortality, life expectancy, and literacy.
The success of that indicator has led to the creation of several other indices, including the Gender Development Index, the Gender Empowerment Measure, and
the Human Poverty Index. In short, the data and analyses undertaken by various
UN agencies are critical for member states' development planning and for UN policy debates.

Setting Goals: The Development Decades.   By the early 1960s, decolonization
had produced the demographic shift in UN membership that dramatically
changed the focus of the organization's agendas and activities to promoting national economic growth—the dominant conception of development at that time.
Although the UN had been heavily involved in generating ideas, policies, and planning for development up to that time, with a push from President John F.
Kennedy's address to the General Assembly in September 1961, the General Assembly proclaimed the 1960s as the "United Nations Development Decade." This
marked a new role: setting goals and targets as a way of mobilizing support "for the
measures required on the part of both developed and developing countries to ac-
celerate progress towards self-sustaining growth of the economy of the individual
nations and their social advancement" (Resolution 1710/XVI).

The first development decade was followed by three subsequent decades. In
each, there were clearly articulated goals: targets for annual aid from developed to
developing states (initially 1 percent of developed countries' gross national product [GNP]); and targets for increases in the average annual growth rates of developing countries (initially 5 percent), as well as their exports, domestic savings, and
agricultural production. Among the outcomes of the first decade were increased
attention to development issues; widespread adoption of national planning as a

development tool; studies of major trends in the international economy, and especially in world trade; new attention to the role of education; and efforts to build capacity for the application of science and technology to the needs of developing countries.[10] In addition, the first decade saw the creation of more institutional structures for development with UNDP, the World Food Programme, the United Nations Conference on Trade and Development (UNCTAD), and the United Nations Industrial Development Organization (UNIDO).

The most recent UN goal-setting initiative involves the Millennium Development Goals (MDGs), established in 2000. This represents a new approach for the twenty-first century and is discussed below.

Trade Issues and the Creation of UNCTAD.   The creation of UNCTAD in 1964 marked the recognition of the centrality of trade issues to economic development. Frustrated by the slow response of the Bretton Woods institutions to their development needs and by the developed countries' dominance of these institutions, developing countries proposed an international conference to establish principles and policies to govern international trade relations and to guide trade policies. The UN Conference on Trade and Development subsequently became a permanent organ reporting to the General Assembly, but with its own secretary-general. UNCTAD supporters resisted becoming a separate specialized UN agency, preferring to draw strength from the General Assembly, where developing countries commanded a majority of votes.

Initially, the Bretton Woods institutions were to include the International Trade Organization. That organization was expected to provide a general framework for trade rules and a venue for ongoing trade discussions, especially for the vexing problems of commodities that are of particular concern to less developed countries. Lack of support in the U.S. Senate, however, killed the proposed organization. In its place, the General Agreement on Tariffs and Trade (GATT) was established "temporarily" to provide a framework for trade negotiations. Only in 1995 did the World Trade Organization come into being following the eighth round of GATT trade negotiations. (See below for more on GATT and WTO.)

Through the 1950s, many less developed countries grew increasingly dissatisfied with GATT's emphasis on trade in manufactured products and its lack of interest in the commodity problem and in trade as a way to transfer economic resources from the rich to the poor countries. Spurred by the work of the Economic Commission for Latin America, which was grounded in Marxist and dependency thinking, the increasingly vocal G-77, established at the founding UNCTAD conference, envisioned that institution as a new venue for addressing trade issues relating to development. Reciprocity in trade relations, a core GATT principle, was viewed as serving only to perpetuate dependency and underdevelopment. The inherently unequal international liberal trading system could not be made more equal without major changes. Thus, the developing countries argued that they needed special concessions—including preferential access to developed country markets—to improve their trade.

UNCTAD's founding conference recommended a number of general principles to govern international trade relations as well as recognizing the need for a system of **trade preferences.** It emphasized that the developed countries had a major role to play in addressing the problems of trade affecting developing countries. And it brought into the open the growing split—which persists today—between North and South, developed and developing countries, over issues relating to trade and development.

UNCTAD continues to meet every four years, and the Trade and Development Board, its permanent governing organ, meets annually. The UNCTAD Secretariat has been important in shaping its work because of its close ties with the G-77; it also provides research, analysis, and training for government officials to remedy the limited expertise of many developing countries' governments on complex international trade issues. UNCTAD's dynamics were long shaped by a pattern of group bargaining, prompted by the G-77's high degree of unity, and the one-state one-vote mode of majority decisionmaking. Despite efforts to develop operational responsibilities, it has functioned largely as a forum for debate, negotiation, and legitimation of new norms. It was the primary forum for articulating the major challenges to the predominant liberal thinking about economic development, including the New International Economic Order, discussed below.[11] Currently, its meetings address such issues as commodity diversification, trade and commercial negotiations, transportation, macroeconomic policies, and debt financing. It has sponsored programs for the least-developed countries, including the landlocked and small-island developing countries. Since the early 1980s, the interests of developing countries have increasingly diverged because some have achieved significant economic growth and others continue to lag. UNCTAD remains important for the least developed, who have resisted suggestions that UNCTAD has outlived its usefulness. Nonetheless, it is less active and its record for more than forty years shows few substantial achievements.

The Bretton Woods Institutions and UN Specialized Agencies.   The nineteen specialized agencies are an integral part of the UN's approaches to international development and trade (see fig. 2.1). Many of them provide technical assistance, UNESCO and the ILO leading the way. The World Bank provides capital investment, the IMF ensures financial and monetary stability, and GATT/WTO foster the opening of markets for trade. Yet trade cannot occur without a physical means to transport goods, hence the need for ocean shipping and air transport. Development depends on communications infrastructure; thus, the International Maritime Organization, the International Civil Aviation Organization, and the

International Telecommunications Union are important players in making the international economic system function. UNIDO has been catalytic for industrial development, and agricultural development has been promoted through a group of UN-related organizations, two of which are specialized agencies: the Food and Agriculture Organization, established in 1945, and the International Fund for Agricultural Development (IFAD), founded in 1977. They are complemented by the World Food Programme, created in 1963, and the Consultative Group on International Agricultural Research (CGIAR), established in 1972, among others.

To illustrate the roles of specialized agencies, we look briefly at the work of the Bretton Woods and food institutions in relationship to trade and development. Whereas total UN technical cooperation assistance is more than $5 billion annually, the World Bank has loaned more than $500 billion since its founding. And although the World Bank is a UN specialized agency, there is a sharp distinction between it (and the IMF) and the rest of the UN system. For reasons that will become clear, the other UN agencies were critical of many activities of the bank and IMF, particularly in the 1980s and 1990s.

The International Bank for Reconstruction and Development (IBRD), or World Bank.   The World Bank's initial task was to facilitate reconstruction in post–World War II Europe. In fact, because the task proved so great, the United States financed the bulk of it bilaterally through the European Recovery Program (or Marshall Plan) rather than multilaterally through the bank. During the 1950s, the bank shifted focus from reconstruction to development. Unlike the UN, where member assessments provide the financing, the bank generates capital funds largely from the international financial markets and, to a lesser extent, from member states. Unlike the UN, which offers grants, the bank lends money at market interest rates to states for major economic development projects. Its lending is not designed to replace private capital but to facilitate its operation by funding projects that private banks would not support, such as infrastructure (dams, bridges, highways), primary education, and health. Unlike private banks, the World Bank attaches conditions to its loans in the form of policy changes it would like to see states make to promote economic development and to alleviate poverty.

To aid the World Bank in meeting the needs of developing countries, the International Finance Corporation (IFC) and the International Development Association (IDA) were created in 1956 and 1960, respectively. IDA provides capital to the poorest countries, usually in the form of no-interest ("soft" or concessional) loans with long repayment schedules (fifty years), to allow the least-developed countries more time to reach "takeoff," sustain growth, and hence develop economically. Such funds have to be continually "replenished" or added to by major donor countries. The creation of the IDA was a direct response to pressure from the developing countries for concessional loans. The IFC provides loans to promote the growth of private enterprises in developing countries. In 1988, the Multilateral Investment Guarantee Agency (MIGA) was added to the World Bank group. This agency's goal—to augment the flow of private equity capital to less developed countries—is met by insuring investments against losses. Such losses may include expropriation, government currency restrictions, and losses stemming from civil war or ethnic conflict. The World Bank family of institutions now also incorporates the International Centre for Settlement of Investment Disputes (ICSID). Like the UN, the bank group has added new institutions and mechanisms to meet new needs and to service new approaches to economic development.

The World Bank, like the other development organizations, the UN itself, and major donor governments, has changed its orientation over time, moving from an emphasis on major infrastructure projects in the 1950s and 1960s to **basic human needs** in the 1970s, and private-sector participation in the 1980s. During the 1980s, the bank and its sister institution, the IMF, pushed a staunchly neoliberal economic agenda of **privatization,** open markets for capital and trade, and structural adjustment. The UN itself was increasingly marginalized in economic matters, a forum for critics of the effects of these priorities, but itself a critic that continued to offer new ideas and approaches concerning issues such as the role of women in economic life, the links between environmental concerns and development, and **poverty alleviation,** as shown below. Thus, by the 1990s, when the bank added environmentally sustainable development, good governance, and poverty alleviation to its priorities, it was the result of influences from elsewhere within the UN system as well as from NGOs.[12]

The International Monetary Fund.   The IMF's chief function at the outset was to stabilize currency exchange rates by providing short-term loans for member states with "temporary" **balance-of-payments** difficulties. Funds to meet such needs were contributed by members according to quotas negotiated every five years and payable both in gold and in local currency. Members could borrow up to the amount they had contributed. The IMF was never designed to be an aid agency, but its role in economic development is crucial insofar as stable currency values and currency convertibility are necessary to facilitate trade. Although some states' balance-of-payments shortfalls are temporary, others experience long-term structural economic problems. Beginning with the 1982 Mexican debt crisis, the IMF took on the role of intermediary in negotiations between creditors and debtor countries, and also became increasingly involved in dictating policy changes as conditions of lending. As a result, the IMF's reach has extended into areas of economic activity that the UN has never touched.

For many less developed countries plagued by persistent high debts, the IMF now provides long-term loans and the "international stamp of approval" for other multilateral and bilateral lenders as well as private banks. In return for assistance, the IMF negotiates **structural adjustment programs,** requiring countries to institute economic policy reforms or achieve certain conditions, often referred to as **conditionality.** These are consistent with liberal economic theory and involve trade liberalization, economic reforms to eliminate subsidies and introduce user fees, and government reforms such as cutting waste and privatizing public enterprises. Once agreement is reached with a government, the IMF monitors the adjustment programs and determines whether performance criteria have been met. During the 1997–1998 financial crisis in Asia, for example, the fund pushed Indonesia to change its entire economic system. In the 1990s, the IMF was also instrumental in the transitions of Russia and other former Communist countries to market economies. The very large size of IMF aid packages for several countries, including Mexico, Russia, and South Korea, effectively placed the IMF in the position of "bailing out" countries on the verge of economic collapse where there were concerns about contagion to other countries.

The World Bank and the IMF are both involved in structural adjustment lending (the fund through short-term emergency loans and its negotiating and monitoring roles, the bank through aid for long-term structural reforms). Both also play key roles in debt renegotiation. Although originally established as institutions having very different tasks, the distinctions between the two have blurred.

The IMF and World Bank Under Attack.   The bank and particularly the fund have been subjected to intense criticism of both governance and issues. By convention, the IMF managing director is always a European and the World Bank president, an American. In both institutions a limited-member executive board decides everyday policies. The executive boards operate under **weighted voting** systems that guarantee the voting power of the major donors commensurate with their contributions. The larger donors, including the United States, Germany, Japan, France, and Great Britain, have often made funding decisions based on domestic political priorities. Thus, domination by the few opens both institutions to trenchant criticism from developing countries that have little power within the respective institutions. That dominance is reinforced in each of the bureaucracies that employ economists trained in Western countries in the same liberal economic tradition as U.S. decisionmakers. That is one of the reasons the less developed countries have strongly supported the UN's development-related institutions and ideas, where they enjoy a louder voice.

Since the 1980s, the most vehement criticisms have focused on structural adjustment programs and the imposition of conditionality; many believe these exact too high social and economic costs and represent a "cookie-cutter" approach to complex problems taken without regard for particular local situations. In this view, bank and fund programs disproportionately affect the already disadvantaged sectors of the population: the unskilled, women, and the poor. Critics are particularly outraged by the fact that these institutions are able to reach deep into areas of domestic policy traditionally protected by state sovereignty.[13] Many of these critics would prefer to see the UN take on more responsibility for development.

For the first time, critics from outside the bank and fund have been joined by officials within the organizations. The question is whether the institutions have been offering the right advice. Officials critical of IMF policies in East Asia have suggested that they brought the world to the verge of a global meltdown. To others, the IMF not only has promoted a culture of bailouts to countries making unwise economic decisions but also has pushed countries to open their economies to the risks in volatile international financial flows.[14]

Trade and the World Trade Organization.   The GATT provided one major approach to international trade based on principles of trade liberalization, nondiscrimination in trade, and reciprocity. With only a loose link to the UN, GATT oversaw trade negotiations in eight successive multilateral rounds. Although the interests of the industrialized countries took precedence, gradually, under pressure from the G-77 and UNCTAD, more favorable, preferential treatment for less developed countries was granted. In the eighth, or Uruguay Round, concluded in December 1993 after seven years of negotiations, two topics previously excluded from the GATT rules but critical for developing countries were covered: agriculture and textiles. The Uruguay Round also resulted in agreement to create a true global trade organization—the World Trade Organization.

Although the WTO has no formal relationship with the UN, it does provide a unified organizational structure for managing the growing complexity of global trade issues. Like GATT, it is based on a contractual framework—the previously negotiated trade agreements—so that joining WTO involves negotiating the terms of a country's accession to those agreements. For example, when China became a member in 2001 after fifteen years of negotiations, the document setting forth the terms of accession was nine hundred pages long and China's government had to revise many laws that restricted foreign access to its economy. WTO membership now stands at 149 because many developing countries and former Communist states have decided to join. To assist the latter, the WTO and UNCTAD secretariats jointly operate the International Trade Centre in Geneva to provide technical cooperation to developing and transitional countries in developing their capacity for trade. But like the bank and the fund, the WTO has been subject to many of the same criticisms, particularly from those who see the organization as unfairly representing the interests of the developed world. That is why the developing world has often turned to the UN specialized agencies. We illustrate their work by looking at agricultural development.

Agricultural Development Through FAO and IFAD. The core organization of the international food regime, the FAO, was established at the end of World War II with the objective of increasing agricultural productivity to eliminate hunger and improve nutrition, address problems of surpluses and shortages, establish common standards, and harmonize national agricultural policies with free trade principles. Based in Rome, it carries out basic research to enhance technical assistance in agriculture and acts as an information center for agricultural activities, including fishing and forestry. During the 1960s, FAO supported the development and dissemination of high-yield strains of grain and rice that produced the "green revolution" for developing countries. In the 1980s and 1990s, sustainable agricultural and rural development became the organization's primary focus.

Although it is not a specialized agency, the World Food Programme has operational capacities that enable it to deliver food aid to food-deficit countries. Initially supported largely by the United States and Canada, WFP grew by the mid-1980s to a budget greater than $1 billion, more than twenty-five donors, and development projects in more than one hundred countries.[15] In 2004, WFP made food distributions to 113 million of the world's poorest and conducted relief operations in 120 countries. With more than 50 percent of all food aid delivered through WFP, its total annual expenditures approached $3 billion. As the need for food relief has accelerated, WFP has spent up to 90 percent of its funds for relief, and 90 percent of its 9,000 employees are involved in relief operations. It has spent less than 10 percent on development aid.

UN-sponsored World Food conferences in 1974, 1996, and 2002 helped bring together various constituencies, and draw attention to persistent hunger, shortfalls in food production, and the need to promote agricultural development, as well as forge new principles of cooperation. At the 2002 World Food Summit, for example, many traditional issues filled the agenda: food aid to end hunger; emergencies; food safety and phytosanitary regulations; and securing food under conditions of limited water supplies. Among the new issues were the New Partnership for Africa's Development (NEPAD) and the International Treaty on Plant Genetic Resources for Food and Agriculture that engaged the debate on genetic engineering of food crops. More than 650 labor, human rights, and farmers groups participated in the conference along with 180 countries. This was a clear signal that collaboration with NGOs would increase along with partnerships with multinational corporations (MNCs) such as the Italian food giant Parmalat, which provided funding for the summit.

The specialized agencies illustrate the UN's tendency, in common with many governments, to create new agencies and programs. Some institutions have been established because thinking about development has changed and new institutions meet new needs more readily than old institutions can be reformed. The result,

PHOTO 5.1   World Food Programme rising to the challenge
of getting earthquake relief to remote villages of Pakistan before winter sets in. *WFP photo 083347, 2005/Peter Harriss.*

however, can be problems of duplication, inefficiency, and lack of coordination. Thus, the UN system has evolved over time in its efforts to meet the mandate to foster cooperation for economic and social development. The newer challenges of globalization and the persistence of poverty heighten the need for economic governance and for better coordination of the different parts of the UN system; however, they do not lessen the value of the UN's long-time role in the development of norms and ideas. We turn, therefore, to a set of policy debates that highlight this role and the interplay of different institutions.

POLICY DEBATES AND ISSUES IN PROMOTING SUSTAINABLE DEVELOPMENT

The UN has played a key role in the development of ideas. By changing the ways issues are viewed, it has provided a focus for the mobilization of various constituencies and forums for policy debates. As a result of the new ideas that have been embedded into UN institutions, the approaches to and the practice of development have sometimes changed. The debates concern the proposed New International Economic Order, the role of women in development, the notion that development must be sustainable, the role of MNCs in development, and the millennium challenge of reducing global inequality and alleviating poverty.

Challenging Economic Liberalism: The Debate over the New International Economic Order

The 1970s were a particularly difficult period for North-South relations and the international economy. The 1973 oil crisis led to sharp increases in the prices of energy and food. The demonstrated power of the oil-producing states in OPEC to control prices and supplies was viewed by American and other Western officials as a direct challenge to the liberal economic order. In 1973 and 1974, the G-77, impatient with the slow progress toward development and bolstered by support from OPEC members—whom the developing countries admired for their challenge to the major oil companies and the North—increased its pressure for restructuring international economic relations. In two successive special sessions of the UN General Assembly in 1974–1975, in global conferences on food, population, and women, as well as in UNCTAD, the G-77 used its wide majority and strong solidarity to secure the adoption of the Declaration on the Establishment of a New International Economic Order and the Charter of Economic Rights and Duties of States. The 1975 Seventh Special Session of the UN General Assembly marked the peak of confrontation between North and South that dominated not only UNCTAD but much of the UN system, including the specialized agencies.

Through the proposed NIEO, the G-77 sought changes in six major areas of international economic relations with the goal of altering the relationship of dependency between the developed and developing countries. It sought changes in international trade, including adjustment in the **terms of trade,** to stabilize the prices of such commodities as coffee, cocoa, bauxite, tin, and sugar, and to link those prices with the price of finished products imported from developed countries. The G-77 also demanded greater authority over natural resources and foreign investment in developing countries, particularly through the regulation of MNCs. It wanted improved means of technology transfer to make it cheaper and more appropriate for the local population. To propel development, the South also demanded increased foreign aid and improved terms and conditions.

Although the G-77 won adoption of the Generalized System of Preferences (GSP) in GATT in 1967, waiving the nondiscrimination rule, GSP schemes were applied unilaterally by the European Community and the United States, and others. They could be withdrawn at any time. Still, this was a step toward establishing the principle of preferential treatment for developing country exports. The G-77 also won more favorable terms for commodity price stabilization. On most other issues, however, the North refused to negotiate. No common fund was established to stabilize commodity prices. No regulations on MNCs were concluded. There were no dramatic increases in development assistance. In fact, by the late 1980s, "donor fatigue" had set in and levels of official development assistance had steadily decreased.

Two other issues pushed by the G-77 remain on the agenda today—debt relief and restructuring the international financial institutions. For the latter, proponents of the NIEO sought changes in the weighted voting structures of the World Bank and International Monetary Fund and the developed-country bias within the GATT. They sought, in short, to alter basic power relationships in international economic affairs. No major changes have been made in decisionmaking within the bank or the fund. And, in fact, developing countries became even more marginalized on major international economic decisions with the creation of the G-7 in the late 1970s. The latter stemmed in part from the G-77's tactics of using its majority to pass resolutions in the UN that fostered disenchantment with the UN among some Western governments, especially the United States. Hence, the issue of restructuring the international financial institutions and decisionmaking on international economic issues persists. Consensus voting in the WTO, however, has increased the influence of developing countries over new trade negotiations, and, although the developed countries still dominate the outcomes, developing countries have become much more skilled at exercising leverage. For example, during the Doha Development Round of trade negotiations in late 2005, rich countries agreed to major concessions eliminating all tariffs and quotas on 97 percent of goods from the fifty poorest countries and ending their agricultural export subsidies by 2013, developments that reflected a surprising show of unity among the developing countries.[16]

The issue of debt relief to developing countries has also been much debated since the early 1970s. In 1980, the debt of all developing countries was $567 billion; by 1992, it had reached $1.6 trillion, and by 2000, $2.2 trillion.[17] There are many reasons for these high levels: loans made during the Cold War for political reasons; the large amount of OPEC petrodollars that commercial banks were eager to lend in the early 1980s; World Bank and IMF structural adjustment loans with tough conditions; falling commodity prices, severe drought in many African countries, and higher interest rates; and increased private capital investment. In short, debtors and creditors both share blame. The consequences, however, for many developing countries, and especially for the least-developed countries, have been severe. Some of the latter spend as much as four times more for debt servicing than on social services or education. When repayment crowds out opportunities for investment in the economy, infrastructure, health care, and education suffer. Poverty increases. The debt burden has increased the dependence of developing countries on foreign creditors and the international financial institutions as well as reduced the ability of their citizens to control their own development policies.

Almost twenty years after the NIEO debate dominated UN agendas, a popular movement known as Jubilee 2000 (now Jubilee Plus)—a coalition of development-oriented NGOs, church groups, and labor groups—launched a campaign to cancel developing countries' debts. In 1996, the IMF and World Bank undertook a major policy shift called the Heavily Indebted Poor Countries Initiative (HIPC). Still, Jubilee Plus pressed the G-7 for "faster, deeper, and broader debt relief." In 2005, the two institutions agreed to cancel $55 billion in debt owed to them by fourteen of the poorest countries. Yet this covers only some of the debt and some of the most heavily indebted poor countries.

Twenty-five years after the NIEO was proposed and many of its key elements rejected, some of the policy debates it engendered, persist. The G-77, however, gradually splintered with the wide acceptance (some say triumph) of economic liberalism, and the diverging interests of many members. But the founding of UNCTAD and subsequent actions by the G-77 within the UN system provided the first fundamental, sustained challenge to the dominant liberal economic ideology.

Modifying Liberalism: The Roles of Women in Development

During the early years of the UN, the Commission on the Status of Women (CSW), one of the original six functional commissions of ECOSOC, focused on ensuring that women had the right to vote, hold office, and enjoy equal legal rights. The idea that women played important roles in development was unrecognized, however. Indeed, UN agencies and liberal economic theorists believed that as development occurred, women's economic status would improve. There was no special reason to target women as actors in the development process.

In the 1970s, Esther Boserup, the activist, academic, and UN consultant, found otherwise. In her landmark book, *Women's Role in Economic Development*, she argued that as technology improves, men benefit economically, but women become increasingly marginalized economically.[18] Thus, by 1975, when the UN-sponsored International Women's Year was launched with the first World Conference on Women in Mexico City, the conventional wisdom held that the development community could not sit idly by and assume that economic development would inevitably benefit all groups. Women needed special attention if they were to become participants and active agents in development. Programs should be designed to reduce women's traditional activities and to expand new activities into economically productive roles for them in agriculture, small business, and industry. UN agencies undertook the huge task of documenting the facts of women's lives; those facts would generate the powerful slogan that women constitute half the world's population, fill two-thirds of its work hours, receive one-tenth of its income, and own less than one-hundredth of its property.[19]

The women-in-development agenda (WID), the International Decade for Women, and the first three UN women's conferences in 1975, 1980, and 1985 were all heavily affected by the North-South conflict of that period and by debates over the proposed NIEO as well as over the political issues of Palestinian rights and Zionism as racism. With governments in the lead at the UN-sponsored conferences, and women's groups working only from the sidelines of parallel NGO meetings, the central issues of women's economic roles and social status were often lost in the process.

Following the approval in 1979 of the Convention on the Elimination of Discrimination Against Women, the UN in 1982 established the International Research and Training Institute for the Advancement of Women (INSTRAW) to implement the women-in-development agenda. Funded by voluntary contributions, INSTRAW's goals are to provide training to integrate and mobilize women in the development process and to act as a catalyst in promoting the role of women. The UN Development Fund for Women (UNIFEM), established in 1975, supports projects run by women, such as one in Mexico for the rural manufacture of a small water pump. In northeast Thailand, UNIFEM helped fund a local lender by extending credit for small silk-weaving businesses; thus the development fund provided an economic alternative to women who otherwise might have become part of Thailand's sex trade.

Virtually all the UN specialized agencies initiated programs for women. The World Bank established the post of adviser on women in 1977. Today, the women-in-development agenda is well integrated into the UN's programs. That integration has been bolstered by the activities of women's groups in the 1990s and by global conferences on the environment, population, human rights, social development, and, of course, women. Women's NGOs pushed for language in the conference declarations and programs of action affirming the centrality of women's roles in sustainable development;[20] for example, the 1994 Cairo Conference on Population and Development declared that the key to population growth and economic development lies in the empowerment of women through education and economic opportunity. It enshrined a new concept of population that gives women more control over their lives by promoting education for girls, a range of choices for family planning and health care, and as greater involvement of women in development planning.

A major attitudinal shift within the UN system now links the social status and political empowerment of women to poverty, violence, the environment, sustainable development, and population control. The Platform of Action unanimously approved by the 1995 Fourth World Conference on Women in Beijing reaffirmed this connection by calling for the "empowerment of all women" through ensuring "women's equal access to economic resources including land, credit, science and technology, vocational training, information, communication, and markets."[21] It, in turn, has been reiterated at the "Beijing Plus Five" and "Beijing Plus Ten" meetings in 2000 and 2005. Furthermore, the Millennium Development Goals set in 2000 specifically call for promoting gender equality and empowering women through promoting women's education and improving the health status of women and children.

The issue of women's roles in development illustrates the ways in which NGOs, UN-sponsored global conferences, and UN studies reshaped thinking about development and had an impact throughout the UN system, including the World Bank and IMF. It also influenced the human-development-centered thinking that emerged in the 1990s, as we shall see shortly. A similar, yet somewhat different, process and dynamics have brought the concept of **sustainable development** to the fore in the UN and on the global agenda.

Reconceptualizing Development: Sustainability

The UN has been at the forefront in the evolution of thinking about development. By the mid-1960s, critics began to question development defined in terms of overall economic growth and the increasing use of resources and technology. There was growing realization that economic development defined narrowly might be accompanied by unintended and unanticipated side effects, including an increasing gap between the rich and the poor, the marginalization of some groups, environmental degradation, and an inability to sustain the level of economic growth into the future.

In 1980, the UN General Assembly adopted the World Conservation Strategy advocating the new but poorly defined concept of sustainable development. That began a reorientation of development. In 1983, the UN General Assembly established the World Commission on Environment and Development (WCED), headed by Prime Minister Gro Harlem Brundtland of Norway and composed of eminent persons from many parts of the world. WCED's task was to formulate a new development approach around the concept of sustainable development. This approach proved politically astute because it recognized that dealing with environmental problems would be ineffectual if global poverty and economic inequalities were not addressed. The 1987 Brundtland Commission Report *(Our Common Future)* called for "development that meets the needs of the present without compromising the ability of future generations to meet their own needs."[22] It sought to balance ecological concerns with the economic growth necessary to reduce poverty. (That idea and its implementation are examined further in chapter 7.) The evolution of the idea of sustainable development, however, points again to the major role that the UN has had in the promotion of ideas.

The Role of MNCs in Development: Obstacle or Aid?

Multinational corporations are actors organized to conduct for-profit business transactions and operations across the borders of three or more states. Although they take many different forms, they all have the ability to invest capital and thus to create jobs. In liberal economic thinking, they are engines of economic development. Yet critics of the liberal economic model have long been dissatisfied with the role multinational corporations play in economic affairs, believing that they occupy a position of preeminence without being subject to international or national controls. Their goal has been to develop ways of regulating MNCs' activities; and, in fact, such regulation was a goal of the NIEO described above.

The UN Commission on Transnational Corporations was established in 1974 and spearheaded the first effort ever to develop information systems about MNCs to help countries negotiate national-level restrictions. It also attempted to draft an international code of conduct to govern the behavior of MNCs more broadly. Some of the specialized agencies also tried to regulate the behavior of MNCs. For example, the World Health Organization sought to limit the marketing of infant formula in developing countries by MNCs. After a long battle, Nestlé Corp., one of those targeted, bowed to pressures to limit its marketing practices. In this and other campaigns against MNCs, NGOs have frequently been lead actors. In recent years, they have targeted sweatshops and child labor, the scuttling of a North Sea oil rig, and cutting of tropical rain forests.

By the mid-1980s, economic liberalism had triumphed, and privatization and deregulation became part of the conditions imposed by the World Bank and IMF under strong U.S. influence. The pressure on MNCs continued, however. Many major corporations implemented their own codes of conduct and monitoring mechanisms. Under pressure from NGO-led grassroots campaigns, these codes of conduct have had to be continually strengthened. Yet, corporations have made concessions that would have been unthinkable in the past. As the *Economist* noted in 1995, "a multinational's failure to look like a good global citizen is increasingly expensive in a world where consumers and pressure groups can be quickly mobilized behind a cause."[23] The search for an international **code of conduct** officially terminated when the Commission on Transnational Corporations was eliminated in 1994, despite the opposition of developing countries. What remained of its work was integrated into UNCTAD.

With the growth of private investment, especially in Asia, as a source of development capital, the mandate changed dramatically: to provide governments interested in attracting foreign investment with the support to do so. Indeed, the UNDP, in collaboration with bilateral donors, began publishing investment guides. This break from the historical approach to MNCs was solidified officially in 1999 when Secretary-General Kofi Annan proposed a global compact at the World Economic Forum in Davos, Switzerland. He hoped to join the UN, relevant UN agencies, research centers, corporations, environmental groups, human rights groups, and labor NGOs (represented by the International Confederation of Free Trade Unions) into a partnership committed to providing the social foundations of a sustainable global economy, encouraging private sector investment in LDCs and promoting good corporate practices.

The **Global Compact** on Corporate Responsibility revolves around nine principles that participating companies have agreed to uphold. These include adherence to international human rights law, rejection of child and forced labor, abolition of discrimination in employment, and promotion of greater environmental responsibility. Several of these principles reflect earlier work of both the ILO and the Office of the High Commissioner for Human Rights. More than 2,000 companies had signed the Compact by 2004, including Petro-Canada, Nokia, Lufthansa, Bayer, Volkswagen, Nike, and Dupont. With this network, MNCs and others learn how other companies have addressed the principles and dialog on best practices. The Global Compact is clearly "an experiment in devising fundamentally new forms of global governance."[24]

The approach is not without its critics. Those individuals and groups point to the fact that some companies have joined that previously opposed standard-setting. Perhaps, they contend, joining is nothing more than a publicity ploy. Others, including many economists, doubt the effectiveness of voluntary mechanisms. Still others point to the fact that the approach does not include any remedies for MNC policies that run counter to the principles.

The Global Compact has not eliminated other efforts to regulate MNCs. UNCTAD still addresses issues of restrictive business practices. WHO has targeted specific MNCs and their marketing practices, most notably the tobacco companies. Coupled with a campaign publicizing the adverse health effects of smoking, the WHO-drafted Framework Convention on Tobacco Control came into effect in 2004. The treaty calls for states to ban advertising tobacco products, set requirements on packaging, and implement broader liability for manufacturers. Pharmaceutical companies, too, have been targeted for various practices, including, most recently, for their failure to provide inexpensive antiretroviral drugs for HIV/AIDS to developing countries suffering a high incidence of the disease. (This issue is addressed in chapter 7.) Yet, in general, there has been a change. The UN seeks to work with MNCs, but still hold them accountable for various practices.

The policy debates illustrate the different roles the UN has played. One group of scholars noted:

> The UN has played an important role as a critic of some of the policies propagated by the international financial organizations and the orthodox economists. The UN critique of stabilization and adjustment policies contributed to growing skepticism about their effectiveness. On the debt issue, UN ideas were largely ignored but have found favor in recent years. On the consequences of globalization, the validity of the more balanced and comprehensive analyses done by the UN agencies is gaining increasing acceptance.[25]

Since the mid-1990s, with greater focus on poverty alleviation, the UN has tried to soften the impact on those most adversely affected by globalization and develop ideas to make development sustainable for the most vulnerable population. The IMF, World Bank, and UN all endorsed the Millennium Declaration, "A Better

World for All," in 2000, setting quantitative objectives for reducing poverty. These ideas have come together in the Millennium Development Goals.

Tackling Poverty and Global Inequality: Millennium Development Goals

The Millennium Declaration adopted at the UN-sponsored Millennium Summit in September 2001 incorporated the set of eight Millennium Development Goals. These represent a conceptual convergence, or what the *Human Development Report 2003* calls a "compact among nations," about reducing poverty and promoting sustainable human development in response to globalization. The mutually reinforcing and intertwined MDGs include halving world poverty and hunger by 2015, reducing infant mortality by two-thirds, and achieving universal primary education. The eighth goal deals with partnerships among UN agencies, governments, civil society organizations, and the private sector as a means to achieving the other seven goals. (See box 5.1 for the complete list.) The goals are disaggregated into eighteen specific targets, specific time frames, and forty-eight performance indicators with an elaborate implementation plan involving ten global task forces, MDG report cards for each developing country, regular monitoring, and a public information campaign to keep pressure on governments and international agencies.

To a large degree, the MDGs are a product of the global conferences in the 1990s. Those conferences stimulated research, introduced new ideas and approaches, and energized civil society on human development issues. They also highlighted the interrelated nature of many development issues such as population, children, food, women, the environment, and human settlements. Consensus on the need for new forms of cooperation and partnerships does not guarantee success of the effort.

One test, however, is whether new resources are forthcoming to support the MDG initiative. At the March 2002 International Conference on Finance for Development in Monterrey, Mexico, the United States announced a "new compact for development" to increase core assistance to less developed countries over a three-year period by 50 percent, a $5 billion annual increase in U.S. bilateral aid. The EU pledged to add $7–8 billion in aid. Funds are to be placed in the new Millennium Challenge Account and used to stimulate economic growth and reduce poverty in selected states that adopt "sound policies." The latter include good governance (stopping corruption, supporting human rights, and rule of law); health and education of the citizenry; and economic policies promoting private enterprise, free trade, and entrepreneurship. Countries must compete for the grants (not loans), according to how well they meet the above criteria. Winners are able to join in partnerships for development involving private-sector firms, foundations, international and local NGOs, and as states and local jurisdictions. The underlying idea behind the initiative is that only countries with good governance will be able to at-

---

BOX 5.1   The Millennium Development Goals and Targets for 2015

Goal 1: Eradicate extreme poverty and hunger
Halve the proportion of people living on less than one dollar a day and those who suffer from hunger.

Goal 2: Achieve universal primary education
Ensure that all boys and girls complete primary school.

Goal 3: Promote gender equality and empower women
Eliminate gender disparities in primary and secondary education preferably by 2005, and at all levels by 2015.

Goal 4: Reduce child mortality
Reduce by two-thirds the mortality rate among children under five.

Goal 5: Improve maternal health
Reduce by three-quarters the ratio of women dying in childbirth.

Goal 6: Combat HIV/AIDS, malaria, and other diseases
Halt and begin to reverse the spread of HIV/AIDS and the incidence of malaria and other major diseases.

Goal 7: Ensure environmental sustainability
Integrate the principles of sustainable development into country policies and programs and reverse the loss of environmental resources.

Reduce by half the proportion of people without access to safe drinking water.

By 2020 achieve significant improvement in the lives of at least 100 million slum dwellers.

Goal 8: Develop a Global Partnership for Development
Develop further an open trading and financial system that includes a commitment to good governance, development, and poverty reduction, nationally and internationally.

Address the special needs of least-developed, landlocked, and small-island developing states.

Deal comprehensively with developing countries' debt problems.

---

tract private investors and be likely to be successful; therefore those countries should be rewarded.

As a result, countries have been encouraged to detail specific plans on how to reduce poverty in affected populations through the development of Poverty Reduction Strategy Papers. This is viewed as mandatory before further development aid is given or debt renegotiated or eliminated. These papers are developed in collaboration with

UNDP, UNICEF, and WFP, all UN programs and agencies with a strong presence and capacity at the country level. And, for the first time, UN agencies have reported information on governance in published reports on governmental corruption. This represents a sea change in attitude because the UN was previously reluctant to criticize member states. With respect to the MDGs, "the UN had returned once again to make distinct and pioneering contributions," noted a group of scholars. "It did so through the global conferences, its new vitality in promoting human rights, the paradigm of human development, and organizing an unprecedented millennium consensus in defining global goals for poverty reduction and mobilizing commitments in support of those goals."[26] What is also most remarkable about the MDGs, Ruggie notes, is that "[i]t is unprecedented for the UN and its agencies, let alone also the Bretton Woods institutions, to align their operational activities behind a unifying substantive framework."[27]

Many conceptual questions have arisen about this initiative. What criteria will be used to measure governance performance? How much does corruption have to be curbed before a state qualifies? To what extent will other assistance money be tied to the same criteria? How open does a state's trading system have to be? What level of cooperation has to exist between the governments, the private sector, and NGOs? These questions have no absolute answer.

Most problematic are the empirical realities; articulating goals is easier than ensuring that policies meet the goals. Africa will have the most difficulty meeting those goals. That continent would have to attain 7 percent average annual growth, doubling the current average. Thirty-two African countries remain in the most-heavily-indebted category, and debt cancellation has been approved for only a few. An assessment of the African predicament one-third of the way toward 2015 shows that the percentage of people whose income is less than $1 a day has risen in Africa, but the percentage in other developing countries has declined. Although the percentage of girls in school has increased significantly, the 2005 goals were not met. Maternal health status remains unclear because of the paucity of reliable data. HIV prevalence has stabilized in Africa, but remains the highest in the world. The number of Africans having access to drinking water has grown, but not at a sufficient rate to meet the 2015 goals. And although IGO-UN partnerships for development have proliferated, substantial remunerative partnerships with the private sector lag far behind.[28] The outlook for achieving the MDG in Africa is not good. On the donor side, overall aid to Africa has been increasing, as has Africa's share of overall foreign aid, both reversing a long downward trend. This reflects in part the progress noted in other regions. Yet the picture is not unequivocal. Donor countries can report disbursement of aid when it is, in fact, debt forgiveness, and there are no new infusions of aid. Most striking is that much of the aid did not go to the priority sectors targeted in the MDG, although that is not true for UN development assistance.[29]

LESSONS LEARNED

The United Nations and its specialized agencies have struggled to be relevant to the major economic issues of the day, including the imperative for economic development. Likewise, the Bretton Woods institutions, the GATT/WTO, and developed countries have been involved in efforts to find an appropriate and effective approach to balancing economic growth and economic equity. The UN was frequently in the forefront of developing new ideas and thinking about economic development, especially in the early years and more recently. It provided forums in several bodies for policy debates. At times, however, the Bretton Woods institutions, with their large resources and the backing of major donors, controlled the agenda of international economic relations, and the UN played the role of critic, constructive to some and obstructionist to others. There has been a move toward convergence with the MDGs, but what lessons have been learned along the way?

First, the UN, as well as the rest of the development community, has learned that international involvement in countries should be based on individual countries' needs. Thus, for example, where countries have experienced lengthy periods of civil conflict, as in Namibia, Cambodia, and Mozambique, the UN's development cooperation activities are part of its wider engagement in political and humanitarian areas. The establishment of the Peacebuilding Commission is designed to continue engagement after conflict has ended. In other situations, the UN's activities are more limited to technical assistance. In countries in transition from socialist economies in the 1990s, more attention was paid to formalizing accountability and increasing transparency, as well as providing technical assistance for banking reforms and formulating property laws. One strategy does not fit all.

Second, the value of coordinating efforts at the grassroots has been recognized. To overcome what was often a fragmented approach by various UN programs and agencies, UNDP now seeks to play a coordinating role within each recipient country. The move to establish a UN House, where the individual agencies and UNDP are located, symbolizes such cooperation. In the small Central Asian republic of Kyrgyzstan, for example, the UN House provides a focal point for UNDP, UN Volunteers, UNHCR, UNICEF, and UNFPA, located in an accessible building on the main street in the capital. The UNDP resident director in Vietnam is responsible for coordinating the work of more than twenty UN agencies as well as joint projects with bilateral donors. Another strategy involves UNDP and World Bank–sponsored international donor conferences to coordinate aid with government needs.

Third, at the substantive level, the UN has incorporated the liberal economic approach, the necessity of market-opening steps for expanding people's choices and ability to help themselves in a sustainable way. Thus, UNDP works with other donors and local officials to develop manuals for countries to use to attract foreign investment. As part of that investment strategy, UNDP conducts surveys of what people in different countries want.

Fourth, almost sixty years of UN development cooperation have shown that poverty is not reduced by general development and economic growth alone. Bilateral and multilateral aid donors must work with the nonstate sector, including foreign direct investors, to promote poverty reduction and with the government to develop capacity for good governance. UNDP has learned also that "the value of educating and training many individuals will remain limited unless the overall policy and institutional environment within which these individuals live and work," and the capacity of the country as a whole, is strengthened.[30] Hence, the UN and other development institutions are now more likely to critique government policies. Indeed, in 2000, UNDP commissioned a study in Kyrgyzstan on corruption in various institutions.[31] This represents a broader view of development, one which potentially infringes on state sovereignty.

Fifth, development is no longer seen as unidimensional. The concept of sustainable development has been firmly established so that development means attention to economic distribution, gender equity, and environmental concerns.

Although lessons have been learned, implementation still presents difficulties. Programs have been initiated, as was noted more than twenty-five years ago, but "legislative provisions are not always matched by adequate enforcement measures and machinery."[32] Action has not always followed rhetoric. The global conferences of the 1990s all concluded with action programs and subsequent special sessions of the General Assembly, and other meetings have reviewed progress. The MDGs have elucidated another set of goals and targets. Financial and human resources, follow-through by national policymakers, and commitment by governments and the UN are all essential if those goals are to be met.

THE PERSISTENT DILEMMAS

Dilemma 1: Expanding Needs Versus the UN's Limited Capacity

The UN has been an important advocate for the international economic issues that have proliferated in this era of globalization. It has shaped thinking about the requirements for development, introduced new issues to the international agenda, facilitated the mobilization of various constituencies, particularly through the global conferences of the 1970s and 1990s, and provided various institutional responses. The capacity of the UN, the specialized agencies, and the Bretton Woods institutions to respond to the UN Charter's broad mandate for economic and social cooperation has developed in fits and spurts, often in an ad hoc manner. New programs and agencies have created a largely unmanageable complex of organizations. With such proliferation inevitably come duplication, contradictory goals, and confusion for donors and recipients alike. Small wonder that coordination has long been an issue for UN economic and social activities and that ECOSOC has never been up to the task.

The main question for the twenty-first century is foreshadowed by Secretary-General Kofi Annan in the opening quotation of this chapter: Is the UN suited to meet these challenges? Can a decentralized, often redundant system become more cohesive? (We return to this issue in chapter 8 when we look at proposed reforms.)

Dilemma 2: The Persistence of and Challenges to Sovereignty

Efforts by UN system institutions to address economic issues and developmental issues increasingly confront the dilemma of respecting state sovereignty versus intervention in the domestic affairs of states. IMF and World Bank conditionality requires that states adjust their economic and fiscal policies in return for assistance. Indeed, the IMF's power to shape the domestic economic policies of countries receiving aid borders on supranational authority and has been soundly criticized as such. Although the UN has been critical of specific policies and has sometimes depended on state prerogatives, UN programs, too, increasingly intrude into areas traditionally reserved for the state, pushing governments to accept a particular economic philosophy and condemning corruption among state officials. Providing technical assistance on issues such as creating a legal system, often with a view about how that system should be constructed, deeply impinges on an area traditionally reserved for states. Coupling economic assistance with calls for reforms of governance and critiquing sitting governments threatens state sovereignty. This is a trend that is likely to continue in the future. Because of that, the space between the international and the domestic will continue to be a contested one, and the boundary between the two less clearly delineated.

Dilemma 3: The Need for Leadership
Versus the Dominance of the United States

Unlike security issues, where the United States is the undisputed dominant power, economic power is more dispersed. Material resources count, but so do intellectual leadership and the strength of numbers in international economic relations. Japan, the European Union, India, Brazil, and emergent China are all economic powers whose involvement is critical for the success of trade negotiations, for example. If the Millennium Development Goals are to be achieved, financial and technical resources as well as leadership and coordination from many quarters will be required. The United States has been notably lukewarm on the MDGs, and its preoccupation with the war on terrorism and Iraq make it unlikely to be a prime mover against poverty. Others have to take up the slack. Several G-7 leaders, including Prime Minister Tony Blair of Great Britain, have been at the forefront; supporting them has been Secretary-General Kofi Annan. These voices for tackling poverty and global inequality have to be followed by financial commitments, however, if any of the ambitious targets are to be met.

For meaningful change to occur, successful leadership also needs broad-based participation by people and grassroots organizations in decisionmaking, as well as implementation, at the lowest possible levels. Hence, there is greater recognition of the importance of civil society and of NGOs in the institutions of the UN system. Implicitly and, increasingly, explicitly, development has also been linked to human rights, as we see in chapter 6.

NOTES

1. Robert L. Heilbroner, *Marxism: For and Against* (New York: Norton, 1980).

2. For early illustrations of the Latin American dependency approach, see Teotonio Dos Santos, "The Structure of Dependence," *American Economic Review* 60, no. 5 (1970): 235–246, and Celso Furtado, *Development and Underdevelopment: A Structural View of the Problems of Developed and Underdeveloped Countries* (Berkeley and Los Angeles: University of California Press, 1964).

3. Richard Jolly et al., *UN Contributions to Development Thinking and Practice* (Bloomington, Ind.: Indiana University Press, 2004), 69. This volume is invaluable for understanding the evolution of development thinking and the UN's contributions.

4. Ibid., 185.

5. Ibid., 191.

6. Ibid., 288–289.

7. General Assembly Resolution 1219 (XII), 17 December 1957.

8. For an extended discussion of the debate over the UN fund, see Jolly et al., *UN Contributions to Development Thinking and Practice,* 66–83.

9. United Nations, *The World's Women: Trends and Statistics 1970–1990* (New York: United Nations, 1991).

10. Jolly et al., *UN Contributions to Development Thinking and Practice,* 88–96.

11. See Marc Williams, *Third World Cooperation: The Group of 77 in UNCTAD* (New York: St. Martin's Press, 1991), and Craig N. Murphy, *The Emergence of the NIEO Ideology* (Boulder: Westview Press, 1984).

12. Michelle Miller-Adams, *The World Bank: New Agendas in a Changing World* (London: Routledge, 1999).

13. See Michael Goldman, *Imperial Nature: The World Bank and Struggles for Social Justice in the Age of Globalization* (New Haven: Yale University Press, 2005); Michel Chossudovsky, *The Globalisation of Poverty: Impacts of IMF and World Bank Reforms* (London: Zed Books, 1997); John Walton and David Seddon, *Free Markets and Food Riots: The Politics of Global Adjustment* (Oxford: Blackwell, 1994).

14. Joseph E. Stiglitz, *Globalizaton and Its Discontents* (New York: W. W. Norton, 2002); William Easterly, *The Elusive Quest for Growth: Economists' Adventures and Misadventures in the Tropics* (Cambridge, Mass.: MIT Press, 2001).

15. Raymond F. Hopkins, "International Food Organizations and the United States: Drifting Leadership and Diverging Interests," in *The United States and Multilateral Institutions: Patterns of Changing Instrumentality and Influence,* ed. Margaret P. Karns and Karen A. Mingst (Boston: Unwin Hyman, 1990), 180.

16. Keith Bradsher, "Trade Officials Agree to End Subsidies for Agricultural Exports," *New York Times,* December 19, 2005.

17. Data from www.johannesburgsummit.org; see also Thomas E. Ambrogi, "Goal for 2000: Unchaining Slaves of National Debt," *National Catholic Reporter* (March 26, 1999): 3–6.

18. Esther Boserup, *Women's Role in Economic Development* (London: George Allen and Unwin, 1970).

19. The first compilation of results from this statistical endeavor was published in 1991: United Nations, *The World's Women 1970–1990: Trends and Statistics.* The report represented a major collaborative undertaking by many UN bodies. The third edition was published in 2000 and a Special Report issued in 2005.

20. On the strategies of women's NGOs, see Ann Marie Clark, Elisabeth J. Friedman, and Kathryn Hochstetler, "A Comparison of NGO Participation in UN World Conferences on the Environment, Human Rights, and Women," *World Politics* 51 (October 1998): 1–35.

21. "Platform for Action," in *An Agenda for Women's Empowerment: Report of the Fourth World Conference on Women* (A/Conf.177/20). This report also contains the Beijing Declaration.

22. World Commission on Environment and Development (Brundtland Commission Report), *Our Common Future* (Oxford: Oxford University Press, 1987), 8.

23. "Multinationals and Their Morals," *Economist* 377, no. 7943 (December 2, 1995): 18.

24. John Gerard Ruggie, "The United Nations and Globalization: Patterns and Limits of Institutional Adaptation," *Global Governance* 9, no. 3 (July-September 2003): 313.

25. Jolly et al., *UN Contributions to Development Thinking and Practice,* 185.

26. Ibid., 299.

27. Ruggie, "The United Nations and Globalization," 305.

28. "Africa and the Challenge of the Millennium Development Goals," *Africa Renewal* (July 2005): 12–13.

29. Ernest Harsch, "Focusing Aid on Africa's Own Priorities," *Africa Renewal* (July 2005): 15–17.

30. UN Development Program, "UNDP in Vietnam: Some Lessons Learned in Supporting the Transition from Poverty to Prosperity," staff paper, September 1997, 18.

31. UN Development Program, *Corruption in Kyrgyzstan* (Bishkek: Center of Pubic Opinion Studies and Forecasts, 2000).

32. UN World Conference of the UN Decade for Women, "Equality, Development, and Peace," 13 August 1980 (A/CONF.94/34).

6

◄O►

Human Rights

Today's human rights violations are the causes of tomorrow's conflicts.

—**Mary Robinson, UN High Commissioner for Human Rights (1998)**

Since the end of World War II, human rights have become a major issue in world politics and "the single most magnetic political idea of the contemporary time," in the words of Zbigniew Brzezinski, the former U.S. national security adviser.[1] This trend is best explained not by realism or liberalism but by constructivism. With the spread of the idea that the protection of human rights knows no boundaries and the international community has an obligation to ensure governments guarantee internationally recognized rights, state sovereignty has been diminished. The end of **apartheid** in South Africa, the recognition that women's rights are human rights, the spread of democracy, and the emerging norm of humanitarian intervention all provide evidence of the trend. At the same time, news headlines regularly remind us that respect for human life and the political, civil, social, and economic rights of individuals and groups are often violated, whether in Uzbekistan, the Sudan, Congo, Burma, or China.

The UN has played an important role in the process of globalizing human rights. It has been central to establishing the norms, institutions, mechanisms, and activities for giving effect to this powerful idea that certain rights are universal. States have seldom been prime movers in this process, although their acceptance and support for human rights is critical. The international human rights movement—a growing network of human-rights-oriented NGOs—and dedicated individuals have been responsible for drafting much of the language of human rights conventions and for mounting transnational campaigns to promote human rights norms. The role of these groups and individuals and the processes by which they have persuaded policymakers in powerful states to adopt human rights policies demonstrate the power of ideas to reshape definitions of national interests, consistent with constructivism.[2] Before we examine the UN and other actors' roles in this process, however, let us look at the historical antecedents in the League of Nations, the International Labour Organization, and key events.

FROM THE LEAGUE OF NATIONS TO THE UNITED NATIONS

Although the League of Nations Covenant made little mention of human rights as such, it nonetheless addressed rights-related issues and set important precedents. For example, the covenant did include specific provision for the protection of minorities and, through the Mandate System, for dependent peoples in colonies of the defeated powers of World War I (Turkey and Germany). A designated victor nation would administer the territory under the league's supervision and so provide a degree of protection from abuses. This reflected the growing sentiment that territories were not to be annexed after wars; rather, the international community had responsibilities over dependent peoples, the eventual goal being self-determination.

The 1919 Paris Peace Conference also produced five agreements, known as the Minority Treaties, that required beneficiaries of the peace settlement (such as Poland, Czechoslovakia, and Greece) to provide protection to all inhabitants regardless of nationality, language, race, or religion. Similar obligations for civil and political rights were imposed on the defeated states. Minority rights became a major agenda item for the League Council, Assembly, and committees, the admission of new members being contingent on a pledge to protect minority rights; special mechanisms were established for monitoring implementation. In addition, the league established principles on assisting refugees and the Refugee Organization. This step marked the first recognition that the international community has responsibility for protecting those forced to flee their homelands because of repression or war. The league also devoted attention to women's and children's rights, as well as the rights to a minimum level of health. And, in the 1930s, the league's assembly discussed the possibility of an international human rights document, but it took no action.

The ILO's mandate to work for the improvement of workers' living conditions, health, safety, and livelihood was consistent with the concepts of economic and social rights. Between 1919 and 1939, the ILO approved sixty-seven conventions that covered such issues as hours of work, maternity protection, minimum age, and old-age insurance; in 1926, it was the first IGO to introduce a procedure for supervising the standards established. This procedure provided an important model for the UN and continues to be a key part of the international human rights regime.

The precedents established by the league and ILO influenced the drafting of the UN Charter's provisions at the end of World War II. In addition, however, the drafters were influenced by wartime Allied goals, the Holocaust, and human rights advocates. First, President Franklin D. Roosevelt's famous "Four Freedoms" speech in 1941 called for "a world founded upon four essential freedoms," and together with his vision of "the moral order," formed a normative base for the Allies in their fight against Germany and Japan.[3] The liberation of Nazi concentration camps in the closing weeks of World War II revealed the full extent of the Holocaust and the deaths of 6 million Jews, gypsies, and other "undesirables." This was a second powerful impetus for seeing human rights as an international issue that required more than talk. Peace itself seemed to rest ultimately on respect for individual rights. In addition, at the UN's founding conference in San Francisco in 1945, a broad spectrum of groups from churches to peace societies, along with delegates from various small states, pushed for the inclusion of human rights language in the Charter. Although they were more weakly worded than these advocates had hoped, seven references to human rights were scattered throughout the final document and, thus, the UN Charter placed the promotion of human rights among the central purposes of the new organization.[4]

UN CHARTER PRINCIPLES AND ORGANIZATIONAL STRUCTURES

One of the primary purposes of the UN, as set forth in Chapter I, Article 1, is international cooperation in solving various international problems, including those of a "humanitarian character," and "in promoting and encouraging respect for human rights and for fundamental freedoms for all without distinction as to race, sex, language, or religion." Articles 55(c) and 56 amplify the UN's responsibility to promote "universal respect for, and observance of, human rights and fundamental freedoms for all" and the obligation of member states to "take joint and separate action in cooperation with the Organization for the achievement of the purposes set forth in Article 55."

These provisions did not define what was meant by "human rights and fundamental freedoms," but they established that human rights were a matter of international concern and that states had assumed an as yet undefined international obligation relating to them. They also contradicted the Charter's affirmation of state sovereignty and the principle of nonintervention in the domestic affairs of states contained in Article 2(7). They provided the UN with the legal authority, however, to undertake the definition and codification of these rights. The foundation for that effort was laid by the General Assembly's passage on 10 December 1948 of the Universal Declaration of Human Rights to "serve as a common standard of achievement for all peoples of all nations."[5] Taken together, the UN

Charter and the Universal Declaration of Human Rights represented a watershed in the revolution that placed human rights at the center of world politics.

General Assembly

The General Assembly's broad mandate to discuss any issue within the scope of the UN Charter led states to use this forum to raise specific human rights issues almost from the beginning. In its first session in 1946, India and other countries introduced the issue of South Africa's treatment of its sizable Indian population; thus began the UN's longest-running human rights issue: apartheid in South Africa. Debates concerning colonial issues, and particularly the right to self-determination of colonial and dependent peoples, occupied a major share of General Assembly agendas in the 1950s and 1960s.[6] During the Cold War, some Western countries pushed issues such as forced labor under communism. Over the years, the General Assembly and almost every other UN body have been pressed by Arab states and their allies to condemn Israel's treatment of the Palestinian people in the Occupied Territories. The fifty-fifth assembly in 2000, for example, adopted more than twenty resolutions on Israeli-related issues; and then, after violent clashes in the territories, it convened in a special emergency session to adopt yet another resolution. In the late 1990s, the assembly repeatedly condemned the Taliban government in Afghanistan for its appalling human rights record. In short, the General Assembly's attention to human rights issues has reflected the majority at any given time. These debates have often spilled over into other organs and specialized agencies, leading to charges of politicization. Yet because the assembly is the primary global forum, its debates and resolutions draw attention to issues and, in naming specific states, may shame them into taking action.

The assembly's power under Article 13(1) "to conduct studies and make recommendations for the purpose of . . . assisting in the realizing of human rights and fundamental freedoms for all without distinction as to race, sex, language, or religion" has been used with respect to a variety of issues. Thus, for example, the General Assembly established the UN Decade for Women (1975–1985) and the UN Decade for Human Rights Education (1995–2005). It has approved rights-related declarations such as the 1959 Declaration on the Right of the Child; the 1967 Declaration on the Elimination of Discrimination Against Women; and the 1993 Declaration on the Elimination of Violence Against Women, which in due course may form the basis for binding international treaties, as happened with the first two of these declarations. Two of the assembly's main committees contribute to the drafting of human rights treaties: the Social, Humanitarian and Cultural (or Third) Committee and the Legal (or Sixth) Committee. In addition, the assembly receives reports from seven so-called treaty bodies established by the parties to select human rights treaties to monitor implementation (see fig. 6.1).

FIGURE 6.1 Human Rights Organizational Structure (Selected Bodies)

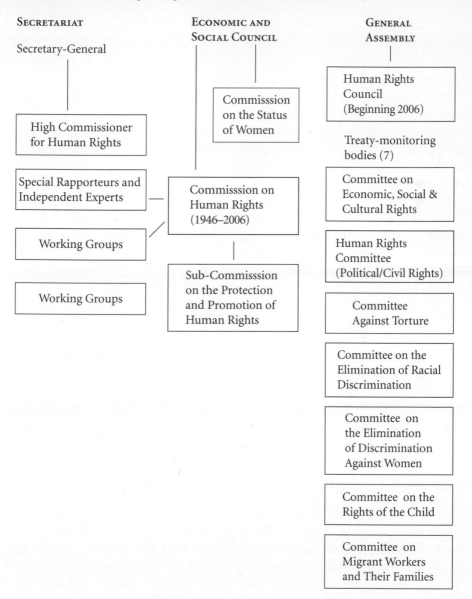

Security Council

The UN Charter left the Security Council free to define what constitutes a threat to international peace and security. Throughout the Cold War years, the council did not link security with human rights violations. Like the General Assembly, it did address issues such as the rights of colonial peoples to self-determination, of the Palestinians in the Occupied Territories, and of black majorities under apartheid in South Africa and in Southern Rhodesia because these were seen as situations that threatened international peace and security. The Cold War's end, greater emphasis on human rights issues throughout the UN system, and egregious human rights violations in various conflicts made it increasingly difficult to separate human rights abuses and threats to peace. In addition, beginning with Secretary-General Pérez de Cuéllar's 1991 report to the General Assembly, each secretary-general has played an active role in urging the Security Council to address the links between human rights and security. As discussed in chapter 4, the Security Council has repeatedly found itself faced with humanitarian crises and demands for intervention under Chapter VII. Ethnic cleansing, genocide, and other crimes against humanity led it to create ad hoc war crimes tribunals for the former Yugoslavia, Rwanda, and Sierra Leone. Peacebuilding operations often needed to address human rights protection.

By the end of the 1990s, the Security Council had definitely embraced human rights and was routinely issuing declarations on issues ranging from child soldiers to the role of women in promoting international peace and stability. Human rights activities have also been incorporated into the mandates for several peacekeeping operations. In late 2005, the council took the further step of agreeing to hear a report from Secretary-General Kofi Annan on human rights violations in Myanmar—a step short of putting the issue formally on the council's agenda, but nonetheless significant.

ECOSOC

The Economic and Social Council was given authority under Article 62 to conduct studies, issue reports, and make recommendations "for the purpose of promoting respect for, and observance of, human rights and fundamental freedoms for all." It has used this authority to address a number of issues such as genocide, the protection of minorities, and, with the ILO, the prevention of forced labor. In addition, Article 68 gave ECOSOC the specific mandate of setting up commissions in the area of human rights, and in 1946 and 1947 it established the Commission on Human Rights, the Commission on the Status of Women, and the Sub-Commission on Prevention of Discrimination and Protection of Minorities (renamed the Sub-Commission on the Protection and Promotion of Human Rights in 1999). These commissions have borne the major responsibility for human rights activities in the UN system. Their work has included conducting studies and issuing reports.

The Commission on Human Rights and Sub-Commission on the Protection and Promotion of Human Rights.   These commissions have been described as "the political cornerstones of the United Nations human rights system."[7] The commission has borne primary responsibility for drafting and negotiating the major documents that elaborate and define human rights norms, including the Universal Declaration on Human Rights, the two international human rights covenants, and treaties on a range of issues from torture to the rights of the child and the rights of migrant workers. Although the UN received thousands of complaints of human rights violations in its early years, ECOSOC denied the Commission on Human Rights the right to review these complaints until 1970, and then only confidentially. States were reluctant to have their human rights records scrutinized. Gradually the commission's responsibilities expanded to include more direct procedures for investigating gross violations as well as individual complaints (through what are known as 1235 and 1503 procedures). The fifty-three member states of the commission, chosen by ECOSOC in accordance with a formula for geographical equity, met annually to hear state complaints and individual petitions and to adopt resolutions on major themes such as racism and violations of human rights in Israeli-occupied Arab territories. The annual meeting drew up to 3,000 delegates from states with seats on the commission, as well as observer states and NGOs.

The commission has often drawn fire for being too political. Critics charged that some countries were singled out for human rights abuses, but others equally as complicit were not scrutinized. Widespread public attention was drawn to the commission in 2001 when the United States lost its seat for the first time. Those who voted against the United States, including some of its allies, did so because of perceived U.S. lack of support for the UN, its continued support of Israel, and its efforts to single out China and Cuba for their human rights abuses. The commission was criticized in recent years when some well-known human rights abusers such as the Sudan, Zimbabwe, Saudi Arabia, Pakistan, Cuba, and Nepal were elected members. It drew still further adverse publicity in 2002 when Libya was elected chair. To restore credibility, the General Assembly approved a proposal in 2006 to replace the commission with a permanent Human Rights Council reporting to the assembly. (This reform is discussed further in chapter 8.)

The Sub-Commission on the Promotion and Protection of Human Rights is much less political because its twenty-six members are chosen for their expertise rather than national affiliation. The sub-commission also meets annually, but its schedule is different from the commission's, and draws many NGOs with ECOSOC consultative status, observer states, and other UN agencies. Its primary functions include studies and recommendations to prevent discrimination and to protect racial, national, religious, and linguistic minorities.

The commission and sub-commission have both created various subsidiary bodies. These include thematic working groups, such as on arbitrary detention or involuntary disappearances, and special rapporteurs charged with investigating a given country (e.g., Iraq, Sudan, and the former Yugoslavia) or a particular problem such as torture or violence against women.

Secretariat: The High Commissioner for Human Rights

An important addition to the UN organizational structure relating to human rights is the Office of the High Commissioner for Human Rights (OHCHR), established in 1993. It provides a visible international advocate for human rights in the same way that the UN High Commissioner for Refugees focuses international attention on that problem. The office is responsible for promotion and coordination, for mainstreaming human rights into the UN system, and for furnishing information to relevant UN bodies. Increasingly, OHCHR is assuming an operational role, providing technical assistance to countries in the form of training courses for judges and prison officials, electoral assistance, and advisory services on constitutional and legislative reform, among other things.[8] With field offices in many countries, OHCHR is able not only to help strengthen domestic institutions but also to promote compliance with international human rights standards and to report directly to the high commissioner on abuses. The high commissioner serves on all four executive committees in the UN Secretariat because of the cross-cutting nature of human rights issues, yet the office is handicapped by its small budget allocation (just 2 percent of the total UN budget). Each year, the high commissioner has had to appeal for voluntary contributions so that OHCHR can perform its tasks.

Of the first three commissioners, the third, Mary Robinson, the former president of Ireland, had sufficient longevity (1997–2002) and strength to be an effective and vocal spokesperson. The fourth, Louise Arbour, the former member of Canada's Supreme Court and chief prosecutor in the international criminal tribunals for the former Yugoslavia and Rwanda, said in her opening briefing in 2004, "There are very few burning issues today that don't have a human rights component."[9] Her reputation for taking on difficult challenges suggests that OHCHR has again found a strong advocate.

Just as we have seen for economic issues in Chapter 5, human rights issues have expanded both conceptually and organizationally within the United Nations. The UN's role initially focused on setting standards—defining and elaborating what constitute the internationally protected rights of individuals. It has expanded to include monitoring activities, promoting respect for human rights norms, and, to a limited degree, enforcement.

PHOTO 6.1   Eleanor Roosevelt holds the Universal Declaration of Human Rights, November 1949. *UN Photo 23783.*

THE ROLE OF THE UN IN HUMAN RIGHTS

Defining Human Rights: Setting Standards and Norms

The UN's role in setting human rights standards began with the General Assembly's unanimous approval of the Universal Declaration of Human Rights on 9 December 1948 and the passage one day earlier of the Convention on the Prevention and Punishment of the Crime of Genocide. Under the tireless leadership of Eleanor Roosevelt, the wife of the late President Franklin D. Roosevelt and chair of the UN Commission on Human Rights, these documents articulated a far-reaching human rights agenda for the UN.

The Universal Declaration, called by some the most important document of the twentieth century,[10] drew on ideas dating from the French and American Revolutions and earlier bills of rights as well as principles of natural rights. Among its catalog of thirty principles, it elucidated rights critical for the exercise of political freedom, rights essential for the preservation of a civil society, and the social and economic rights of individuals. The declaration listed those claims as a first step toward the articulation of international human rights standards. Since the declaration was only a General Assembly resolution, the expectation was that these rights would be set forth in a covenant (or treaty) that would bind states to respect them.

Three Generations of Rights

Because human rights norms have evolved from diverse traditions and over time, it is customary to refer to three generations of rights. So-called **first-generation human rights** are those associated with political and civil rights. They were the first rights to be incorporated into national constitutions and are "negative rights" in that they are intended to block government authorities from interfering with private individuals in civil society. They are linked to Western liberalism and include the right to free speech, freedom of religion, a free press, and the right to congregate at will. In contrast, **second-generation human rights** build upon the socialist view that emphasizes economic and social rights such as the right to employment, to health care, and to social security. Sometimes referred to as "positive rights," these are the basic material benefits that the state must provide to individuals. The designation "second-generation" stems from the association of these benefits with the twentieth-century idea of governments' responsibility for social welfare. The Universal Declaration incorporated both sets of rights, but the conflict between Western and socialist views blocked conclusion of a single treaty that would define them further. Two covenants were ultimately drafted to surmount the political and ideological impasse.

The International Covenant on Economic, Social, and Cultural Rights and the International Covenant on Civil and Political Rights were both approved by the General Assembly in 1966 and became operative in 1976 following the necessary number of ratifications to bring them into force. By 2005, more than 150 countries were parties to both covenants, not including the United States, which has yet to ratify the Covenant on Economic, Social, and Cultural Rights. The two covenants together with the Universal Declaration are often referred to as the **International Bill of Rights.**

Both prior to and following the approval of the covenants, the UN has brought into being an array of other human rights treaties that systematically articulate a variety of first- and second-generation rights. Some of these evolved from the work of the specialized UN agencies, including the ILO; most were drafted by the Commission on Human Rights. Subjects include women, slavery and forced labor, torture, refugees, racial discrimination, and children. A list of selected UN human rights conventions is found in table 6.1.

Third-generation human rights center on the idea that certain groups, such as minorities, indigenous peoples, colonial peoples, women, and children, have collective rights such as self-determination, the protection of distinctive cultures, and economic and social development. In addition, there have been moves to recognize collective rights to a safe environment, to peace, to democracy, and to development. The latter, for example, was endorsed by the 1993 World Conference on Human Rights in Vienna.

Disagreements about the relative priority of the three generations of rights are a primary reason for the lack of political will for the enforcement of international hu-

TABLE 6.1   Selected UN Human Rights Conventions

Convention (grouped by subject)	Year Opened for Ratification	Year Entered Into Force	Number of Ratifications, Accessions, Acceptances (2006)
General Human Rights			
International Covenant on Civil and Political Rights	1966	1976	156
International Covenant on Economic, Social, and Cultural Rights (private petition)	1966	1976	153
Racial Discrimination			
International Convention on the Elimination of All Forms of Racial Discrimination	1966	1969	70
International Convention on the Suppression and Punishment of the Crime of Apartheid	1973	1976	106
Rights of Women			
Convention on the Political Rights of Women	1952	1954	111
Convention on the Elimination of All Forms of Discrimination Against Women	1979	1981	182
Slavery and Slave-Like Practices			
Slavery Convention of 1926, as amended in 1953	1953	1955	95
Supplementary Convention on the Abolition of Slavery, the Slave Trade, and Institutions and Practices Similar to Slavery	1956	1957	119
Convention for the Suppression of the Traffic in Persons and Exploitation of the Prostitution of Others	1950	1951	74
Refugees and Stateless Persons			
Convention Relating to the Status of Refugees	1951	1954	142
Protocol Relating to the Status of Refugees	1967	1967	142

(continues)

TABLE 6.1   Selected UN Human Rights Conventions *(continued)*

Convention (grouped by subject)	Year Opened for Ratification	Year Entered Into Force	Number of Ratifications, Accessions, Acceptances (2006)
Rights of Children			
Convention on the Rights of the Child	1989	1990	192
ILO Convention (No. 182) Concerning the Prohibition and Immediate Action for the Elimination of the Worst Forms of Child Labour	1999	2000	160
Optional Protocol to the Convention on the Rights of the Child on the Involvement of Children in Armed Conflicts	2000	2002	107
Optional Protocol to the Convention on the Rights of the Child on the Sale of Children, Child Prostitution and Child Pornography	2000	2002	106
Other			
Convention on the Prevention and Punishment of the Crime of Genocide	1948	1951	138
Convention Against Torture and Other Cruel, Inhuman or Degrading Treatment or Punishment	1984	1987	141
ILO Convention (No. 169) Concerning Indigenous and Tribal Peoples in Independent Countries	1989	1991	17
Convention on the Protection of the Rights of All Migrant Workers and Members of Their Families	1990	2003	34

SOURCES: International Labour Organization, *ILOLEX: Database of International Labour Standards*, http://www.ilo.org/ilolex/english/convdisp1.htm. UNCHR *Treaty Body Database*, http://www.unhchr.ch/tbs/doc.nsf.

man rights. In addition, just as the West has dominated international economic relations, it has tried to dominate the setting of standards for human rights. Thus, the strongest international and regional human rights mechanisms protect civil and political rights, but the other two generations have received less attention. It is also far more difficult to establish standards of compliance for economic and social rights and politically far more difficult to secure agreement on third-generation rights.

The Universality of Human Rights Versus Cultural Relativism

Are all human rights truly universal, that is, applicable to all peoples, in all states, religions, and cultures? The debate over **universal rights** versus **cultural relativism** has been a perennial one. In the 1990s, a number of Asian states argued that the West was interfering in their internal affairs with its own definition of human rights because the principles in the Universal Declaration represented Western values. Yet Amartya Sen, an Indian economist and winner of the 1998 Nobel Prize in Economics, surveyed the diverse Asian cultural and religious traditions from Confucianism to Buddhism and found no "grand dichotomy."[11] The legal scholar and activist Abdullahi An-Na'im, however, noted that "detailed and credible knowledge of local culture is essential for the effective promotion and protection of human rights in any society."[12]

Much of the debate was political and took place between authoritarian states concerned about human rights intervention in their domestic affairs and Western democratic states eager to promote political change. The debate over universality versus cultural relativism is particularly sensitive, however, with respect to issues of religion, culture, women's status, the protection of children, family planning, divorce, and practices such as female circumcision.

The Final Declaration and Programme of Action of the Vienna World Conference on Human Rights, issued on 24 June 1993, stated: "All human rights are universal, indivisible and interdependent and interrelated." Regional arrangements, the declaration stated, "should reinforce universal human rights standards, as contained in international human rights instruments, and their protection." Secretary-General Kofi Annan more recently observed, "It was never the people who complained of the universality of human rights, nor did the people consider human rights as a Western or Northern imposition. It was often their leaders who did so."[13]

Articulation of standards is not enough, however, to ensure the observance of human rights. Those rights have to be effective in national settings where states are not only the creators of human rights norms but also the primary violators. The UN has moved in bits and pieces from articulating norms to monitoring, promoting, and enforcing the standards.[14]

From Articulating Human Rights Norms to Monitoring

The first period of UN involvement in human rights from 1948 to 1968 focused on setting human rights standards. Monitoring the implementation of those standards requires procedures for receiving complaints of violations from affected individuals or interested groups as well as reports of state practice. It may also be accompanied by the power to comment on reports, make recommendations to states, appoint working groups or special rapporteurs, and vote on resolutions of condemnation. Publicity and public "shaming" are key tools of multilateral monitoring of state compliance.

As noted earlier, the ILO was the first international organization to establish procedures for monitoring human rights within states—in this instance, workers' rights. In 1926, the ILO instituted the system of annual meetings of the Committee of Experts to examine state reports on treaty implementation that continues today. When problems are found, the committee may seek further explanation or call for a change in state policies. The tripartite structure of representation (government, labor, and management) in the ILO facilitates this monitoring by making it easier to criticize state (governmental) practices.

With only governments represented in the UN and on the former Commission on Human Rights and the new Human Rights Council, however, monitoring is much more problematic than standard setting. Nevertheless, developments in the 1970s outside of the UN provided major impetus for the further evolution of international human rights protection. First, the number of human rights NGOs increased dramatically; they emerged as a powerful political force that gathered and publicized information on human rights violations in many countries and pressed for action by governments, the UN, and regional organizations. Second, events in several parts of the world fueled activists' efforts. Among these were the repressive military regimes that came to power in Chile and Argentina and launched brutal reigns of terror; apartheid's deepening repressiveness in South Africa; and the 1975 Helsinki Accords between the Soviet Union, Eastern European countries, Western Europe, and the United States, which opened the Communist countries to scrutiny and pressure for political liberalization. Third, several countries, including the United States, introduced human rights into their foreign policies in the 1970s. President Jimmy Carter's public support for human rights provided a major boost. Fourth, a broad coalition of West, East, and nonaligned states helped bring much greater attention to UN human rights activities. Most states then found it impossible politically not to give at least some token support to international human rights efforts.

In 1967, the Commission on Human Rights was empowered for the first time to examine gross violations of human rights in South Africa and Southern Rhodesia. Further investigations against specific states followed, setting precedents for monitoring. In 1970, ECOSOC Resolution 1503 authorized the commission to undertake confidential investigations of individual complaints that suggest "a consistent pattern of gross and reliably attested violations." This "1503 Procedure," however, only provided for examination of complaints in private and terminated with a report to the commission. Nonetheless, the commission significantly expanded its activities during the 1970s, creating working groups to study specific civil rights problems such as forced disappearances, torture, religious discrimination, and the situation in Chile after the 1972 coup.[15] In 2000, ECOSOC revised the procedures to give the OHCHR and the sub-commission roles in the screening process and the commission itself several options for handling cases, including appointing an independent expert and the possibility of conducting public procedures. Although the 1503 procedure can handle only a fraction of the complaints received each year, it does provide means for placing pressure on offending governments as well as encouraging dialogue to address the complaints.

The sub-commission also was reactivated in the 1970s after several years of dormancy. With the advantage of being composed of independent experts, it plays a major role in screening petitions from individuals and NGOs before their consideration by the commission.[16] In this connection, it has been an important forum for NGO activities. Since 1982, its Working Group on Indigenous Populations has been the central forum for promoting indigenous peoples' rights. Other working groups focus on slavery, minorities, the administration of justice, transnational corporations, and communications (complaints consistent with a pattern of gross violations of human rights). Studies and reports also form a major part of the sub-commission's work. Topics range from the rights of noncitizens and traditional practices affecting the health of women and the girl child to realization of the right to safe drinking water and sanitation.

The other primary mode for UN monitoring is through the treaty bodies created in connection with specific human rights treaties.[17] The first of these, the Human Rights Committee (not to be confused with the now defunct ECOSOC Commission on Human Rights or the new Human Rights Council), was provided for by the Covenant on Civil and Political Rights; others were linked to the conventions on the rights of the child and of migrant workers, and on the elimination of racial discrimination, torture, and discrimination against women. Each requires states to submit periodic reports of their progress toward implementation of the treaty. Committees of independent experts elected by the parties to each treaty review the reports, engage in dialogue with governments, and issue concluding comments. Human rights NGOs frequently prepare their own "shadow reports," which provide the committees with an independent assessment of whether governments are fulfilling their commitments and put additional pressure on governments. OHCHR is now providing assistance with follow-up and hosting regional meetings for each treaty body to assist the cumbersome reporting processes.

The human rights treaties vary in their provision for individual or group petitions and complaints. Even where there is such a provision, states themselves are generally reluctant to accept it. For example, only about one-third of the states that are party to the International Covenant on Civil and Political Rights have accepted the optional provision that allows individual petitions, and the same is true for the Convention Against Torture. The record is even worse with respect to the Convention on the Elimination of Racial Discrimination: Only a dozen of the parties permit petitions, and of those only a few are African states. No Asian states have accepted this provision. A further problem arises from the limited number of petitions that can be handled in a given year. Out of the 5,000 or so complaints relating to civil and political rights filed with the secretary-general in 2004, only a small fraction could be considered by the Human Rights Committee.[18]

Most scholars agree that the various UN systems for monitoring are in need of reform. The commissions and treaty bodies are overburdened with work, making effective follow up impossible. States are bogged down by multiple reporting requirements; late and incomplete reports remain a persistent problem. And even if reports are adequate, many of the UN monitoring systems lack the mandate and capacity to push implementation to the next level.

Do UN investigations, reports, and resolutions make a difference? One argument contends that, over time, repeated condemnations (often referred to as "naming and shaming") can produce change; this was true to some extent in South Africa. Another argument is that enforcement through economic sanctions or other actions is required to effect change. Still a third point of view holds that public condemnations can antagonize states and harden their position—the opposite of the intended effect. For example, sixteen years of General Assembly resolutions linking Zionism with racism only antagonized Israel and the United States, and it had no effect on the rights of Palestinians in Israel or the Occupied Territories.

Since the 1990s, there have been several significant developments in UN monitoring. These include the first human rights monitoring in conjunction with a peacekeeping mission following the end of civil wars in El Salvador and Guatemala as well as extensive UN involvement in election monitoring in conjunction with complex peacekeeping/peacebuilding missions in more than twenty countries. In addition, beginning in 1992, the Human Rights Committee decided to publish its general conclusions after reviews of states' reports, thus removing the veil of secrecy. It has also appointed rapporteurs and special missions to deal with massive human rights violations in countries such as Rwanda, Georgia, Colombia, the former Yugoslavia, and the Democratic Republic of Congo.

In short, although UN human rights monitoring has come a long way in the last forty years, it has also remained limited in its measurable impact. It is one thing to point to complex procedures, quite another to link those procedures to changes in attitudes and behavior. The case of China suggests the difficulties. Following the 1989 Tiananmen Square massacre in China, the Sub-Commission on the Prevention of Discrimination approved a resolution criticizing human rights in China— the first direct action ever against a major power. Thereafter, China became a regular target of the sub-commission's attention, NGO interventions, and pressure from Western nations. Yet China fought back: It challenged the more aggressive monitoring actions by the sub-commission and drew strong support from many developing countries. Together, they challenged the extent of NGO involvement, the independence of the sub-commission members, the open proceedings, and the secret voting. Beginning in 1993, China successfully blocked all action on U.S.-

introduced resolutions dealing with its human rights situation, thereby demonstrating the limits of UN monitoring of ongoing, systematic abuse of human rights by a powerful state.[19] Only in 2005, after ten years of effort, did the special rapporteur on torture, for example, secure China's agreement for an official visit. He found abuse "still widespread" and accused the Chinese authorities of obstructing his work.[20] China, in turn, attempted to get the rapporteur to alter the report.

Translating norms and rhetoric into actions that go beyond stopping violations to change long-term attitudes and behavior is the challenge of promoting human rights. UN efforts in this sphere have been scattered throughout the UN system.

From Monitoring to Promotion

Since the end of the 1980s, the UN has promoted democratization through its electoral assistance programs in conjunction with peacebuilding missions such as those in Namibia, Nicaragua, and Cambodia. These missions "drafted reforms of judicial and security institutions and oversaw their implementation, to ensure long-term conformity with international standards on human rights."[21] In addition, the UN Electoral Assistance Division, created in 1992, has provided technical assistance of various kinds to more than 140 countries. Previously, the Cold War and the predominance of nondemocratic governments among UN members precluded the UN from taking an active role in promoting democratization and political rights. Now, member states often seek assistance on the legal, technical, administrative, and human rights aspects of organizing and conducting democratic elections as well as in supporting the international observation of an electoral process.

Since the early 1990s, the language of second- and third-generation human rights has increasingly been linked to development activities and programs across the entire UN system. Secretary-General Boutros-Ghali's *Agenda for Development* (1995) helped to make this connection through its emphasis on the right to development that had been endorsed by the General Assembly in 1986 (A/41/128). Now the World Bank promotes "good governance," including political and civil rights, among its aid recipients, along with the empowerment of women and participation by civil society. UNDP's annual *Human Development Report* includes numerous indices that measure gender empowerment, life expectancy, literacy, wellbeing, and other variables linked to "human," not just economic, development. The 2003 report, for example, noted in connection with its gender empowerment measures, "When women can take collective action to demand more rights—to education, health care, equal employment—these positive synergies [e.g., fewer children, work outside the home, high productivity] are even more likely."[22] The Millennium Development Goals discussed in chapter 5 join all three generations of rights to the goals of eradicating poverty; promoting human dignity; achieving peace, democracy, and environmental sustainability; and involving people in decisions affecting them and their communities.

This rights-based promotion of development is rooted in the language of the Universal Declaration of Human Rights, namely, "The peoples of the United Nations . . . have determined to promote social progress and better standards of life in larger freedom." It is a way of thinking about the processes of human development based on the international human rights standards defined in various treaties. And, most important, it is geared operationally to promoting those rights in a proactive way by integrating the norms, standards, and principles of the international human rights system into the plans, policies, and processes of development. The eight Millennium Development Goals incorporate a set of targets for each MDG goal (box 5.1), quantitative measures for progress, and systems for review of states' progress. OHCHR has linked each MDG goal to relevant provisions of existing human rights treaties.

Thus, the rights-based approaches of the MDGs engage much of the UN system in active promotion of the full range of interdependent civil, cultural, economic, political, and social rights. They make clear that development projects or activities that have the effect of violating rights are unacceptable and that "trade-offs" between development and rights are unacceptable. OHCHR noted:

> Such approaches also provide for the development of adequate laws, policies, institutions, administrative procedures and practices, and mechanisms of redress and accountability that can deliver on entitlements, respond to denial and violations, and ensure accountability. They call for the translation of universal standards into locally determined benchmarks for measuring progress and enhancing accountability.[23]

The work of forging the conceptual links between the ideas and norms of human rights and the relevant operational activities of many parts of the UN system can be attributed to the High Commissioner for Human Rights assuming the mantle of coordination and the leadership of Secretary-General Kofi Annan.

From Promotion to Enforcement

As noted in chapter 4, the foundation for UN enforcement actions is found in the Charter's Chapter VII. On the two occasions during the Cold War when the council authorized enforcement, it was in response to the persistent, gross violations of the rights of black majorities by white minority governments, first in the breakaway British colony of Southern Rhodesia (1966–1980), and then in South Africa (1978–1993). In neither case, however, did the council make an explicit linkage between human rights violations and security threats. Since 1989, however, the UN's member states have been much more willing to link international peace and security with human rights and to consider multilateral intervention. For example, when the Security Council authorized a U.S.-led peacekeeping operation to restore the democratically elected government of Haiti in 1993, it signaled a willingness to enforce the emerging right to democracy—one of the third-generation rights.[24] Thus, "something very suggestive of human rights enforcement did take place in the 1990s, in El Salvador, Guatemala, Namibia, Haiti, and Cambodia . . . [showing that] under certain circumstances the international community can now enforce human rights."[25]

Since 1990, a series of enforcement actions have been authorized under Chapter VII to deal with humanitarian emergencies in northern Iraq after the Gulf War, Somalia, Bosnia, Rwanda, Sierra Leone, East Timor, and Haiti. As noted in chapter 4, the Security Council did not authorize action in Kosovo and has not taken enforcement action to address the genocide in the Darfur region of Sudan except to refer those guilty of crimes against humanity to the International Criminal Court. With the emergence of a new norm of humanitarian intervention, then, in *select* cases, the Security Council has explicitly linked egregious human rights violations that result in large-scale humanitarian crises to security threats and authorized enforcement action without the consent of the states concerned. From a human rights point of view, these actions represented a substantial step beyond the kind of humanitarian relief the UN has long provided for refugees through UNHCR and the UN Relief and Works Agency for Palestine Refugees in the Near East (UNRWA). These humanitarian interventions have employed UN peacekeeping forces to protect relief workers, guard medical and food supplies, run convoys, and shield civilians from further violence and suffering in so-called "safe areas" that often were far from safe due to inadequate numbers of UN troops and unwillingness to employ armed force.

Many governments are suspicious of strengthening the UN's power to intervene in what many still regard as their domestic jurisdiction. Still, the evolution of complex peacebuilding missions and the debate over an emerging norm of humanitarian intervention have set some important precedents for UN enforcement action in the human rights field since the Cold War's end.

We cannot understand the UN's roles in setting standards and in monitoring, promoting, and even enforcing human rights in specific cases, however, without taking a look first at the roles of NGOs involved in human rights and humanitarian activities. It was the increasingly influential activity of NGOs more than political events that produced the shift in UN responses from the 1970s to the 1990s.

THE ROLE OF NONGOVERNMENTAL ORGANIZATIONS

Much of the UN's success in defining human rights norms, monitoring respect for human rights, and promoting human rights has depended on the activities of the growing international human rights network of NGOs. They perform a variety of functions and roles: providing information and expertise in drafting human rights conventions, monitoring violations, implementing human rights norms, mobilizing public support within countries for changes in national policies, mounting publicity campaigns and protests, lobbying, and bringing petitions before international bodies. Human rights advocates have been instrumental in getting governments to incorporate human rights norms into their concepts of national interest. Networks of advocates, and the NGOs of which they are a part, have gotten international responses to human rights violations by motivating governments to cooperate. Humanitarian NGOs not only perform similar roles in calling attention to humanitarian crises but also deliver relief aid to refugees and victims.

Many human rights NGOs were established in the late 1970s after the two international covenants went into effect and after the 1975 Helsinki Accords were signed. The Helsinki Accords gave Western governments and NGOs a basis for monitoring human rights in Eastern Europe and the Soviet Union. This helped weaken Communist regimes in those states and contributed to political and social liberalization. Similarly, the large number of disappearances and other human rights abuses under dictatorships in Chile, Argentina, and other Latin American countries in the 1970s spurred the growth of human rights NGOs. This converged with a greater interest among members of the U.S. Congress in linking human rights with U.S. foreign policy, including foreign economic assistance. They, in turn, relied on NGOs for expertise and information.[26] In the late 1970s and 1980s, many of those same NGOs gained experience in mobilizing and lobbying when they sought to change U.S. policies in Central America.

The number of international human rights NGOs has grown exponentially since the 1970s. Their activities cover an increasingly diverse range: from mere reporting and publicizing violations to promotion, supervisory, and enforcement activities—activities in which the UN, as an intergovernmental body, cannot easily engage. Although the larger and more well known of the human rights NGOs have ECOSOC consultative status, others often draw on their grassroots connections to gain informal access and serve as information sources for the UN system. Most international human rights NGOs, regardless of whether they are accredited, have endeavored to have representatives in Geneva during the sessions of the Commission on Human Rights and the sub-commission as well to participate in official and informal meetings. These have been described as "a time when ideas get generated and contacts made."[27] One UN official noted, "Eighty-five percent of our information came from NGOs. We did not have the resources or staff to collect information ourselves."[28]

NGOs provided much of the momentum for the 1993 World Conference on Human Rights in Vienna and the 1995 Fourth World Conference on Women in Beijing.[29] Their activities were directed at both shaping the official conference outcomes and organizing the parallel NGO conferences. NGOs provided information for official delegates, lobbied governments and international policymakers, and networked with delegates and other NGOs. Some NGOS were also represented on official delegations. Yet, because human rights NGOs, like groups in other issue areas, have traditionally been enormously diverse and diffuse in their efforts, coordinated initiatives are difficult.

The best-known international human rights NGO is Amnesty International (AI), founded in 1961. AI gained attention for identifying specific political prisoners in countries without respect to political ideology and for conducting publicity and letter-writing campaigns to pressure governments on their behalf. This was a new tool in the human rights arsenal, one that the UN itself could not exercise. AI earned a reputation for scrupulous neutrality by investigating and censuring governments of all types and by precluding its chapters from lobbying or investigating in their own countries.[30] Other key human rights NGOs include the International Commission of Jurists and Human Rights Watch (HRW).[31] Many human rights NGOs, however, are dedicated to specific issues such as indigenous peoples or India's Dalits. The links between local grassroots groups and the larger international organizations form a dense transnational network. Abuses come to light because information is reported through these links and, in turn, responses are coordinated through the network.

Humanitarian NGOs have been concerned traditionally not with rights but with alleviating human suffering, such as by providing food during famines as in Niger or Mozambique, aiding innocent victims of war, and coordinating relief efforts following the 2004 tsunami. They are distinguished from human rights groups because of their nonadvocacy positions and their active participation in providing relief aid in wartime, famine, and natural disasters, during which they often work alongside the UN relief agencies. Their neutrality permits them to take a variety of actions that may be unavailable to governments.

The first humanitarian organization to gain recognition in the nineteenth century was the International Committee of the Red Cross (ICRC) (and its affiliated Red Crescent Societies in predominantly Muslim states). Working closely with governments during times of armed conflict, the ICRC is known for its neutrality, which has facilitated its work behind the scenes to ensure that prisoners of war receive fair treatment and to assist victims of war by providing medical care, clothing, shelter, and food. Following the 2003 Iraq War, for example, the ICRC inspected facilities where prisoners of war were being held by American authorities, quietly pressured the U.S. government to follow the Geneva Conventions, and, when they were unable to effect changes in prisoner treatment, leaked reports of prisoner abuses to the international press.[32] Other prominent humanitarian NGOs include Oxfam, Save the Children, Doctors Without Borders (also known in French as Médecins sans Frontières), and CARE. The International Crisis Group does not deliver aid, but has become an important source of information and has worked to raise awareness of humanitarian crises in conflict situations such as the Darfur region of Sudan. All the major humanitarian relief groups have been active in providing aid for victims of genocide in Darfur.

NGOs have become increasingly important in the promotion and enforcement areas. They have been active in providing education on human rights in Central America, Cambodia, Afghanistan, and other postconflict areas. During the 1992–1995 war in Bosnia-Herzegovina, human rights groups were instrumental in generating and sustaining public interest in the unfolding tragedy of ethnic cleansing. AI, for example, issued three reports on widespread human rights abuses between October 1992 and January 1993, and it was among the NGOs that pressed the Security Council to establish the war crimes tribunal for the former Yugoslavia in 1994. An umbrella group of more than a thousand NGOs, the Coalition for the International Criminal Court, played an important role in mobilizing international support in 1997 and 1998 to create the International Criminal Court and, more recently, to secure its ratification.

NGOs, therefore, through monitoring and promoting human rights and humanitarian norms, have become important actors within and alongside the UN system in the development of human rights standards. Yet NGOs (and concerned individuals and states) are frequently frustrated when governments fail to act, or when they limit NGO access to official UN meetings to protect nation-state prerogatives and interests.

In all four case studies of UN human rights activity that follow, the UN has provided a forum for getting the issue onto the international agenda and for setting and monitoring standards. In one case, it undertook enforcement. In another, it is now promoting implementation of norms. In each case, NGOs have played key roles, working both within and outside the UN system.

CASE STUDIES OF THE UN SYSTEM IN ACTION

The Anti-Apartheid Campaign

One of the major human rights issues faced by the UN from 1946 to the early 1990s was the apartheid policy of the Republic of South Africa. A political and economic policy supporting the legal "separateness" of the races, apartheid was embodied in a series of South African laws dating from 1948 that enveloped the country's black majority population as well as its coloreds and Asians in increasingly restrictive regulations that violated all human rights standards. To quell domestic opposition, the government used detention, torture, and state-sanctioned murder.

These gross violations of human rights directed against the black majority by the white minority provoked an international campaign against apartheid that was conducted inside and outside the UN by a core group of Third World states and a group of NGOs. The UN General Assembly, the main forum for the campaign, passed its first resolution on the subject in December 1946. Led by India, the assembly approved annual resolutions that rejected South Africa's claims that the Charter's human rights provisions constituted no special obligations for member states and that there was no widely accepted definition of these rights and freedoms.

When South African troops fired on demonstrators in the Sharpeville massacre of 1960, the international community was outraged. Twenty-six newly independent African countries, along with other countries, began in 1962 to call for members to break diplomatic ties with South Africa and impose economic sanctions. This marked an acceptance by a majority of the UN's members that enforcement was necessary. In 1963, a voluntary embargo on military sales to South Africa was adopted by the Security Council. Other assembly resolutions called for sanctions against oil, trade, investment, and International Monetary Fund credits, as well as diplomatic and cultural isolation. The Commission on Human Rights created the first monitoring body, the Ad Hoc Working Group on Southern Africa. When ECOSOC agreed to allow the commission to examine gross violations of human rights in 1967, the practice of apartheid was the focus of investigation.

Beginning in 1974, South Africa was prohibited from taking its seat in the General Assembly; subsequently, the assembly granted observer status to two of the opposition groups—the African National Congress (ANC) and the Pan African Congress. These resolutions passed by large majorities, and pressure mounted for enforcement action by the Security Council. In 1976, the International Convention on the Suppression and Punishment of the Crime of Apartheid went into effect, establishing apartheid as an international crime. In 1977, after a series of particularly egregious actions by the South African government, including the death in detention of the well-known black activist Steve Biko, a mandatory arms embargo was approved by the Security Council under Chapter VII. Pressure for economic sanctions continued, and the General Assembly declared 1982 the International Year of Mobilization for Sanctions Against Apartheid.

The three Western permanent members of the Security Council—the United States, Great Britain, and France—had economic and security interests at stake, however; they persistently opposed assembly resolutions calling for economic sanctions and thereby thwarted further Security Council action. Britain and France were major trading partners of South Africa, and the United States was loathe to apply pressure for a change in regime and thereby risk political instability. These examples illustrate that states often have priorities that conflict with concern for human rights, particularly when there is pressure for enforcement actions.

The international campaign against apartheid took other directions as well, some orchestrated by the General Assembly's Special Committee on Apartheid.[33]

For example, there were UN aid programs for victims of apartheid-related abuse through the UN Trust Fund for South Africa. Virtually every international meeting held under UN auspices singled out apartheid for examination. The WHO scrutinized health care for blacks; the ILO probed labor practices. During the 1970s and 1980s, South Africa became a "pariah" state, its sports teams banned from international competition and its cultural activities boycotted, all owing to the egregious violation of the human rights of its own majority population.

The campaign was joined by NGOs such as the World Council of Churches, the World Peace Council, the International Confederation of Free Trade Unions, and the International League for Human Rights; all lobbied governments to approve sanctions and isolate South Africa. Numerous national and subnational NGOs, including church groups, university students, trade unions, and women's and civil rights groups, joined these international NGOs in support of the cause.[34] One tactic was to promote better working conditions for black South Africans by getting American corporations that invested in South Africa to adopt a code of conduct. Another pressured universities, state pension funds, and local governments to refrain from doing business with companies that had investments in South Africa and/or to divest (sell their stocks in those companies).

The UN and NGOs also provided aid to groups resisting apartheid and became instrumental in publicizing and educating the world about apartheid. Scholarships were given to black South African students, legal aid was provided for those imprisoned for apartheid-related offenses, and relocation was offered for refugees from the regime. This UN support enabled the exiled South African opponents of apartheid to survive decades of severe repression.[35]

In the 1980s, the campaign against apartheid inside and outside the UN grew stronger as apartheid itself became more repressive. Media coverage of violence in South Africa increased public awareness of the problem. High-profile black leaders in South Africa who were not imprisoned, such as Bishop Desmond Tutu, the winner of the 1985 Nobel Peace Prize, actively advocated economic sanctions. In the United States, for example, public pressure and a campaign of civil disobedience by prominent politicians and civil rights activists led both liberal Democrats and conservative Republicans in Congress to approve the Comprehensive Anti-Apartheid Act, including sanctions, over a presidential veto. Britain followed suit in imposing sanctions. This was one instance where grassroots pressure and the strength of moral condemnation mattered.

In 1990, the white-controlled South African regime announced a political opening that led to the dismantling of apartheid and the change to black majority rule. Nelson Mandela, the ANC leader, was freed from prison after twenty-seven years. Open elections were held in 1994, and a black majority government has governed South Africa since then. Apartheid laws have been systematically eliminated; sanctions and the country's diplomatic isolation ended; and, although racism persists in South Africa, the long process of promoting human rights among blacks and whites is under way.

What role did the UN and the international anti-apartheid campaign, including economic sanctions, play in this change? For one, the UN General Assembly and other UN bodies where majority voting was the rule were crucial forums for sustained criticism of South Africa over almost forty years; for isolating the apartheid government diplomatically; and for giving the domestic opposition and exiles visibility, legitimacy, and material aid. The Western permanent members of the Security Council, however, used their veto power to block Third World proposals for comprehensive sanctions, approving only the 1978 arms embargo. The imposition of sanctions by Britain and the United States in the 1980s was a morale boost for the anti-apartheid campaign as well as a means to inflict pain on the South African business community and, through them, on the government. Enlightened white leaders realized that internal opposition could no longer be suppressed and that sanctions were having a damaging effect on the economy.[36] In testimony to the UN's role in delegitimizing and defeating apartheid, Nelson Mandela made one of his earliest public speeches after being freed to the UN General Assembly, thanking members for their support.

In some sense, apartheid might be considered an "easy" case. The discrimination was systematic and egregious, and the campaign against apartheid found early and widespread support for which the UN provided an important forum.

Women's Rights as Human Rights

Women have faced various forms of discrimination in virtually every country and culture. In the 1940s, however, women's rights were viewed as separate and different from human rights, even though Article 2 of the Universal Declaration of Human Rights states that "rights and freedoms set forth in this Declaration" must be given without distinction as to race, color, sex, or language. Eleanor Roosevelt and her Latin American colleagues, who pushed to include gender in the Declaration, intended to use that statement to address the problem of women's subordinate status in many countries. Yet only in the 1990s were women's rights fully incorporated into the general human rights rubric. The United Nations and its specialized agencies have been agenda setters on women's issues and in the process of recognizing women's rights as human rights.

Initially, it was the political status of women that appeared on the UN agenda because the Western liberal democracies and the socialist states agreed on the importance of granting women political rights. The Commission on the Status of Women, created at the same time as the Commission on Human Rights in 1946, had primary responsibility for ensuring women's right to vote, hold office, and enjoy various legal rights. For example, ECOSOC's sixth session in 1952 addressed the status of women in public and private law and led to the drafting of the Conventions on the Political Rights of Women (1952), Nationality of Married Women (1957), and Consent to Marriage (1962).

During the 1960s and 1970s, more attention was given to elevating the status of women as economic actors through the women in development initiatives (see chapter 5). That discussion, however, was never framed in terms of women's rights as human rights.

During the 1980s and 1990s, a major change occurred in the discussion of women's issues as women's rights were increasingly viewed within the rubric of universal human rights.[37] The shift began with the 1979 Convention on the Elimination of All Forms of Discrimination Against Women (CEDAW), which set the standard for states "to eliminate discrimination against women in the political and public life of the country (Article 7) [and] to modify the social and cultural patterns of conduct of men and women, with a view to achieving the elimination of prejudices and customary and all other practices which are based on the idea of inferiority or the superiority of either of the sexes or on stereotyped roles for men and women (Article 5[a])." CEDAW did not, however, establish a system for reviewing complaints of violations of women's rights; and it addressed the issue of violence against women only by prohibiting trafficking and prostitution. The four successive UN-sponsored World Conferences on Women in Mexico City (1975), Copenhagen (1980), Nairobi (1985), and Beijing (1995), as well as the activities of the UN Decade for Women (1975–1985), raised awareness of women's rights and mobilized action at new levels. They also provided impetus for the expansion of the women's international NGOs from sixteen in 1973 to sixty-one in 1993 and for the formation of new networks of women's NGOs, the nexus of a vibrant international women's movement.[38] These new groups represented every hue in the ideological rainbow from secular to religious, radical, conservative, grassroots, and elite. They were engaged in delivering welfare and development services to women, organizing women for change, researching women's lives and work, and advocating change for women. They were local, national, regional, and international.[39]

Representing this expanding social movement, 6,000 people attended the 1975 Mexico City NGO forum; 13,500 registered for the 1985 forum in Nairobi; and 300,000 attended the Beijing forum ten years later.[40] With growing numbers and experience with UN conference procedures, women's groups became more effective in their lobbying efforts. Analyzing the changes between the mid-1980s and mid-1990s, one scholar wrote, "The international women's movement has been able to forge remarkable consensus and coalitions around specific issues that affect women, namely environment, human rights and population."[41]

The networks of women's NGOs, such as the International Feminist Network and the Asian Women's Research and Action Network, have become key actors in the UN system. They organized participation in preparatory meetings for the global conferences, developed strategies to push selected issues, gathered information, and monitored governments' positions. By cross-mobilizing ninety human rights and women's NGOs through the Global Campaign for Women's Human Rights prior to the 1993 Vienna World Conference on Human Rights, the women's groups successfully linked women's rights to human rights.[42] A major element in that strategy was their focus on "gender-based violence against women as the issue which demonstrates most clearly and urgently what it means to expand human rights to incorporate women."[43] To dramatize the issue of violence against women, they organized the Global Tribunal on Violations of Women's Human Rights: Four international judges heard the testimony of women from twenty-five countries who put a human face on domestic violence, torture, political persecution, and denial of economic rights.

The joint efforts of women's and human rights groups produced Article 18 of the Vienna Declaration and Programme of Action, which declared: "The human rights of women and of the girl-child are an inalienable, integral and indivisible part of universal human rights. . . . The human rights of women should form an integral part of the United Nations human rights activities, including the promotion of all human rights instruments relating to women." Violence against women and other abuses in situations of war, peace, and domestic family life, including sexual harassment, were also identified as breaches of both human rights and humanitarian norms. Their elimination was to be pursued with legal measures, through national and international action. Later in 1993, the General Assembly approved the Declaration on the Elimination of Violence Against Women, and called for the appointment of a special rapporteur on violence against women, and for states to take steps to combat violence in accordance with provisions of that declaration. This marked a further intrusiveness of international human rights norms. States are now responsible for providing and enforcing human rights guarantees to women not only in public life but also in private life in the sanctity of the home. Dr. Radhika Coomeraswamy of Sri Lanka was appointed as the first Special Rapporteur on Violence Against Women in 1994.

The 1994 UN Conference on Population and Development in Cairo and the 1995 Fourth World Conference on Women in Beijing both confirmed that women's rights are human rights. The Cairo declaration, for example, affirmed women's right "to control all aspects of their health, in particular their own fertility" as a basic ingredient to their empowerment and to addressing the problem of population growth. The Beijing Platform for Action emphasized the need to bring women into positions of power because "it is only through power that you renegotiate the discrimination which you face."[44]

Following the 1995 Beijing conference, the General Assembly mandated the Commission on the Status of Women to review regularly the critical areas in the Beijing Platform for Action and to play a catalytic role in mainstreaming a gender

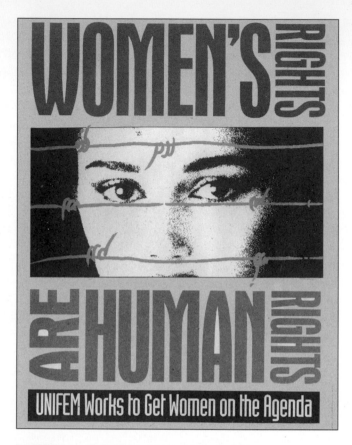

POSTER 6.1   UNIFEM poster on women's rights.

perspective in UN activities. A special assembly session in 2000, "Women2000: gender equality, development and peace for the twenty-first century" (also known as "Beijing Plus Five"), reviewed progress toward implementation and approved further actions. The commission, now enlarged from fifteen to forty-five members, has organized its work around the Beijing goals, and its 2005 meeting, dubbed "Beijing Plus Ten," involved an extensive review and appraisal by governments and NGOs of progress and impediments to the implementation of the Platform for Action's goals in twelve areas. In addition, concerns about women's status and rights infuse the Millennium Development Goals, two of which exclusively target women: Goal 3—Promote gender equality and empower women, and Goal 5—Improve maternal health.

Inevitably the debates concerning women's rights and roles have raised issues of cultural and other differences. When women's NGOs lobbied for attention to particular issues of violence against women, other groups opposed their inclusion on grounds of cultural relativism. The preamble to the Beijing declaration attempted to put to rest the argument over cultural relativism by affirming: "While the significance of national and regional particularities and various historical, cultural and religious background must be borne in mind, it is the duty of states, regardless of the political, economic and cultural systems, to promote and protect all human rights and fundamental freedoms." Yet, CEDAW has the largest number of substantive reservations of any of the human rights treaties, indicating continuing disagreements rooted in cultural and religious differences.

The role the UN has played and NGO skill and persistence have placed women's empowerment through the human rights agenda on a firm trajectory. UN activities relating to women (including the Commission on the Status of Women) have now been consolidated under the UN Division for the Advancement of Women, which has three functions: analysis of gender issues, promotion of women's human rights, and coordination and outreach. The Optional Protocol to CEDAW that entered into force in 2000 provides procedures for individual and group complaints of discrimination. Yet the UN does not have enforcement capabilities. NGOs will have to do much of the work of influencing and monitoring national policies and programs. Promoting observance of women's rights as human rights has become the task of people and governments everywhere.

Slavery and Slave-Like Practices

Slavery is an ancient institution. Most readers probably assume that it has long since disappeared. Unfortunately, it has not, and efforts to eradicate it, along with what are called slave-like practices of forced labor and trafficking in persons, continue today. The ILO, for example, estimates that 12.3 million people, half of them children, are "enslaved" in forced labor, and of those, some 2.4 million are trafficked.[45]

Anti-slavery groups were among the first human rights advocates. In the late eighteenth century, abolitionists in the United States, Great Britain, and France organized to end the slave trade. Although not powerful enough by themselves to effect immediate international change, the group was strong enough in Great Britain to force Parliament in 1807 to ban the slave trade for British citizens. Less than a decade later, the Final Act of the Congress of Vienna in 1815 included an Eight Power Declaration that the slave trade was "repugnant to the principles of humanity and universal morality."[46] Willingness to sign onto a norm prohibiting slavery did not mean that states were ready to take specific measures to abolish the practice, however.

In the early twentieth century, the Anti-Slavery and Aborigines' Protection Society (now known as Anti-Slavery International) vigorously lobbied the League of

Nations on the slavery issue. As a result, the league conducted a study of slavery and established a Temporary Slavery Commission whose report led to the Slavery Convention of 1926. The convention defined slavery in vague terms, however, and the permanent Advisory Committee of Experts on Slavery intended to monitor the abolition of the practice had no effective means of doing so.

It has been under UN (and ILO) aegis that more extensive action against slavery and related practices has been taken with a series of treaties. The Universal Declaration on Human Rights included the rights to be free from slavery or servitude among the articles addressing civil rights. The 1949 Convention on Suppression of International Trafficking prohibited trafficking in persons for the purpose of prostitution (even with their consent). In 1953, the assembly amended the 1926 Slavery Convention. In 1956, it explicitly identified contemporary practices that were considered "slave-like," among them serfdom, forced marriage, child labor, debt bondage, and trafficking in human beings, when it approved the Supplementary Convention on the Abolition of Slavery, Slave Trade and Institutions and Practices Similar to Slavery. The ILO banned forced labor in a 1957 convention, and addressed abuses of migrant workers in a 1975 convention. Other related UN actions include the 1962 convention proscribing early and forced marriages, CEDAW, the 1990 Convention on the Rights of the Child, and the Optional Protocols on Children in Armed Conflict and on the Sale of Children, Child Prostitution, and Child Pornography (2002).

In 1990, the General Assembly approved the International Convention on the Protection of the Rights of All Migrant Workers, which went into effect in 2003. In addition, the Convention Against Transnational Organized Crime (2003) contains provisions that protect migrants and target traffickers; a supplementary optional protocol dealing specifically with trafficking came into force in 2003. In short, the UN has actively sought to ban recruiting, transporting, and harboring individuals for the purpose of exploitation, by use of threat or use of coercion or as slave-like practices.

Many of these conventions did not include procedures for monitoring compliance, for state reporting, or for individual communications. Those that did include CEDAW and its Optional Protocol, which went into effect in 2000; the Convention on the Rights of the Child and its two optional protocols on child prostitution and children in armed conflict; and the recent convention on migrant workers. The latter, for example, has provision for individual communications, but the procedure becomes effective only when ten states have accepted it. As of 2005, no state had made the necessary declaration. Thus, although standard-setting took much of the twentieth century, effective monitoring and enforcement are tasks for the twenty-first century.

To generate publicity about slave-like practices, the UN General Assembly declared the year 2004 as the International Year to Commemorate the Struggle against Slavery and Its Abolition, and sponsored programs, exhibits, and educational programs. Likewise, the ILO has undertaken major studies in 2001 and 2005 of forced labor, including human trafficking. The 2005 report highlighted the fact that "Forced labour is ubiquitous. . . . Yet, paradoxically, it is 'the most hidden problem of our times.'" Both reports link human trafficking with globalization, but the 2005 report reveals ways in which globalization actually promotes forced labor in various environments, such as the pressure to cut costs, the surplus of migrant workers, and the deregulation of labor markets.[47] By titling its report "A Global Alliance Against Forced Labour," the ILO calls for a broad effort to eliminate forced labor within ten years.

The primary mechanisms for monitoring are the Working Group on Contemporary Forms of Slavery under the Sub-Commission on Promotion and Protection of Human Rights and the ILO's procedures. The Working Group is comprised of five independent experts from the sub-commission rather than state representatives and meets once a year; often it focuses on one issue, such as bonded labor and debt bondage (2000) or trafficking (2001). In the process, it receives reports from NGOs such as Anti-Slavery International and from other UN agencies such as UNESCO, FAO, UNICEF, and Interpol. It has often appointed special rapporteurs to investigate and make recommendations on particular problems such as the sale of children and trafficking in persons, especially women and children. In recent years, it has called attention to child trafficking in the United Arab Emirates, the problem of forced or bonded labor in India, Nepal, and Pakistan, the exploitation of Indonesian migrant labor, and forced labor/slavery in the Sudan. The group also serves a monitoring function by receiving information from states on steps they have taken to implement slavery-related conventions. At the recommendation of the Working Group, the General Assembly established the UN Voluntary Trust Fund on Contemporary Forms of Slavery in 1991 to provide financial assistance to NGOs dealing with these issues in meeting with the Working Group, and to provide aid to individuals whose human rights have been violated by contemporary forms of slavery.

The ILO is regarded as having the most effective system of monitoring. Governments report on practices covered under the various ILO conventions; ILO staff then prepare comments on these reports for the Committee of Experts and may use direct contacts, reports of other UN bodies, and reports from both employers' and workers' groups to supplement government reports. The findings of the Committee of Experts, although not binding on states, are then conveyed to a conference committee for a final report. The ILO sometimes investigates allegations of state non-compliance through its Commission of Inquiry. For example, in 1998, the Commission of Inquiry found that Myanmar had not complied with the forced labor conventions; this led to condemnation and the denial of ILO development funds. Although ILO procedures can lead to enforcement, the norm is not to utilize coercive measures but to work with the country in question to improve compliance with standards.

In sum, slave-like practices have proved to be a persistent problem. They are aggravated now by the ease of moving people across borders, the pressures to keep labor costs low, persistent poverty in many parts of the world, and the high profitability of the sex trade. The UN, including the ILO, has actively tried to expose and end these human rights abuses, but that remains a persistent challenge.

Genocide, Crimes Against Humanity, and War Crimes

During the twentieth century, millions were victims of genocide, ethnic cleansing, other crimes against humanity, and war crimes. The Holocaust is often singled out for the deaths of some 6 million Jews, gypsies, and other "undesirables" under the Nazi German regime, but there were other incidents of what is now called **genocide** before World War II as well as several since. The post–World War II trials of war criminals held in Nuremburg, Germany, and Tokyo, Japan, organized by the victors made it painfully obvious that there was no international law prohibiting genocide. In fact, prior to 1944, the term "genocide" did not exist. It was coined by a Polish lawyer, Raphael Lemkin, who, along with Chilean and Greek jurists, was largely responsible for drafting the genocide convention as part of the Ad Hoc Committee on Genocide created by ECOSOC. Some countries believed that such a convention was worthless because it could never be enforced. In 1948, however, the General Assembly unanimously adopted the Convention on the Prevention and Punishment of Genocide. The treaty defines the crime of genocide and lists acts that are prohibited. It calls for persons committing genocide to be punished, for states to enact legislation, and for persons charged to be tried either in the state where the crimes were committed or by an international tribunal. (See box 6.1 for key provisions.)

The Genocide Convention was rapidly signed and ratified and widely recognized as a major advance in international human rights law. Yet it contained ambiguities that could create problems with interpretation and enforcement. For example, it does not specify how many people have to be killed for the incident to be considered genocide, but only addresses the intention on the part of the perpetrators to destroy a group of people "in whole or in part." In contrast to later human rights treaties, the convention created no permanent body to monitor situations or provide early warnings of impending or actual genocide. And, for many years, it seemed to have little effect. In Cambodia, Sudan, China, and former East Pakistan (now Bangladesh), millions of people were killed or forced to flee their homelands as a result of war or deliberate government actions. The international community paid little attention. Still, the norm had been established.

Along with the legal prohibition against genocide came the codification of other **crimes against humanity** and crimes committed during warfare, albeit outside the UN system. These norms are contained in four 1949 Geneva Conventions, two additional protocols concluded in 1977, and related treaties dealing with use of specific weapons. They are designed to protect civilians, prisoners of war, and wounded soldiers, as well as to ban particular methods of war (e.g., bombing hospitals) and certain weapons that cause unnecessary suffering (e.g., poisonous gases). Together these form the foundations of **international humanitarian law** and establish the legal basis for **war crimes.** International human rights law— including the Universal Declaration of Human Rights, the Covenant on Political and Civil Rights, and the conventions on torture, genocide, refugees, and children—and the fundamental principle of nondiscrimination between peoples enshrined in Article 1 of the UN Charter establish the basis for crimes against humanity. These are all now incorporated in Article 8 of the International Criminal Court Statute (see box 6.2).

The enforcement of norms against genocide, crimes against humanity, and war crimes has proven problematic. Only in the 1990s, with the humanitarian crises in the former Yugoslavia, Rwanda, and Sierra Leone, did the international community begin to pay attention to evidence of ethnic cleansing, genocide, and other crimes and demand action, although too late to prevent huge harm and loss of life. Only then was there pressure to create mechanisms for prosecuting those accused of crimes against humanity and of war crimes, initially on an ad hoc basis and then through the ICC.

The former Yugoslavia illustrates the dilemmas associated with application of the conventions against genocide, crimes against humanity, and war crimes. During the Yugoslav civil war, the term "ethnic cleansing" was coined to refer to systematic efforts by Croatia and the Bosnian Serbs to remove peoples of another group from their territory, but not necessarily to wipe out the entire group, or part of it, as specified in the Genocide Convention. In Bosnia, Muslim civilians were forced by Serb troops to flee towns for Muslim areas within Bosnia or for neighboring countries. Some were deported to neighboring Macedonia, others placed in concentration camps. Sixty thousand Bosnian women were raped by Serb forces.

The UN Commission on Human Rights appointed envoys to investigate the situation. Initially, in 1992, they reported "massive and grave violations of human rights." Several months later, another report concluded that Muslims were the principal victims and were being threatened with extermination. In December 1992, the General Assembly passed a resolution describing Serbia's ethnic cleansing of Bosnia's Muslims as a form of genocide and condemned its actions. In 1993, the International Court of Justice issued a unanimous order to Serbia to follow the Genocide Convention, and the World Conference on Human Rights appealed to the Security Council to take measures to end the genocide in Bosnia. The council

BOX 6.1   The Genocide Convention

Article I . . . genocide, whether committed in time of peace or in time of war, is a crime under international law which they undertake to prevent and punish.

Article II . . . genocide means any of the following acts committed with intent to destroy, in whole or in part, a national, ethnical, racial or religious group, as such:

(a) Killing members of the group;
(b) Causing serious bodily or mental harm to members of the group;
(c) Deliberately inflicting on the group conditions of life calculated to bring about its physical destruction in whole or in part;
(d) Imposing measures intended to prevent births within the group;
(e) Forcibly transferring children of the group to another group.

Article III The following acts shall be punishable:
(a) Genocide;
(b) Conspiracy to commit genocide;
(c) Direct and public incitement to commit genocide;
(d) Attempt to commit genocide;
(e) Complicity in genocide.

Article IV Persons committing genocide or any of the other acts enumerated in article III shall be punished, whether they are constitutionally responsible rulers, public officials or private individuals.

Article V The Contracting Parties undertake to enact . . . the necessary legislation to give effect to the provisions of the present Convention and to provide effective penalties for persons guilty of genocide or any of the other acts enumerated in article III.

created a Commission of Experts, which heard hundreds of hours of taped testimony and sifted through intelligence information, concluding that although all sides were committing war crimes, only the Serbs were conducting a systematic campaign of genocide. It also created the International Criminal Tribunal for the Former Yugoslavia, imposed an arms embargo on all parties, and imposed trade sanctions on Serbia, condemning it for human rights violations.

Was ethnic cleansing in Bosnia equivalent to genocide? If so, who was guilty? The UN Commission of Experts, the ICJ, and the UN Human Rights Commission all said yes, and that Serbia alone had a conscious policy of systematic genocide. A number of NGOs maintained that all sides were guilty. In reality, Security Council members lacked the political will to stop the killing in Bosnia. The same was true

---

BOX 6.2   Crimes Against Humanity

Attack against or any effort to exterminate a civilian population

Enslavement

Deportation or forcible transfer of population

Imprisonment or other severe deprivation of physical liberty

Torture

Rape, sexual slavery, forced prostitution, pregnancy, and sterilization

Persecution of any group or collectivity based upon political, racial, national, ethnic, cultural, religious, or gender grounds

Enforced disappearance of persons

---

in 1994 in Rwanda, where the evidence of genocide was much clearer.[48] As noted in chapter 4, the response again was too little and too late for the victims, but a second international tribunal was created to try those charged with crimes. Although UN members failed to stop, let alone prevent, genocide in Rwanda, ethnic cleansing in Bosnia, and crimes against humanity or war crimes, in other situations, the idea of individual responsibility for such crimes was revived in the face of the atrocities committed during conflicts in the former Yugoslavia, as well as in Rwanda and Sierra Leone.

International War Crimes Tribunals.   To bring those responsible for crimes during interstate or civil wars to justice, the Security Council under Chapter VII of the Charter established the International Criminal Tribunal for the Former Yugoslavia (ICTY) in 1993, followed in 1994 by the International Criminal Tribunal for Rwanda (ICTR). In a somewhat different procedure, the UN negotiated an agreement with the government of Sierra Leone in 2002 to establish the Special Court for Sierra Leone. Still another approach was used by the UN to establish the Khmer Rouge Tribunal in agreement with the Cambodian government. Initially, these ad hoc courts lacked established structures and procedures, as well as actual criminals in custody. Yet they recruited prosecutors, investigators, administrators, and judges, devised rules of procedure and evidence, and worked to gain the cooperation of states to carry out their tasks. Deciding whom to indict, arresting those individuals, and trying them in a timely fashion have been ongoing challenges. Let us look briefly at two of the tribunals: ICTY and ICTR.

Employing fourteen judges and three separate proceedings, as well as more than six hundred staff members from around the world, the ICTY developed answers to questions of authority, jurisdiction, evidence, sentencing, and imprisonment that have aided other tribunals. By mid-2005, 162 individuals had been indicted, 55 had received judgments, and 9 were on trial, including Slobodan Milosevic, the former Serbian president who died in custody in 2006 before the conclusion of his trial. Seventy-eight cases were awaiting trial.[49] One scholar wrote, "The real success of the ICTY lies in the fact that . . . it is a functioning international criminal court that is providing a forum for victims to accuse those who violated civilized norms of behavior . . . stigmatizing persons . . . and forcing them to relinquish any official power . . . and generating a body of jurisprudence that will undoubtedly continue to build over time."[50] Its judgments have elaborated on the Geneva Conventions, for example, by defining sexual violence, and especially rape, as a war crime, the elements of crimes of genocide and torture, and the application of international humanitarian law to internal armed conflicts.

The Rwandan tribunal has also had problems securing cooperation in arresting suspects and been slow in processing cases. By 2005, it had convicted twenty defendents, acquitted three, and had twenty-six cases in progress.[51] ICTR's most important contributions to international criminal law are the convictions for using media to incite and coordinate Hutu violence against the Tutsis, and of Jean Kambanda, the former prime minister of Rwanda, for the crime of genocide—the first such conviction of a head of government. Still, because there are more than 120,000 people in custody awaiting trial in Rwanda, it is uncertain how either ICTR or Rwandan courts will process all the cases.

The International Criminal Court. In 1998, in light of the difficulties posed by the ad hoc nature of the Yugoslav and Rwandan tribunals, and in response to a long-standing movement to create a permanent international criminal court, UN members concluded the Rome Statute for the International Criminal Court. The statute had been drafted by the International Law Commission over several years at the request of the General Assembly. The coalition for the ICC (a group of more than 1,000 NGOs) played an important role in mobilizing international support for the ICC and, later, in promoting ratification.

In contrast to the ICJ, the ICC has not only compulsory jurisdiction but also jurisdiction over individuals. Called by one "the most ambitious initiative in the history of modern international law,"[52] the new court only has jurisdiction over "serious" war crimes that represent a "policy or plan" rather than just random acts in wartime. They must also have been "systematic or widespread," not single abuses. Four types of crimes are covered: genocide, crimes against humanity, war crimes, and crimes of aggression (undefined). No individuals (save those younger than eighteen) are immune from jurisdiction, including heads of states and military leaders. The ICC functions as a court of last resort and hears cases only when national courts are unwilling or unable to deal with grave atrocities. Prosecution is forbidden for crimes committed before July 1, 2002, when the court came into being, and individuals must be present during the trial. Furthermore, the ICC may act only in cases where the state on whose territory the crime was committed, or whose nationals are accused, has ratified the treaty. Anyone—an individual, a government, a group, or the UN Security Council—can bring a case before the ICC. In 2003, the court became operational. As of 2005, 139 states had signed the Rome Statute and 100 had ratified it. Among those who had not were the United States, China, India, Iraq, and Turkey.

Although the United States has historically supported international accountability for war crimes, it opposes the ICC. One major concern is the possibility that the ICC might prosecute U.S. military personnel, or even the president, without American approval. Thus, the U.S. Department of Defense has strongly insisted that the United States cannot participate; the Bush and Clinton administrations, as well as Congress, have deferred to their judgment. The United States also objects to the aggression clause as undefined and vague. It objects more generally on the grounds that the ICC infringes on U.S. sovereignty, and, hence, it would prefer an international court whose powers depended upon approval by the UN Security Council where it has veto power. To protect itself, the United States has taken advantage of the treaty's Article 98 and negotiated bilateral immunity agreements with more than fifty states not to send Americans to the court for prosecution.

It is significant, however, that the ICC came into being and began to operate in spite of American objections. Its establishment moves international adjudication and international law far more in the direction of accepting individuals and nonstate entities such as terrorist and criminal groups as subjects of international law, where only states historically have enjoyed such status. Although not an official part of the UN system, the ICC signed an agreement with Secretary-General Kofi Annan in 2004 that gives it observer status in the General Assembly, mechanisms for cooperation with the Security Council, and access to UN conference and other services.

At the end of 2005, five cases were pending before the ICC. All involved crimes committed in African countries: Democratic Republic of Congo, Uganda, Central African Republic, Côte d'Ivoire, and the Darfur region of Sudan. With the exception of Darfur, all involve conflicts and atrocities that have attracted little attention in the Western media. The Congo's case, for example, involves the deaths of more than 4 million people, mostly women and children, since 1998. That in Uganda involves the abduction and enslavement of more than 30,000 children by The Lord's Resistance Army of Northern Uganda. The Darfur situation is the first to be referred by the Security Council to the ICC, an important precedent, especially as the United States first opposed the referral because of its objections to the ICC in general, and then abstained.

In sum, the UN has been central to efforts to codify standards relating to genocide, crimes against humanity, and war crimes. It has also been instrumental to more recent efforts to apply those standards in preventing these egregious crimes and to establishing judicial bodies to try those accused of committing them.

EVALUATING THE UN'S HUMAN RIGHTS RECORD

These four case studies illustrate the variations in the UN's role with respect to human rights issues. They also show the complex processes by which human rights norms have gained acceptance as well as the challenges of promoting their application and enforcement. The UN's inability to prevent the well-publicized human rights tragedies in Bosnia, Rwanda, and the Sudan has called into question the organization's human rights record, just as did its earlier inability to put a prompt end to apartheid in South Africa. Unquestionably, the UN has failed to address many egregious human rights violations. When it has cataloged abuses, its follow-up activities have too often been weak and ineffectual. The monitoring mechanisms may be too diverse and state-dominated to be effective. The funds allocated for these activities are limited—about 1 percent of the regular budget. But this harsh indictment does not tell the whole story.

The UN has played a central role in institutionalizing human rights norms in world politics. In 1948, only slavery, genocide, and abuses against aliens were legally proscribed. By 2000, that list had expanded to include extensive protection for individuals as well as women, children, minorities, and indigenous peoples. The vast majority of states have ratified the two international covenants and many of the other human rights conventions. It is broadly recognized that human rights are internationally protected and universally applicable, even if enforcement still lags.

The UN itself has moved a long way from the time when mere reporting by states themselves was the only mechanism of monitoring and enforcement. The focus of public monitoring of violations and activities has moved far beyond the long-time pariah states of South Africa and Israel. NGOs have played a key role in this process, providing independent monitoring of human rights activities, filing petitions on behalf of victims, publicizing gross violations in a way that the UN cannot, promoting ratification of human rights treaties, and mounting international campaigns against gross violators, including boycotts and sanctions. Moreover, human rights NGOs have been increasingly integrated into the work of the various UN bodies. In this respect, there is a partnership between the UN and NGOs representing civil society.

The UN's activities on human rights have been complemented by the even more extensive development of human rights norms and institutions at the regional level. By far the most developed is the human rights regime in Europe, where governments are held accountable for actions against their citizens through the European Court of Human Rights. Although the Americas have also witnessed substantive innovations, human rights regimes are weak in Africa, and nonexistent in Asia and the Middle East.

UN and other international efforts to address human rights issues confront challenges relating to our three dilemmas because states traditionally were free to treat their own citizens however they chose. And although liberalism provides a basis for explaining the UN's role and the expansion of international human rights law, it is constructivism that provides the framework for understanding how new norms emerge and become widely accepted.

Dilemma 1: Expanding Need for Governance Versus the UN's Weakness

With the expansion of democracy, global economic integration, and the communication revolution, there is much greater knowledge about violations of human rights in different areas of the world and demands for international action by victims and human rights advocates. Those demands for action face the reality, however, that the UN's monitoring and enforcement mechanisms are weak instruments. The UN has been even less successful in enforcement, precisely because enforcement offends the states that are its constituents. Thus, the UN has been slow to use the "naming" and "shaming" approach that human rights NGOs frequently employ. The 1990s marked a major shift in this regard, but it is still a relatively small number of violators that get singled out for action, especially by the Security Council.

Dilemma 2: Human Rights at the Nexus of State Sovereignty

Attempts to protect individuals and groups from human rights abuses occurring within the borders of states directly challenge traditional interpretations of state sovereignty and Article 2(7) of the UN Charter that proscribes intervention in matters within the domestic jurisdiction of states. Thus, key to the increased UN attention to human rights is a shift in the understanding of what states are free to do and in the evolving interpretation of what the international community through the UN can and ought to do. Through its role as a forum for bringing human rights into the center of world affairs, the UN has sharpened the sovereignty dilemma. States still periodically assert the principle of noninterference in internal affairs, but that justification is heard less often. More often, states such as China, a strong proponent of the sovereignty argument, expend enormous amounts of diplomatic capital to defend themselves and to avert the publicity of public criticism.

Dilemma 3: The Need for Leadership versus the Dominance of a Sole Superpower

The establishment of the ICC over the active objections of the United States clearly demonstrated the unwillingness of many states to allow the world's sole superpower to prevent the advance of international criminal law. In fact, historically, no major power has played a leading role in promoting human rights through the UN. The United States has a poor record for signing and ratifying human rights conventions. Instead, leadership has come from the Netherlands, Norway, India, Canada, Costa Rica, and a handful of other states. NGOs such as Amnesty International and the International Commission of Jurists, the Women's Caucus, and Anti-Slavery International have been prime movers, and grassroots groups of all stripes are important sources of information and advocacy. Thus, human rights are an area where leadership does not depend on traditional sources of power and where, indeed, the seemingly powerless have proved capable of making a difference.

It is because of the evolution of international human rights norms that new conceptions of security have emerged. These conceptions reject the idea that security applies only to states and embrace the notion that poverty, disease, gross violations of human rights, and environmental degradation threaten the security and wellbeing of human beings.

NOTES

1. Zbigniew Brzezinski, *The Grand Failure: The Birth and Death of Communism in the Twentieth Century* (New York: Charles Scribner's Sons, 1989), 256.

2. Kathryn Sikkink, "Transnational Politics, International Relations Theory, and Human Rights," *PS: Political Science and Politics* 31, no. 3 (September 1998): 517–521.

3. "Address by the President," 87, *Congressional Record* 44 (1941): 46–47.

4. The seven references appear in Articles 1, 13(1), 55, 56, 62, 68, and 76.

5. Mrs. Franklin D. Roosevelt, "General Assembly Adopts Declaration of Human Rights," statement before the General Assembly, 9 December 1948, *Department of State Bulletin* (19 December 1948), 751.

6. On the UN and colonialism, see Rupert Emerson, *From Empire to Nation: The Rise to Self-Assertion of Asian and African People* (Cambridge, Mass.: Harvard University Press, 1960), and Harold K. Jacobson, "The United Nations and Colonialism: A Tentative Appraisal," *International Organization* 16 (Winter 1962): 27–56.

7. Julie A. Mertus, *The United Nations and Human Rights: A Guide for a New Era* (New York: Routledge, 2005), 48. This is an excellent resource on all aspects of the UN human rights system, particularly chapters 3 and 4 on the functioning of different parts of the organizational structure and the various treaty bodies.

8. See Ibid., 17–18.

9. Quoted in Ibid., 41.

10. Louis Henkin, "The Universal Declaration and the U.S. Constitution," *PS: Political Science and Politics* 31, no. 3 (September 1998): 512.

11. Amartya Sen, "Human Rights and Asian Values," Sixteenth Morgenthau Memorial Lecture on Ethics and Foreign Policy, Carnegie Council on Ethics and International Affairs, 1997, 27, 30.

12. Abdullahi A. An-Na'im, "The Cultural Mediation of Human Rights: The Al-Arqum Case in Malaysia," in *The East Asian Challenge for Human Rights,* ed. Joanne R. Bauer and Daniel A. Bell (Cambridge: Cambridge University Press, 1999), 147. This volume is an excellent set of critical essays on the Asian values debate.

13. Quoted on the Web site for the UN High Commissioner for Human Rights, http://www.unhchr.ch.

14. On this evolution, see Thomas Buergenthal, "The Normative and Institutional Evolution of International Human Rights," *Human Rights Quarterly* 19 (1997): 703–723, and Paul Gordon Lauren, *The Evolution of International Human Rights: Visions Seen,* 2nd ed. (Philadelphia: University of Pennsylvania Press, 2003), chaps. 8 and 9.

15. See Howard Tolley Jr., *The UN Commission on Human Rights* (Boulder: Westview Press, 1987), and Mertus, *The United Nations and Human Rights,* 56–64.

16. See Asborjn Eide, "The Subcommission on Prevention of Discrimination and Protection of Minorities," in *The United Nations and Human Rights: A Critical Appraisal,* ed. Philip Alston (Oxford: Clarendon Press, 1992).

17. For extensive discussion of the treaty bodies, see Mertus, *The United Nations and Human Rights,* chap. 4.

18. Lorna Davidson and Jacques Fomerand, "Human Rights and Humanitarian Assistance: Ensuring Individual Liberties, Delivering Necessary Relief," *Global Agenda: Issues Before the 60th General Assembly of the United Nations,* ed. Angela Drakulich (New York: UNA/USA, 2005), 149. On the work of the Human Rights Committee and individual petition procedures, see Ineke Boerefijn, "Towards a Strong System of Supervision: The Human Rights Committee's Role in Reforming the Reporting Procedure Under Article 40 of the Covenant on Civil and Political Rights," *Human Rights Quarterly* 17 (1995): 766–793, and Liz Heffernan, "A Comparative View of Individual Petition Procedures Under the European Convention on Human Rights and the International Covenant on Civil and Political Rights," *Human Rights Quarterly* 19 (1997): 78–112.

19. Ann Kent, "China and the International Human Rights Regime: A Case Study of Multilateral Monitoring, 1989–1994," *Human Rights Quarterly* 17 (1995): 1–47.

20. "UN: China Torture Still Widespread," http://www.cbsnews.com/stories/2005/12/02/world/main1093457.shtm.

21. Susan Burgerman, *Moral Victories: How Activists Provoke Multilateral Action* (Ithaca: Cornell University Press, 2001), 2.

22. United Nations Development Program, *Human Development Report 2003. Millennium Development Goals: A Compact among Nations to End Human Poverty* (New York: United Nations, 2003), 8.

23. See http://www.unhchr.ch/development/approaches–04.html.

24. See Thomas M. Franck, "The Emerging Right to Democratic Governance," *American Journal of International Law* 86, no. 1 (1992): 46–91.

25. Burgerman, *Moral Victories,* 3–4.

26. Ibid., 11–15.

27. Quoted in Mertus, *The United Nations and Human Rights,* 66.

28. Margaret E. Keck and Kathryn Sikkink, *Activists Beyond Borders: Advocacy Networks in International Politics* (Ithaca: Cornell University Press, 1998), 96.

29. For a study of the roles and strategies of NGOs in three global conferences, see Ann Marie Clark, Elisabeth J. Friedman, and Kathryn Hochstetler, "The Sovereign Limits of Global Civil Society: A Comparison of NGO Participation in UN World Conferences on the Environment, Human Rights, and Women," *World Politics* 51 (October 1998): 1–35. The discussion in this section draws heavily on the analysis in this article. For a more extensive treatment, see Elisabeth Jay Friedman, Kathryn Hochstetler, and Ann Marie Clark, *Democracy, Sovereignty, and Global Civil Society* (Albany, N.Y.: SUNY Press, 2005).

30. On Amnesty International, see Ramesh Thakur, "Human Rights: Amnesty International and the United Nations," *Journal of Peace Research* 31, no. 2 (1994): 143–160; see also Ann Marie Clark, *Diplomacy of Conscience: Amnesty International and Changing Human Rights Norms* (Princeton: Princeton University Press, 2001); and for Amnesty's own voluminous publications, go to http://www.amnesty.org.

31. On the International Commission of Jurists, see Howard Tolley, *The International Commission of Jurists: Global Advocates for Human Rights* (Philadelphia: University of Pennsylvania Press, 1994).

32. David Forsythe, *The Humanitarians: The International Committee of the Red Cross* (Cambridge: Cambridge University Press, 2005).

33. See Audie Klotz, *Norms in International Relations: The Struggle Against Apartheid* (Ithaca: Cornell University Press, 1995).

34. For a comprehensive treatment of the actions of international, national, and local NGOs, see Janice Love, *The U.S. Anti-Apartheid Movement: Local Activism in Global Politics* (New York: Praeger, 1985).

35. Klotz, *Norms in International Relations,* 53.

36. For an analysis of the role sanctions played in the end of apartheid, see ibid., chap. 9.

37. See Charlotte Bunch, "Women's Rights as Human Rights: Toward a Re-Vision of Human Rights," *Human Rights Quarterly* 12, no. 4 (November 1990): 486–498, and Radhika Coomaraswamy, *Reinventing International Law: Women's Rights as Human Rights in the International Community* (Cambridge, Mass.: Harvard Law School Human Rights Program, 1997).

38. Keck and Sikkink, *Activists Beyond Borders,* 11.

39. Martha Alter Chen, "Engendering World Conferences: The International Women's Movement and the UN," in *NGOs, The UN, and Global Governance,* ed. Thomas G. Weiss and Leon Gordenker (Boulder: Lynne Rienner, 1996), 141.

40. Clark, Friedman, and Hochstetler, "The Sovereign Limits of Global Civil Society," 9.

41. Chen, "Engendering World Conferences," 142.

42. Donna J. Sullivan, "Women's Human Rights and the 1993 World Conference on Human Rights," *American Journal of International Law* 88 (1994): 152.

43. Charlotte Bunch, "Organizing for Women's Human Rights Globally," in *Ours by Right: Women's Rights as Human Rights,* ed. Joanna Kerr (London: Zed Books, 1993), 146.

44. Devaki Jain, quoted in *The Power of UN Ideas: Lessons from the First 60 Years,"* ed. Richard Jolly, Louis Emmerij, and Thomas G. Weiss (New York: The United Nations Intellec-

tual History Project, 2005), 30. See also Devaki Jain, *Women, Development, and the UN: A Sixty-Year Quest for Equality and Justice* (Bloomington, Ind.: Indiana University Press, 2005).

45. "New ILO Report: A Global Alliance Against Forced Labour," http://www-ilo-mirror.cornell.edu/public/english/bureau/inf/magazine/54/forcedlabour.htm.

46. Lauren, *The Evolution of International Human Rights*, 40.

47. "New ILO Report."

48. There are many good sources on the failure of international responses to genocide, among them, see Samantha Power, *"A Problem from Hell": America and the Age of Genocide* (New York: Basic Books, 2002), and Michael Barnett, *Eyewitness to a Genocide: The United Nations and Rwanda* (Ithaca: Cornell University Press, 2002).

49. Lawrence C. Moss, "International Law: Treaty-Making, Governance and the Advancement of Justice," in *Global Agenda: Issues Before the 60th General Assembly of the United Nations*, ed. Angela Drakulich (New York: UNA/USA, 2005), 258.

50. Sean D. Murphy, "Progress and Jurisprudence of the International Criminal Tribunal for the Former Yugoslavia," *American Journal of International Law* 93, no. 1 (January 1999): 96–97.

51. Moss, "International Law," 260.

52. Marlise Simons, "World Court for Crimes of War Opens in The Hague," *New York Times*, March 12, 2003.

7

Human Security:
The Environment and Health

The concept of security must change—from an exclusive stress on national security to a much greater stress on people's security, from security through armaments to security through human development, from territorial security to food, employment, and environmental security.

—1993 *Human Development Report*

Traditionally, international peace and security has meant states' security and the defense of states' territorial integrity from external threats or attack. Yet out of the people-oriented concept of sustainable human development, articulated in the late 1980s and early 1990s, and the evolution of international human rights norms has come the broader concept of human security. "Making human beings secure," it is argued, "means more than protecting them from armed violence and alleviating their suffering."[1] This new conceptualization has major implications not only for how the UN and its member states think about security, but also for how the UN and other multilateral institutions are organized and conduct their work, for a human security-oriented approach cuts across traditional divisions between peace and security issues and economic and social issues. Some states, such as Canada, have adopted it as a foundation of their foreign policies.

AN EXPANDED VIEW OF SECURITY

Although some scholars argue that the concept of human security lacks precision and is too expansive,[2] it has been increasingly accepted within the UN system as a useful way to conceptualize a variety of threats that affect states, groups, and individuals. In 2000, for example, the Millennium Declaration set the goal of attaining "freedom from fear" and "freedom from want" for all people. In 2004, the High-level Panel on Threats, Challenges and Change incorporated many ideas relating to human security in its report. Among the threats it identified were poverty, infectious diseases, and environmental degradation, in addition to such traditional threats as interstate conflict, civil war, genocide, nuclear weapons, terrorism, and transnational organized crime. This evolution in thinking about security "has recognized the security needs of individuals and the responsibilities of states and organizations in attending to those needs."[3] An important part of that evolution involves the roles of nonstate actors—NGOs, civil society, private corporations, scientists, and IGOs in empowering individuals and communities to act on their own behalf. "Correspondingly," as two members of the Commission on Human Security noted, "human security requires strong and stable states."[4]

Viewed in this way, human security has already been addressed in the previous four chapters through the examination of humanitarian intervention, terrorism, and other threats to peace and security; efforts to eradicate poverty, reduce economic inequalities, and promote human and sustainable development; and the promotion of greater respect for human rights. In this chapter, the focus is on the need for protecting the environment and human health. Neither of these issues is new on the international agenda; indeed, health is one of the oldest areas of functional cooperation. What has changed is recognition that failure to address either environmental degradation or major threats to health has a fundamental impact on human security. They can also have "a direct impact on peace and stability within and between states."[5] In short, issues once perceived as "merely environmental" or "merely social" have far-reaching security implications when people rather than states become the primary concern. These issues are increasingly at the forefront of the UN's agenda in the twenty-first century.

PROTECTION OF THE ENVIRONMENT

The desire to protect the environment dates from the nineteenth century when commissions were established between neighboring states to coordinate cross-border environmental issues (such as the United States and Canada on the Great Lakes and interstate river commissions in Europe). NGOs also formed to protect specific species (for example, the Society for the Protection of Birds in 1898) or to promote general environmental awareness (the Sierra Club in 1892). At the close of the twentieth century, the threat posed by major environmental degradation was much greater. As one scholar noted, "climate change, land degradation and desertification, the largest wave of species extinctions since the dinosaurs, and multifarious pollutants are real and growing sources of insecurity."[6] International cooperation in pursuit of environmental security had also grown, especially with the proliferation of environmental treaties. At the forefront have been NGOs, industries, scientists, the UN and other IGOs, and industries. Much of this activity has taken place since the early 1970s, and much of it has been "too little and too late."

Although some states and a few NGOs recognized the need for environmental protection at the time, neither the League of Nations Covenant nor the UN Charter contained specific provisions to that effect. This is not surprising because environmental issues did not emerge on most states' agendas until the late 1960s. Inspired by books such as Rachel Carson's *Silent Spring* and Garrett Hardin's essay, "Tragedy of the Commons,"[7] and photographs of the earth taken by Apollo 2 astronauts in 1969, an entirely new image of the planet as a single ecosystem began to emerge. Concerns about the consequences of economic growth on the earth's environment and on human health grew. The UN, responding to this growing environmental consciousness, played a key part in the emergence of an international environmental agenda. The UN's role included the development of a global policy-making framework as a result of UN-sponsored global conferences, the articulation of new norms, and the drafting of numerous environmental conventions. NGOs, industries, and major scientific and professional groups have all had important inputs along with developed and developing states. From the beginning, North-South divisions have marked the politics of environmental issues.

In response to scientists' growing concerns about the biosphere, the UN Educational, Scientific and Cultural Organization sponsored the first international environmental conference in 1968. In that same year, Sweden offered to host a larger UN conference. The 1972 UN Conference on the Human Environment (UNCHE), or Stockholm Conference, was the first UN-sponsored conference on a major issue of global concern. At this time, there was little recognition that environmental degradation might become so severe that it would lead to conflict between states and among individuals for precious resources, let alone threaten human security.

The Genesis of an Idea: The Stockholm Conference

The Stockholm Conference put environmental issues on the UN and global agendas, as well as on many national governments' agendas. It initiated a process that has led to the piecemeal construction of international environmental institutions, expansion of the global environmental agenda, increasing acceptance by states of international environmental standards and monitoring regimes, and extensive involvement of both NGOs and scientific and technical groups in policymaking efforts. Putting environmental issues on the UN's agenda was an innovation as important to development as peacekeeping was to the UN's role in maintaining international peace and security.

During the preparatory meetings for the 1972 conference, UNCHE Secretary-General Maurice Strong, a Canadian businessman, provided the leadership for trying to bridge the divergent interests of North and South. The developed countries saw environmental issues as stemming from the population explosion in the less-developed countries. Increasing population leads to greater pressures for natural resource utilization, and hence greater strains on the environment. States must be willing to pay the costs for a safe and healthy environment. In contrast, the developing countries blamed environmental problems on the over-utilization of natural resources and the pollution caused by the consumption excesses of the developed countries. The less developed countries feared that environmental regulation could hamper economic growth and divert resources from economic development. Many developing countries were reluctant even to attend the Stockholm Conference; indeed, they had to be persuaded that environmental problems were neither a concern simply of developed, industrialized countries nor a plot to keep developing countries underdeveloped. It was incumbent on Strong and others to forge conceptual links between development and the environment.

The Stockholm Declaration suggested such a conceptual link: the principle that it is states' obligation to protect the environment and their responsibility not to cause damage to the environment of other states or areas beyond their national jurisdiction. Delegates also endorsed the principle that environmental policies should enhance developing countries' development potential and not hamper the attainment of better living conditions for all. Environmental concerns are not to be used to justify discriminatory trade practices or as a way to restrict access to domestic markets. Finally, the conference called for the creation of a new UN body to coordinate environmental activities and promote intergovernmental cooperation. That body—the UN Environment Programme (UNEP)—is discussed below.

The Stockholm Conference also inaugurated the important practice of a parallel forum of NGO representatives, run simultaneously with the official conference. This has proven critical for generating new ideas and involving a key set of actors. The almost two hundred groups that participated in the NGO forum at Stockholm set important precedents for similar forums in conjunction with future UN-sponsored global conferences.

Solidification of an Idea: Sustainable Development

The ideas generated at Stockholm on integrating the environment and development continued to be challenged during the next decade. A series of other UN-sponsored global conferences dealt with specific issues such as food, population, desertification, water, human settlements, and climate (see box 2.2). The tension between the developing countries that sought economic growth and developed states that were increasingly questioning the costs and the unintended side effects of economic growth led the UN General Assembly in 1983 to establish the World Commission on Environment and Development (WCED, or Brundtland Commission) (discussed in chapter 5). Its report *Our Common Future* called for "development that meets the needs of the present without compromising the ability of future generations to meet their own needs."[8] It sought to balance ecological concerns with the economic growth necessary to reduce poverty; that became sustainable development. The report underscored that the South cannot develop in the same way the industrialized countries did because humanity could not survive a similarly radical transformation in the environment.

The Brundtland Commission's approach was adopted in 1987 by UNEP, and later by the World Bank, NGOs, and many national development agencies; it became the rallying cry of the environmental movement articulated by academics, state officials, and leading scientists. The commission acknowledged that poverty is a critical source of environmental degradation; it required that people think about critical links between agriculture, trade, transportation, energy, and the environment; and it called attention to the long-term view. The commission also called for a second global conference on the environment twenty years after Stockholm.

The Rio Conference and Sustainability. The 1992 UN Conference on the Environment and Development (UNCED)—or Earth Summit—in Rio de Janeiro and its extensive preparatory process were major outgrowths of the debate over sustainable development and the necessity of balancing economic growth with preserving the environment. Just as the Stockholm conference had occurred because of growing public awareness of environmental issues, the Rio Conference and its preparatory process were influenced by a series of important scientific findings during the 1980s, including the discovery of the ozone hole over Antarctica, the growing evidence of global warming, or climate change, and the accumulating data on loss of biodiversity and depletion of fisheries. Rio was further influenced by three agreements dealing with ozone depletion: the 1985 Vienna Convention for Protection of the Ozone Layer, the 1987 Montreal Protocol on Substances that Deplete the Ozone Layer, and the 1990 London amended protocol phasing out ozone-depleting chemicals. The largest developing countries, most notably China, India, Brazil, and Indonesia, were successful in bargaining with the industrialized countries for unprecedented guarantees of technology and resource transfers from North to South as well as for input into financing decisions—a major victory for the South.

These developments shaped the Rio Conference agenda and were crucial steps in the continuing struggle to get North and South working together to address environmental issues without lessening the shared commitment to promoting economic growth and greater well-being for rich and poor.

The 1992 Rio Earth Summit was the largest of the UN-sponsored global conferences not only in the number of participants but also in the scope of the agenda. As with other conferences, a series of preparatory meetings were used to articulate positions, hammer out basic issues, and negotiate the text for all conference documents. NGOs played significant roles in the preparatory process as well as in the conference. Although the environmental movement began in the North and continued to be dominated by Northern NGOs, by the 1980s it had spread in the South. UNCED provided even further impetus through opportunities for networking among the unprecedented number of participating NGOs. The 1,400 accredited environmental organizations included not only traditional, large, well-financed NGOs, such as the World Wide Fund for Nature and the International Union for the Conservation of Nature, but also many new groups pursuing grassroots activities in developing countries that typically were poorly financed and had few previous transnational linkages.

In retrospect, what did the Rio Earth Summit accomplish? First, it is credited with integrating environmental and development policies worldwide by demonstrating the interconnections between various human activities such as industry, agriculture, and consumption patterns and the environment. The outcomes, summarized in box 7.1, included the Rio Declaration of Twenty-seven Principles, Agenda 21, the UN Convention on Biological Diversity, and the UN Framework Convention on Climate Change. The South succeeded in integrating broader issues of global economic reform into Agenda 21, Chapters 2, 3, 4, and 12. Each program area (debt, structural adjustment, trade and commodities, poverty, and multinational corporations) needs to include not only cost evaluations but also human resource development and capacity building. The South reaffirmed the principle of sovereignty over natural resources such as forests. Yet it also accepted that deforestation, the degradation of water supplies, atmospheric pollution, and desertification were threats to global security and that states were responsible for exercising control over environmentally damaging activities within their boundaries. Second, the linkage between development and the environment was made not only in the UN but also in the trade and development agenda of the WTO and the gradual "greening" of World Bank programs. This suggests a growing consensus around the concept of sustainable development both in the UN system and beyond.

A third outcome of Rio was the acceptance of direct NGO participation in dealing with environmental issues. The goal of sustainable development depends not only on governments, businesses, and IGOs, but also on ordinary people whose interests NGOs often purport to represent. Although the member states excluded NGOs from negotiations concerning the most important final documents, NGOs' persistence paid off. Section II (Chapter 4) of Agenda 21 recognized the unique capabilities of

BOX 7.1   Main Outcomes of the 1992 UN Conference on the Environment and Development

Major Principles Adopted:

Sovereign right of states to exploit their resources

Right of states to develop

Cooperation among states to eradicate poverty

Priority of the needs of the less developed countries

Responsibility of developed countries for global environmental problems

More financial assistance to poorer countries

Implement Agenda 21 based on principles of universality, democracy, cost effectiveness, and accountability

Main Institutional Outcomes:

Two treaties: UN Framework Convention on Climate Change and UN Convention on Biological Diversity

Creation of the Commission on Sustainable Development

The UN General Assembly established as the supreme policymaking forum

UN Secretary-General acts as high-level coordinator

Regional and sub-regional commissions established to foster capacity building for achieving sustainable development

States should produce national reports and action plans for sustainable development

Nongovernmental organizations are integrated as partners in sustainable development efforts

Main Financial Outcomes:

Developed countries to commit 0.07 percent of GNP ratio to foreign assistance by 2000

Agreement to strengthen the Global Environmental Facility

Developed countries pledge new financial assistance to less developed countries at a rate of $607 billion per year to implement the conventions

Adapted from Robert O. Matthews, "United Nations Reform in the 1990s," *ACUNS Reports and Papers,* no. 5, 1993, 15–38, and Peter S. Thatcher, "Evaluating the 1992 Earth Summit," *Security Dialogue* 23, no. 3 (1992): 117–126.

NGOs and recommended that they participate at all levels, from policy- and decisionmaking to implementation. What began as a parallel informal process of participation within the UN system evolved into a more formal role. Indeed, NGO
participation at UNCED stimulated a review of their relationship with the UN.
Many NGOs had been admitted to UNCED even though they did not have official
consultative status with ECOSOC. Some states and long-established NGOs argue
that the proliferation of NGOs, many of which do not have international experience
or logistical capacity, has undermined and delegitimized their consultative status
with ECOSOC. The newer NGOs, many of them small, grassroots organizations
from the South, see participation in the UN system as a significant breakthrough,
one that makes the UN more representative of the "peoples of the world." Rio
marked a high point for NGOs and the international environmental movement.

Finally, just as Stockholm led to the establishment of UNEP, Rio led to the creation of the Commission on Sustainable Development (CSD) in 1993 as the body
to encourage and monitor the implementation of Agenda 21. CSD is discussed below. As one observer remarked, "institutionalization of sustainable Third World
development within the UN system may be the most important consequence of
Rio for the less industrialized world."[9]

Beyond Rio: The Challenges of Implementing Sustainable Development.
Moving from promises and commitments to implementing sustainable development as articulated in the Rio documents has proven difficult. For the most part,
only a fraction of the requisite resources have actually been committed. In the
mid-1990s, for example, development assistance, including funding for environmentally related activities, dropped to its lowest level in decades. When the General
Assembly convened its Special Session, "Earth Summit Plus Five," in 1997, the
global environment was worse than ever and too few concrete steps had been taken
to halt rising levels of greenhouse emissions, toxic pollution, solid waste, and the
unsustainable depletion of water, soil, fisheries, and other resources. The Review
Conference itself was disappointing. Conflicting interests among and between developed and developing countries over the core issues of sustainable development
blocked agreement on all but a few general goals. In the words of General Assembly President Razali Ismail of Malaysia, "There was a clear acknowledgment by all
. . . that progress . . . remains insufficient."[10]

The Millennium Declaration and the Millennium Development Goals adopted
in September 2001 represented a major effort to integrate environmental concerns
with other threats to human security (see box 5.1). MDG 7 calls for ensuring environmental sustainability. The stated targets are to integrate principles of sustainable development into country policies and programs and reverse the loss of
environmental resources, to halve by 2015 the proportion of people without sus-

tainable access to safe drinking water and sanitation, and by 2020 to achieve a major improvement in the lives of 100 million slum dwellers.

In 2002, another summit was convened in Johannesburg, South Africa, the UN World Summit on Sustainable Development, also known as Rio Plus 10. The 2002 summit, however, is generally seen as disappointing compared to previous gatherings. Although the gathering was large (a hundred presidents and prime ministers, 10,000 delegates, and almost 1,000 NGOs, including 8,000 members from civil society), there had been few preparations. Only the European Union held preparatory meetings. States avoided making postsummit commitments for curbing the use of energy resources or for changing forest, soil, and water management practices. The summit's Plan of Implementation included some targets, like access to clean water and proper sanitation, that were consistent with MDGs; others focused more specifically on environmental issues such as the restoration of fisheries by 2015, the reduction of biodiversity loss by 2010, and the better use of chemicals by 2020, as well as more use of renewable energy, but no target or plan was specified. These goals with long time horizons were to be achieved through partnerships between governments, citizen groups, and business (called action coalitions), many of which had already been forged before Johannesburg. The Europeans supported specific targets and timetables, but the United States argued that targets were unnecessary. The South sought more aid for economic growth; the North disagreed. Partnerships were a key strategy for achieving summit outcomes, yet NGOs were still not permitted to be full participants at the meetings.

Part of the explanation for the disappointing results was that by the time the Johannesburg Summit convened in 2002, there was increasing disillusionment with the notion of sustainable development. The term was perceived as a "buzzword largely devoid of content," and some officials, especially in the developing world, had begun to argue that "sustainable" refers to continuity of economic growth without even acknowledging the term's environmental dimension.[11] The timing is especially ironic because, just as disillusionment set in during the early years of the new millennium, there was growing recognition that environmental degradation can cause conflicts between states. In the Middle East, the degradation of water resources has exacerbated conflict between Israel and Jordan, as well as between Turkey and Syria; in Asia, water conflicts linked to degradation have led to conflicts between India and Bangladesh and states around the Caspian and Aral Seas. A widely read book, *Collapse,* argues that environmental degradation and the ensuing struggle for scarce resources led not only to the collapse of states and empires in the past but also to state failure in Rwanda and Haiti.[12] And, as the Indian Ocean tsunami (2004), hurricane Katrina in the United States (2005), and the earthquake in Kashmir (2005) illustrate, humans living in environmentally fragile zones are vulnerable to natural disasters, some of which may be linked to global climate change.

The Institutional Framework for Environmental Protection

The creation of international environmental institutions, including new organizations and a large number of environmental treaties, has been a permanent legacy of UN-sponsored activities since the early 1970s. These have set standards and contributed to the evolution of key ideas. The organizations coordinate initiatives, encourage and support treaty negotiations, monitor state behavior, aid member states, NGOs, and other IGOs in the promotion of environmental standards, and, occasionally, enforce environmental norms. One scholar put it this way: "The clearest evidence for the ecological turn in world politics is the astonishing array of recent treaties on a host of environmental problems, including marine pollution, acid rain, stratospheric ozone depletion, loss of biodiversity, and the export of toxic waste to developing countries"[13] (see table 7.1).

Global environment-related conferences and world summits such as UNCHE in Stockholm, UNCED in Rio, and Rio Plus 10 in Johannesburg, as well as others on food, water, population, and desertification, have played major roles in this evolution of institutions and ideas. Because the topics were new to the international agenda when the process began in the 1970s, the UN used these global conferences "to highlight the interconnections between issues that had previously been treated in isolation[,] . . . to mobilize concern about new problems, to coordinate national actions to study and monitor environmental quality and human activities with environmental consequences, and to develop joint measures."[14] Inevitably, some conferences have been more productive than others, as we have seen. Because the goals and outputs have often been ambiguous, it can be difficult to measure the impact on states' behavior, let alone on the environment. As one scholar noted, however, "it is equally unreasonable to assign blame to conferences for failing to reverse environmental decline."[15] Among the more concrete outcomes have been new organizations.

United Nations Environment Programme.   The United Nations Environment Programme was the chief product of Stockholm and was established by the General Assembly in 1972. With Maurice Strong as its first executive director, UNEP became the champion of the emerging environmental agenda and, by establishing its headquarters in Nairobi, Kenya, it became the first UN agency based in a developing country. With a relatively small professional staff and an annual budget of about $200 million, its mandate is to promote international cooperation in the field of the environment, serve as an "early warning system" to alert the international community to environmental dangers, provide guidance for the direction of environmental programs in the UN system, and review implementation of these programs. UNEP's Governing Council sets general policy and reports to the General Assembly through ECOSOC. Its fifty-eight members are elected by the UN General Assembly for four-year terms.

TABLE 7.1   UN Environmental Agreements

Year	Convention
1971	Convention on Wetlands of International Importance Especially as Waterfowl Habitat
1972	Convention for the Protection of the World Cultural and Natural Heritage
1973	Convention to Regulate International Trade in Endangered Species of Wild Fauna and Flora (CITES)
1979	Convention on the Conservation of Migratory Species of Wild Animals
1982	UN Convention on the Law of the Sea
1985	Vienna Convention for the Protection of the Ozone Layer
1987	Montreal Protocol on Substances that Deplete the Ozone Layer
1987	Convention on Long-Range Transboundary Air Pollution Concerning the Control of Emissions of Nitrogen Oxides or Their Transboundary Fluxes
1989	Convention on the Control of Transboundary Movements of Hazardous Wastes and Their Disposal
1991	Protocol on Environmental Protection to the Antarctic Treaty
1992	UN Convention on Biological Diversity
1992	UN Framework Convention on Climate Change
1994	UN Convention to Combat Desertification in Those Countries Experiencing Serious Drought and/or Desertification, Particularly in Africa
1997	Kyoto Protocol to UN Framework Convention on Climate Change
1998	Convention on the Prior Informed Consent Procedure for Certain Hazardous Chemicals and Pesticides in International Trade
2000	Convention on the Conservation and Management of the Highly Migratory Fish Stocks of the Western and Central Pacific
2001	Stockholm Convention on Persistent Organic Pollutants

Although it has no direct programmatic responsibilities, UNEP has played a proactive role. In the mid-1980s, Executive Director Mustafa Tolba provided leadership for the negotiation of the Montreal Protocol on Substances that Deplete the Ozone Layer and the 1990 London Amendment that further tightened states' agreement to phase out ozone-depleting chemicals. UNEP co-sponsored the negotiations for the Basel Convention on Hazardous Waste Substances (1989) and provides secretariat support for that convention as well as for the UN Convention on Biological Diversity (1992) and the Montreal Protocol. For the latter convention, UNEP's Multilateral Fund assists less developed countries in meeting the costs of compliance. UNEP also oversees the implementation and coordination of the International Registry of Toxic Chemicals, the Global Environmental Monitoring System, and the Regional Seas Program. And it works closely with other UN specialized agencies. Together with the World Meteorological Organization, it monitors atmospheric quality; ocean quality monitoring is shared with the International Oceanographic Council. UNEP, FAO, and WHO jointly conduct studies of freshwater quality.

During its early years, UNEP was strengthened by the dynamic leadership of its first two executive directors, Maurice Strong and Mustafa Tolba. In the process leading to the successful negotiations on ozone, Tolba mobilized an international constituency and initiated consultations with key governments, private interest groups, and international organizations. He argued for flexibility, applied pressure, and floated his own proposals as a stimulus to participants. He organized the negotiating process and procedures expeditiously, subdividing the issues into smaller problems.[16] More recently, UNEP's Executive Director Klaus Toepfer has helped keep environmental concerns on the global agenda. The environment "is the oxygen breathing life into all the Goals (MDG)," he argued at the 2005 World Summit. "It is the red ribbon running around our common aspirations for a healthier, more stable and just world. It is also critical to the economies of countries and regions, a fact that governments have yet to fully take on board but which they ignore at their economic peril."[17]

Although UNEP is often given credit for its role in the ozone "solution," it has been handicapped in other areas by its limited leverage over the specialized agencies and national governments, its location in Nairobi far removed from other UN centers, and its nominal budget. Not only are the funds relatively modest, but the budget is divided between a very small regular budget provided by the UN, the Environment Fund comprised of entirely voluntary contributions, the Trust Fund for very specific purposes, UN Foundation support mainly for biodiversity and climate change, and partnership agreements with major donors for earmarked funds. UNEP, like many UN agencies and programs, has been a venue for North-South confrontation. The developed countries fear that the UNEP bureaucracy has been captured by LDC interests. Rather than supporting a strong and independent UNEP bureaucracy, they have preferred to strengthen the role of national environmental ministers in determining UNEP policies.

Commission on Sustainable Development.   The Commission on Sustainable Development (CSD) was created following the 1992 Rio Conference to encourage and monitor implementation of Agenda 21, review reports from states, and coordinate sustainable development activities within the UN system, overlapping in part with UNEP. Since it first convened in 1993, an important task for the CSD has been strengthening the participation of major societal groups, including NGOs, indigenous peoples, local governments, workers, businesses, women, and the young, in decisionmaking and pioneering innovative arrangements for civil society participation. Located in New York, the commission, with its fifty-three members, is the venue for discussing issues related to sustainable development. Every two years, it focuses on a cluster of issues, most recently on energy for sustainable development, industrial development, and climate control. Yet the CSD, like UNEP, lacks both the power to make binding decisions and necessary financial resources. It is the economic institutions like the World Bank which exercise that power.

Global Environmental Facility.   In 1991, the Global Environmental Facility (GEF) was created at the suggestion of France and Germany. Serving as a catalyst, GEF provides funds for environmental projects with global benefits in low- and middle-income countries. Although the World Bank is the dominant partner in administering the facility, organizing the application process, and implementing projects using facility funds, two other UN agencies participate in implementation. UNEP provides scientific oversight and helps in selecting priorities and UNDP coordinates with other bilateral donors. NGOs are involved in the planning and the execution of projects. As a result, the GEF has emerged as a useful complement to other sources of financial assistance for environmental projects in less developed countries. It has enabled the World Bank to call itself a "green" institution and has augmented the amount of funding for environmental activities.

GEF funds are designed to induce the developing countries to take environmental actions, covering the cost differential between a project initiated with environmental objectives and an alternative project undertaken without attention to global environmental concerns. In addition, through a series of small grants ($50,000–$250,000), the GEF subsidizes grassroots groups, thereby building on its commitment to NGO participation.

GEF's four priorities are ozone, international waters, biodiversity, and climate change. It provides the financial mechanisms for the UN Convention on Biological Diversity and the UN Framework Convention on Climate Change as well as operational guidance on international waters and ozone activities. Two new focal areas have recently been added: land degradation and persistent organic pollutants. With respect to the latter, the GEF helps states destroy harmful pollutants and aids states in making implementation plans.

The GEF Council, comprised of sixteen states from the developing world, fourteen from developed countries, and two from the transitional economies, operates by consensus. That arrangement was developed in the mid-1990s to accommodate contending interests. NGOs enjoy an open invitation to participate, a unique priv-ilege not often found in other international institutions. Every three years, the GEF Assembly meets with all countries to review general policies. The monitoring and evaluation of programs is particularly critical, and there has been an effort made to conduct continuous reviews, including independent evaluations.

Yet the GEF, like UNEP, has encountered political problems, though the prob-lems are different. To many countries in the South, GEF, because of its association with the World Bank, has come to over-represent the interests of the industrialized North, and it fails to address more localized problems, such as soil erosion and ur-ban air pollution, in the South. Despite the organizational changes described above, problems continue, including a dearth of financial resources.

The Difficulties of Halting Environmental Degradation and Promoting Human Security: Lessons Learned

Institutions are in place. The goals for environmental sustainability have been elu-cidated in a variety of UN-related documents and bodies. Multilateral and bilateral financial resources have been allocated, though not nearly enough to meet the de-mands. Global successes have included reducing the threat to the ozone layer caused by chlorofluorocarbons, cleaning up international waters, developing stan-dards to decrease the prevalence and malevolent effects of persistent organic pollu-tants, and joining in fruitful partnerships with state and local institutions to mitigate soil erosion and plant emissions.

Looming large on the international agenda as a threat to human security is global warming. What lessons can be drawn from the above successes, especially in dealing with the ozone problem, which may be relevant for global warming?[18] Four stand out. First, the environmental problem needs to be acknowledged. Ozone depletion was thrust onto the international agenda in 1975 when two American scientists submitted a report attributing the depletion of the ozone layer to use of chlorofluorocarbons (CFCs). The correlation between use of CFCs and ozone depletion was contested for several years among scientists. But in a little less than a decade, following publication of new data confirming a widening ozone hole over Antarctica, most states and scientific experts acknowledged the problem. In contrast, the issue of global climate change, or greenhouse warming, has proven more complicated. The scientific facts are indisputable. Most greenhouse gas emis-sions come from automobile emissions and from the burning of fossil fuels in the industrialized northern countries (and, increasingly, in China, India, and other rapidly growing countries) for power generation, but the deforestation of the trop-ics is also a contributing factor. The models of climate change, however, are com-plex, yet still rudimentary. There is dispute about whether global temperatures have actually risen and by how much. Although most agree that the globe's temperature appears to be between 0.3 and 0.6 degrees centigrade higher than in 1990, scientists disagree about projected increases in the future and what impacts they will have. Global warming may positively affect some, but negatively impact others, such as small-island states and the polar regions. Only in the early years of the millennium has global warming been widely accepted by the scientific community as a major environmental threat to human security.

Second, key states need to support action. The United States and European states were not only the major producers of CFCs but also the major consumers, although usage in the new industrializing countries of India, China, Brazil, and Mexico was rising at about 10 percent annually. U.S., Canadian, and Norwegian leadership was critical to success in negotiating the Montreal Protocol and subsequent amendments. The support of those countries rested on a mobilized public that articulated the issue and on supportive NGOs. The U.S. government was particularly active, and the two important American-based multinational corporations that produced CFCs, Dow Chemical and Dupont, found suitable substitutes for most uses and, hence, did not oppose phasing out those chemicals.

Concerning global warming, the United States has raised major objections to the Kyoto Protocol and to the 1992 UN Framework Convention on Climate Change, and has refused to support any international agreement calling for specific cutbacks in emissions. It believes that the costs of compliance would be too high and that the U.S. economy would be adversely affected. The United States has objected to the fact that developing countries (especially China and India) are excluded from Kyoto's emission limits. In contrast, the Europeans and Japanese have all signed the protocol and have already made significant efforts to reduce emissions. Russia's ratification allowed the protocol to come into force in early 2005 (with 156 parties accounting for 55 percent of greenhouse gas emissions), and Canada hosted the first meeting of parties in Montreal in December 2005. Although the United States continued to oppose binding commitments on emissions, one outcome of the meeting was agreement on negotiations for a new climate treaty that would include both the United States and China. Other outcomes included compliance rules for dealing with countries that do not meet their targets and agreement to promote carbon capture and sequestration technologies for using coal. The Montreal meeting also called for serious efforts to adapt to the consequences of climate change—an important outcome for human security.

Third, multilateral institutions are needed to monitor provisions and settle controversies. For ozone, such institutions developed slowly. In approving the 1985 Vienna Framework Convention, states promised to cooperate on research and data acquisition. The 1987 Montreal Protocol and the 1990 London Amendment further strengthened states' commitment to phase out ozone-depleting chemicals. The industrialized countries agreed to pay for the incremental costs of compliance for developing countries, creating the Multilateral Fund for the Implementation of the Montreal Protocol. The GEF has provided financial assistance to Central and Eastern European countries. More than $12 billion in funds have been allocated to 3,300 projects in 121 countries. The Implementation Committee handles cases of noncompliance. In addition, there is a procedure for states to ask UNEP's Ozone Secretariat (after consultation with a technical committee) for relief should specific industries be adversely affected by the chemical restrictions.

In contrast, with the eight-year lag between conclusion of the Kyoto Protocol and its entry into force, very little institutional structure has yet been created to aid in implementation. There is a Compliance Committee with both facilitative and enforcement tasks. Parties found to be noncompliant are not entitled to use the flexible mechanisms to offset emission standards. Authority has been given to the GEF to finance projects for increasing energy efficiency and energy conservation and for promoting renewable energy sources. Since 1991, GEF has allocated $1.74 billion to climate-change projects, projects that have been matched by more than $9.5 billion in co-financing. Yet without the participation of the largest industrialized countries and largest emitter, the United States, these institutions are clearly weakened.

Fourth, international environmental agreements need flexibility—a way to change standards when new scientific information becomes available—without renegotiating the entire treaty. The Montreal Protocol (and the subsequent London and Copenhagen Amendments) is a flexible instrument that can and has been made more restrictive as the scientific evidence warranted; its provisions could also be relaxed should the ozone problem become less severe.

Likewise, the Kyoto Protocol provides flexible mechanisms for states to meet emission requirements, including emission trading permits, investment credits for the joint implementation of projects, and credits for forested land. Yet the commitments embedded in it expire in 2012. Accordingly, a major agenda item at the 2005 Montreal meeting was to set the framework for negotiations on the second commitment period. Even though it has not ratified Kyoto, the United States was a participant, but a difficult one and it continued to object to fixed emissions targets. Only after former U.S. President Bill Clinton addressed the delegates and suggested that the Bush administration was out of touch with American public opinion and the actions of several American states and corporations were participants able to agree on two negotiating tracks. The first will address second round commitments; the other will seek a climate treaty that includes both the United States and China. One reporter injected a note of irony in his headline: "Glacial Gains in Global Talks on Cleaner Air."[19]

The contrasting cases of ozone depletion and climate change illustrate the difficulties of halting environmental degradation and promoting human security. Preliminary evidence continues to show some improvement in the ozone layer, but the final verdict on whether ozone depletion has been permanently curbed is still out. The same cannot be said for global warming. Emissions continue to increase not only from the parties to the agreement but also from developing countries not covered under the current agreement. The rapid growth in China's emissions is particularly pronounced. An optimistic assessment suggests that now at least more states realize the costs of not taking action. Given current global dependence on oil and gas as major sources of energy to sustain economic growth, the issue of climate change is perhaps the most closely linked to concerns about sustainability and human security. It is also perhaps the toughest to address. Hence, the *Economist* may have been right when it suggested that the "enduring legacy" of the 2005 Montreal conference "may be greater . . . if it results in serious efforts around the world to adapt to the inevitable consequences of climate change."[20]

One of the challenges in addressing environmental threats to human security is the long time lag before major effects may be felt; indeed, this tends to decrease the sense of urgency in addressing the sources of degradation. Such is not the case with infectious diseases and health threats.

HEALTH AND HUMAN SECURITY

Public health and disease are hardly new issues, but globalization has had a dramatic effect on the transmission, incidence, and vulnerability of individuals and communities to disease through migration, air transport, trade, and troop movements. Intensified human mobility poses major problems for containing outbreaks of cholera, influenza, HIV/AIDS, tuberculosis, West Nile virus, Severe Acute Respiratory Syndrome (or SARS), avian (bird) influenza, and other diseases that can be carried in a matter of hours from one part of the globe to another long before symptoms may appear. Globalization has thus exacerbated the urgency and the scope of the threats infectious diseases can pose to human security. The issue is not only vulnerability to large-scale loss of life, however; it is also one of disease impeding development and weakening societies, as the WHO-appointed Commission on Macroeconomics and Health has argued.[21]

Rudimentary international rules to prevent the spread of epidemics, including procedures for instituting quarantines, date back hundreds of years, and institutionalized collaboration can be traced to 1851. With the HIV/AIDS epidemic and recent outbreaks of SARS and avian flu, there has been a substantial strengthening of global health governance just since 2003. The linkage of health and human security was made most directly by the UN Security Council in its first ever special session devoted to the challenge of HIV/AIDs in January 2000. Three of the MDGs deal with health; MDG 6 specifically targets HIV/AIDs, malaria, and other diseases.

Developing International Responses to Health Issues

Between 1851 and 1903, a series of eleven international conferences developed procedures to prevent the spread of contagious and infectious diseases. In 1907, the Office International d'Hygiène Publique (OIHP) was created with a mandate to disseminate information on communicable diseases such as cholera, plague, and yellow fever. More than a decade later, at the request of the League of Nations Council, the International Health Conference met to prepare for a permanent International Health Organization, but OIHP did not become part of this new health organization. Following the UN's creation, in 1948, the World Health Organization (WHO) came into being.

In membership and budget, the WHO is one of the largest UN specialized agencies, a sign of the universality of health concerns. With its strong regional offices located on every continent, it is also one of the more decentralized functional organizations. The WHO secretariat, located in Geneva, is highly technical, the director-general, other secretariat officials, and many delegates being medical doctors. The medical and allied health communities form a strong epistemic community based on their technical expertise and training.

The main decisionmaking body is the World Health Assembly (WHA) comprised of three delegates from each member state, including delegates from the scientific, professional, and nongovernmental communities. Each country, however, has only one vote, unlike the ILO where representatives of each functional group have a separate vote. The Executive Board is a smaller group of thirty members elected by the WHA. By "a gentlemen's agreement," at least three of the Security Council members are supposed to be represented.

WHO Initiatives.   WHO has undertaken several campaigns to eradicate specific diseases. These include the widely acclaimed and successful eradication of smallpox. The last case was reported in 1977. With the global war on terrorism, however, there has been renewed concern over protecting the few remaining smallpox stockpiles. Another campaign, undertaken with the support of Rotary International, the Bill and Melinda Gates Foundation, and other groups, has targeted polio. In 1988, there were 350,000 cases of polio reported in 125 countries. With WHO vaccination programs, polio was close to eradication in 2003. In that year, however, religious objections to vaccination in northern Nigeria contributed to a resurgence of the disease. Cases of polio have since turned up in ten previously polio-free African countries, as well as in Indonesia and Yemen. An earlier campaign against malaria proved unsuccessful, but that endemic disease, too, has been targeted by the international community.

Another area of WHO activity involves regulation. One of the most controversial issues was infant formula regulation. In 1981, the WHA adopted the Code of Marketing for Breast-Milk Substitutes; this called for states to adopt regulations banning marketing and advertising of infant formula that discouraged breastfeeding, but it acknowledged a "legitimate market" for breast milk substitutes. Developing countries have also been concerned that imported drugs were of sufficient quality, and they have sought technical assistance in monitoring quality control. WHO approved guidelines for drug manufacturing quality control in 1970, covering such issues as labeling, self-inspection, and reporting adverse reactions. In the late 1990s, the accessibility and affordability of drugs in developing countries appeared on WHO's agenda. Of particular concern is the antiretroviral "cocktail" of drugs used to treat HIV/AIDs that has been far too costly for use in regions such as Africa without special pricing arrangements and relaxing regulations on licensing generic drugs. That story is told below.

At its root, WHO still is most concerned with the issues that brought about its establishment—the transmission of infectious diseases. Because efforts to deal with the HIV/AIDS epidemic have involved many more UN agencies and other actors than just WHO, we address it separately. The SARS epidemic of 2003, however, reminded the international community of the dangers in rapid contagious transmission. It was "a prime example of the effects of globalization on health security."[22] Although the epidemic killed fewer than 1,000 individuals, the potential for a global pandemic was widely recognized and the economic repercussions on the most affected countries—China, Vietnam, Singapore, and Canada—were significant. During the SARS epidemic, WHO issued a global health alert detailing the disease and its probable method of transmission. Working with public health officials in the United States, Canada, Europe, and Asia, WHO was the conduit for reports on research and governmental actions. WHO officials visited affected countries, helped establish national monitoring systems, advised on infection control methods, and provided technical assistance.

The experience with SARS demonstrated the tension between sovereign states and the UN. China initially suppressed information on the outbreak and was slow to permit WHO officials to visit potentially affected areas. Between November 2002 and February 2003, it refused to admit that the epidemic had spread and did not undertake preventive measures until April of that same year. Canada objected that WHO travel advisories on visiting Toronto were unnecessary.

Referring to SARS, Gro Harlem Brundtland, the former director general of WHO, noted, "It has never been clearer than today that a secure healthy future for us all depends on cooperation across borders and between institutions."[23] Not only did SARS demonstrate that existing international health regulations, last updated in 1969, were seriously outdated by requiring the reporting only of three infectious diseases—cholera, plague, and yellow fever—but it also highlighted the problem that under these regulations, reporting was the exclusive domain of governments. As one scholar noted, "the SARS epidemic had a profound impact on international health governance."[24] In May 2003, the WHA empowered WHO to "take into account reports from sources other than official notifications."[25] In short, nonstate actors are now major players, providing and disseminating information without the consent of governments. In addition, with the SARS epidemic, WHO clearly took upon itself the authority to issue travel advisories and alerts. Building on these precedents, the 2005 assembly approved a new set of international health regulations to help WHO maximize protection against public health emergencies of global concern while minimizing disruptions of trade and tourism.

Brundtland's remarks are just as appropriate for the 2005–2006 outbreaks of avian flu. In response to the possibility that the H5N1 strain of avian influenza could mutate and result in rapid human-to-human transmission, potentially setting off a world flu pandemic, WHO established a new Strategic Operations Center for the Global Outbreak Alert and Response Network. This is a medical strike force, a "fire brigade," that has the capacity to send experts, on six hours notice, to distribute antiviral drugs in an area affected by an outbreak. Longer term, the aim is to train nationals in developing countries to identify outbreaks, provide essential technology for surveillance, and encourage states to develop national plans. Regional offices of WHO, national health institutes, and developed states are all involved in this urgent initiative.[26] The reality is, however, that many countries affected by avian flu have neither the surveillance systems nor the diagnostic tools needed to provide early warning and rapid response. Few governments are prepared for a widespread health emergency. To underscore the seriousness of the threat a global pandemic of influenza could pose to human security, UN Secretary-General Kofi Annan used his 2005 report, *In Larger Freedom,* to indicate his willingness to use Article 99 of the UN Charter to ask the Security Council to deal with "any overwhelming outbreak of infectious disease that threatens international peace and security."[27]

There are other infectious diseases, some old and endemic, such as malaria and tuberculosis, others new, such as Ebola and Marburg hemorrhagic fever. WHO is at the forefront of efforts to address these and, with the lessons of SARS in mind, launched a three-year effort in 2004 to strengthen its capacity for responding to health crises of all types, including those resulting from natural disasters such as earthquakes and hurricanes.

The international health agenda has expanded well beyond the issues of the nineteenth century, and the WHO's central role has been complemented by other IGOs, NGOs, private groups, and governments and public health authorities. In the 1980s, the World Bank emerged as the largest external financier of health programs in developing countries. In the 1990s, other groups took the initiative in AIDS, as we shall see below. Since 2000, international funding has increasingly been funneled through major research institutes and foundations, such as the Gates Foundation, and administered by NGOs. The change has been motivated in part by the challenges posed by the HIV/AIDS epidemic, which, more than any other health issue, has demonstrated how infectious disease in particular threatens human security.

The Challenge of AIDS

The greatest challenge for global governance generally is the HIV/AIDS epidemic. Not just a health or humanitarian problem, it threatens economic development and social stability in the world's poorest regions. There is no cure. The disease is highly mutable, and some mutations are resistant to drugs. It is disproportionately affecting those in the most productive years between fifteen and forty-five years, including military personnel. Indeed, soldiers serving in peacekeeping forces in Africa have helped spread the disease. States with overwhelming economic problems are apt to fail, and failed states are ripe for conflict. In the twenty-five years since its emergence, more than 25 million people have died, 3.1 million in 2005 alone. More than 40 million individuals are currently living with the disease; and, with infection rates rising in India, China, Central Asia, Russia, Eastern Europe, and the Caribbean, as well as much of Africa, where some 70 percent of affected adults currently live, those numbers will rise further. Only a few countries, such as Thailand, Uganda, Senegal, and Brazil, have succeeded in slowing or reversing the rate of infection. A 2001 International Crisis Group report made this statement: "Where it reaches epidemic proportions, HIV/AIDS can be so pervasive that it destroys the very fibre of what constitutes a nation: individuals, families and communities; economic and political institutions; military and police forces. It is likely then to have broader security consequences."[28]

International responses to the AIDS epidemic have mirrored evolving awareness of the multifaceted nature of the problem. Initially, in 1986, the World Health Organization took the lead. The earliest WHO actions, for example, were to stimulate the creation of national AIDS programs. That was based on the idea that governments' willingness to acknowledge HIV/AIDS as a major problem and their commitment to enlarging public health budgets would be vital steps needed to address the problem. Yet both measures were controversial because some states refused to acknowledge the problem and others did not have the resources to devote to it.

Other UN agencies gradually became involved when it became evident that the effects of AIDS reached beyond health. In 1996, the Joint Programme on HIV/AIDS, or UNAIDS, was created by UNICEF, UNDP, the UN Fund for Population Activities, UNESCO, WHO, and the World Bank—with the UN Drug Control Programme, WFP, and the ILO subsequently joining—to be the lead agency for global action. UNAIDS illustrates the importance of network approaches through partnerships among UN agencies, national governments, corporations, religious organizations, grassroots groups, and NGOs. It tracks the epidemic, monitors responses, distributes strategic information, mobilizes resources, and reaches out to diverse groups. Illustrative of the variety of partnerships that AIDS-related initiatives require, the Global Alliance for Vaccines and Immunization (GAVI), which is

CARTOON 7.1   The Spectre of AIDS. KAL, the *Economist*. *KAL, CartoonArts International/CWS.*

supporting efforts to develop an AIDS vaccine, receives funding from the Bill and Melinda Gates Children's Vaccine Program, the Rockefeller Foundation, and the International Federation of Pharmaceutical Manufacturers Associations, as well as UNICEF, WHO, and the World Bank.

The UN has convened global AIDS conferences every two years to raise awareness and mobilize responses. Three UN Security Council sessions in 2000 and 2001, along with reports by the International Crisis Group and others, increased global awareness of AIDS. In 2000, for example, UN Security Council Resolution 1308 identified the AIDS pandemic as a threat to global security, the first time a health issue was elevated to such status. The 2001 Special Session of the General Assembly resulted in unanimous adoption of a Declaration of Commitment and the Global HIV/AIDS and Health Fund with a target of $7–10 billion in annual expenditure by 2005 in the most affected poor and middle-income countries, a target that has not been met. Including HIV/AIDS in the MDGs makes fighting it a top global priority.

Preventive measures cause relatively little controversy, but the same is not true for treatment measures. In the mid-1990s, the development of antiretroviral multi-drug "cocktails" raised economic and ethical questions that the UN proved ill-equipped to handle. The expense of the drugs made their use in Africa and Asia problematic; yet the budgets of the UN and related specialized agencies were inadequate to subsidize long-term expensive drug treatments. The pharmaceutical companies were reluctant to cooperate, citing the need to protect intellectual property rights against cheaper generic substitutes manufactured in Brazil and India. Intellectual property rights protections are enshrined in the World Trade Organization's international trading rules. Developed countries that might provide additional financing or relax trade rules have been reluctant to commit the necessary sums, and their efforts are limited by pressures from domestic pharmaceutical companies. The U.S. government has been particularly reluctant to allow the wider distribution of generic, low-cost drugs manufactured in India and Brazil.

Faced with an outpouring of pressure from NGOs, IGOs, and affected developing countries, the major pharmaceutical companies first adopted two strategies: one of creating partnerships with individual countries for exclusive distribution at reduced prices and another that involved lawsuits against states that wanted to make cheaper substitutes. The first approach, adopted by five companies working with WHO, initially reached far fewer people than anticipated, and prices were still too high for most Africans. The second approach gained public attention but became a public relations nightmare. "There has been a world-wide revolt of public opinion," UN Secretary-General Kofi Annan told African leaders in the African Summit on HIV/AIDS and Other Related Infectious Diseases in April 2001. "People no longer accept that the sick and dying, simply because they are poor, should be denied drugs which have transformed the lives of others who are better off."[29]

NGOs such as Oxfam, the AIDS Coalition to Unleash Power (ACT UP), and Africa Action, as well as student activists, created the transnational Treatment Action Campaign to exert more pressure on the pharmaceutical companies to reduce prices of antiretrovirals for developing countries in general, and African states in particular—a strategy that has resonated with many people. The pharmaceutical manufacturers were forced to alter pricing strategies in poor countries and stop their efforts to thwart the sale of generics.

To increase attention to AIDS-related issues, Secretary-General Kofi Annan appointed four regional special representatives on AIDS and has spoken out frequently. He has organized meetings with the pharmaceutical companies and officials from UNAIDS and WHO, and has sought to convince MNCs operating in Africa to participate in AIDS prevention by offering counseling, condoms, and treatment, including the antiretroviral cocktail, for affected employees. Annan pushed for the creation of the Global Fund to Fight AIDS, Tuberculosis and Malaria in 2002. This is a unique public-private effort to gather and distribute funds to the most severely affected countries. As of 2005, the fund had committed $3 billion in

128 countries and approved funding for some 1.6 million people to receive anti-retroviral treatment and still more to be tested for infection. It is also enabling training of several hundred thousand people for a variety of prevention programs.[30] In addition to working to increase resources available for fighting HIV/AIDS, Annan and his representatives have been more willing to criticize governments that have not taken sufficient responsibility for responses to the epidemic. For example, Stephen Lewis, the secretary-general's special envoy to Africa on AIDS, strongly criticized the South African government and President Thabo Mbeki for his "bewildering" set of policies and that country's "lackadaisical" approach.[31]

The UN's recognition that the AIDS epidemic and other health issues directly link to human security is illustrated by their inclusion in the Millennium Development Goals. Goal 6 calls for combating HIV/AIDS, malaria, and other diseases, with the major target of halting and reversing the spread of HIV/AIDS by 2015. Goal 4 calls for the reduction of child mortality, and Goal 5 addresses the need for the improvement of maternal health. Until those goals are reached, health issues will continue to pose major challenges for the UN system. Even then, as one scholar noted, "although new technologies and breakthroughs may allow us to cure once devastating diseases, new contagions and long-dormant ones will pose new threats."[32]

DILEMMAS IN HUMAN SECURITY

Environmental degradation and health threats are only two of many human security issues. Adverse impacts of technology, population pressures, and growing poverty are among other threats to human security. Such disparities have critical ramifications, as a UN panel warned several months before the September 11, 2001, attacks: "In the global village, someone else's poverty very soon becomes one's own problem: of lack of markets for one's products, illegal immigration, pollution, contagious disease, insecurity, fanaticism, terrorism."[33] Because they represent new needs for governance that cut across traditional ways of defining issues, challenge state sovereignty, and require leadership, human security issues pose major dilemmas for the United Nations system.

Dilemma One: Needs for Governance Versus the UN's Weakness

Human security issues are now widely accepted as a permanent part of the UN's agenda, though framing environmental degradation and health as human security issues has occurred only since the mid-1990s. Institutionalization, however, has tended to be ad hoc and piecemeal, often with little thought to how coordination was to occur. There is a perennial shortage of funds to tackle the governance challenges posed by human security issues. Debate continues on whether there should be greater centralization of these international activities under UN authority, or whether a more decentralized approach is more effective.

The debate over environmental governance exemplifies this dilemma. On one side are those who argue for the greater centralization of environmental institutions through a world or global environmental organization. They note that UNEP's weak mandate, insufficient powers, and inadequate resources to address problems mean the UN system only addresses certain issues. They believe problems such as lack of resources and coordination can be resolved by creating a global or world environmental organization.[34] On the other side are those who suggest that restructuring or creating a new architecture will divert attention from the major institutional and policy issues, including confusion over the norm of sustainable development and the challenge of integrating nonstate actors and civil society into the governance process. In all likelihood, the only suitable approach to international environmental issues is a multilevel one with a wide variety of partnerships.[35] The UN and its specialized agencies play valuable roles, but their weaknesses as institutions mean they cannot accomplish the tasks alone, either in the environment or in health. There will continue to be decentralized approaches and partnerships among global, regional, national, and local entities, public and private, with the UN a central, but not always the most important, actor.

Dilemma Two: Sovereignty Versus Challenges to Sovereignty

Human security issues are boundary-spanning issues because epidemics and pollution do not stop at states' borders. As a result, these issues and, most especially, responses to them, challenge state sovereignty. That challenge is just as fundamental as it is to human rights issues and to humanitarian intervention. States, quite predictably, continue to be wary of such challenges, just as they have feared interference in their domestic affairs on other issues. Although the hard shell of sovereignty has been breached, the tension still remains and the shell is not yet broken. The SARS epidemic illustrates the necessity of using all possible sources of information on infectious disease regardless of whether governments admit there is a problem or whether they cooperate with WHO to provide data. Ozone depletion and climate change illustrate the potential for cooperation when there is shared recognition of a problem and a willingness to provide assistance in dealing with it, as well as the variety of factors, including a powerful state, that can block action.

Dilemma Three: Need for Leadership Versus Dominance of Sole Superpower

All issues require leaders who seize the issue as their own, publicize it, mobilize constituencies, forge potential solutions, and work for implementation. On human security issues that may come from a particular state, such as Canada, which has made human security an integral part of its foreign policy, or a group of states, such as those that have ratified the Kyoto Protocol and demonstrated their determination to forge ahead in its implementation even without the participation of the United States. Leadership can come from the UN secretary-general, as Kofi Annan has demonstrated on repeated occasions, the executive-director of UNEP, the director-general of WHO, the head of UNAIDS, or an ambassador such as Richard Holbrooke, who played a key role in convening the first Security Council session on the threat of HIV/AIDS. Given the wide recognition of threats to human security now, it is not necessarily vital for the world's sole superpower to be leader or initiator. Nonstate actors of various kinds are important partners in addressing these issues. Commitments of governmental funding are important, but private foundations such as the Bill and Melinda Gates Foundation have shown how much can be done with private initiative.

The challenges posed by human security issues reinforce what we have seen with respect to peace and security issues, economic development, and human rights, namely, that reform of the UN system is imperative to strengthen the UN system's capacity to deal with contemporary governance needs. It is to that topic we now turn.

NOTES

1. Thomas G. Weiss, David P. Forsythe, and Roger A. Coate, *The United Nations and Changing World Politics,* 4th ed. (Boulder: Westview Press, 2004), 278.

2. See, for example Roland Paris, "Human Security: Paradigm Shift or Hot Air?" *International Security* 26, no. 2 (Fall 2001): 87–102.

3. Richard Jolly, Louis Emmerij, and Thomas G. Weiss, *The Power of UN Ideas: Lessons from the First 60 Years* (New York: United Nations Intellectual History Project, 2005), 34.

4. Sadako Ogata and Johan Cels, "Human Security—Protecting and Empowering the People," *Global Governance* 9, no. 3 (July-September 2003): 275. Sadako Ogata was co-chair of the Commission on Human Security and former UN High Commissioner for Refugees. Johan Cels was the commission's project coordinator for conflict.

5. Edward Newman, "Human Security and Constructivism," *International Studies Perspectives* 2, no. 3 (August 2001): 241. For a somewhat different approach to the link between environmental degradation and state security, see Thomas Homer-Dixon, *Environment, Scarcity, and Violence,* 2nd ed. (Princeton: Princeton University Press, 1999). Also see Michael T. Klare, *The New Landscape of Global Conflict* (New York: Metropolitan/Owl Book, 2001).

6. Karen T. Litfin, "Constructing Environmental Security and Ecological Interdependence," *Global Governance* 5, no. 3 (July-September 1999), 364.

7. See Rachel Carson, *Silent Spring* (Cambridge, Mass.: Houghton Mifflin, 1962) and Garrett Hardin, "The Tragedy of the Commons," *Science* 162 (13 December 1968): 1243–1248.

8. World Commission on Environment and Development, *Our Common Future,* 8.

9. Craig N. Murphy, "The United Nations Capacity to Promote Sustainable Development: The Lessons of a Year That 'Eludes All Facile Judgment,'" in *The State of the United Nations: 1992,* ed. Albert Legault, Craig N. Murphy, and W. B. Ofuatey-Kodjoe, ACUNS Reports and Papers, no. 3 (1993), 60.

10. "Grey Is the Theory, But Green Is the Tree of Life," *UN Chronicle* 3 (1997): 22.

11. Daniel C. Esty, "A Term's Limits," *Foreign Policy* 126 (September-October 2001): 74.

12. Jarod Diamond, *Collapse. How Societies Choose to Fail or Collapse* (New York: Penguin, 2005).

13. Litfin, "Constructing Environmental Security and Ecological Interdependence," 367.

14. Peter M. Haas, "UN Conferences and Constructivist Governance of the Environment," *Global Governance* 8, no. 1 (January-March 2002): 78.

15. Ibid., 81.

16. Richard Elliot Benedick, *Ozone Diplomacy: New Directions in Safeguarding the Planet,* enlarged ed. (Cambridge, Mass.: Harvard University Press, 1998).

17. Klaus Toepfer, "Nature's Capital Must Be at Centre of Poverty Eradication," UNEP News Centre, 12 September 2005, http://www.unep.org/Documents.Multilingual/Default.asp?DocumentID=452&ArticleID=4925&l=en.

18. See Michele M. Betsill, "Global Climate Change Policy: Making Progress or Spinning Wheels?" in *The Global Environment. Institutions, Law, and Policy,* ed. Regina S. Axelrod, David Leonard Downie, and Norman J. Vig, 2nd ed. (Washington D.C.: CQ Press, 2005), 103–124.

19. Andrew C. Revkin, "Glacial Gains in Global Talks on Cleaner Air," *New York Times,* December 11, 2005.

20. "Pricking the Global Conscience," *Economist* 377, no. 8457 (December 17, 2005): 77.

21. World Health Organization, *Macroeconomics and Health: Investing in Health for Economic Development,* Report of the Commission on Macroeconomics and Health (Geneva: World Health Organization, 2001), http://www.who.int/macrohealth/documents/en. For an extended treatment on health and security, see Andrew T. Price-Smith, *The Health of Nations: Infectious Disease, Environmental Change, and Their Effects on National Security and Development* (Cambridge, Mass.: MIT Press, 2002).

22. Ilona Kickbusch and Lea Payne, "Ensuring Health Security in an Interdependent World," in *Global Agenda: Issues Before the 59th General Assembly of the United Nations,* ed. Angela Drakulich (New York: United Nations Association of the USA, 2004), 12.

23. Quoted in Lawrence K. Altman, "No Cases of SARS Have Been Transmitted on Airlines Since March, W.H.O. Report," *New York Times,* May 20, 2003.

24. Yanzhong Huang, "Commentary: International Health Regulations—the SARS Example," in *Global Agenda: Issues Before the 60th General Assembly of the United Nations,* ed. Angela Drakulich (New York: United Nations Association of the USA, 2005), 216.

25. Quoted in ibid.

26. David Brown, "Preparing for the Worst," *Washington Post National Weekly Edition,* December 5–11, 2005.

27. *In Larger Freedom: Towards Development, Security and Human Rights for All,* Report of the Secretary-General, 21 March 2005, http://www.un.org/largerfreedom.

28. International Crisis Group, "HIV/AIDS as a Security Issue," 2001, www.intl-crisis-group.org.

29. Kofi Annan, "From the Secretary-General: Facing It Head-On. We Can. We Must," *UN Chronicle* 38, no. 1 (March 2001): 5.

30. Yanzhong Huang, "Health: Preventing Infectious Diseases, Securing Well-being," *Global Agenda: Issues Before the 60th General Assembly of the United Nations,* ed. Angela Drakulich (New York: United Nations Association of the U.S.A, 2005), 203.

31. Sharon LaFraniere, "U.N. Envoy Sharply Criticizes South Africa's AIDS Program," *New York Times,* October 25, 2005.

32. Octavio Gomez-Dantes, "Health," in *Managing Global Issues: Lessons Learned,* ed. P. J. Simmons and Chantal de Jonge Oudraat (Washington D.C.: Carnegie Endowment for International Peace, 2001), 417.

33. United Nations General Assembly, *Report of the High-level Panel on Financing for Development Appointed by the United Nations Secretary-General,* Fifth-fifth Session, Agenda item 101, 26 June 2001, A/55/1000, 3, www.un.org/esa/ffd/a55–1000.pdf.

34. Haas, "UN Conferences and Constructivist Governance of the Environment," 87–88.

35. See Adil Najam, "The Case Against a New International Environmental Organization," *Global Governance* 9, no. 3 (July-September 2003): 367–384.

8

◄○►

The Future of the United Nations

Reform is a process, not an event. . . . The UN is not a house in which revolutionaries flourish.

—Secretary-General Kofi Annan (1997, 1998)

Excellencies, we have come to a fork in the road. This may be a moment no less decisive than 1945 itself, when the United Nations was founded.

—Secretary-General Kofi Annan (2003)

For many, the future of the United Nations is closely linked to the fate of efforts to reform the institution and, thereby, enhance its legitimacy, accountability, and effectiveness. Over the UN's sixty-year history, there have been periodic calls for reform, including Charter revision. In the 1970s, the thrust was on improving the coordination of economic and social programs in the UN system; in the 1980s, calls for financial reforms dominated the agenda. Since the 1990s and into the new millennium, several factors have driven the reform agenda, including the need for more resources caused by expansion of UN obligations, particularly for peace-keeping, the counterpressures within the U.S. government for reduction of the UN budget and for managerial reforms, and the election of an activist secretary-general whose platform called for reform and whose legitimacy has been based on reform. Thus, the call for reform goes to the heart of the first dilemma: the need for governance (and the funding for those activities) versus the UN's weaknesses. Reforms are designed to remedy those weaknesses.

Yet the demands the UN has faced since the Cold War's end and in the early twenty-first century for dealing with threats to international peace and security, alleviating poverty and promoting economic and social development, halting environmental degradation, and protecting human rights have revealed its weaknesses more than ever. The UN, to be sure, has expanded the functions of peacekeepers, articulated the Millennium Development Goals, met humanitarian emergencies, created the Office of the High Commissioner for Human Rights, and implemented other reforms within the Secretariat—all without amending the Charter. To many observers, however, the UN is still hamstrung by pre–Cold War structures, redundant agencies, inadequate personnel policies, a lack of accountability and transparency, and the inability to meet the needs of a changing world. The sixtieth anniversary in 2005 appeared to be an opportune moment to press for fundamental changes in policy, institutions, and internal management. By examining some of these major proposals for reform, we gain insights into the problems that need fixing and the politics of achieving change.

How can UN reform occur? First, changes in the major organs of the UN require amending the UN Charter. This has happened on only two occasions thus far: in 1963 when the Security Council membership was increased from eleven to fifteen, its voting majority changed from seven to nine, and ECOSOC enlarged from eighteen to twenty-seven members; and again in 1971, when ECOSOC was expanded to fifty-four members. Today's UN membership is more than three times that of 1945, and the world has changed in fundamental ways. The rise in demands for UN actions reflects many of those changes. Like many constitutions, the UN Charter is designed to be difficult to amend, however. Under Articles 108 and 109, amendments must be approved and ratified by two-thirds of the UN member states, including all five permanent members of the Security Council. The principal reforms under discussion that would require Charter amendment include the size and composition of the Security Council and deletion of the Military Staff Committee and the Trusteeship Council. The first of these is the most controversial.

Many changes, however, can and have been accomplished without amending the UN Charter, as we have seen throughout earlier chapters. This includes the creation of new bodies to meet new demands, addressing coordination and management issues, transparency and accountability issues, and the termination of those that have outlived their usefulness. In 1997, for example, Secretary-General Kofi Annan merged three departments into one Department of Economic and Social Affairs, and all the Geneva-based human rights programs into the Office of the High Commissioner for Human Rights. He reduced the size of the Secretariat by almost 4,000, created the post of deputy secretary-general, grouped the central offices into five executive groups (their heads forming a cabinet), and promoted the idea of UN "houses" in developing countries to bring UN development agencies and programs together. In short, incremental changes are easier to effect than revolutionary changes.

Among the major reforms currently being initiated are the Peacebuilding Commission to enhance the UN's capacity to support and coordinate complex peacebuilding missions; the Human Rights Council to replace the Commission on Human Rights; and various changes to enhance the UN's ability to meet new security threats, including poverty, infectious diseases, terrorism, environmental degradation, and organized crime. The oil-for-food scandal has raised issues of accountability and transparency. None of these changes requires amending the Charter. Management reform within the Secretariat can be accomplished by the secretary-general; the creation of a new commission or program requires General Assembly action. Shifts in priorities and enhancing UN capacity generally require action by one of the major organs and the Secretariat. Changes that require new resources need the support of contributing states and, in the social and economic field, the support of private funders, such as the Gates Foundation on health initiatives, or corporations such as the major pharmaceuticals in the case of HIV/AIDS, or the establishment of effective partnerships where the UN is only one of many partners.

In the wake of the U.S.-led invasion of Iraq in March 2003, when speculation about the UN's future was widespread, Secretary-General Kofi Annan made his famous "fork in the road" address to the General Assembly. He suggested that it might be a moment as decisive as 1945. "Now," he said, "we must decide whether it is possible to continue on the basis agreed then, or whether radical changes are needed. And we must not shy away from questions about the adequacy, and effectiveness, of the rules and instruments at our disposal."[1] To examine contemporary global threats and recommend measures for ensuring effective action in the future, "including but not limited to a review of the principal organs of the United Nations," he established the High-level Panel on Threats, Challenges and Change (HLP). Among the distinguished individuals on the sixteen-member panel were former presidents and prime ministers and former heads of UN agencies. Their report, submitted in December 2004, became the focus of the reform debate during the UN's sixtieth anniversary year, 2005.[2] Some of their recommendations will be discussed below.

In the sections that follow, we look at some key reform issues as well as at the politics of achieving change in the UN. The latter includes both the politics of getting agreement on reforms and the challenges of implementation.

KEY REFORM ISSUES

For this brief concluding chapter, we have chosen to focus on two types of UN reform issues. First is the issue of representation, or participation, most particularly on the Security Council. This issue is regarded by many inside and outside the UN as the most important and urgent issue of UN reform because it relates to the legitimacy of the Security Council's role as the principal decisionmaking body with respect to enforcement and the use of force in international politics. Another type of representation issue concerns the involvement of NGOs in the UN system. Second is the issue of institutional capacity and effectiveness, which also encompasses management, coordination, accountability, and financing. In the peace and security area, the new Peacebuilding Commission represents a positive step, as does the new Human Rights Council. The MDGs have done a great deal to increase the level of coordination and cooperation among various UN bodies, including specialized agencies and the World Bank—more than many past reform efforts, but whether that initiative will be successful will not be known for many years.

Representation

Security Council Membership and Voting.   No UN reform issue is as controversial as the question of changing the Security Council's membership and voting rules. With the P-5 still limited to the five major victor nations of World War II and their veto power over substantive issues, the Security Council has been viewed for many years as something of an anachronism. The P-5 underrepresent the majority of the world's population and the principal financial contributors to the UN; Europe is overrepresented at the expense of Latin America, Africa, and Asia; China is the only Third World and Asian country; Germany and Japan contribute more financially than Russia, China, Great Britain, and France.

Should Security Council membership be expanded and diversified to accord more with representative principles? What arrangements can satisfy the criteria of representation and efficiency? Should voting be modified to alter the antidemocratic bias of the veto power? Would the legitimacy of Security Council actions be enhanced by diversifying the geographic representation and altering the voting structure? With the council's greater activity since the end of the Cold War, these issues have gained increasing urgency as the Asian, African, and Latin American states have challenged their exclusion from permanent seats and the disproportionate representation of developed countries, and as some developed countries have challenged their exclusion as well. The issue gained new visibility with the divisive Security Council debate over U.S.-led war with Iraq in 2003.

Given the UN's enlarged membership, virtually all groups agree that more states should be added to the Security Council. The addition of more members would begin to alleviate the present-day inequities. The key is to increase the number of members for geographic representation and enhanced legitimacy while maintaining a small enough size to ensure efficiency.[3] A second issue concerns whether or not the distinction between permanent and nonpermanent members should be

CARTOON 8.1 "Musical Chairs: Who Gets the Security Council Seat?" By Beata Szpura for the *Independent,* a publication of the UN Association of the United States. Reprinted with permission.

kept. Closely related is the question of whether new permanent members will have veto power. Some proposals would give no veto power to the new permanent members; others would limit veto power to Chapter VII questions; still others would grant veto power comparable to what the P-5 currently enjoy; some would eliminate the veto entirely on the grounds that it is undemocratic. The latter is a nonstarter for all permanent members, and Britain and France are hardly eager to give up their seats. In reality, as one observer noted, "new veto-wielding permanent members would only increase the likelihood of blockage and still further paralyze the organization."[4] Another noted that "without first tackling working methods [of the council], no real reform is proposed at all."[5] Box 8.1 summarizes the debate over Security Council reform.

Resolving the representation and permanent member issues has proven impossible thus far. There is no agreement on what process or formula should be used

BOX 8.1   The Debate over Security Council Reform

ISSUE

Representation
> Council needs greater representation of Africa, Asia, Latin America
> Permanent members should better reflect geopolitics and economics
>> Proposed additions: Germany and Japan
>> One member each from Asia and Latin America, two from Africa, but who and how to select?
> No permanent members
> No new permanent members
> Veto power
>> Eliminate veto entirely
>> Reduce scope for its use to Chapter VII decisions
>> Keep current P-5, but not give new permanent members veto power
>> Give all permanent members veto power

Openness
> More open Council meetings
> More information on when Council meets, nature of discussions, draft resolutions, presidential statements, actions
> More consultations with interested states and NGOs

Efficiency
> Size should be large enough to allow greater representation, but small enough to preserve the ability to act
> Proposed size: 22–26 members

WHO DECIDES
> Reform of council membership requires Charter Amendment, which takes a vote of two-thirds of the General Assembly members and must be ratified in accordance with their respective constitutional processes by two-thirds of the members of the UN, including all permanent members of the Security Council (Chapter XVIII, Article 108)
> Reforms in methods of work may be made by the Security Council itself

to determine who would get new permanent seats. The Open-ended Working Group established by the General Assembly in 1994 has jokingly been referred to as the "never-ending working group."[6] There are three likely African candidates for permanent membership (Nigeria, Egypt, and South Africa). Countries (such as Pakistan) that know a rival (such as India) is more likely to be a candidate tend to oppose adding any permanent seats. Thus Italy has opposed a seat for Germany, and Argentina challenges Brazil's candidacy. The United States used to support permanent seats for both Germany and Japan, but came out in opposition to Germany because of its stance on the Iraq War. China declared its opposition to a seat for Japan in 2005, and even encouraged grassroots demonstrations and petitions organized through the Internet and signed by 22 million Chinese. The Chinese position is an excellent illustration of how that country's political interests prevent Security Council reform. China champions Latin American and African participation as indicative of its support for developing countries, but it opposes more participation from Asia. It is willing to support India's admission to the Security Council over Japan's only if India agrees to oust Tibet's Dalai Lama, a significant issue between the two countries. Not surprisingly, China opposes any reforms linked to democratization. In short, China prefers to keep the size of the council small, to maintain its veto for "historic reasons," and to be the sole representative of a major continent.[7]

The High-level Panel provided a set of recommendations on the issue of Security Council reform (though no single formula), and with the sixtieth anniversary in 2005, Secretary-General Kofi Annan and a number of member states pressed hard to get a resolution. Other proposals have also emerged. Four countries that have quietly and sometimes not-so-quietly campaigned for permanent seats—Japan, Germany, India, and Brazil—went public on the issue in an effort to take advantage of what appeared to be the best opportunity in decades to line up votes. This so-called Group of Four suggested a twenty-five-member council, including six permanent seats, four of which would be reserved for themselves. The Africa Union supported a different plan, adding eleven seats, including six permanent ones, two of which would be reserved for Africa. Still another group of middle powers, including Italy and Pakistan, proposed a twenty-five-member council with ten new rotating seats.

There are also sharp divisions about whether to grant veto power to new permanent members. Many small countries would prefer to abolish the veto power entirely. The African Union went on record in 2005 supporting veto power for all new permanent members. The United States, on the other hand, has not taken a position on the veto for any new members.

In short, there is no agreement precisely because the issue of Security Council representation is so important. As Luck pointed out:

> [It involves] profound and persistent divisions about which and how many countries should sit around the table; whether permanent status should be extended; what the balance among regions and groups should be; whether the veto should be retained, modified, or eliminated; how decisions should be made; and whether its working methods should be further refined. . . . The very fact that none of this has been resolved . . . testifies . . . to the

divergent perspectives and interests among member states, and to the value capitals place on the work of the council.[8]

 Despite the frustration and disappointment in some quarters when the 2005 discussions came to naught, the issue will persist: "It would be a grave error for those who think that Security Council reform will go away," Nirupam Sen of India reminded us. "They believe it would be like the Cheshire cat, where you have the smile without the cat, but they will find that the cat has nine lives."[9] The final lesson, however, may be that formal reforms such as this are difficult to achieve and likely to come only at glacial speed.

Despite these deep divisions and the widely expressed concerns in 2003 that the feared loss of legitimacy as a result of the debate about Iraq might permanently paralyze the Security Council, new peacekeeping missions have been authorized, such as in the Democratic Republic of Congo, and others have been expanded, as in Côte d'Ivoire, as discussed in chapter 4. And when crises break out, such as the nuclear programs of North Korea and Iran, the international community calls for action by the Security Council. States want to be where the action is; states still want to become nonpermanent members. Participation is seen as a mark of status and prestige for a state and its diplomats. States attach symbolic importance to Security Council endorsement of regional peacekeeping operations, such as the African Union's in the Sudan. Thus, the Security Council continues to be seen as the most authoritative body in the international community and to retain considerable legitimacy despite its unrepresentative composition.

NGO Representation.   Security Council membership is not the only representation issue at the UN, however. NGOs have come to play increasingly important roles in the UN system through their influence on decisionmaking in conferences and summits, and the delivery of economic, social, and humanitarian assistance in collaboration with UN agencies. Although not truly representative in a democratic sense, they frequently promote the concerns of peoples over those of states. In earlier chapters, we saw NGOs' roles in humanitarian interventions and peacebuilding, in implementing the sustainable development and women in development agendas, in the articulation, promotion, and monitoring of international human rights, and in addressing environmental and health issues. As one scholar noted, "they are being asked to substitute for the UN in a variety of ways because of UN Secretariat, and UN peacekeeping, shortages of people and money."[10] Added Lloyd Axworthy, the former Canadian foreign minister, "At last count, there were over 25,000 human rights organizations around the world. The co-operative and cohesive voice of that number of people demands notice. . . . It is this organized force that will drive the policy decisions that must be made. . . . Unless the will of the people is reflected in the decision making, then can we really call it reform?"[11]

Should NGOs gain an enhanced role in the UN system? Will a greater variety of NGOs be represented? Will they be able to utilize and influence the UN system to even greater effect than they have in the past? Will they be given more responsibility to implement UN decisions? Or will the concerns of many developing countries that the majority of NGOs are based in Western developed countries and therefore do not represent the poor or people in less developed countries generally lead to restrictions on the access and roles of NGOs? Although NGOs may not automatically be more representative of the peoples of the world than governments of states, they reflect the growth in popular social movements. Many early twenty-first-century problems call for novel approaches that are more likely to be found in NGOs than in states or IGOs such as the UN.

NGOs can be given a more formal role in the UN system without major Charter revision. Already changes have taken place in the accreditation process, in the expanded roles that NGOs play in UN-sponsored global conferences, and in their follow-up activities, as delineated in earlier chapters. Other suggestions require more extensive actions, perhaps even Charter amendment. For example, in the mid-1990s, the Commission on Global Governance proposed an annual forum of civil society meeting before the General Assembly. Another proposal would create a council of petitions that would be instrumental in humanitarian early warning systems by providing information on developing crises.

Among the most innovative suggestions emerged from the 2003 Cardoso Report, headed by Fernando Henrique Cardoso, the former Brazilian president. That report argued for a conceptual shift in thinking about both the UN as a body and NGO participation. To protect itself from the erosion of multilateralism, the UN must become a convener of multiple constituences, facilitating rather than undertaking operations. Its work must include more actors, including local ones, going beyond its intergovernmental nature. Thus, NGOs would become core participants in engagement, as exemplified by the Global Compact and partnerships with civil society.[12]

Yet this conceptual shift has not been made, and a mechanism for systematic engagement with civil society organizations has not yet emerged. The 2005 World Summit went only so far as to "welcome" the contributions of civil society and NGOs, especially in development and human rights programs, and to "stress the importance of their continued engagement with Governments, the United Nations and other international organizations in these key areas."[13]

Institutional Capacity and Effectiveness

Over the past decades, enhancing the UN's institutional capacity and effectiveness has long been a key reform issue, one with many different facets. Some of these relate to specific UN activities, such as peacekeeping or development; others relate to the operations of various bodies, such as ECOSOC, the Commission on Human Rights, and the Secretariat itself.

Peacekeeping and Peacebuilding.   Managing large, complex peacekeeping and peacebuilding operations requires capacities that the UN Secretariat never had before the Cold War's end. Thus, many of the problems and shortcomings that arose in the 1990s were not surprising given the increased demand for peacekeeping operations and sanctions. Secretary-General Boutros-Ghali's 1992 *An Agenda for Peace*, commissioned by the Security Council, led to major reforms of the UN Department of Peacekeeping Operations, including the addition of military staff from member states and experts in demining, training, and civilian police.[14] In 2000, the Brahimi Report, commissioned by Secretary-General Annan, called for strengthening the planning and management of complex peace operations, the Secretariat's information gathering and analysis capacity to improve conflict prevention, and the size and competence of DPKO. The report also called for doctrinal changes, namely, the need to prepare for more robust peacekeeping—a lesson learned from the experiences in Somalia, Bosnia, and elsewhere in the 1990s.[15] Many of that report's recommendations have been implemented, including the creation of strategic deployment stocks and rapid deployment teams.

The 2004 Report of the High-level Panel called for "getting serious about prevention" and for creating a Peacebuilding Commission to coordinate international efforts to rebuild states (a new idea), and for strengthening the secretary-general's role in mediation and peacebuilding. The report characterized the UN's postconflict efforts as "countless ill-coordinated and overlapping bilateral and United Nations programmes, with inter-agency competition preventing the best use of scarce resources."[16] When the PBC's creation was approved in December 2005, General Assembly President Jan Eliasson of Sweden said, "That word, historic, is often over-used, but in this case, I have no doubt that it is merited. . . . This resolution would, for the first time in the history of the United Nations, create a mechanism which ensures that for countries emerging from conflict, post-conflict does not mean post-engagement of the international community."[17]

The new PBC is to have thirty-one members, including seven Security Council members, seven members of ECOSOC elected from regional groups, five top contributors to UN budgets, funds, and programs, five top providers of military personnel and civilian police to UN missions, and seven other members elected by the General Assembly, with particular consideration for states that have already experienced postconflict recovery. It is intended to be an intergovernmental advisory body that will propose strategies for stabilization, economic recovery and development, and overall coordination of UN system efforts. Secretary-General Annan stressed that the hard work of making the commission function properly lies ahead "if it is truly to make a difference, not in these halls but in the countries where its help is needed."[18]

The High-level Panel's report also made recommendations to address problems in the UN's capacity for more effective peacekeeping, among them the shortage of adequately trained personnel and the slow deployment of police contingents. It called for the creation of "a small corps of senior police officers and managers (50–100) personnel" for the early stages of peace operations. This was endorsed by the 2005 World Summit, as was a call for the EU and other regional bodies to develop their capacities for rapid deployment and a ten-year plan for capacity building with the African Union. Only time will tell whether these are implemented and, most importantly, make a difference in the UN's ability to field sufficient police and peacekeeping troops in a timely manner.

Promoting Sustainable Development.   Coordinating UN system activities in the economic development area has proven a monumental task. Because the specialized agencies are individually funded and autonomous, ECOSOC's coordinating function was undermined from the outset. In 1969, the Jackson Report warned that "the machine as a whole has become unmanageable. It is becoming slower and more unwieldy like some prehistoric monster."[19] In 1978, a director-general for development and international economic cooperation was appointed but given few resources. ECOSOC has been systematically bypassed, and its work has been duplicated in the General Assembly. The programs of action for various global conferences compounded the problems. The Commission on Global Governance in the mid-1990s proposed a more revolutionary approach by focusing on the lack of a coherent economic policy framework. Peter Sutherland, the founding head of the WTO, stated, "Neither the [Group of Seven nor] the [Group of Fifteen] reflects a perspective that adequately represents the world economic community. We have . . . a structural deficit in the world economy, in terms both of the making of policies and of their execution."[20] The commission proposed an Economic Security Council under the UN's umbrella to provide a framework for sustainable development across the range of UN organizations, Bretton Woods institutions, and the private sector. To enhance the proposed council's status, finance ministers would meet with heads of state annually. The idea never took hold, however.

Several incremental changes have been made to further UN system coordination for sustainable development. In 2002, the Administrative Committee on Coordination was reorganized into the UN Chief Executives Board for Coordination. This body provides a forum for twenty-eight heads of organizations and programs to meet. Included are the heads of the World Bank, IMF, WTO, WHO, WFP, UNEP, UNDP, FAO, UNIDO, and IAEA, among others, along with a permanent coordinating committee. That change brings together the Bretton Woods institutions and other UN agencies in an unprecedented way. This change has facilitated the global consensus on fighting poverty embodied in the Millennium Development Goals. This approach permits the coordination of development initiatives whose key components are interdisciplinary in nature and require synchronized actions.

In addition, the High-level Panel suggested that ECOSOC abandon much of its traditional agenda dealing with administrative issues and program coordination to focus on major themes in the Millennium Declaration. The 2005 World Summit outcome endorsed this approach and further called for ECOSOC to "serve as a quality platform for high-level engagement among Member States and with the international financial institutions, the private sector and civil society on emerging global trends, policies and action and develop its ability to respond better and more rapidly to developments in the international economic, environmental and social fields."[21] Once again, only time will tell whether ECOSOC's methods of work change and it becomes a more effective body for coordinating and supporting the UN's vast array of development-related programs.

Human Rights.   When the Commission on Human Rights met for the spring 2005 session, its membership was once again the target of criticism from human rights NGOs and a number of states. Among the members were Zimbabwe, Indonesia, China, Sudan, Russia, Saudi Arabia, Cuba, and Nepal, all of which were noted for human rights abuses and for their efforts to avert discussion of those records. Paula Dobriansky, the U.S. undersecretary of state for global affairs, stated at the time, "We need to put a stop to the trend of the world's worst human rights abusers securing membership on the Commission to deflect criticism of their abuses at home."[22] This situation fueled pressure to replace the commission with a smaller body and to set criteria for membership.

The High-level Panel Report noted that the Commission on Human Rights "suffers from a legitimacy deficit that casts doubts on the overall reputation of the United Nations." Membership was identified as a key problem, and the panel recommended expanding that to include all UN member states and encouraging states to designate prominent human rights figures as heads of delegations. It further suggested creating a small advisory council of independent experts.[23] Secretary-General Kofi Annan, in his own report, *In Larger Freedom: Towards Development, Security and Human Rights for All,* recommended replacing the commission with a smaller, standing Human Rights Council; its members would be elected by a two-thirds majority in the General Assembly and they would be expected to abide by human rights standards.[24]

The proposed Human Rights Council was endorsed by the 2005 World Summit, which called upon the General Assembly's president to conduct negotiations to establish the mandate, size, and other modalities. Secretary-General Annan undertook an active diplomatic role in those discussions, particularly in urging the G-77 to come to an early agreement on the council. In 2006, the General Assembly overwhelmingly approved the creation of the new forty-seven-member Human Rights Council (HRC), in spite of strong opposition from the United States to what it saw as a weakened proposal. The HRC members will be selected in a secret ballot by a majority of the assembly's members (currently, ninety-six votes) for three-year, renewable terms with seats distributed among the five recognized regional groups. By contrast, the fifty-three members of the Commission on Human Rights were selected by regional groups and elected by acclamation, without a vote. Members of the new HRC will be expected to "uphold the highest standards in the promotion and protection of human rights." Where the commission met just once a year for six weeks, the HRC will meet for at least ten weeks throughout the year and will report to the General Assembly not ECOSOC. To address the problem of having human rights violators among the membership, all HRC members' human rights records are subject to scrutiny and the council can suspend members suspected of abuses with a two-thirds vote. Secretary-General Kofi Annan commented, "This gives the United Nations the chance—a much-needed chance—to make a new beginning in its work for human rights around the world."[25]

Whether the new council is stronger than the old commission will depend in part on whether states agree to the possibility of more UN interference in the domestic sphere of human rights. That is the heart of the second dilemma: sovereignty versus challenges to sovereignty. Whether the HRC will be more accountable and representative, as Annan hopes, is a question for the future.

Efforts to address the coordination and management issues have led to greater centralization of activities. These steps are controversial, as any proposal to bring agencies under more effective centralized control conflicts with the deliberately decentralized nature of the system. In addition, although each proposal for change advantages some agencies, states, and NGOs, it disadvantages others. Because the General Assembly has to approve many of these changes, including creating a new office or department or eliminating overlapping programs or agencies, these are controversial reforms. One observer noted, "Reforms are possible and needed, but they must proceed by complex bargaining, so that all member states feel they are winning at least something in the process."[26]

The Secretariat and Office of the Secretary-General.   In chapter 2, we examined the growth of the Secretariat that led Sir Brian Urquhart, a former UN undersecretary-general, to observe in the early 1990s that "too many top-level officials, political appointments, rotten boroughs, and pointless programs had rendered the Secretariat fat and flabby over the years."[27] We also discussed a number of the changes that Secretary-General Kofi Annan instituted with his 1997 "quiet revolution." By the early twenty-first century, other changes in the Secretariat were underway, including the creation of the UN System Integrated Plan on AIDS in 2001 that linked AIDS-related budgets and work plans of twenty-nine UN funds, programs, and agencies. In the area of peacekeeping, following the Brahimi Report, the General Assembly approved a 50 percent increase in staff and more flexibility in administration for the Department of Peacekeeping Operations. In 2002, a new system went into effect for recruiting, placing, and promoting staff that gave more emphasis to merit, competence, and accountability for results than tenure and precedent. Yet as Julius K. Nyerere, former president of Tanzania, observed in 1995, "We all want to see the United Nations well managed. But it is not a business; its operations cannot be judged solely by 'efficiency' in money terms."[28]

In the final year of his second term, Kofi Annan proposed still more reforms to modernize the UN Secretariat, improve the information and communications system, improve recruitment and training, and create a mobile corps of peacekeeping specialists that could be sent rapidly on urgent missions. His proposals also called for delegating more authority for management and operational matters to the deputy secretary-general. Speaking of the secretary-general's responsibilities, he said, "In short, I am expected to be the world's chief diplomat and at the same time to run a large and complex organization, as it were, in my spare time. This will hardly be less true for my successors."[29]

There are also limits to what reforms of the Secretariat can accomplish. It will always be subject to the political will of states, for such is the nature of the intergovernmental organizations—they exist and operate because states want them to. Experience with two recent scandals—the Oil-for-Food Programme and the sexual exploitation by UN peacekeepers in the Congo—is illustrative. The Secretariat has now taken steps to limit the damages and to prevent recurrence. It instituted a zero-tolerance policy in dealing with sexual exploitation, fired ten UN personnel with oversight responsibilities, repatriated eighty-eight peacekeepers, and pressured offending states to punish individuals responsible.[30]

In response to the OFFP scandal, the Secretariat introduced measures to improve the performance of senior management, including a better selection system for senior officials, the monitoring of individual performance, and a new Office of Internal Oversight Services. With the adoption of policies covering antifraud and corruption, whistleblower protection, financial disclosure, conflict of interest, and procurement contracts, the Secretariat is being reorganized to prevent the type of personnel abuses found in the oil-for-food scandal. The establishment of the first ombudsman in 2002 represents one of the specific responses. The task of the independently appointed individual is to hear complaints from staff on employment conditions and harassment, and to protect whistleblowers.

At the same time, although the UN could have prevented contract abuses in the Oil-for-Food Programme, states were responsible for enforcing the sanctions by monitoring Iraq's borders and they failed to do so. Even if the Secretariat were perfectly organized to coordinate peacebuilding in Kosovo or East Timor, states would still control the financing of reconstruction efforts and the seconding of troops, civilian police, and other personnel. Relatively little has been done to end the problem of sexual abuse by peacekeepers because the Secretariat cannot force member states to prosecute offenders or to impose discipline on their troops. In short, the Secretariat has only limited independent capability and any reforms must be designed to better utilize that capability. The UN's 2005 summit failed to strengthen that capability significantly because developing countries in particular fear that Westerners would dominate the senior staff positions even more than at present if the General Assembly gave the secretary-general more authority over hiring and firing personnel.

Solving the UN's Financial Problems. As we discussed in Chapter 2, the UN has had long-standing financial problems because it has no independent source of financing and depends solely on its members for assessed and voluntary contributions. Since the mid-1980s, however, the UN has been in a state of chronic budget crisis. The heart of the problem lies in the failure of the United States and other countries to pay their assessed dues in a timely fashion, and in the reluctance of states to grant the UN authority to raise money independently. The implementation of the MDGs depends on the willingness of developed donor countries to meet the 0.7 percent of GNP target for official development assistance.

With the high demand for peacekeeping operations since 1990 and the recognition of the need for rapid deployments in crisis situations and natural disasters, efforts have been made to create funds for emergencies. Historically, the UN has had to wait for members to volunteer troops and logistical support, and the members in turn must wait for reimbursement of the costs for providing forces. For example, Secretary-General Boutros-Ghali's *An Agenda for Peace* called for a peacekeeping reserve fund of $50 million. Most recently, the High-level Panel called for a multiyear standing Peacebuilding Fund funded by voluntary contributions. This is intended to ensure immediate availability of resources for launching peacebuilding activities and recovery efforts. The panel also called for DPKO to make further use of "strategic deployment stockpiles, standby arrangements, trust funds and other mechanisms . . . to meet the tighter deadlines necessary for effective deployment." And it called on the Security Council and General Assembly to authorize funding from assessed budgets for tasks such as disarmament and demobilization.[31] Although the sixtieth General Assembly in 2005 did not act on the panel's proposal for a Peacebuilding Fund, it did create the Central Emergency Response Fund (CERF) to replace the earlier Central Emergency Revolving Fund; this was an effort to ensure swifter and more equitable responses to humanitarian emergencies such as the 2004 tsunami, hurricanes, floods, and drought with funds, expected to total $500 million, made available within three to four days.

The purpose of all proposals on UN financing is to provide a steady and predictable flow of resources. Yet the UN's financing problems are not just about money; they are also about political influence. Suggestions for sources of revenue other than states' assessed and voluntary contributions have been put forward, such as fees for use of international waterways, the resources of Antarctica, the oceans, seabeds, and outer space. Many member states, however, especially the United States and other major powers, oppose the loss of control such independent revenues would entail. Nonetheless, Secretary-General Annan has been creative in exploring partnerships with the corporate community and major philanthropists such as Ted Turner and Bill Gates. In late 2005, he welcomed the decision of the French National Assembly to place a levy on airline tickets to benefit the health sector in developing countries as an innovative source of financing to help developing countries achieve the MDGs.[32]

There has been no shortage of proposals for changing structures and methods of financing as well as for enhancing oversight and efficient use. States, however, are a key source of the problem. In the mid-1990s, Ingvar Carlsson, co-chairman of the Commission on Global Governance, noted, "The United Nations is not a third party, somehow separate from member governments. It is not the property of the officials appointed to head its secretariat or agencies. The United Nations belongs to its members—with all the benefits, problems, and above all, responsibilities of ownership."[33] If a majority of members refuse to consider whether the UN should still have a decolonization unit, for example, no amount of good management skills or reform proposals will effect change. The Secretariat cannot destroy even the smallest committee. If the UN's most powerful member and largest contributor, the United States, opposes adoption of the UN's budget unless the costs of new reform proposals are included, as happened in late 2005, it can provoke a crisis unless a compromise is found. This leads us to look at the challenges of achieving change in the UN.

THE POLITICS OF ACHIEVING CHANGE

States have always played an essential role in reform. They must not only be committed to maintaining and reinvigorating the institution in the abstract but must also provide resources and leadership for the task. As Secretary-General Annan remarked on the eve of the 2005 World Summit, when the draft declaration had been turned into a pale shadow of the proposals he had put forward, "with 191 member states, it's not easy to get an agreement."[34] States are deeply divided over many UN reforms because changes can enhance or diminish their influence. With respect to implementing many UN initiatives, such as the Millennium Development Goals, sustainable development, or peacebuilding, the capacity of states to carry out their own changes is also at issue. Among the states, the United States has long been one of the UN's most vocal critics and advocates of change. We briefly examine some of these issues in the new millennium.

The United States and UN Reforms

In 1992, the United States welcomed Secretary-General Boutros-Ghali's *An Agenda for Peace* as an "extremely valuable contribution to both the consideration—and actual construction—of the United Nations' future role in international security."[35] Upon assuming office in 1993, the Clinton administration was even more optimistic about the possibilities of a reformed and renewed UN. It openly supported Security Council membership for Japan and Germany and enhanced responsibilities for the council. Strengthening the UN was consistent with the Clinton administration's policy of assertive multilateralism: The United States could no longer be the world's policeman; responsibilities should be more equally shared with other countries. The UN was the appropriate vehicle for sharing such burdens.

The optimism proved short-lived. In his September 1993 speech to the General Assembly, President Clinton evidenced a growing skepticism about the ability of the UN to manage all the demands placed on it. "The United Nations simply cannot become engaged in every one of the world's conflicts," he said. "If the American people are to say yes to UN peacekeeping, the United Nations must know when to say no."[36] The loss of American soldiers in Somalia led to a more circumspect view of UN peacekeeping, and especially of U.S. participation. A second phase of U.S. post–Cold War foreign policy had begun. The optimism for a UN–centered world and for assertive multilateralism waned and then was decisively killed in November 1994 when the newly elected Republican Congress led an all-out assault on the UN, attacking peacekeeping operations, reducing American funding of the organization, and imposing strict limits on the president's power to put troops under UN command. The UN was once again marginalized in U.S. foreign policy.

The problem of Congress's refusal to pay U.S. dues and arrearages unless UN administrative and budgetary reforms were undertaken persisted throughout the rest of the 1990s. Which reforms needed to be taken, however, was a question left purposefully vague. The Congress disputed the amount owed, called for the reimbursement of peacekeeping support, and proposed unilaterally to reduce the U.S. assessment to 20 percent. This pattern of withholding was resolved only in 2000 shortly before the Clinton administration left office. These actions made it clear that the United States had adopted more unilateralist policies, reversing the multilateralism of the early 1990s and undermining the U.S. ability to exercise leadership.

The record of the Bush administration in the UN has likewise been a mixed one. After the September 11, 2001, terrorist attacks, the United States clearly recognized the UN's value in the war on terrorism, then squandered that support with the Bush administration's willingness to go to war against Iraq in 2003 without Security Council authorization. A major indicator, however, of the seriousness with which the United States viewed the High-level Panel's report and proposals for change was the appointment of a Senior Advisor on UN Reform in March 2005. Noted one observer, "It would also appear that in looking more closely at the reform proposals currently under discussion—especially in Kofi Annan's text, which includes a more explicit commitment than the panel to democracy promotion, a favoured theme of the Bush administration, and proposes the creation of a Human Rights Council—administration officials have found much that they approve of."[37] Still, the Bush administration's record on multilateralism remains a mixed one. Although the appointment of John Bolton as the U.S. permanent representative to the UN was linked to U.S. desire to reform the UN, it was widely interpreted as boding ill for U.S.-UN relations, given his past hostility to the body. Bolton's initial act of proposing hundreds of last-minute amendments in the draft document for the 2005 summit reinforced that view. In addition, a significant portion of the U.S. Congress continues to be hostile to the UN and willing to use the tool of withholding U.S. assessed dues to force change, even proposing to fund the UN for six month periods until reforms are implemented.

U.S. support for reforms that enhance efficiency, oversight, and accountability reflects the interests of a state that provides more than 20 percent of the UN's funding. Those interests frequently clash with the concerns of many other states who want to ensure that their voices are heard and that the United Nations does not become solely a tool of the world's only superpower. This takes us to the heart of the third dilemma: the need for leadership in a world dominated by a single superpower and one whose historical record on multilateralism is full of "mixed messages."[38] To be sure, the United States looms large at the UN. "Nothing can be done without the concurrence of the United States," remarked a French diplomat in 2002.[39] Yet one long-time UN observer noted that it is the Western bloc more generally that dominates the UN, not just the United States, and their shared adherence to liberal ideas "decisively affects and patterns outcomes in global political, economic, military, social and cultural affairs." In this context, he noted, "the primary and continuing role of the United States . . . has been, and continues to be, that of an enforcer . . . [and] the primary role of the United Nations under the hegemony of the West is to validate the liberal world order."[40] Richard Holbrooke, the former U.S. ambassador to the UN, warned, "Yes, everyone has to understand that the U.N. without America behind it doesn't work, but at the same time the U.N. cannot serve as America's tool. The U.N. has to represent a poor farmer in Burkina Faso as well as a senator from Minnesota."[41] That is the essence of UN legitimacy.

The Secretary-General's Role in Reform

Not long after Kofi Annan became secretary-general in 1997, he noted that he was being criticized for not reforming the UN in six weeks. "'But what are you complaining about?' asked the Russian ambassador: 'You've had more time than God.' Ah, Mr. Annan quipped back, 'but God had one big advantage. He worked alone without a General Assembly, a Security Council and [all] the committees.'"[42]

Former Secretary-General Boutros-Ghali and Secretary-General Annan both devoted considerable amounts of their time in office to reforming the institution. Boutros-Ghali's pathbreaking *An Agenda for Peace* (1992) provided the framework for much of the 1990s debate on reform to meet security needs. *An Agenda for Development* (1994), though less innovative, shaped debate on reform in the economic arena. In 1997, in the document "Renewing the United Nations: A Program for Reform," Secretary-General Annan unveiled his plans for sweeping UN reforms, many of which were taken immediately under his leadership, others of which required action by the General Assembly. In each of these cases, the secretary-general was pushed by key states and governments. Annan had the advantage of long experience within the organization, including a stint as head of personnel and later as head of peacekeeping operations.

Kofi Annan departed from the practice of his predecessors, however, in endeavoring to play a much more active role in pushing member states to act on specific reform proposals. His 2003 "fork in the road" speech quoted at the beginning of the chapter marked his opening step in the most recent reform effort. This was followed by the appointment and report of the High-level Panel, which, in turn, was followed by Annan's own recommendations contained in the document, *In Larger Freedom*, issued in March 2005 and a further set of reforms in 2006.[43] Among his mistakes, in the view of critics, was to push too hard for Security Council reform when there are profound and persistent divisions about the nature of that reform. "Was he aware," one asked, "that none of his predecessors had dared to tread on this territory, traditionally reserved for member states, by becoming outspoken advocates for an expanded council?"[44] Similarly, Annan suggested that member states accept the various proposals he and the High-level Panel put forward as a package. "What I am proposing," he said, "amounts to a comprehensive strategy."[45] Noted one longtime observer: "The history of UN reform also tells us that, although broad packages of steps are sometimes proposed, they are never adopted. The member states, understandably, like to pick and choose. Some elements of comprehensive plans are always more politically ripe than others . . . [and] if six decades of trying to reform the UN have a central lesson, it is that modest expectations are in order."[46] These criticisms of Annan's handling of the 2005 reform proposals underscore the tightrope a secretary-general must walk in exercising leadership for the process of reforming the UN. In addition to having made strategic errors, Annan was pushing for change in a political context of sharp divisions among member states, an oil-for-food scandal that weakened the institution and his own credibility, and the approaching end of his term in late 2006. Ironically, some would argue that it is the process for selecting the secretary-general that is most in need of reform.

CONCLUSION

The obstacles to amending the UN Charter are not procedural but political. The Charter's provisions on membership and representation in the Security Council and other bodies, on contributions, and on voting power were carefully worked out compromises. The major provisions of the Charter were drafted by Americans and a small number of representatives from other countries, who in turn worked on behalf of a group of countries representing less than one-third the total number of current UN members. Consensus and agreement were far easier to achieve under those circumstances than they would be today, when the number of states and the diversity of interests and points of view are far greater. Charter amendment has thus always been like the proverbial Pandora's box: Once the box was opened, neither the agenda (the issues that would be discussed) nor the outcome could be controlled.

Discussion of ways to increase the capacity of the Office of the Secretary-General and of the Secretariat invokes fears of centralizing powers in a single, powerful leader and of diminishing states' control. Changing Security Council membership and altering the veto elicits fears of some current permanent members about losing their status, either by having to resign from the council or, more generally, by having their power diluted with the addition of new permanent members. Equally sensitive is the question of which states should gain permanent membership on the Security Council. There is also the anxiety of decentralizing power further from the few toward the many—from Europe and North America to Latin America, Asia, and Africa; from the wealthy to the poorer; from whites to people of color. And from the developing countries' perspective, increasing the role of the Security Council reduces their influence and "could well mean . . . the freedom [for the United States], through UN legitimacy, to impose its own values and world view on the vast majority of those member-states constituting the Third World."[47]

Proposals for greater efficiency and coordination may meet the interests of major contributors, but will hardly address concerns over inadequate funding of UN economic and social programs, let alone over the management of international economic relations. The G-77 may have fragmented and the NIEO largely disappeared from UN agendas, but the political battle between North and South is not over. Proposals for budgetary reforms giving more power to those with economic resources continue to elicit charges of great-power domination. And altering the reform process itself—making the procedure "easier"—challenges the basic organizational compromises, leading to potential crises within the organization.

We are no more likely to see fundamental changes in the twenty-first century than we were in the preceding post–Cold War era. As Kofi Annan himself said early in his first term as secretary-general, "reform is not an event; it is a process."[48] The process is an incremental one of strengthening and enhancing the UN's capacity to meet the demands of an increasingly globalized, complex world. Today, that process is of more serious concern perhaps because of the danger that the UN will become more marginalized in world politics with a sole superpower willing to use military force without Security Council sanction and economic decisionmaking centered outside the UN system.

The issues of UN reform, however, are not just debates over how to make an organization more efficient, effective, and representative. They are deeply political and philosophical questions of values and power. As one UN expert suggested, "in many respects, the struggles in the UN over the years were grounded in north-south differences as much, if not more than in east-west tensions."[49] The gulf between North and South remains, although for the moment at least the East-West divide has disappeared. The major industrialized countries, led by the United States, may well be able to gain support for some types of reforms in the UN, with or without amending the Charter, though they do not appear to be committed to moving in this direction. Nevertheless, the fault lines in debates over these reforms, as well as over economic and social programs, the environment, human rights, and peace and security activities, are likely to be along the North-South axis, even though at times it may seem like the United States versus the rest of the world. Underlying and shaping the debates will be the three dilemmas: needs for global governance versus the UN's weaknesses, the persistence of state sovereignty and challenges to it, and the need for leadership versus the dominance of a sole superpower.

NOTES

1. Secretary-General's Address to the UN General Assembly, 23 September 2003.

2. For the High-level Panel's Report, see United Nations, *A More Secure World: Our Shared Responsibility,* Report of the Secretary-General's High-level Panel on Threats, Challenges and Change (New York: United Nations, 2004), http://www.un.org/secureworld.

3. Peter Wallensteen, "Representing the World: A Security Council for the Twenty-first Century," *Security Dialogue* 25, no. 1 (1994): 67.

4. James A. Paul, "Security Council Reform: Arguments about the Future of the United Nations System," 1995, http://www.globalpolicy.org/security/pubs/secref.htm.

5. Edward C. Luck, "The UN Security Council," in *Irrelevant or Indispensable? The United Nations in the 21st Century,* ed. Paul Heinbecker and Patricia Goff (Waterloo, Canada: Wilfred Laurier Press, 2005), 148.

6. Simon Chesterman, "Reform: Managing Peace and Security in the 21st Century," *Global Agenda: Issues Before the 60th General Assembly of the United Nations,* ed. Angela Drakulich (New York: United Nations Association of the United States of America, 2005), 4.

7. J. Mohan Malik, "Security Council Reform: China Signals Its Veto," *World Policy Journal* (Spring 2005): 19–29.

8. Edward C. Luck, "How Not to Reform the United Nations," *Global Governance* 11, no. 4 (October–December 2005): 407–414.

9. Quoted in Warren Hoge, "U.N. Envoys See Loss of Steam For Expanding Security Council," *New York Times,* November 18, 2005.

10. Chadwick F. Alger, "The Emerging Roles of NGOs in the UN System: From Article 71 to a People's Millennium Assembly," *Global Governance* 8, no. 1 (January–March 2002): 116.

11. Lloyd Axworthy, "Making the Case for Change," in *Irrelevant or Indispensable? The United Nations in the 21st Century,* ed. Paul Heinbecker and Patricia Goff (Waterloo, Canada: Wilfred Laurier Press, 2005), 173.

12. Panel of Eminent Persons on United Nations–Civil Society Relations, *We the Peoples: Civil Society, the United Nations and Global Governance,* UN document A/58/817 (New York: United Nations, 21 June 2004).

13. 2005 World Summit Outcome adopted by the General Assembly, 15 September 2005, (A/60/L.1).

14. Boutros Boutros-Ghali, *An Agenda for Peace: Preventive Diplomacy, Peacemaking, and Peacekeeping* (New York: United Nations, 1992).

15. United Nations General Assembly and Security Council, *Report of the Panel on United Nations Peace Operations,* A/55/305-S/2000/809, 21 August 2000, http://www.un.org/peace/ reports/peace_operations.

16. United Nations, *A More Secure World,* http://www.un.org/secureworld.

17. "UN Press Release," http://www.un.org/ps/newstory.asp?NewsID=16990&Cr=reform &C41.

18. Ibid.

19. Quoted in Jacques Fomerand, *Strengthening the UN's Economic and Social Programs: A Documentary Essay,* ACUNS System Report, no. 2 (1990), 2.

20. Quoted in Ingvar Carlsson, "The United Nations: A Time to Reform," *Foreign Policy,* no.100 (Fall 1995): 8. For the full text, see Commission on Global Governance, *Our Global Neighborhood* (Oxford: Oxford University Press, 1995).

21. 2005 World Summit Outcome.

22. U.S. Department of State press release, March 17, 2005.

23. UN, *A More Secure World.*

24. *In Larger Freedom: Towards Development, Security and Human Rights for All,* Report of the Secretary-General to the General Assembly, March 21, 2005, para. 183.

25. Warren Hoge, "US Dissents as U.N. Approves New Human Rights Council," *New York Times,* March 15, 2006.

26. James A. Paul, "UN Reform: An Analysis," Global Policy Forum, 1997, 1–2, http://www.globalpolicy.org/reform/analysis.htm.

27. Brian Urquhart, *A Life in Peace and War* (New York: W. W. Norton, 1991), 352.

28. Yves Beigbeder, "The United Nations Secretariat: Reform in Program," in *The United Nations at the Millennium: The Principal Organs,* ed. Paul Taylor and A.J.R. Groom (New York: Continuum, 2000), 207.

29. Warren Hoge, "Annan Offers His Blueprint to Make the U.N. More Efficient," *New York Times,* March 8, 2006.

30. UN Security Council, "Press Release," SC/8649, 23 February 2006, http://www.un.org/ News/Press/docs/2006/sc8649, doc.htm.

31. UN, *A More Secure World,* paras. 218 and 227.

32. UN Secretary-General Kofi Annan, "Secretary-General Welcomes France's Levy on Airline Tickets to Benefit Health Sector Of Developing Countries," UN Department of Public Information SG/SM/10284, 27 December 2005, http://www.un.org/News/Press/docs/2005/sgsm10284.doc.htm.

33. Carlson, "The United Nations: A Time to Reform," 3.

34. "Better Than Nothing," *Economist* 376, no. 8444 (September 17, 2005): 33.

35. Judy Aita, "U.S. Supports Stronger UN Peacekeeping Operations," United States Information Agency no. 247189, 10 October 1992.

36. President Bill Clinton, Address to UN General Assembly, 27 September 1993, excerpted in the *New York Times,* September 28, 1993.

37. Mats Berdal, "The UN's Unnecessary Crisis," *Survival* 47, no. 3 (Autumn 2005): 25.

38. Edward C. Luck, *Mixed Messages: American Politics and International Organization 1919–1999* (Washington, D.C.: Brookings Institution Press, 1999).

39. Quoted in Donald J. Puchala, "World Hegemony and the United Nations," *International Studies Review* 7, no. 4 (December 2005): 574.

40. Ibid., 581.

41. Quoted in Warren Hoge, "U.N. Is Transforming Itself, but Into What is Unclear," *New York Times,* February 28, 2005.

42. "United Nations Reform Better than Nothing," *Economist* 376, no. 8444 (September 17, 2005): 33.

43. Kofi Annan, *In Larger Freedom: Towards Security, Development and Human Rights for All,* UN Doc. A/59/2005, 21 March 2005.

44. Luck, "How Not to Reform the United Nations," 410.

45. Kofi Annan, "Secretary-General Proposes Strategy for UN Reform to General Assembly, Giving Equal Weight to Development, Security, Human Rights," press release, SG/SM/9770, 21 March 2005.

46. Luck, "How Not to Reform the United Nations," 411–412.

47. K. P. Saksena, *Reforming the United Nations: The Challenge of Relevance* (New Delhi: Sage, 1993), 194.

48. Kofi Annan, *Renewing the United Nations: A Program for Reform,* Report of the Secretary General, A/51/1950, 14 July 1997, 87.

49. Gene M. Lyons, "Rethinking the United Nations," *Mershon International Studies Review* 38, supp. 1 (April 1994): 98.

Appendix

Charter of the United Nations (Selected Selections)

The Charter of the United Nations was signed on 26 June 1945, in San Francisco, at the conclusion of the UN Conference on International Organization, and it came into force on 24 October 1945. The Statute of the International Court of Justice is an integral part of the Charter.

Amendments to Articles 23, 27, and 61 were adopted by the General Assembly on 17 December 1963 and came into force on 31 August 1965. A further amendment to Article 61 was adopted by the General Assembly on 20 December 1971 and came into force on 24 September 1973. An amendment to Article 109, adopted by the General Assembly on 20 December 1965, came into force on 12 June 1968.

Preamble to the Charter of the United Nations

WE THE PEOPLES OF THE UNITED NATIONS DETERMINED

to save succeeding generations from the scourge of war, which twice in our lifetime has brought untold sorrow to mankind, and

to reaffirm faith in fundamental human rights, in the dignity and worth of the human person, in the equal rights of men and women and of nations large and small, and

to establish conditions under which justice and respect for the obligations arising from treaties and other sources of international law can be maintained, and

to promote social progress and better standards of life in larger freedom,

AND FOR THESE ENDS

to practice tolerance and live together in peace with one another as good neighbours, and

to unite our strength to maintain international peace and security, and

to ensure, by the acceptance of principles and the institution of methods, that armed force shall not be used, save in the common interest, and

to employ international machinery for the promotion of the economic and social advancement of all peoples,

HAVE RESOLVED TO COMBINE OUR EFFORTS TO ACCOMPLISH THESE AIMS.

Accordingly, our respective Governments, through representatives assembled in the city of San Francisco, who have exhibited their full powers found to be in good and due form, have agreed to the present Charter of the United Nations and do hereby establish an international organization to be known as the United Nations.

CHAPTER I

Purposes and Principles

Article 1

The Purposes of the United Nations are:

1. To maintain international peace and security, and to that end: to take effective collective measures for the prevention and removal of threats to the peace, and for the suppression of acts of aggression or other breaches of the peace, and to bring about by peaceful means, and in conformity with the principles of justice and international law, adjustment or settlement of international disputes or situations which might lead to a breach of the peace;

2. To develop friendly relations among nations based on respect for the principle of equal rights and self-determination of peoples, and to take other appropriate measures to strengthen universal peace;

3. To achieve international co-operation in solving international problems of an economic, social, cultural, or humanitarian character, and in promoting and encouraging respect for human rights and for fundamental freedoms for all without distinction as to race, sex, language, or religion; and

4. To be a centre for harmonizing the actions of nations in the attainment of these common ends.

Article 2

The Organization and its Members, in pursuit of the Purposes stated in Article 1, shall act in accordance with the following Principles.

1. The Organization is based on the principle of the sovereign equality of all its Members.

2. All Members, in order to ensure to all of them the rights and benefits resulting from membership, shall fulfill in good faith the obligations assumed by them in accordance with the present Charter.

3. All Members shall settle their international disputes by peaceful means in such a manner that international peace and security, and justice, are not endangered.

4. All Members shall refrain in their international relations from the threat or use of force against the territorial integrity or political independence of any state, or in any other manner inconsistent with the Purposes of the United Nations.

5. All Members shall give the United Nations every assistance in any action it takes in accordance with the present Charter, and shall refrain from giving assistance to any state against which the United Nations is taking preventive or enforcement action.

6. The Organization shall ensure that states which are not Members of the United Nations act in accordance with these Principles so far as may be necessary for the maintenance of international peace and security.

7. Nothing contained in the present Charter shall authorize the United Nations to intervene in matters which are essentially within the domestic jurisdiction of any state or shall require the Members to submit such matters to settlement under the present Charter; but this principle shall not prejudice the application of enforcement measures under Chapter VII.

CHAPTER II

Membership

Article 3

The original Members of the United Nations shall be the states which, having participated in the United Nations Conference on International Organization at San Francisco, or having previously signed the Declaration by United Nations of 1 January 1942, sign the present Charter and ratify it in accordance with Article 110.

Article 4

1. Membership in the United Nations is open to all other peace-loving states which accept the obligations contained in the present Charter and, in the judgment of the Organization, are able and willing to carry out these obligations.

2. The admission of any such state to membership in the United Nations will be effected by a decision of the General Assembly upon the recommendation of the Security Council.

Article 5

A Member of the United Nations against which preventive or enforcement action has been taken by the Security Council may be suspended from the exercise of the rights and privileges of membership by the General Assembly upon the recommendation of the Security Council. The exercise of these rights and privileges may be restored by the Security Council.

Article 6

A Member of the United Nations which has persistently violated the Principles contained in the present Charter may be expelled from the Organization by the General Assembly upon the recommendation of the Security Council.

Chapter III

Organs

Article 7

1. There are established as the principal organs of the United Nations: a General Assembly, a Security Council, an Economic and Social Council, a Trusteeship Council, an International Court of Justice, and a Secretariat.

2. Such subsidiary organs as may be found necessary may be established in accordance with the present Charter.

Article 8

The United Nations shall place no restrictions on the eligibility of men and women to participate in any capacity and under conditions of equality in its principal and subsidiary organs.

Chapter IV

The General Assembly

Composition

Article 9

1. The General Assembly shall consist of all the Members of the United Nations.

2. Each Member shall have not more than five representatives in the General Assembly.

Functions and Powers

Article 10

The General Assembly may discuss any questions or any matters within the scope of the present Charter or relating to the powers and functions of any organs provided for in the present Charter, and, except as provided in Article 12, may make recommendations to the Members of the United Nations or to the Security Council or to both on any such questions or matters.

Article 11

1. The General Assembly may consider the general principles of co-operation in the maintenance of international peace and security, including the principles governing disarmament and the regulation of armaments, and may make recommendations with regard to such principles to the Members or to the Security Council or to both.

2. The General Assembly may discuss any questions relating to the maintenance of international peace and security brought before it by any Member of the United Nations, or by the Security Council, or by a state

which is not a Member of the United Nations in accordance with Article 35, paragraph 2, and, except as provided in Article 12, may make recommendations with regard to any such questions to the state or states concerned or to the Security Council or to both. Any such question on which action is necessary shall be referred to the Security Council by the General Assembly either before or after discussion.

3. The General Assembly may call the attention of the Security Council to situations which are likely to endanger international peace and security.

4. The powers of the General Assembly set forth in this Article shall not limit the general scope of Article 10.

Article 12

1. While the Security Council is exercising in respect of any dispute or situation the functions assigned to it in the present Charter, the General Assembly shall not make any recommendation with regard to that dispute or situation unless the Security Council so requests.

2. The Secretary-General, with the consent of the Security Council, shall notify the General Assembly at each session of any matters relative to the maintenance of international peace and security which are being dealt with by the Security Council and shall similarly notify the General Assembly, or the Members of the United Nations if the General Assembly is not in session, immediately the Security Council ceases to deal with such matters.

Article 13

1. The General Assembly shall initiate studies and make recommendations for the purpose of:

A. promoting international co-operation in the political field and encouraging the progressive development of international law and its codification;

B. promoting international co-operation in the economic, social, cultural, educational, and health fields, and assisting in the realization of human rights and fundamental freedoms for all without distinction as to race, sex, language, or religion.

2. The further responsibilities, functions, and powers of the General Assembly with respect to matters mentioned in paragraph 1(b) above are set forth in Chapters IX and X.

Article 14

Subject to the provisions of Article 12, the General Assembly may recommend measures for the peaceful adjustment of any situation, regardless of origin, which it deems likely to impair the general welfare or friendly relations among nations, including situations resulting from a violation of the provisions of the present Charter setting forth the Purposes and Principles of the United Nations.

Article 15

1. The General Assembly shall receive and consider annual and special reports from the Security Council; these reports shall include an account of the measures that the Security Council has decided upon or taken to maintain international peace and security.

2. The General Assembly shall receive and consider reports from the other organs of the United Nations.

Article 16

The General Assembly shall perform such functions with respect to the international trusteeship system as are assigned to it under Chapters XII and XIII, including the approval of the trusteeship agreements for areas not designated as strategic.

Article 17

1. The General Assembly shall consider and approve the budget of the Organization.

2. The expenses of the Organization shall be borne by the Members as apportioned by the General Assembly.

3. The General Assembly shall consider and approve any financial and budgetary arrangements with specialized agencies referred to in Article 57 and shall examine the administrative budgets of such specialized agencies with a view to making recommendations to the agencies concerned.

Voting
Article 18

1. Each member of the General Assembly shall have one vote.

2. Decisions of the General Assembly on important questions shall be made by a two-thirds majority of the members present and voting. These questions shall include: recommendations with respect to the maintenance of international peace and security, the election of the non-permanent members of the Security Council, the election of the members of the Economic and Social Council, the election of members of the Trusteeship Council in accordance with paragraph 1(c) of Article 86, the admission of new Members to the United Nations, the suspension of the rights and privileges of membership, the expulsion of Members, questions relating to the operation of the trusteeship system, and budgetary questions.

3. Decisions on other questions, including the determination of additional categories of questions to be decided by a two-thirds majority, shall be made by a majority of the members present and voting.

Article 19

A Member of the United Nations which is in arrears in the payment of its financial contributions to the Organization shall have no vote in the General Assembly if the amount of its arrears equals or exceeds the amount of the contributions due from it for the preceding two full years. The General Assembly may, nevertheless, permit such a Member to vote if it is satisfied that the failure to pay is due to conditions beyond the control of the Member.

Procedure
Article 20

The General Assembly shall meet in regular annual sessions and in such special sessions as occasion may require. Special sessions shall be convoked by the Secretary-General at the request of the Security Council or of a majority of the Members of the United Nations.

Article 21

The General Assembly shall adopt its own rules of procedure. It shall elect its President for each session.

Article 22

The General Assembly may establish such subsidiary organs as it deems necessary for the performance of its functions.

CHAPTER V
The Security Council
Composition
Article 23

1. The Security Council shall consist of fifteen Members of the United Nations. The Republic of China, France, the Union of Soviet Socialist Republics, the United Kingdom of Great Britain and Northern Ireland, and the United States of America shall be permanent members of the Security Council. The General Assembly shall elect ten other Members of the United Nations to be non-permanent members of the Security Council, due regard being specially paid, in the first instance to the contribution of Members of the United Nations to the maintenance of international peace and security and to the other purposes of the Or-

ganization, and also to equitable geographical distribution.

2. The nonpermanent members of the Security Council shall be elected for a term of two years. In the first election of the nonpermanent members after the increase of the membership of the Security Council from eleven to fifteen, two of the four additional members shall be chosen for a term of one year. A retiring member shall not be eligible for immediate reelection.

3. Each member of the Security Council shall have one representative.

Functions and Powers

Article 24

1. In order to ensure prompt and effective action by the United Nations, its Members confer on the Security Council primary responsibility for the maintenance of international peace and security, and agree that in carrying out its duties under this responsibility the Security Council acts on their behalf.

2. In discharging these duties the Security Council shall act in accordance with the Purposes and Principles of the United Nations. The specific powers granted to the Security Council for the discharge of these duties are laid down in Chapters VI, VII, VIII, and XII.

3. The Security Council shall submit annual and, when necessary, special reports to the General Assembly for its consideration.

Article 25

The Members of the United Nations agree to accept and carry out the decisions of the Security Council in accordance with the present Charter.

Article 26

In order to promote the establishment and maintenance of international peace and security with the least diversion for armaments of the world's human and economic resources, the Security Council shall be responsible for formulating, with the assistance of the Military Staff Committee referred to in Article 47, plans to be submitted to the Members of the United Nations for the establishment of a system for the regulation of armaments.

Voting

Article 27

1. Each member of the Security Council shall have one vote.

2. Decisions of the Security Council on procedural matters shall be made by an affirmative vote of nine members.

3. Decisions of the Security Council on all other matters shall be made by an affirmative vote of nine members including the concurring votes of the permanent members; provided that, in decisions under Chapter VI, and under paragraph 3 of Article 52, a party to a dispute shall abstain from voting.

Procedure

Article 28

1. The Security Council shall be so organized as to be able to function continuously. Each member of the Security Council shall for this purpose be represented at all times at the seat of the Organization.

2. The Security Council shall hold periodic meetings at which each of its members may, if it so desires, be represented by a member of the government or by some other specially designated representative.

3. The Security Council may hold meetings at such places other than the seat of the Organization as in its judgment will best facilitate its work.

Article 29

The Security Council may establish such subsidiary organs as it deems necessary for the performance of its functions.

Article 30

The Security Council shall adopt its own rules of procedure, including the method of selecting its President.

Article 31

Any Member of the United Nations which is not a member of the Security Council may participate, without vote, in the discussion of any question brought before the Security Council whenever the latter considers that the interests of that Member are specially affected.

Article 32

Any Member of the United Nations which is not a member of the Security Council or any state which is not a Member of the United Nations, if it is a party to a dispute under consideration by the Security Council, shall be invited to participate, without vote, in the discussion relating to the dispute. The Security Council shall lay down such conditions as it deems just for the participation of a state which is not a Member of the United Nations.

CHAPTER VI
Pacific Settlement of Disputes

Article 33

1. The parties to any dispute, the continuance of which is likely to endanger the maintenance of international peace and security, shall, first of all, seek a solution by negotiation, enquiry, mediation, conciliation, arbitration, judicial settlement, resort to regional agencies or arrangements, or other peaceful means of their own choice.

2. The Security Council shall, when it deems necessary, call upon the parties to settle their dispute by such means.

Article 34

The Security Council may investigate any dispute, or any situation which might lead to international friction or give rise to a dispute, in order to determine whether the continuance of the dispute or situation is likely to endanger the maintenance of international peace and security.

Article 35

1. Any Member of the United Nations may bring any dispute, or any situation of the nature referred to in Article 34, to the attention of the Security Council or of the General Assembly.

2. A state which is not a Member of the United Nations may bring to the attention of the Security Council or of the General Assembly any dispute to which it is a party if it accepts in advance, for the purposes of the dispute, the obligations of pacific settlement provided in the present Charter.

3. The proceedings of the General Assembly in respect of matters brought to its attention under this Article will be subject to the provisions of Articles 11 and 12.

Article 36

1. The Security Council may, at any stage of a dispute of the nature referred to in Article 33 or of a situation of like nature, recommend appropriate procedures or methods of adjustment.

2 The Security Council should take into consideration any procedures for the settlement of the dispute which have already been adopted by the parties.

3. In making recommendations under this Article the Security Council should also take into consideration that legal disputes should as a general rule be referred by the parties to the International Court of Justice in accordance with the provisions of the Statute of the Court.

Article 37

1. Should the parties to a dispute of the nature referred to in Article 33 fail to settle it by the means indicated in that Article, they shall refer it to the Security Council.

2. If the Security Council deems that the continuance of the dispute is in fact likely to endanger the maintenance of international peace and security, it shall decide whether to take action under Article 36 or to recommend such terms of settlement as it may consider appropriate.

Article 38

Without prejudice to the provisions of Articles 33 to 37, the Security Council may, if all the parties to any dispute so request, make recommendations to the parties with a view to a pacific settlement of the dispute.

Chapter VII

Action with Respect to Threats to the Peace, Breaches of the Peace, and Acts of Aggression

Article 39

The Security Council shall determine the existence of any threat to the peace, breach of the peace, or act of aggression and shall make recommendations, or decide what measures shall be taken in accordance with Articles 41 and 42, to maintain or restore international peace and security.

Article 40

In order to prevent an aggravation of the situation, the Security Council may, before making the recommendations or deciding upon the measures provided for in Article 39, call upon the parties concerned to comply with such provisional measures as it deems necessary or desirable. Such provisional measures shall be without prejudice to the rights, claims, or position of the parties concerned. The Security Council shall duly take account of failure to comply with such provisional measures.

Article 41

The Security Council may decide what measures not involving the use of armed force are to be employed to give effect to its decisions, and it may call upon the Members of the United Nations to apply such measures. These may include complete or partial interruption of economic relations and of rail, sea, air, postal, telegraphic, radio, and other means of communication, and the severance of diplomatic relations.

Article 42

Should the Security Council consider that measures provided for in Article 41 would be inadequate or have proved to be inadequate, it may take such action by air, sea, or land forces as may be necessary to maintain or restore international peace and security. Such action may include demonstrations, blockade, and other operations by air, sea, or land forces of Members of the United Nations.

Article 43

1. All Members of the United Nations, in order to contribute to the maintenance of international peace and security, undertake to make available to the Security Council, on its call and in accordance with a special agreement or agreements, armed forces, assistance, and facilities, including rights of passage, necessary for the purpose of maintaining international peace and security.

2. Such agreement or agreements shall govern the numbers and types of forces, their degree of readiness and general location, and the nature of the facilities and assistance to be provided.

3. The agreement or agreements shall be negotiated as soon as possible on the initiative of the Security Council. They shall be concluded between the Security Council and Members or between the Security Council

and groups of Members and shall be subject to ratification by the signatory states in accordance with their respective constitutional processes.

Article 44

When the Security Council has decided to use force it shall, before calling upon a Member not represented on it to provide armed forces in fulfilment of the obligations assumed under Article 43, invite that Member, if the Member so desires, to participate in the decisions of the Security Council concerning the employment of contingents of that Member's armed forces.

Article 45

In order to enable the United Nations to take urgent military measures, Members shall hold immediately available national air-force contingents for combined international enforcement action. The strength and degree of readiness of these contingents and plans for their combined action shall be determined within the limits laid down in the special agreement or agreements referred to in Article 43, by the Security Council with the assistance of the Military Staff Committee.

Article 46

Plans for the application of armed force shall be made by the Security Council with the assistance of the Military Staff Committee.

Article 47

1. There shall be established a Military Staff Committee to advise and assist the Security Council on all questions relating to the Security Council's military requirements for the maintenance of international peace and security, the employment and command of forces placed at its disposal, the regulation of armaments, and possible disarmament.

2. The Military Staff Committee shall consist of the Chiefs of Staff of the permanent members of the Security Council or their representatives. Any Member of the United Nations not permanently represented on the Committee shall be invited by the Committee to be associated with it when the efficient discharge of the Committee's responsibilities requires the participation of that Member in its work.

3. The Military Staff Committee shall be responsible under the Security Council for the strategic direction of any armed forces placed at the disposal of the Security Council. Questions relating to the command of such forces shall be worked out subsequently.

4. The Military Staff Committee, with the authorization of the Security Council and after consultation with appropriate regional agencies, may establish regional sub-committees.

Article 48

1. The action required to carry out the decisions of the Security Council for the maintenance of international peace and security shall be taken by all the Members of the United Nations or by some of them, as the Security Council may determine.

2. Such decisions shall be carried out by the Members of the United Nations directly and through their action in the appropriate international agencies of which they are members.

Article 49

The Members of the United Nations shall join in affording mutual assistance in carrying out the measures decided upon by the Security Council.

Article 50

If preventive or enforcement measures against any state are taken by the Security Council, any other state, whether a Member of the United Nations or not, which finds itself confronted with special economic problems arising from the carrying out of those measures shall have the right to consult the

Security Council with regard to a solution of those problems.

Article 51

Nothing in the present Charter shall impair the inherent right of individual or collective self-defence if an armed attack occurs against a Member of the United Nations, until the Security Council has taken measures necessary to maintain international peace and security. Measures taken by Members in the exercise of this right of self-defence shall be immediately reported to the Security Council and shall not in any way affect the authority and responsibility of the Security Council under the present Charter to take at any time such action as it deems necessary in order to maintain or restore international peace and security.

Chapter VIII

Regional Arrangements

Article 52

1. Nothing in the present Charter precludes the existence of regional arrangements or agencies for dealing with such matters relating to the maintenance of international peace and security as are appropriate for regional action provided that such arrangements or agencies and their activities are consistent with the Purposes and Principles of the United Nations.

2. The Members of the United Nations entering into such arrangements or constituting such agencies shall make every effort to achieve pacific settlement of local disputes through such regional arrangements or by such regional agencies before referring them to the Security Council.

3. The Security Council shall encourage the development of pacific settlement of local disputes through such regional arrangements or by such regional agencies either on the initiative of the states concerned or by reference from the Security Council.

4. This Article in no way impairs the application of Articles 34 and 35.

Article 53

1. The Security Council shall, where appropriate, utilize such regional arrangements or agencies for enforcement action under its authority. But no enforcement action shall be taken under regional arrangements or by regional agencies without the authorization of the Security Council, with the exception of measures against any enemy state, as defined in paragraph 2 of this Article, provided for pursuant to Article 107 or in regional arrangements directed against renewal of aggressive policy on the part of any such state, until such time as the Organization may, on request of the Governments concerned, be charged with the responsibility for preventing further aggression by such a state.

2. The term "enemy state" as used in paragraph 1 of this Article applies to any state which during the Second World War has been an enemy of any signatory of the present Charter.

Article 54

The Security Council shall at all times be kept fully informed of activities undertaken or in contemplation under regional arrangements or by regional agencies for the maintenance of international peace and security.

Chapter IX

International Economic and Social Cooperation

Article 55

With a view to the creation of conditions of stability and well-being which are necessary for peaceful and friendly relations among nations based on respect for the principle of equal rights and self-determination of peoples, the United Nations shall promote:

A. higher standards of living, full employment, and conditions of economic and social progress and development;

B. solutions of international economic, social, health, and related problems; and international cultural and educational cooperation; and

C. universal respect for, and observance of, human rights and fundamental freedoms for all without distinction as to race, sex, language, or religion.

Article 56

All Members pledge themselves to take joint and separate action in cooperation with the Organization for the achievement of the purposes set forth in Article 55.

Article 57

1. The various specialized agencies, established by intergovernmental agreement and having wide international responsibilities, as defined in their basic instruments, in economic, social, cultural, educational, health, and related fields, shall be brought into relationship with the United Nations in accordance with the provisions of Article 63.

2. Such agencies thus brought into relationship with the United Nations are hereinafter referred to as "specialized agencies."

Article 58

The Organization shall make recommendations for the co-ordination of the policies and activities of the specialized agencies.

Article 59

The Organization shall, where appropriate, initiate negotiations among the states concerned for the creation of any new specialized agencies required for the accomplishment of the purposes set forth in Article 55.

Article 60

Responsibility for the discharge of the functions of the Organization set forth in this Chapter shall be vested in the General Assembly and, under the authority of the General Assembly, in the Economic and Social Council, which shall have for this purpose the powers set forth in Chapter X.

Chapter X

The Economic and Social Council

Composition

Article 61

1. The Economic and Social Council shall consist of fifty-four Members of the United Nations elected by the General Assembly.

2. Subject to the provisions of paragraph 3, eighteen members of the Economic and Social Council shall be elected each year for a term of three years. A retiring member shall be eligible for immediate reelection.

3. At the first election after the increase in the membership of the Economic and Social Council from twenty-seven to fifty-four members, in addition to the members elected in place of the nine members whose term of office expires at the end of that year, twenty-seven additional members shall be elected. Of these twenty-seven additional members, the term of office of nine members so elected shall expire at the end of one year, and of nine other members at the end of two years, in accordance with arrangements made by the General Assembly.

4. Each member of the Economic and Social Council shall have one representative.

Functions and Powers

Article 62

1. The Economic and Social Council may make or initiate studies and reports with re-

spect to international economic, social, cultural, educational, health, and related matters and may make recommendations with respect to any such matters to the General Assembly, to the Members of the United Nations, and to the specialized agencies concerned.

2. It may make recommendations for the purpose of promoting respect for, and observance of, human rights and fundamental freedoms for all.

3. It may prepare draft conventions for submission to the General Assembly, with respect to matters falling within its competence.

4. It may call, in accordance with the rules prescribed by the United Nations, international conferences on matters falling within its competence.

Article 63

1. The Economic and Social Council may enter into agreements with any of the agencies referred to in Article 57, defining the terms on which the agency concerned shall be brought into relationship with the United Nations. Such agreements shall be subject to approval by the General Assembly.

2. It may co-ordinate the activities of the specialized agencies through consultation with and recommendations to such agencies and through recommendations to the General Assembly and to the Members of the United Nations.

Article 64

1. The Economic and Social Council may take appropriate steps to obtain regular reports from the specialized agencies. It may make arrangements with the Members of the United Nations and with the specialized agencies to obtain reports on the steps taken to give effect to its own recommendations and to recommendations on matters falling within its competence made by the General Assembly.

2. It may communicate its observations on these reports to the General Assembly.

Article 65

The Economic and Social Council may furnish information to the Security Council and shall assist the Security Council upon its request.

Article 66

1. The Economic and Social Council shall perform such functions as fall within its competence in connection with the carrying out of the recommendations of the General Assembly.

2. It may, with the approval of the General Assembly, perform services at the request of Members of the United Nations and at the request of specialized agencies.

3. It shall perform such other functions as are specified elsewhere in the present Charter or as may be assigned to it by the General Assembly.

Voting
Article 67

1. Each member of the Economic and Social Council shall have one vote.

2. Decisions of the Economic and Social Council shall be made by a majority of the members present and voting.

Procedure
Article 68

The Economic and Social Council shall set up commissions in economic and social fields and for the promotion of human rights, and such other commissions as may be required for the performance of its functions.

Article 69

The Economic and Social Council shall invite any Member of the United Nations to participate, without vote, in its deliberations on any matter of particular concern to that Member.

Article 70

The Economic and Social Council may make arrangements for representatives of the specialized agencies to participate, without vote, in its deliberations and in those of the commissions established by it, and for its representatives to participate in the deliberations of the specialized agencies.

Article 71

The Economic and Social Council may make suitable arrangements for consultation with non-governmental organizations which are concerned with matters within its competence. Such arrangements may be made with international organizations and, where appropriate, with national organizations after consultation with the Member of the United Nations concerned.

Article 72

1. The Economic and Social Council shall adopt its own rules of procedure, including the method of selecting its President.

2. The Economic and Social Council shall meet as required in accordance with its rules, which shall include provision for the convening of meetings on the request of a majority of its members.

CHAPTER XI
Declaration Regarding Non-Self-Governing Territories

Article 73

Members of the United Nations which have or assume responsibilities for the administration of territories whose peoples have not yet attained a full measure of self-government recognize the principle that the interests of the inhabitants of these territories are paramount, and accept as a sacred trust the obligation to promote to the utmost, within the system of international peace and security established by the present Charter, the well-being of the inhabitants of these territories, and, to this end:

A. to ensure, with due respect for the culture of the peoples concerned, their political, economic, social, and educational advancement, their just treatment, and their protection against abuses;

B. to develop self-government, to take due account of the political aspirations of the peoples, and to assist them in the progressive development of their free political institutions, according to the particular circumstances of each territory and its peoples and their varying stages of advancement;

C. to further international peace and security;

D. to promote constructive measures of development, to encourage research, and to co-operate with one another and, when and where appropriate, with specialized international bodies with a view to the practical achievement of the social, economic, and scientific purposes set forth in this Article; and

E. to transmit regularly to the Secretary-General for information purposes, subject to such limitation as security and constitutional considerations may require, statistical and other information of a technical nature relating to economic, social, and educational conditions in the territories for which they are respectively responsible other than those territories to which Chapters XII and XIII apply.

Article 74

Members of the United Nations also agree that their policy in respect of the territories to which this Chapter applies, no less than in respect of their metropolitan areas, must be based on the general principle of good-neighbourliness, due account being taken of the interests and well-being of the rest of the world, in social, economic, and commercial matters.

Chapter XIV
The International Court of Justice

Article 92

The International Court of Justice shall be the principal judicial organ of the United Nations. It shall function in accordance with the annexed Statute, which is based upon the Statute of the Permanent Court of International Justice and forms an integral part of the present Charter.

Article 93

1. All Members of the United Nations are ipso facto parties to the Statute of the International Court of Justice.

2. A state which is not a Member of the United Nations may become a party to the Statute of the International Court of Justice on conditions to be determined in each case by the General Assembly upon the recommendation of the Security Council.

Article 94

1. Each Member of the United Nations undertakes to comply with the decision of the International Court of Justice in any case to which it is a party.

2. If any party to a case fails to perform the obligations incumbent upon it under a judgment rendered by the Court, the other party may have recourse to the Security Council, which may, if it deems necessary, make recommendations or decide upon measures to be taken to give effect to the judgment.

Article 95

Nothing in the present Charter shall prevent Members of the United Nations from entrusting the solution of their differences to other tribunals by virtue of agreements already in existence or which may be concluded in the future.

Article 96

1. The General Assembly or the Security Council may request the International Court of Justice to give an advisory opinion on any legal question.

2. Other organs of the United Nations and specialized agencies, which may at any time be so authorized by the General Assembly, may also request advisory opinions of the Court on legal questions arising within the scope of their activities.

Chapter XV
The Secretariat

Article 97

The Secretariat shall comprise a Secretary-General and such staff as the Organization may require. The Secretary-General shall be appointed by the General Assembly upon the recommendation of the Security Council. He shall be the chief administrative officer of the Organization.

Article 98

The Secretary-General shall act in that capacity in all meetings of the General Assembly, of the Security Council, of the Economic and Social Council, and of the Trusteeship Council, and shall perform such other functions as are entrusted to him by these organs. The Secretary-General shall make an annual report to the General Assembly on the work of the Organization.

Article 99

The Secretary-General may bring to the attention of the Security Council any matter which in his opinion may threaten the maintenance of international peace and security.

Article 100

1. In the performance of their duties the Secretary-General and the staff shall not seek or receive instructions from any government or from any other authority external to the Organization. They shall refrain from any action which might reflect on their position as international officials responsible only to the Organization.

2. Each Member of the United Nations undertakes to respect the exclusively international character of the responsibilities of the Secretary-General and the staff and not to seek to influence them in the discharge of their responsibilities.

Article 101

1. The staff shall be appointed by the Secretary-General under regulations established by the General Assembly.

2. Appropriate staffs shall be permanently assigned to the Economic and Social Council, the Trusteeship Council, and, as required, to other organs of the United Nations. These staffs shall form a part of the Secretariat.

3. The paramount consideration in the employment of the staff and in the determination of the conditions of service shall be the necessity of securing the highest standards of efficiency, competence, and integrity. Due regard shall be paid to the importance of recruiting the staff on as wide a geographical basis as possible.

CHAPTER XVIII

Amendments

Article 108

Amendments to the present Charter shall come into force for all Members of the United Nations when they have been adopted by a vote of two-thirds of the members of the General Assembly and ratified in accordance with their respective constitutional processes by two-thirds of the Members of the United Nations, including all the permanent members of the Security Council.

Article 109

1. A General Conference of the Members of the United Nations for the purpose of reviewing the present Charter may be held at a date and place to be fixed by a two-thirds vote of the members of the General Assembly and by a vote of any nine members of the Security Council. Each Member of the United Nations shall have one vote in the conference.

2. Any alteration of the present Charter recommended by a two-thirds vote of the conference shall take effect when ratified in accordance with their respective constitutional processes by two-thirds of the Members of the United Nations including all the permanent members of the Security Council.

3. If such a conference has not been held before the tenth annual session of the General Assembly following the coming into force of the present Charter, the proposal to call such a conference shall be placed on the agenda of that session of the General Assembly, and the conference shall be held if so decided by a majority vote of the members of the General Assembly and by a vote of any seven members of the Security Council.

Suggested Readings

General Sources on International Organizations and the United Nations

Bailey, Sydney D., and Sam Daws. *The Procedure of the UN Security Council.* 3rd ed. New York: Oxford University Press, 1999.

Barnett, Michael, and Martha Finnemore. *Rules for the World: International Organizations in Global Politics.* Ithaca: Cornell University Press, 2004.

Bennett, A. LeRoy. *International Organizations: Principles and Issues.* 7th ed. Englewood Cliffs, N.J.: Prentice-Hall, 2002.

Claude, Inis L., Jr. *Swords into Plowshares: The Problems and Progress of International Organization.* 4th ed. New York: Random House, 1984.

Fasulo, Linda. *An Insider's Guide to the UN.* New Haven: Yale University Press, 2004.

Karns, Margaret P., and Karen A. Mingst. *International Organizations. The Politics and Processes of Global Governance.* Boulder: Lynne Rienner, 2004.

Malone, David, ed. *The UN Security Council: From the Cold War to the 21st Century.* Boulder: Lynne Rienner, 2004.

Marin-Bosch, Miguel. *Votes in the UN General Assembly.* The Hague: Kluwer Law International, 1998.

Muldoon, James P., Jr., *The Architecture of Global Governance: An Introduction to the Study of International Organizations.* Boulder: Westview Press, 2004.

Newman, Edward. *The UN Secretary-General from the Cold War to the New Era: A Global Peace and Security Mandate?* New York: St. Martin's Press, 1998.

Peterson, M. J. *The General Assembly in World Politics.* Boston: Unwin Hyman, 1986.

Reinalda, Bob, and Bertjan Verbeek, eds. *Decision Making Within International Organizations.* London: Routledge, 2004.

Schlesinger, Stephen C. *Act of Creation: The Founding of the United Nations.* Boulder: Westview Press, 2003.

Smith, Courtney B. *Politics and Process at the United Nations: The Global Dance.* Boulder: Lynne Rienner, 2006.

Taylor, Paul, and A. J. R. Groom, eds. *The United Nations at the Millennium: The Principal Organs.* New York: Continuum, 2000.

United Nations Association of the USA, eds. *Global Agenda: Issues Before the General Assembly of the United Nations.* New York: UNA-USA (published annually).

Weiss, Thomas G., David P. Forsythe, and Roger A. Coate. *The United Nations and Changing World Politics.* 4th ed. Boulder: Westview Press, 2003.

Ziring, Lawrence, Robert Riggs, and Jack Plano. *The United Nations: International Organization and World Politics.* 3rd ed. New York: Harcourt College, 2000.

An excellent source of material on the United Nations is The UN, *Chronicle,* published bimonthly by the UN Department of Public Information, New York.

Actors In The United Nations System: States and NGOs

Alger, Chadwick F., Gene M. Lyons, and John E. Trent, eds. *The United Nations and the Politics of Member States.* Tokyo: United Nations University Press, 1995.

Dore, Ronald. *Japan, Internationalism, and the UN.* London: Routledge, 1997.

Florini, Ann M., ed. *The Third Force: The Rise of Transnational Civil Society.* Tokyo and Washington: Japan Center for International Exchange and the Carnegie Endowment for International Peace, 2000.

Friedman, Elizabeth, Kathryn Hochstetter, and Ann Marie Clark. *Democracy, Sovereignty and Global Civil Society.* Albany, N.Y.: SUNY Press, 2005.

Karns, Margaret P., and Karen A. Mingst, eds. *The United States and Multilateral Institutions: Patterns of Changing Instrumentality and Influence.* Boston: Unwin Hyman, 1990.

Keck, Margaret E., and Kathryn Sikkink. *Activists Beyond Borders: Advocacy Networks in International Politics.* Ithaca: Cornell University Press, 1998.

Krause, Keith, and W. Andy Knight, eds. *State, Society, and the UN System: Changing Perspectives on Multilateralism.* Tokyo: United Nations University Press, 1995.

Luck, Edward C. *Mixed Messages: American Politics and International Organization 1919–1999.* Washington D.C.: Brookings Institution Press, 1999.

Nye, Joseph S., Jr. *The Paradox of American Power: Why the World's Only Superpower Can't Go It Alone.* Oxford: Oxford University Press, 2002.

Ostrower, Bary B. *The United Nations and the United States.* Old Tappan, N.J.: Twayne, 1998.

Paolini, Albert J., eds. *Between Sovereignty and Global Governance: The United Nations, the State and Civil Society.* Basingstoke, U.K.: Palgrave, 2003.

Patrick, Stewart, and Shepard Forman, eds. *Multilateralism and U.S. Foreign Policy: Ambivalent Engagement.* Boulder: Lynne Rienner, 2002.

Schechter, Michael G. *United Nations Global Conferences.* London: Routledge, 2005.

Weiss, Thomas G., and Leon Gordenker, eds. *NGOs, the UN, and Global Governance.* Boulder: Lynne Rienner, 1996.

Another excellent source on U.S. participation is the United Nations Association of the United States. See www.unausa.org.

Peace and Security

Abiew, Frances Kofi. *The Evolution of the Doctrine and Practice of Humanitarian Intervention.* The Hague: Kluwer Law International, 1999.

Boulden, Jane, and Thomas G. Weiss, eds. *Terrorism and the UN: Before and After September 11.* Bloomington, Ind.: Indiana University Press, 2004.

Chesterman, Simon. *You, The People: The United Nations, Transitional Administration, and State-Building.* New York: Oxford University Press, 2004.

_____. *Just War or Just Peace? Humanitarian Intervention and International Law.* N.Y.: Oxford University Press, 2001.

Cortright, David, and George A. Lopez. *Sanctions and the Search for Security.* Boulder: Lynne Rienner, 2002.

Diehl, Paul F. *International Peacekeeping.* Baltimore: Johns Hopkins University Press, 1993.

Dobbins, James, et al. *The UN's Role in Nation-Building: From the Congo to Iraq.* Santa Monica, Calif.: Rand Corp, 2005.

James, Alan. *Peacekeeping in International Politics.* London: Macmillan, 1990.

Jentleson, Bruce W. *Opportunities Missed, Opportunities Seized: Preventive Diplomacy in the Post–Cold War World.* Lanham, Md.: Rowman and Littlefield, 1999.

Mayall, James, ed. *The New Interventionism, 1991–1993: United Nations Experience in Cambodia, Former Yugoslavia, and Somalia.* Cambridge: Cambridge University Press, 1996.

Price, Richard M., and Mark W. Zacher, eds. *The United Nations and Global Security.* N.Y.: Palgrave Macmillan, 2004.

Pugh, Michael, and Waheguru Pal Singh Sidhu. *The United Nations and Regional Security: Europe and Beyond.* Boulder: Lynne Rienner, 2003.

Ratner, Steven R. *The New UN Peacekeeping: Building Peace in Lands of Conflict After the Cold War.* New York: St. Martin's Press, 1996.

Sorenson, David S., and Pia Christina Wood, eds. *The Politics of Peacekeeping in the Post–Cold War Era.* London: Frank Cass, 2005.

Stedman, Stephen John, Donald Rothchild, and Elizabeth M. Cousens. *Ending Civil Wars: The Implementation of Peace Agreements.* Boulder: Lynne Rienner, 2002.

Thakur, Ramesh, and Albrecht Schnabel, eds. *United Nations Peacekeeping Operations: Ad Hoc Missions, Permanent Engagement.* Tokyo: United Nations University Press, 2001.

United Nations. *The Blue Helmets: A Review of United Nations Peace-Keeping.* 3d ed. New York: UNDPI, 1996.

Weiss, Thomas G., ed. *Beyond UN Subcontracting: Task-Sharing with Regional Security Arrangements and Service-Providing NGOs.* New York: St. Martin's Press, 1998.

Weiss, Thomas G., and Cindy Collins. *Humanitarian Challenges and Intervention: World Politics and the Dilemmas of Help.* 2nd ed. Boulder: Westview Press, 2000.

An excellent source on peacekeeping is the journal *International Peacekeeping,* published by Frank Cass and Co., London.

Economic Development and Sustainablility

Ayres, Robert. *Banking on the Poor: The World Bank and World Poverty.* Cambridge, Mass.: MIT Press, 1983.

Boas, Morten, and Desmond McNeill, eds. *Global Institutions and Development: Framing the World?* London: Routledge, 2004.

Goldman, Michael. *Imperial Nature: The World Bank and Struggles for Social Justice in the Age of Globalization.* New Haven: Yale University Press, 2005.

Grunberg, Isabelle, and Sarbuland Khan, eds. *Globalization: The United Nations Development Dialogue, Finance, Trade, Poverty, Peacebuilding.* Tokyo: UNU Press, 2000.

Hoekman, Bernard M. *The Political Economy of the World Trading System: From GATT to WTO.* Oxford: Oxford University Press, 1995.

Honeywell, Martin, ed. *The Poverty Brokers: The IMF and Latin America.* London: Latin America Bureau, 1983.

Jain, Devaki. *Women, Development, and the UN: A Sixty-Year Quest for Equality and Justice.* Bloomington, Ind.: Indiana University Press, 2005.

Jolly, Richard, Louis Emmerij, Dharam Ghai, and Frederic Lapeyre. *UN Contributions to Development Thinking and Practice.* Bloomington, Ind.: Indiana University Press, 2004.

Kapur, Devesh, John P. Lewis, and Richard Webb, eds. *The World Bank: Its First Half Century.* Vol. 1, *History;* vol. 2, *Perspectives.* Washington, D.C.: Brookings Institution Press, 1997.

Miller-Adams, Michelle. *The World Bank: New Agendas in a Changing World.* London: Routledge, 1999.

Nelson, Paul J. *World Bank and NGOs: The Limits of Apolitical Development.* New York: St. Martin's, 1995.

O'Brien, Robert, Anne Marie Goetz, Jan Aart Scholte, and Marc Williams. *Contesting Global Governance: Multilateral Economic Institutions and Global Social Movements.* New York: Cambridge University Press, 2000.

Peet, Richard. *Unholy Trinity: The IMF, World Bank and WTO.* New York: Zed Books, 2003.

Schott, Jeffrey J., ed. *The WTO After Seattle.* Washington, D.C.: Institute of International Economics, 2000.

Srinivasan, T. N. *Developing Countries and the Multilateral Trading System: From GATT to the Uruguay Round and the Future.* Boulder: Westview Press, 1998.

Stiglitz, Joseph E. *Globalization and Its Discontents.* New York: W. W. Norton, 2002.

Tabb, William K. *Economic Governance in the Age of Globalization.* New York: Columbia University Press, 2004.

Ul Haq, Mahbub, et al., eds. *The UN and the Bretton Woods Institutions.* New York: St. Martin's Press, 1995.

Williams, Marc. *Third World Cooperation: The Group of 77 in UNCTAD.* New York: St. Martin's Press, 1991.

Human Rights

Alston, Philip, ed. *The United Nations and Human Rights: A Critical Appraisal.* Oxford: Clarendon Press, 1992.

Barnett, Michael. *Eyewitness to Genocide: The United Nations and Rwanda.* Ithaca: Cornell University Press, 2002.

Devaki, Jain. *Women, Development, and the UN: A Sixty-Year Quest for Equality and Justice.* Bloomington, Ind.: Indiana University Press, 2005.

Donnelly, Jack. *Universal Human Rights in Theory and Practice.* 2nd ed. Ithaca: Cornell University Press, 2003.

Forsythe, David. *The Humanitarians. The International Committee of the Red Cross.* New York: Cambridge University Press, 2005.

Hopgood, Stephen. *Keepers of the Flame: Understanding Amnesty International.* Ithaca: Cornell University Press, 2006.

Kerr, Joanna, ed. *Ours by Right: Women's Rights as Human Rights.* London: Zed Books, 1993.

Lauren, Paul Gordon. *The Evolution of International Human Rights: Visions Seen.* 2nd ed. Philadelphia: University of Pennsylvania Press, 2003.

Lischer, Sarah Kenyon. *Dangerous Sanctuaries: Refugee Camps, Civil War and the Dilemmas of Humanitarian Aid.* Ithaca: Cornell University Press, 2005.

Mertus, Julie A. *The United Nations and Human Rights: A Guide for a New Era.* London: Routledge, 2005.

Meyer, Mary K., and Elisabeth Prugl, eds. *Gender Politics in Global Governance.* Lanham, Md.: Rowman and Littlefield, 1999.

Neuffer, Elizabeth. *The Key to My Neighbor's House: Seeking Justice in Bosnia and Rwanda.* N.Y.: Picador, 2001.

Peterson, V. Spike, and Anne Sisson Runyan. *Global Gender Issues.* 2nd ed. Boulder: Westview Press, 1999.

Pietila, Hilkka, and Jeanne Vickers. *Making Women Matter: The Role of the United Nations.* London: Zed Books, 1990.

Smith, Jackie, Charles Chatfield, and Ron Pagnucco, eds. *Transnational Social Movements and Global Politics: Solidarity Beyond the State.* Syracuse, N.Y.: Syracuse University Press, 1997.

United Nations. *The United Nations and the Advancement of Women, 1945–1996.* Blue Book vol. 6. New York: United Nations, 1997.

_____. *The United Nations and Apartheid, 1948–1994.* Blue Book vol. 1. New York: United Nations, 1995.

_____. *The United Nations and Human Rights, 1945–1995.* Blue Book vol. 7. New York: United Nations, 1996.

Winslow, Anne, ed. *Women, Politics, and the United Nations.* Westport, Conn.: Greenwood Press, 1995.

Human Security

Benedict, Richard Elliot. *Ozone Diplomacy: New Directions in Safeguarding the Planet.* Enlarged ed. Cambridge, Mass.: Harvard University Press, 1998.

Conca, Ken, and Geoffrey D. Dabelko. *Green Planet Blues: Environmental Politics from Stockholm to Kyoto.* 2nd ed. Boulder: Westview Press, 1998.

Garrett, Laurie. *The Coming Plague.* New York: Farrar, Straus, and Giroux, 1994.

_____. "The Next Pandemic?" *Foreign Affairs* 84, no. 4 (July-August, 2005): 3–64.

Homer-Dixon, Thomas. *Environment, Scarcity, and Violence.* 2nd ed. Princeton: Princeton University, 1999.

Price-Smith, Andrew T. *The Health of Nations: Infectious Disease, Environmental Change, and Their Effects on National Security and Development.* Cambridge, Mass: The MIT Press, 2002.

Rich, Bruce. *Mortgaging the Earth: The World Bank, Environmental Impoverishment and the Crisis of Development.* Boston: Beacon Press, 1994.

Simmons, P. J., and Chantal de Jonge Oudraat, eds. *Managing Global Issues. Lessons Learned.* Washington D.C.: Carnegie Endowment for International Peace, 2001.

Sitarz, Daniel, ed. *Agenda 21: The Earth Summit Strategy to Save Our Planet.* Boulder: Earthpress, 1994.

Tolba, Mostafa K., with Iwona Rummel-Bulska. *Global Environmental Diplomacy: Negotiating Environmental Agreements with the World, 1973–1992.* Cambridge, Mass.: The MIT Press, 1998.

World Commission on Environment and Development. *Our Common Future* (Brundtland Commission report). Oxford: Oxford University Press, 1987.

Young, Oran R. *International Governance: Protecting the Environment in a Stateless Society.* Ithaca: Cornell University Press, 1994.

UN Reform

Alger, Chadwick F., ed. *The Future of the United Nations System: Potential for the Twenty-first Century.* Tokyo: United Nations University Press, 1998.

Commission on Global Governance. *Our Global Neighborhood.* Oxford: Oxford University Press, 1995.

Evans, Gareth. *Cooperating for Peace: The Global Agenda for the 1990s and Beyond.* St. Leonards, Australia: Allen and Unwin, 1993.

Heinbecker, Paul, and Patricia Goff, eds. *Irrelevant or Indispensible? The UN in the 21st Century.* Waterloo, Canada: Wilfred Laurier Press, 2005.

Luck, Edward C. *Reforming the UN: Lessons from a History in Progress.* New Haven: Academic Council on the UN System, 2003.

Mueller, Joachim W., ed. *Reforming the United Nations: The Quiet Revolution.* The Hague: Kluwer, 2001.

Ogata, Shijuro, and Paul Volcker. *Financing an Effective United Nations: A Report of the Independent Advisory Group on UN Financing.* New York: Ford Foundation, 1993.

Weiss, Thomas G. *Overcoming the Security Council Reform Impasse: The Implausible Versus the Plausible.* Occasional paper no. 14. Berlin: Friedrich-Ebert-Stiftung, 2005.

Internet Resources

Offiial UN Web Sites

UN homepage: **www.un.org**
UN system of organizations: **www.unsystem.org**
UNAIDS: **www.unaids.org**
Commission on Sustainable Development: **www.un.org/esa/sustdev/csd/review.htm**
UN Conference on Trade and Development: **www.unctad.org**
UN Development Programme: **www.undp.org**
UN Department of Peacekeeping Operations: **www.un.org/Depts/dpko/home.htm**
UN Division for Sustainable Development: **www.un.org/esa/sustdev**
UN Environment Programme: **www.unep.org**
Food and Agriculture Organization: **www.fao.org**
Human Development Reports: **www.hdr.undp.org**
UN Inter-Agency Network on Women and Gender Equality: **www.un.org/womenwatch**
International Atomic Energy Agency: **www.iaea.org**
International Court of Justice: **www.icj-cij.org**
International Labour Organization: **www.ilo.org**
International Monetary Fund: **www.imf.org**
UN Framework Commission on Climate Change: **http://unfccc.int/2860.php**
UN Global Compact: **www.unglobalcompact.org**
UN High Commissioner for Human Rights: **www.unhchr.ch**
UN High Commissioner for Refugees: **www.unhcr.org**
UN Johannesburg Summit: **www.johannesburgsummit.org**
UN Millennium Development Goals: **www.un.org/millenniumgoals.org**
UN Office for the Coordination of Humanitarian Affairs: **http://ochaonline.un.org**
UN Reform: **www.un.org/reform**
World Bank: **www.worldbank.org**
World Food Programme: **www.wfp.org**
World Health Organization: **www.who.org**

Academic and Policy-Related Web Sites

Academic Council on the United Nations System: **www.acuns.org**
American Society of International Law: **www.asil.org**
United Nations Association of the United States: **www.unausa.org**
UN Foundation/UN Wire: **www.unfoundation.org/unwire**

Carnegie Endowment for International Peace: **www.carnegieendowment.org**
Global Policy Forum: **www.globalpolicy.org**
United States Institute of Peace: **www.usip.org**

Peace and Security Issues

International Commission on Intervention and State Sovereignty: **www.dfait-maeci.gc.ca/**
   iciss-ciise
International Crisis Group: **www.crisisgroup.org**
International Relations and Security Network: **www.isn.ethz.ch**
Stockholm International Peace Research Institute: **www.sipri.org**

Economic Development

Institute of Development Studies: **www.ids.ac.uk**
World Trade Organization: **www.wto.org**

Human Rights

Amnesty International: **www.amnesty.org**
Anti-Slavery International: **www.antislavery.org**
Human Rights Watch: **www.hrw.org**
International Commission of Jurists: **www.icj.org**
International Committee of the Red Cross: **www.icrc.org**

Human Security

Global Environment Facility: **www.gefweb.org**
Human Security Bulletin: **www.humansecurity.info**
Montreal Protocol: **www.unep.org/ozone/montreal.html**
The UN Framework Convention on Climate Change and Kyoto Protocol:
   www.unfcc.int.2860.php
U.S. Centers for Disease Control and Prevention: **www.cdc.gov**

Glossary

Advisory opinion   An opinion issued by the International Court of Justice based on a request by an international organization for advice on a general question of international law.

Agenda 21   A document adopted as part of UNCED that presented detailed work plans, objectives, responsibilities, and financial estimates for achieving sustainable development.

Apartheid   An Afrikaans term meaning "separateness"; the policy in South Africa from the 1950s to 1992 of official discrimination touching all aspects of public and private life, designed to keep the different races separate.

Arms control and disarmament   Efforts to induce states to limit, reduce, or eliminate specific types of weapons and armaments.

Arrearages   Unpaid assessed contributions to an international organization.

Balance of payments   The flow of money into and out of a country from trade, tourism, foreign aid, sale of services, profits, and so on.

Basic human needs approach   Proposals in the development community to shift from emphasizing economic growth to progress in meeting the population's basic needs, including better health care, education, and water supplies.

Bretton Woods institutions   The international economic institutions—the World Bank and the International Monetary Fund—created in 1944 to promote global monetary stability and economic growth. Also includes the trade procedures established under the General Agreement on Tariffs and Trade (GATT), now the World Trade Organization (WTO).

Coalition of the willing   An ad hoc group of states that volunteer to carry out a peace-enforcement or humanitarian mission with or without Security Council authorization.

Codes of conduct   Formal or informal rules by which multinational corporations agree to conform to acceptable practices, such as the treatment of labor and environmental policies.

Collective legitimation   The garnering of votes at the UN in support of a particular state's policy or a new international norm.

Collective security   The concept behind the League of Nations and the United Nations, namely, that aggression by one state is aggression against all and should be defeated collectively.

Complex peacekeeping   Multidimensional operations employing both military and civilian personnel; often includes traditional peacekeeping as well as peacebuilding activities; dangerous operations because not all parties have given consent and some use of force may be required. Also referred to as second- and third-generation peacekeeping, or muscular peacekeeping.

Concert of Europe, or Concert system   The nineteenth-century practice of multilateral meetings of leaders of major European powers to settle problems.

Conditionality   A strategy by the IMF and the World Bank to link further financial assistance to borrowers to the application of specified policy changes. See also structural adjustment programs.

Constructivism   Approach to study of international relations which examines how shared beliefs, rules, norms, organizations, and cultural practices shape state and individual behavior.

Crimes against humanity   International crimes which include murder, enslavement, forcible transfer of populations, ethnic cleansing, and torture.

Cultural relativism   The belief that morality and ethics are determined by cultures and history, and that values and rights are therefore not universal.

Democratization   The process whereby states become increasingly democratic; that is, citizens vote for representatives who rule on their behalf and the political system is marked by the rule of law.

Dependency theory   Derived from Marxism, an explanation of poverty and underdevelopment in less developed countries based on their historical dependence on and domination by rich countries.

Economic liberalism   The theory that the free interplay of market forces leads to a more efficient allocation of resources, to the benefit of the majority.

Enforcement actions   The use of direct actions—economic sanctions, withdrawal of aid, or military force—by the UN to ensure compliance with Security Council directives.

Exceptionalism   Belief held in the United States that because of its tradition of democracy and adherence to human rights norms that it has a unique role to play in international relations and is not subject to the same restraints as others.

First-generation human rights, or negative rights   The civil or political rights of citizens that prevent governmental authority from interfering with private individuals in civil society.

Functionalism   The belief that cooperation in solving social and economic issues can be separated from politics but will ultimately contribute to peace. UN specialized agencies are functionalist organizations.

Genocide   The systematic killing or harming of a group of people based on racial, religious, or ethnic characteristics, with the intention of destroying the group.

Global civil society   The notion that individuals and groups like NGOs are acting outside states to form nascent bonds among people across borders; facilitated by telecommunication revolution.

Global Compact   Voluntary principles which multinational corporations agree to accept and work toward in cooperation with the UN and NGOs.

Global governance   The rules, norms, activities, and organizations designed to address the international problems that states alone cannot solve.

Globalization   The idea that economies, social relations, and cultures are rapidly being linked by international market processes, international institutions, and NGOs in such a way that state sovereignty and distinctiveness are undermined; the internationalization of the capitalist economy in which states, markets, and civil society are restructured to facilitate the flow of capital.

Grotian tradition   Derived from the writings of Hugo Grotius, the idea that order in international relations is based on the rule of law.

Group of 7 (G-7)   The major economic powers, which meet annually to address world economic problems.

Group of 8 (G-8)   The seven industrialized states and Russia.

Group of 77 (G-77)   A coalition of LDCs that pressed for reforms in economic relations between developing and developed countries; also referred to as "the South." Now includes 132 countries.

Hague system   A system derived from conferences in 1897 and 1907 that established the principle of universality (all states should participate), rules for war, and dispute settlement mechanisms.

Human development   The concept that economic growth alone does not ensure improvement in human standards of living; measured by such indicators as average life expectancy, infant mortality, adult literacy, and per capita nutritional level.

Human security   The idea that security includes not only the security of the state and territory but also security of individuals from civil and economic turmoil, and health and environmental threats.

Humanitarian intervention   UN or individual states' actions to alleviate human suffering during violent conflicts without necessarily obtaining the consent of the host country.

Interdependence   The sensitivity and vulnerability of states to each other's actions resulting from increased interactions generated by trade, monetary flows, telecommunications, and shared interests.

International Bill of Rights   A term for the three primary human rights documents: the Universal Declaration of Human Rights, the Covenant on International Civil and Political Rights, and the Covenant on Economic, Social, and Cultural Rights.

International humanitarian law   International laws holding states and individuals accountable for actions during war, specifically including protection of and assistance to military and civilian victims of war.

International intergovernmental organizations (IGOs)   International agencies or bodies set up and controlled by member states to deal with areas of common interest.

Liberalism   A theoretical perspective, based on the goodness of the individual and the value of political and legal institutions, holding that there are multiple actors in international politics and that the state has many different, sometimes conflicting, interests.

Marxism   A social theory formulated by Karl Marx according to which class conflict between owners and workers will cause the eventual demise of capitalism.

Mercantilism, or statism   The belief that world politics is influenced by a competition for wealth, resources, and power, which should be mobilized to further states' interests and political goals.

Millennium Development Goals (MDGs)   Goals agreed to by UN member states in 2000 to improve the economic and social conditions of people; includes specific targets and a procedure for tracking progress toward attainment of the goals.

Multilateralism   The conduct of international activities by three or more states in accordance with shared general principles, often through international or multilateral institutions.

Multinational corporations   Private enterprises with production facilities, sales, or activity in more than one country; also called transnational corporations.

New International Economic Order (NIEO)   A list of demands by the G-77 to reform economic relations between the North and the South, that is, between the developed countries and the less developed countries.

Newly industrializing countries (NICs)   Countries previously at low levels of economic development but that now are approaching developed-country levels of economic growth.

Nonaligned Movement (NAM)   Group of developing countries held together by principles of anticolonialism, opposition to racism, and neutrality toward the Cold War.

Noncompulsory jurisdiction   When states are not obligated to bring disputes to a body such as the International Court of Justice for settlement.

Nongovernmental organizations (NGOs)   Private associations of individuals or groups that engage in political activity, often across national borders.

Nonintervention   The principle that obliges states and international organizations not to interfere in matters within the domestic jurisdiction of other sovereign states.

Partnerships   UN strategy in the new millennium to work with states as well as with the business community and NGOs for common goals.

Peacebuilding   Postconflict activities to strengthen and preserve peace settlements, such as development aid, civilian administration, and election and human rights monitoring.

Peaceful settlement   Various techniques by which disputes are settled, including adjudication, arbitration, mediation, conciliation, and good offices.

Peacekeeping   The use of multilateral forces to achieve several different objectives: observation of cease-fire lines and cease-fires, separation of forces, promotion of law and order, and humanitarian aid and intervention.

Politicization   The linkage of different issues for political purposes, as in the introduction of a clearly political topic to an organization dealing with health problems.

Poverty alleviation   Programs designed to improve food supply, nutrition, health, housing, and standard of living for the poorest people, particularly in remote areas of developing countries, and in minority groups whose poverty is not reduced by general economic growth and development.

Preventive diplomacy   The practice of engaging in diplomatic actions to prevent the outbreak of conflict; the monitoring of hot spots before conflict erupts.

Privatization   Belief held by economic liberals that economies function more efficiently if there is private ownership of industries and services.

Realist theory, or realism   A theory of world politics that emphasizes states' interest in accumulating power to ensure security in an anarchic world.

Regime   The rules, norms, and decisionmaking procedures developed by states and international organizations to address common concerns and to organize common activities relating to specific issue areas or problems, such as human rights, trade, or nuclear proliferation.

Responsibility to protect   Emerging norm in response to massive human rights abuses that the international community has the responsibility to help individuals suffering at the hands of their own state or other states.

Second-generation human rights, or positive rights   The social and economic rights that states are obligated to provide for their citizenry. May include right to an education, right to decent housing, and right to medical care.

Self-determination   The principle according to which nationalities and colonial peoples have the right to determine who will rule them; thought to minimize war for territorial expansion.

Sovereignty   The authority of the state, based on recognition by other states and nonstate actors, to govern matters within its own borders that affect its people, economy, security, and form of government.

Specialized agencies   UN-related organizations established by separate agreements to deal with specific issues, such as health, working conditions, weather, air and sea transport, and education.

Statism   See mercantilism.

Structural adjustment programs   IMF policies and recommendations to guide countries out of payment deficits and economic crises through changes in domestic economic policies and practices. See also conditionality.

Sustainable development   An approach that tries to reconcile current economic growth and environmental protection with future needs and resource supplies.

Technical assistance   The provision of human skills and resources necessary for economic development, including education, training, and expert advice.

Terms of trade   The ratio of the price of imports to the price of exports. When import prices are greater than the value of exports, a state experiences adverse or declining terms of trade.

Theory   Generalized statements about political, social, or economic activities that seek to describe and explain those activities; used also as a basis for prediction.

Third-generation human rights   The collective rights of groups, such as the rights of children or indigenous people; includes the right to democracy and to development.

Trade preferences   The granting of special trade arrangements usually giving trade advantages to less developed countries.

Traditional peacekeeping   The use of unarmed or lightly armed troops stationed between hostile forces to monitor truces and troop withdrawals and to provide buffer zones. Used with parties' consent. Also referred to as first-generation peacekeeping.

Unilateralism   The practice of states acting alone, without consulting other states.

United Nations system   Includes not only the UN based in New York but also the specialized agencies and other autonomous organizations headquartered in different parts of the world.

Uniting for Peace Resolution   The resolution that enables the General Assembly to assume responsibility for peace and security issues if the Security Council is deadlocked.

Universal rights   The belief that moral values like human rights are basically the same at all times and in all countries and cultures.

Veto   A negative vote cast in the UN Security Council by one of the permanent members that effectively defeats a decision.

Voting blocs   Groups of states voting together in the UN General Assembly or in other international bodies.

War crimes   Illegal activities committed during war, including deliberately targeting civilians, abusing prisoners of war, and committing crimes such as torture and rape.

Weighted voting systems   Systems in which states have unequal votes, based on financial contributions, population, or geographic representation. Used in the Bretton Woods institutions.

Westphalian tradition   The tradition, dating to the Peace of Westphalia in 1648, that emphasizes state sovereignty within a territorial space.

Index